DD096930

ABOUT THE AUTHORS

MARC GONSALVES is a former member of the United States Air Force, who worked as a civilian military contractor for four years. He has a daughter, Destiney, and two stepsons, Cody and Joey. He lives in Connecticut.

KEITH STANSELL is former Marine in the United States Marine Corp. He lives with his daughter, Lauren; his son, Kyle; his twins, Keith Jr. and Nick; and his fiancée, Patricia, in Bradenton, Florida.

TOM HOWES has been a pilot working in the United States and South America for over twenty years. He currently lives with his son, Tommy, in Merritt Island, Florida.

GARY BROZEK is a freelance writer. He lives in Evergreen, Colorado.

OUT OF
CAPTIVITY

Marc Gonsalves,

Keith Stansell,

and Tom Howes

with Gary Brozek

HARPER

NEW YORK • LONDON • TORONTO • SYDNEY

OUT OF CAPTIVITY

Surviving **1,967** Days in the Colombian Jungle

HARPER

Photographs 1–8, 18–24, 33–39 courtesy of the authors; photographs 11–13, 17, 26 courtesy of Wade Chapple; photographs 25, 32, 33 by Newt Porter; photographs 27–31 by Doug Sanders.

A hardcover edition of this book was published in 2009 by William Morrow, an imprint of HarperCollins Publishers.

OUT OF CAPTIVITY. Copyright © 2009 by Marc Gonsalves, Keith Stansell, and Tom Howes. All rights reserved. Printed in the United States of America. No part of this book may be used or reproduced in any manner whatsoever without written permission except in the case of brief quotations embodied in critical articles and reviews. For information address HarperCollins Publishers, 10 East 53rd Street, New York, NY 10022.

HarperCollins books may be purchased for educational, business, or sales promotional use. For information please write: Special Markets Department, HarperCollins Publishers, 10 East 53rd Street, New York, NY 10022.

First Harper paperbacks edition published 2010.

Designed by Sunil Manchikanti

Library of Congress Cataloging-in-Publication data is available upon request.

ISBN 978-0-06-176953-5 (pbk.)

10 11 12 13 14   NMSG/RRD   10 9 8 7 6 5 4 3

For Tommy Janis, who made the ultimate sacrifice: Your skill
and courage under fire saved all our lives. Your actions brought
honor to you, your family, and your country.
For Sergeant Luis Alcedes Cruz, who didn't make it out.
For our families, who were waiting for us when we did.
For the thousands still held in captivity in Colombia and elsewhere
around the world.
None of you is forgotten.

Contents

Authors' Note   xi

Selected FARC Guerrillas 2003–2008   xiii

Prologue: A Place to Crash   xv

1   Choices and Challenges   1

2   Changes in Altitude   30

3   ¿*Quién Sabe?*   60

4   The Transition   82

5   Settling In   115

6   Proof of Life   141

7   Caribe   167

8   Broken Bones and Broken Bonds   197

9   Ruin and Recovery   230

10   Getting Healthy   255

11   Dead   281

12   Running on Empty   298

13   Reunited   321

14   The Swamp   345

15   Politics and Pawns   372

16   Fat Camp   399

17   Freedom   413

18   Homecoming   430

Acknowledgments   453

Authors' Note

This story is not over. At the very moment that you are reading this, another world exists deep inside the vast jungles of Colombia. Hundreds of hostages are still held there, twenty-eight of them are our companions. They are chained, they are starving, and all they want is to go home. Let them not be forgotten:

Civilians
Alan Jara (captive since July 15, 2001)
Sigifredo López (April 11, 2002)

Police and Military Prisoners
Pablo Emilio Moncayo Cabrera (December 20, 1997)
Libio José Martínez Estrada (December 20, 1997)
Luis Arturo García (March 3, 1998)
Luis Alfonso Beltrán (March 3, 1998)
William Donato Gómez (March 8, 1998)
Robinson Salcedo Guarín (March 8, 1998)
Luis Alfredo Moreno (March 8, 1998)
Arbey Delgado Argote (March 8, 1998)
Luis Herlindo Mendieta (January 11, 1998)
Enrique Murillo Sánchez (January 11, 1998)
César Augusto Lasso Monsalve (January 11, 1998)

Jorge Humberto Romero (June 10, 1999)

José Libardo Forero (June 10, 1999)

Jorge Trujillo Solarte (June 10, 1999)

Carlos José Duarte (June 10, 1999)

Wilson Rojas Medina (June 10, 1999)

Álvaro Moreno (December 9, 1999)

Elkin Hernández Rivas (October 14, 1998)

Edgar Yezid Duarte Valero (October 14, 1998)

Guillermo Javier Solózano (June 4, 2007)

William Yovani Domínguez Castro (January 20, 2007)

Salin Antonio San Miguel Valderrama (May 23, 2008)

Juan Fernando Galicio Uribe (June 9, 2007)

José Walter Lozano (June 9, 2007)

Alexis Torres Zapata (June 9, 2007)

Luis Alberto Erazo Maya (December 9, 1999)

Selected FARC Guerrillas 2003–2008

Teófilo Forero Mobile Column
Sonia
Farid
Uriel
Johnny

27th Front
Milton
Ferney (The Frenchman)
Rojelio
Mono
The Plumber
Eliécer
Cereal Boy
2.5
Smiley
Vanessa
Songster
Tatiana
Mona
Alfonso
Costeño
Pidinolo

1st Front
Enrique
Jair
Moster
Asprilla
LJ
Mario
Tula the dog

FARC Leaders 2003–2008
Manuel Marulanda
Raul Reyes
Mono Jojoy
Fabian Ramirez
Burujo
Iván Rios
Sombra (Fat Man)
Ernesto
Alfredo
Cesár
Alfonso Cano
Joaquin Gomez

A Place to Crash

KEITH

"*That,* sir, is an engine failure."

From our pilot Tommy Janis's tone, you wouldn't have known that anything serious was wrong. He had flown all kinds of aircraft all around the world. Tommy J was a real larger-than-life guy with more stories to tell than I have hairs on my head—and I've as full and thick a mane as anybody. His response wasn't borderline sarcastic; it came from a place about as deep into irony country as we were into Colombia.

The "that" he was referring to wasn't so much a thing as it was an absence of a thing—the steady throbbing pulse of the single 675-horsepower Pratt and Whitney turboprop engine that until a few seconds before had been powering our Cessna Grand Caravan. It didn't take someone like me, a guy who'd been in avionics and aircraft maintenance for all his adult life, to recognize that the relative silence in the cabin was not a good thing.

I closed the biography of Che Guevara I'd been reading and looked over at my buddy and coworker Marc Gonsalves. He'd been busy at his station, practicing with the camera gear and the computer. I wasn't sure if he'd been so involved in what he was doing that he noticed anything at all. The poor guy had only been flying with us for just a few missions and now we had a damn engine failure to deal with. I knew that Tommy Janis and our copilot Tom Howes would instantly flip the switch to figure out if we were going to be able to get this bird over the mountains and to the airport at Larandia, where we were scheduled to refuel.

In my twenty-plus years of flying, I'd had all kinds of training in a variety of different military and civilian aircraft. I'd been in tight spots before and now I slipped easily into a don't-panic-just-focus mindset.

"Marc," I told him, "make the mayday call."

"I'm too new to make a call this important," Marc said. "I think you better do it."

I couldn't blame the guy for not wanting to make that initial call. I immediately got on the SATCOM radio to relay our location to the guys back at the base. The first thing I needed to do to was to let our command posts know our location coordinates.

"Magic Worker, this is Mutt 01, do you read me?"

I waited but got no response. I tried them again. Silence.

This was not good. Magic Worker was responsible for our command and control. Normally, they responded almost instantly every time we called in at our appointed half-hour intervals. The thought of possibly going in on an emergency landing without anyone knowing we had a mayday was not something any of us wanted to do. I made another call to a Department of Defense group based in Florida called JIATF East.

"Mutt 01. This is JIATF East. How many souls on board?"

"JIATF East, there are five." I listed them and spelled each of the names: Tom Janis, Tom Howes, Marc Gonsalves, Sergeant Luis Alcedes Cruz, and myself—Keith Stansell.

I kept calling out the coordinates to them as we descended from twelve thousand feet over the rugged Cordilleria Oriental Mountains, south of Bogotá. A few minutes later we reached Ed Trinidad, who was a part of our Tactical Analysis Team back at the embassy in Bogotá. He was trying to stay cool and calm, but I could hear the stress in his voice.

Breaking with usual radio transmission protocol, I said, "Ed, bro, we're just looking for a place to crash. Make sure you tell all our families that we love them."

Just saying those words made it hard for me to look at Marc, so I glanced toward the cockpit, where Tommy J and Tom Howes were busy figuring out how to save our asses—or at least keep them from being scattered over a half mile of godforsaken mountain jungle.

Through the cockpit window I could see we were lined up for our landing. I then focused on the two Tommys sitting there. Tommy J was spot on, man. He showed no panic, just a precision to his every move. The ground was coming at us quick. Marc and I checked our straps one more time. I took a quick look over Tom's shoulder, then linked my arm with Marc's. I'd been in communication with Ed pretty much throughout our roughly four-minute descent, and I said to him, "Hey, Ed, I'm going to have to get off. We're about to crash."

At that point, I flashed back to a conversation I'd had with one of my supervisors in the company. I'd been in the military and had had some basic survival training, but flying with Northrop Grumman, I was supposed to take the next level up. I told this company guy that I wouldn't do it. When he asked why, all I said was, "With this piece-of-shit aircraft we've being asked to fly in, there's no way I'm going to survive a crash. A dead man doesn't need to know how to survive."

TOM

When I heard the engine spooling down, I immediately looked at the instruments and then scrutinized the terrain for an emergency landing spot. I didn't see anything close to suitable, so I reached for a map. I was barely aware of the ambient noise in the cabin. I knew Keith was on the radio, but the sound of his voice in my headphones and the presence of the three men behind me were definitely on the periphery of my consciousness. Our altitude was a little more than twelve thousand feet and I needed to determine if we could make the glide, clear the mountains, and land at our refueling site, Larandia.

I looked over at the gauges to find out what our current airspeed, altitude, and rate of descent were. From the map, I plotted a point approximating our location and our destination. My gut had told me instantly that we were not going to make it over the ridge and into the airport. The calculations I did simply confirmed my suspicions.

"I see a clearing." Tommy J's voice rose in pitch just a bit.

"I see it, too," I said.

We were going down in a steep valley bordered by two ridgelines. Just above the one to the north was a clearing less than the size of a football field. I'm not a spiritual or religious person, but when I calculated the odds of there being any patch of ground that was clear of trees on the thickly forested slopes of the Cordilleria Mountains, I'd say it was pretty damn close to a miracle. The spot was no bigger than a postage stamp, but it was our only option. Put it this way: If we were falling down a deep well, that clearing was like finding a tiny ledge just a few inches above bottom.

The first thing I did was to make contact with the aviation authorities at two nearby airports, reaching the towers at Florencia and Larandia. Between calls, I remembered a brief conversation Keith and Marc had had about today being February 13. Keith had told Marc that he'd have plenty of time when we returned to order flowers for his wife, Shane. I thought of my own wife, Mariana, waiting for me back in

Florida; I didn't want to think about our five-year-old son, Tommy, and what my death might do to him.

To keep my thoughts from going darker and to make sure we explored every option, I asked Tommy J if we should go through a restart procedure. I'd held off raising the question until things calmed down a bit. Tommy J agreed it was worth a shot. I reset the fuel control, power and prop levers, reduced the electrics, checked the engine temperature, and then tried a restart. As the revolutions climbed I introduced fuel, but the engine stopped winding up.

Tommy J did a flawless job of bringing us down and having us just clear the tops of the trees. I was more concerned that he'd overshoot the landing area than I was that he'd come up a bit short. As we'd gotten closer to the clearing I saw that our landing strip ended at the edge of a cliff. Gliding above the ground, I yelled to Tommy J, "Plant it!"

A moment later, my world went dark.

MARC

What spooked me the most was the eerie sound of the wind rushing past and through the plane's surfaces. The noise was a lot like the sound you hear when you are driving at a decent speed in your car. When you raise the windows and the glass is just about ready to make contact with the top of the frame, you hear a high-pitched whining whistle.

Keith had instructed me to secure as many of the loose things in the cabin as I could. Any small object could become a deadly projectile in a crash landing. We had a couple of bottles of water, our cameras and lenses in hard cases, our backpacks, and some other essential gear. I secured them behind the crash barrier. When I was done, I returned to my station, and using the GPS to track our position, I radioed in our coordinates. Keith checked to make sure that I was strapped in and then he did the same for Sergeant Cruz. I was about to go through my first emergency landing, so I couldn't imagine what Cruz was thinking. I literally didn't know because he hardly spoke any English and I spoke little Spanish. From the looks we exchanged, it was clear that we both understood what was happening and that our outlook was grim.

"We are no longer maneuvering. We are searching for a flat spot to crash-land in," I radioed back to Ed Trinidad.

I could feel the plane banking, what seemed to me to be steeply, to the left. We were obviously making a turn and I felt my guts shifting a bit. I recognized that we were lining up for an approach and took a few deep breaths.

A few seconds after we came out of that first turn, the stall warning sounded. We immediately went into a right-hand turn, a less drastic maneuver, and I shut my eyes and said a quick prayer. I asked Jesus to forgive me for my sins, made a quick promise to reform, and asked that He protect my wife, my kids, and my family. My list was suddenly cut off.

"We are going in," I heard someone yell. I braced myself.

When I felt first contact, I opened my eyes. In the back of the cabin, we could see out a row of windows. I saw slashes of sunlight and dark vegetation for a few seconds, heard the scream of tearing metal, and felt a ferocious thunk followed by a second even more violent impact, which must have been the landing gear being sheared off and the fuselage raking across the rock-strewn terrain. We were sliding and everything in my vision was bouncing. I saw a slit of light pour through the front of the aircraft as the cabin was torn open like a can of tuna.

I don't know how long we slid for, but just as it happened when the engine quit, we settled into silence. I could only make out shadows and flashes for a few seconds—the sun came streaming in, lighting up the dust that was flying everywhere. I reached for our bag of pistols and looked up to see Keith and Sergeant Cruz kicking and shouldering the door so we could get out. We all had one thing on our minds—fire. I gathered up more of my gear and some vital paperwork, and after a few seconds with my heart in my throat, I heard the door give way. Keith was gone and Sergeant Cruz stood in the opening, glancing anxiously around.

"Bring this to Keith." I gestured toward the front of the aircraft, where I assumed Keith had gone. Cruz nodded and I was left alone in the back of the plane to gather our other weapons, my survival vest, and my personal backpack with my expense report in it. I wanted to be certain that it got filed.

I worked my way up the pitted hill toward the front of the aircraft. I was surprised to see a cow staring at me. I looked for the pistol bag so that I could arm myself. I didn't see it, and hustled back down the slope to the aircraft, assuming that Cruz hadn't understood me and left it behind.

Glancing into the cockpit from the outside, I saw Tom slumped over in the copilot's seat, his head twisted in such a way that I thought his neck was broken. He was pinned up against the Plexiglas, looking like a bloody tissue sample placed on a slide. Everything around him in the copilot's area was covered in blood. I could see that he had a huge gash above his eye and a flap of skin, like a turkey's wattle, dangling down. I started beating on the glass and calling his name, but I wasn't getting anything back from him. I figured he had to be dead.

Above my own shouting, I heard Sergeant Cruz's voice and the sound of gunfire raining down from above. Then I figured out what Cruz was yelling; he was shouting, "FARC! FARC! FARC!"

Out of the corner of my eye, I saw Tommy J raise his head and then slump back down. Keith ran around to Tommy J's side to get him out, and ended up pulling out Tom Howes as well.

With Tommy J and Tom pulled safely from the plane and bullets flying all around us, it didn't take long for us to figure out that we'd just landed in the middle of a cadre of FARC guerrillas. I couldn't believe it. We'd survived the crash only to find ourselves in a situation that was arguably worse.

Tommy J and Tom were both in a bloodied daze off to the side of the plane. Tom glanced over at Keith.

"What do you think?" Tom asked.

Keith didn't hesitate, figuring it was better to let me, as the newly minted operations officer, know the reality as he saw it.

"We, sir, are fucked."

ONE

Choices and Challenges

February 13, 2003

MARC

The predawn hours in Bogotá are about as peaceful as the day ever gets there. A chaotic city just about any other time, it is nearly deserted at that hour. Few cars are on the road, and even fewer people. The only living things around seem to be the occasional feral cats and stray dogs who wander the streets—but even most of them know they'd be better off asleep.

With such light traffic, I always sailed through stoplights on my way to work—we all did. There was an unofficial but spirited drive time competition going on at the office among Keith, Tom, and the other guys. Win or lose, those morning drives were a great way to start my day. They gave me a chance to prepare myself for what was in store.

Cruising through the desolate Bogotá roads on the morning of the crash, I was thinking about what I had missed the night before when

Keith Stansell, our pilot Tommy Janis, and Tommy's wife, Judith, had asked me to join them for dinner. Living alone, good food wasn't always easy to come by, but for some reason, I hadn't gone with them. Now, with a slight grumble in my stomach, I was regretting that choice and realizing my meager breakfast that morning wouldn't tide me over for long. With my stomach in mind, I listed the inventory of things I'd stuffed into my backpack that morning—a fleece pullover, the expense report I needed to mail that day, and some homework for the Spanish class I was taking. On top of that was my trusty can of tuna just in case Keith didn't have my back (stomach) by bringing me one of his famous sandwiches and a Snickers bar.

Mostly, though, I was thinking about how fortunate I was to be doing a job I enjoyed, working with people I liked, and anticipating the remaining twenty-two days of this twenty-eight-day rotation. I hadn't been on this job for long, but part of its appeal was that it gave me two weeks off for every four weeks of work. Those two weeks between tours in-country had a lot to do with why I'd decided to switch jobs in the first place. No matter how good the work was, nothing could beat spending time with my wife, Shane, and my kids back in the Florida Keys.

I rolled down the window of my Chevy Rodeo (a re-badged Isuzu) and the cool breeze that came in was crisp and dry. I didn't mind. I needed anything to stay alert. Ever since I'd been in-country, I'd been struggling to sleep. Tom Howes told me that my response was typical of people adjusting to life at altitude. I'd gone from Florida flat to 8,200 feet high in Bogotá. My body was going to need some time to get used to it. As tired as I was, I enjoyed flying through traffic light after traffic light, the streets empty except for a couple of delivery trucks. That morning was a particularly good one, and I thought I'd be able to end a string of drive-time defeats at the hands of Keith and Tom.

I wasn't in a reflective mood that morning, just riding a literal and figurative high. I had a new job that paid me well. I was working with people I had come to respect for their service to our country, but who did not take themselves too seriously. I was also getting to know a culture and a place far different from my own, and a few times a week my coworkers and I would fly over some of the most beautiful countryside I'd seen.

During those flights, we were mostly looking for coca fields and drug-processing labs under the control of the principal revolutionary group in Colombia, the Fuerzas Armadas Revolucionarias de Colombia (FARC). The FARC had been around for nearly forty years, beginning initially as the military wing of the Colombian Communist Party. Their Marxist insurgency had ebbed and flowed over the years in terms of numbers and influence, but though their ranks had dwindled of late, their tactics had solidified. Their primary means of waging and funding their "war" was through extortion, kidnapping, and drug running. By gathering intelligence on the FARC's drug connections, I was doing my part in the U.S.'s efforts to eradicate the coca crops and drug-trafficking infrastructure in Colombia. In 2002, 650 metric tons of cocaine were processed in Colombia, and the vast majority of the 494 metric tons of cocaine that made its way into the U.S. came from there. That was down more than 20 percent over 2001 figures, so whatever the joint effort between the U.S. and Colombia had been doing, it had been a success.

I'd only been on the job since November of 2002, and four months into it, I was still very much in a honeymoon period. I was living in an apartment in the vibrant and historic Colombian capital. Though there were quite a few Americans in the city—embassy workers, contract workers, and other international personnel—our employer arranged for us to live in buildings that were occupied by Colombian nationals to minimize the danger to us.

As Americans, we were always considered a kidnapping risk, and if anyone suspected that we were doing intelligence work on behalf of the U.S. government, our value as captives would rise. Colombia's reputation as a place where for-profit kidnapping thrived was well deserved.

The number of prominent military, political, and civilian captives being held by various groups, primarily the FARC, was troubling to say the least. By 2003, the number of yearly kidnappings had declined from the more than 3,500 committed in 2000, but the number of hostages still in captivity was among the highest in the world.

I'd weighed this risk before deciding to go to Bogotá, and despite this threat, I didn't find the place unsafe once I was there. I never walked around with my head on a swivel, suspecting that around every corner there was someone lurking who wanted to do me harm. In fact, it didn't take me long to appreciate the culture of the city and the universal friendliness of the Colombian people. During those first few months on the job, there was little doubt in my mind that I had made the right choice for my life and my career. I'd always been told that life was all about the choices you make. While I don't think that anyone would ever choose to go through a plane crash and become the hostage of a Marxist revolutionary group, I believed then, and do so even more strongly today, that things happen for a reason, that God has a plan for all of us.

The plan that brought me to the jungles of Colombia on February 13, 2003, began when I joined the air force right out of high school. Eight years later, I left active duty and began working for a private defense contractor doing counternarcotic intelligence analysis. I enjoyed the work, though sometimes sitting at a desk staring at a computer screen and editing hours of video surveillance footage down to a ten-minute presentation got tedious. The rewards, financial and personal, offset whatever boredom I felt. I was doing what I considered to be important work, operating at a crucial rear-command position in America's war on drugs. Being paid a more than decent wage and being able to provide a comfortable life for Shane; my sons, Cody and Joey; my daughter, Destiney, meant a lot to me. Living in and working in Key West, Florida, at the Joint Interagency Task Force (JIATF) East was better than slogging through winters back home in Connecticut.

I'm no adrenaline junkie, so when the opportunity eventually came up for me to switch from intelligence analyzing to intelligence gathering in Colombia, I really had to think about it. The job interest was from a government contractor called California Microwave, which was a subsidiary of a larger government contractor called Northrop Grumman. I would receive a significant bump in pay, but strings were attached. I consulted with Shane. I would have to be separated from my family for weeks at a time. The last thing I wanted was to be away from them, but my father, George, had always drummed it into my head that you have to do whatever is necessary to provide for your loved ones. That's what he did for my brother, Mike, and me and that's what I wanted to do for my family. My kids and my wife weren't starving, but rising prices and the prospect of the enormous cost of a college education for three kids were definitely weighing on my mind and my bank account. Being away from them would be hard, but if it meant they'd get the education they needed, it'd be worth it.

If the separation wasn't enough, this new job also carried the risk of physical harm, which gave me pause. My old work consisted of sitting behind a computer reviewing footage and documents. Now I would be in the thick of things, in the middle of the intelligence-gathering process, where a whole lot more could go wrong. California Microwave had been contracted to do aerial surveillance on the Colombian drug trade by the Department of Defense. The fact that I'd be working for Northrop reassured me that accepting the offer was the right move. Several subcontractors did this kind of work for the government, but knowing that we had the support of Northrop gave me the quiet confidence I needed to take this potentially hazardous job. Northrop took care of their employees, and I knew that if anything happened, they'd take care of me and my family.

Ultimately, after assessing the risks and the increased salary with Shane, I signed on with California Microwave, and in November of 2002, I traveled to Colombia to be trained on the company's Forward

Looking Infra-Red (FLIR) surveillance equipment. I'd been flying and working down there—four weeks on, two weeks off—like clockwork ever since.

When I arrived at the airport on the morning of the thirteenth, I showed my ID and passed through a series of security checkpoints to get to our operations headquarters. The road through the checkpoints was a collection of zigzags, almost like a maze, designed to keep your speed down so you couldn't get up enough momentum to crash through a barrier. The last checkpoint was at Fast Eddie's, a cluster of shipping containers that a guy we called Fast Eddie had converted into office space. He'd divided the structure into an administrative section where his daughter and brother handled the paperwork and phones for many of Eddie's varied operations.

Not only did Eddie believe in keeping business in the family, he believed in being in everybody's business all the time—in the best way possible. Eddie was what some would call a fixer. A Colombian-born U.S. citizen who served in our air force, Fast Eddie was a consummate businessman, the real connection between the U.S. State Department and the Colombian government. He was our go-to guy who could make just about anything happen with a phone call. His white button-down and cuff links were his trademark uniform, and he had an air about him that immediately reassured you and made you wonder at the same time. But as fast as Eddie was, he didn't play both sides—he was there for us and for U.S. efforts 24/7.

The girls who did the administrative work for Fast Eddie—one of whom was his daughter Natalie—weren't in yet, and I passed through their space into the recreation area, where the pool table and couches sat unused at this early hour. I walked out onto the tarmac past a row of civilian airplanes, most of them operated by U.S. companies and agencies. My first responsibility was to check the radio on our aircraft to be sure it was operational. After I completed that task, I contacted the folks at JIATF East to let them know the mission was a go and walked back into Fast Eddie's, where I saw Keith sitting with Tom and Tommy Janis at a table in the rec area.

Keith had indirectly been a part of my decision to come to Colombia. I had first met him when he came though Key West with another aircraft that California Microwave had set up to do drug interdiction work. Keith was one of the people responsible for overseeing the upgrades necessary to convert the Cessna Grand Caravan into a surveillance plane. For a few years, his outfit at California Microwave had provided my company with the raw intelligence I turned into reports. The first time I met Keith I was struck by his presence. At six foot two, he was nearly four inches taller than I was. He still wore his hair in a Marine's brush cut, and his authoritative voice was just slightly tinged with a Florida drawl. His ability to convey both a seriousness and a good-ol'-boy casualness was impressive. He'd been there and done *a lot* of that, but he only told you about it when you asked.

From the start, I liked and respected Keith, but despite our first meeting, I knew him more through reputation than firsthand knowledge. Still, the respect must have been mutual, since later on he told me that he and a common friend of ours had recommended me for the job at California Microwave. When I joined the crew in Colombia, he said he'd been hoping the company could find someone like me—someone with experience in knowing what the various agencies did with the raw intelligence these field operations gathered.

In lots of ways, Keith and I couldn't have been more different. As a northerner geographically and temperamentally, born to two first-generation immigrant parents, I tend to be a little bit quiet and reserved. I like to keep the peace at the expense of expressing my views or desires. Keith had no trouble making his opinions known, and he had the knowledge and experience to back up his claims about the work we were all doing. He'd been in Colombia for four years, first working for DynCorp, where Tom had also worked. Keith had also worked in other parts of the Colombia mission—interdiction through U.S. customs, out of Homestead Air Force Base while in the Marines—in all kinds of avionics-technician and aircraft-maintenance positions through the National Guard and in private industry. In the closed world of our occupation, he was someone with a good reputation who switched from maintenance to operations and had been flying missions for California Microwave the last two years.

Tom Howes was just as different from Keith as I was. Though he'd never been in the military, on the surface he reminded me of some of my air-force colleagues. Outwardly more quiet and reserved than Keith, Tom possessed a sly sense of humor that you had to pay close attention to. He was like a master doctor who could give you the needle so expertly that you wouldn't know you'd been jabbed until he walked away. Tom was several years older than Keith and me, and his glasses along with his wide, genial smile always helped his quick-strike wit catch you off guard. Along with his sense of humor came a studied seriousness about aviation and a breadth of knowledge about the region that impressed me. Tom's passions seemed to be food and flying, and everyone benefited from his experience with both.

Ever since I'd left the air force, one of the things I'd missed was the camaraderie. While a lot of the people I worked with prior to coming to Colombia were former active-duty military, there was something about being in-country that upped the we're-all-in-this-together mentality. From my arrival, Keith had included me in the tightly knit group of men that made up the contract workers flying out of Bogotá International Airport. Nobody was outwardly rah-rah and gung ho, but you could tell that the shared experiences and similar dedication to an ideal formed a kind of locker-room bond. I was on my home cycle when a team photo was taken just a couple of weeks before the crash, but I'd seen it. There were a bunch of positive, happy, and good folks in that picture. I was only beginning to learn about the rough-and-tumble, hard living (and I mean that in the best sense) experiences some of them had.

I'd flown with Keith and Tom only a few times prior to February 13, and both of them were, as far as my limited experience told me, real professionals who knew the coca-plant-eradication spraying programs and surveillance quite well. Essentially, we were providing the intel that would let those spraying units know where the coca fields were, while also giving the intelligence agencies the locations of the cocaine production labs, so that they could be destroyed. Wherever we flew, whatever we photographed or videotaped, the U.S. government had the ultimate control over our activities. Primarily the Department of Defense (DOD) called our shots, telling us where to go and what to look for. Whatever we produced, the DOD was supposed to share that information with other federal agencies like the Drug Enforcement Administration, the Bureau of Alcohol, Tobacco and Firearms, and the FBI. We had some latitude on our flights, but not much. The whole time we had to be in near-constant radio communications with the DOD so they could verify our position.

There is never a good time for anyone to experience an engine failure, crash landing, and capture, but this was particularly bad timing for both Keith and Tom. Keith was only into the third day of his current rotation, and after our mission that day, he was scheduled to fly back to the States to do some maintenance work on other aircraft that California Microwave leased. This was to be the only flight mission that Keith would participate in on this rotation.

As for Tom, he found out shortly before takeoff that he'd be able to go home a week early, because he wouldn't be flying any more missions this rotation, either. He was happy about the news. Late in 2002, after more than a few years as a vagabond pilot, he'd moved into his dream house in Merritt Island, Florida. Since that time, he'd only spent a total of twelve days in it. He was looking forward to some serious R&R after going through the drama of home-buying and moving.

Seeing Keith, Tom, and Tommy sitting at Fast Eddie's, I knew that the day's flight would be getting under way soon. That morning while

I'd been driving in and doing the initial radio check, Keith had gone to the U.S. embassy. Keith and I were to be the rear seaters on this mission, but given Keith's experience on the job, he was to be the mission commander that day. In a sense, this was a practice mission for me, giving me more time behind the camera actually operating the equipment. Keith had called me the night before to go over some procedures, and with our scheduled 0700 departure, I knew that he had to be at the embassy by 0500 hours to meet with our Tactical Analysis Team (TAT). They would give him our target package—the places we'd be flying over and photographing and videoing—for the day, and these targets came straight from Southern Command, one of the groups within the Department of Defense that guided our missions. Because of the security risk of being in possession of the targets, we always had to go to the TAT on the morning of the flights.

I'd done all this before, and when Keith and I flew together, we alternated who did the preflight at the airport and who went to our TAT at the embassy. On that morning it had been Keith's turn, and when I saw him sitting with the two Toms, he had a familiar look on his face.

"They were late?" I asked.

"Yep. I can't believe I have to sit there and wait. What am I doing getting my ass up at 'o dark early' if I just have to sit there for twenty minutes? That's twenty minutes of beauty rest I could have had."

"You could have used that," Tom said, smiling at Tommy J and me.

Keith pointed at me.

"That hat, bro. That's not really working for you."

I tugged at the brim of my Tampa Bay Buccaneers Super Bowl Champion hat and smiled at the thought of the team finally going all the way after so many years of futility. I tried to think of something to say in return, but watching Keith twirl a couple of CDs around his index finger had me mesmerized for a bit.

Before Keith could go on to explain whom he was going to be listening to today, a couple of Colombians walked in. We did our work only with the full cooperation and approval of the Colombian government. Some people's perceptions of our work as subcontractors was that we were like cowboys riding all over the range doing whatever we wanted. That's just not true. Every flight we went on, a representative of the Colombian government, either a military guy or a civilian, joined us. They were known as "host-nation riders."

The two Colombians said hello and introduced themselves. They were dressed in civilian clothes, even though one of them introduced himself as Sergeant Luis Alcedes Cruz. Both seemed to be personable guys. Like most of the Colombians we worked with and knew, they seemed eager to make a good impression.

Because there wasn't enough room in the plane and he was mission commander, Keith let them know that only one of them could go up with us. Tom, who'd done a lot of aviation work all over South America and the Caribbean, spoke Spanish, and he interpreted for Keith, relaying to us that Sergeant Cruz had stepped up and let the other guy have the day off. Cruz sat in on our meeting, and with our broken Spanish, his broken English, and Tom's capable translating, we let him know what our target package was for the day. With that message communicated—as much a courtesy as anything else, since he really had no say so at this level to alter our plan—we loaded up.

As usual, during takeoff, we were pretty quiet and on task. Once we were airborne and on our way to the refueling point, the chatter began. I noticed that Tom could barely make it into the first half hour of the flight without dipping into his lunch. His wife, Mariana, was a legend—a Peruvian woman who was a marvelously good cook. Every one of us would have admitted to needing to shed a few pounds, and I knew that Tom was on meds for his high blood pressure, the cause of which he attributed more to Mariana's good cooking than to the stress of being a pilot.

While I was busy checking the equipment, I could hear everybody communicating over the headsets. Tommy J reported that the dinner

I missed was spectacular, "Mama's full of food. I dropped her off at the terminal this morning on my way in. She's happy, and I'm going to see her shortly at home." Tommy J pivoted in his seat and I saw the big grin on his face. The man clearly loved his wife and spoke of her in glowing terms every time I was around him. I remember thinking that the guy was fifty-six years old, but he had the body of someone who was twenty-five. I didn't know how he did it, but I wouldn't have minded doing it myself.

By that time, the smell of Tom's lunch had wafted to the back of the aircraft—garlic, some pungent cheese—and that got Keith and me drooling a bit. Keith showed me the chicken Parmesan sandwich that he'd ordered along with his dinner the night before, and I started wishing again that I'd joined them. My meager can of tuna didn't stand up to the pleasures these guys brought on board. Those smells also didn't make it any easier for me to think about eating better, shedding a few of the pounds the good life had helped me pack on. I couldn't help myself, though. I was about four hours into my day and had barely eaten a thing since the night before.

"Keith, you've got to give me your recipe for tuna-salad sandwiches," I said to him.

As legendary as Tom's wife's cooking was (we could always tell whether she was in Colombia or the States based on the quality of Tom's lunches), Keith's tuna-salad recipe had earned a reputation for excellence company-wide and beyond.

Keith laughed and said, "No can do, sir. It's a can for you. My recipe is classified information. You don't have the proper clearance."

"But you brought the stuff, right? You brought the tuna, too?"

The irony of me talking like a junkie to my dealer wasn't lost on any of us, but those sandwiches of Keith's were just that good.

"Yeah. I got the tuna fish, too, bro. You can calm yourself. Everything's right in our world."

KEITH

Up until the point when our engine died, everything had been right in our world, but to be honest, when I stepped out of the skeletal remains of our bird, I wasn't thinking much about good or bad or right or wrong. I wasn't thinking that we were the best in the business, better than the National Security Agency, the CIA, the air force. Though I believed that was the truth, I didn't have the time to consider that we often flew the lowest, had a low-budget platform, covered the same territory so many times we acquired superior local knowledge, and knew what the customer wanted. All of that was out the door.

We were truly low-level now—not at the five thousand feet above the deck like our missions—but right there on the ground in the trees and on the jagged slopes of those mountains that had looked so different through our FLIR equipment. Marc, Tom, and I may not have been able to use infrared to detect the heat signature a human body throws off, but we knew we were right smack-dab in the middle of the shit.

I'd known we were in trouble as soon as the engine failed. I was glad that twenty minutes before we launched, I had called home to check on my kids, Lauren and Kyle, and my fiancée, Malia. I'd been a single parent for a few years and I wanted to be sure that everyone was up, everyone was getting ready for school. Before I hung up, I had told them that I loved them. Standing on the floor of the jungle looking at the wreckage of your plane, there's not much that can make you feel good about your situation, but I was happy I'd done that and had always told them that they were going to be okay if something happened to me.

When I spilled out of that downed aircraft, I was thinking about one thing—surviving. Though I didn't have time to dwell on it, I was one grateful American at that point. Not too many people can say that they are two-time survivors of aircraft accidents. I'd previously been on board a helo that went down in the States. I'd made it out of that scrape alive and now it seemed I'd gotten out of another all in one piece.

Call me a two-time loser or a twice-lucky SOB, it didn't matter. Within minutes, rounds were firing at us from all directions, and standing at the wreckage of our shattered Cessna Grand Caravan, we all had more important things on our minds. I'd seen a few guerrillas coming up the hill toward our position. Behind them, a whole platoon was making their way toward us. Given the steepness of the terrain and the distance they had to traverse, I knew we only had a couple of minutes to figure out a plan.

Cruz handed me all of our weapons and ammo, and I pitched them down a slope next to the wreckage. This was no time for any of us to fancy himself a gunslinger. This was about making the most expedient choices possible and assessing the situation with one goal and one goal only in mind—get to the end of the day. I knew that with a couple of pistols and a single M-4 rifle we were seriously outmanned and out-equipped. Things were so chaotic that I didn't realize Marc hadn't seen me dispose of our weapons. He still thought we had more on board and he went searching everywhere, inside the cabin, under the wing, under the fuselage.

While he was gone, Cruz and I were standing at the front of the plane, our backs to the sheer drop-off. Sergeant Cruz was understandably worked up, and I told him to calm down. I knew this was no fight we could win, but Cruz was Colombian military. If the FARC guerrillas found that out, he'd be in bad shape. The FARC were known for kidnapping military types, since they were primo bargaining chips in prisoner exchanges.

When Cruz saw me ditch our weapons, he changed tactics.

"Please say I am American! Please tell them!"

I nodded. I could tell that Cruz was seriously hurt. We were all shaken up, and the terrain was difficult to get a solid footing on, but Cruz was limping badly. The odd thing was, he didn't seem to be in any pain. I watched as he hobbled off a few feet away to bury some papers.

Like it was doing for Cruz, the adrenaline pumping through our systems was keeping us from feeling the pain from our injuries. Glancing at the cockpit, I saw that Tom Howes had an obvious head wound. Marc would later tell me that he had a badly banged-up hand, and I had done something to my back or my side. I added that factor to the equation, and decided it was best to just see what would develop and not do anything to make the situation worse.

Marc returned while I was trying to calm down Cruz.

"We can't go anywhere without the pilots," I said to Marc.

Marc then had the presence of mind to remember why we were there in the first place.

"Our target package. I've got to get that." Our target deck had been placed in a metal clipboard we call the pan. "I hid it under the seat. They're going to search it and find it." Our targets were FARC-controlled and -operated drug labs, one of which we knew to be under the command of Mono JoJoy, one of the FARC's major players.

While Marc was off retrieving that sensitive and potentially damning evidence, I helped Tommy Janis and Tom Howes out of the wreckage. Tommy J was obviously dazed, but I said to him anyway, "Tommy J, bro, that was incredible what you just did. Thanks."

Marc had returned without the clipboard, so I assumed he'd destroyed the paperwork. I looked at him and saw that he had his backpack with him. Tom Howes was standing there as well. Cruz was done with tearing through the hold for his papers and the five of us stood in a group waiting. The guerrillas were marching toward us, and it was only a matter of minutes before they arrived.

When they were within a hundred meters, I put my hands up and took a step forward, shouting in my best Spanish-lesson oral-practice voice, "*No armas! No armas!*" Everybody else did the same. I didn't want to be spokesperson, but if Cruz spoke up, they'd immediately recognize his Colombian accent, if they hadn't already tagged him as that based on his skin color and hair. Tom Howes had the best Spanish of any of us, but I could tell by looking at him—the flap of flesh was dangling over his eye, and blood continued streaming from his wound and down his face—that he was basically out on his feet.

By then I could see that there were between fifty and sixty heavily armed guerrillas coming at us. The members of this large platoon-size group were a ragtag-looking bunch wearing an odd assortment of cammo gear, T-shirts, sweatpants, and bandannas, but I was more interested in the weapons they carried. Not the latest or the greatest, but still capable of tearing a hole in any one of us—Israeli Galils, AK-47s, old M-14s. Worse, they had an M–70 grenade launcher and an old Chinese piece-of-crap 308.

When they reached us, four of them approached, their faces completely expressionless. I did a quick scan of the whole bunch. None of them could have been more than twenty years old, ranging from what I guessed was about fourteen. At gunpoint, they led Tom and me downhill and away from the aircraft. I didn't like the idea of us being separated and wondered if this was how they were going to execute us. Then I saw one of the guerrillas take off a scarf he was wearing and hand it to Tom. The scarf was cammo on one side and the other side was checked like a PLO scarf only in the colors of Colombia's flag—red, blue, and yellow.

I was surprised the guy gave it up. The scarf was obviously taken from someone in the Colombian military. A lot of the FARC had them, and it was a way of counting coup—to show that they'd either captured or killed a Colombian counterguerrilla soldier. I also figured if he was bothering to hand that over, it could be a good thing or a bad thing. Either he knew he was going to be getting it back a few minutes after he shot us, or he was trying to take good care of a prisoner. In either case, Tom wrapped the thing around his head to stanch the flow of blood. He leaned back and I could see him wobble a bit.

Tom and I sat down about fifty yards from the plane and watched as one of the group's leaders—a woman we eventually learned was named

Sonia—searched the plane, tossing stuff out of it and onto the ground. I could also see Marc standing with Tommy J and Sergeant Cruz. They started to move Marc away from Tommy J and Cruz and down the hill toward us. I could tell that Marc didn't want to go, but the FARC guard on him was nudging him with his weapon. At one point Marc stopped and turned back, and I followed his gaze up the slope. There, at the top of the hill, stood Tommy J—worn out and injured. He limped over to Sergeant Cruz and put his arm around Cruz's shoulders.

That was the last we saw of them.

The FARC led Tom and me down the hill a little bit farther. The going wasn't any easier, but we managed to make it another four hundred yards or so to a small building made of rough-hewn lumber with a corrugated tin roof. Tom and I stood there for a few minutes and then Marc joined us. A young female guerrilla—she couldn't have been more than eighteen—brought out a large aluminum *ola*, or pot. In it was water with a few lemon seeds floating in it. She handed each of us a small cup of the liquid. I was surprised at how sweet it tasted. FARC lemonade was about as sugary as any sweet tea I'd had at home. I looked over the rim of my cup and all I could see was dark eyes framed by mustaches and black hair. I was struck by the odd assortment of hats they wore and the half-ass assortment of ways they wore them. What kind of terrorist organization was this?

We descended more of the slope, and after we'd gone several steps we stopped. The next thing I knew, the FARC were pawing me, searching for any weapons and indicating that we needed to strip down. They spread out a sheet, and Tom, Marc, and I did as we were told. Pretty soon we were in our underwear. I could barely contain my anger at the hypocrisy the FARC then demonstrated when one of the "idealistic" communists took the money out of my wallet and put it in his pocket. Here was this supposed guerrilla organization that was founded on Marxist principles, and yet the second they come into contact with private property, they jumped to take it for themselves. Each according to his needs, I guess. Worse was the fact that I had a photo in my wallet of my son, just a tiny little snapshot. I indicated that I wanted to keep that, but they wouldn't let me. They did the same to Tom and Marc, taking all their personal possessions except their clothes.

"I guess this is better than being dead," Tom said.

Marc shook his head and added, "What is this? Look at these guys. What a motley crew. They look more like a bunch of kids dressed up for Halloween than soldiers. And the cow that was mooing at us when we first got out of the plane? How surreal."

With everything else going on, I had almost forgotten about the cow, which had made a chaotic setting that much stranger. They may have looked like a bunch of kids at Halloween, but they'd been firing some high-power weapons not too long ago. Those rounds were real and could do serious damage to any one of us. But things were about to get even weirder.

Each of us had a guerrilla come back to search us again, this time probing our hair and our underarms, between our toes. Another FARC member separated himself from the group and stepped forward and said something in vehement Spanish. I understood only two words—*chip* and *mato*. Tom translated for us: "He says that if he finds a microchip on us, he's going to kill us." I didn't like hearing those words, but I was glad that Tom was finally getting more of his wits about him. The blow to his head could have been a hell of a lot worse, but now that he was able to speak in both languages and process thoughts more completely, I was relieved. We needed Tom's input and knowing that he was on his way back to full strength was a good thing.

A few hours later, when we all had our first chance to really speak to one another, we agreed that of all the bizarre moments we experienced the day of the crash, this comment about the microchip was the most puzzling. These people actually thought that we had microchips embedded in our bodies. They assumed that, as Americans, we had some kind of tracking system that enabled our people back in the

States or even in Colombia to trace our every movement. Even when they had finished searching us and should have been satisfied that we didn't have such a thing, they continued to threaten us with death if they discovered a chip. The little fucks were so young they could have thought that a bit of toe jam was a microchip and opened fire. They'd sure as shit never seen a microchip before, so how would they know if they'd found one? It was unsettling on every level, and the idea that we were dealing with such heavily-armed people with this level of competence did not sit well with me.

For the same reason, they also tried to prevent us from speaking too loudly, convinced that American satellites could pick up the sound of our voices. During the course of the next few days, we'd learn that they thought that we were somehow endowed with superpowers, that every American was a snake-eatin', ass-kickin' John Rambo type. (One guard even went so far as to ask us about the movie *Matrix* and how we Americans could do that. Not how do the people in Hollywood create that special effect, but how the three of us were able to dodge bullets like that.)

After we put our clothes back on, we climbed up to the ridge opposite the crash site. Sonia, who was wearing a red jacket either to make herself a better target or to lead someone flying over to believe she was some kind of emergency personnel, was still picking through the wreckage. Marc muttered "HCL lab" and "targets" and looked down at the ground, shaking his head slowly, but I didn't have time to respond to his concerns.

"Helos. A long way off," I said.

Tom and I had been around aircraft for so long that we had fine-tuned our hearing to the sound of them. From the distinctive *whup whup* of the rotors, I could tell that they were UH 1s—Colombian military helos on a rescue mission for us. This is when we knew it was going to get dangerous. We all stood up, knowing that it was time to pop smoke and get the hell out of there.

TOM

I couldn't hear the helos far off in the distance myself, but when Keith mentioned them, it was as if someone had taken a cloth and wiped clean the fog that had been clouding my mind since the crash. Even though I was operating at less than full capacity, I knew we were in a tough spot. I was simply relieved that we'd survived the crash and I tried to keep that thought foremost in my mind. But the sound of those helos coming in and the urgency with which the FARC responded made me realize that though we had lived through the crash, we weren't anywhere close to safe yet.

We were on a hill opposite the crash site in a tiny space that was surrounded by thickly wooded and steeply sloped terrain. Below us was the small ramshackle building near where we'd been stripped and searched. To our left, down another ravine and up on another high point, was an open-area ranch building. The building appeared to have been built into the side of the mountain. Between that larger clearing was another small one with a trail joining them. As we moved toward this building, the helos passed right over us. Marc and Keith were a few yards ahead of me, escorted by a couple of FARC guerrillas. I couldn't move as fast as they were moving, and soon the distance between us increased. I didn't like being separated from them, but I also figured a larger cluster of us made for an easier target.

The helo banked into a turn and then circled us again, this time with its weapons firing. The Colombian military was taking aim at the FARC who were on the perimeter. I was still close enough to hear Marc shout to Keith about what was going on. Keith told him that the helo's gunner was firing a minigun. I could hear rounds zinging through the trees above our heads. I continued to stumble and run, aiming for the path that led from the small clearing to the large one where the building sat. The FARC guarding me pushed me to the side off of the trail and into some denser vegetation and trees. Keith and Marc were right there with their guards, and the hills surrounding us were being peppered with rounds from the minigun.

Marc said to Keith, "Fuck me, I'm getting out of this shit. This is our chance."

"That thing's spitting out two thousand rounds a minute. We've got to consider another option, Marc."

We all knew that the best time for escape was within the first few minutes of being taken, before our captors could get fully organized. This was a pretty chaotic scene and in that sense a good opportunity to flee, but now, with all that gunfire landing right where we wanted to go, it was better to stay put.

Keith was standing and he extended his arm to brace himself against the trunk of a tree. Sunlight reflected off the dial of his wristwatch and caught my eye. It must have also caught the attention of one of the guerrillas near Keith. "*Deme su reloj*," the guy said.

Keith stared at the guy in disbelief and began to unclasp his Seiko diver's watch.

"Here, take the thing," Keith said. "Just let's get the fuck out of here before we get killed."

That theft was just another of the absurdities of the day. Why hadn't they taken it before? Why would a FARC guerrilla choose to steal it during the middle of a firefight? We'd eventually come to the understanding that the FARC didn't operate by anything resembling the logic or values we did.

We stood there for a few minutes, and across the large clearing, I could see a small campesino house the FARC were hoping to get us to. By the word *clearing*, I mean a typical Colombian jungle slash-and-burn type of clearing. Clumps of vegetation, tree stumps, and deadfall lay scattered around the nearly five hundred feet to the structure. While the canopy above us was open, the field itself was the tangled nest of an obstacle course. Sprinting across it would be the equivalent of doing a combination of a high hurdle race mixed in with the long jump, the high jump, and the triple jump—all on a steeply sloped patch of ground.

The guerrillas were gesturing with guns and making it obvious that they wanted us to take off across the clearing. One of them held his gun in the firing position to show us that even though they were letting us run free, we were still going to have their weapons trained on us. What they were also telling us was that they weren't about to go out into that clearing and expose themselves to weapons fire. Finally, one of the FARC grabbed Marc and another grabbed me. They gave us a shove into the slash-and-burn. We took off running and jumping and dodging as best we could. Fortunately for us, the helo was upslope of us and we safely reached a point about halfway between Keith's position and the structure. We crouched down near a stump. From my vantage point, I could see another guard at the house waving at us to come the rest of the way.

At that moment, for some reason, I remembered a conversation I had with my wife, Mariana, a week or so before the crash. She and I were talking about the risks of my job and we were both wondering whether it was worth it. I was making good money, and we both ultimately decided that I should stick it out a bit longer—at least through what was left of that rotation. Funny how the mind works and why that thought would come to me just then. I was worried about her feeling guilty if I didn't make it. Worried that she might think she unduly influenced me.

I didn't have much time to contemplate things. Marc looked at me and nodded, and the two of us headed for the house. It was like we were playing a deadly version of the video game Frogger. We'd hear the helos coming our way, so we'd take cover behind whatever we could. One helo would move off, and we'd zig and zag our way to another bit of cover. After what seemed like twenty minutes or more, we had covered the 500 feet of the clearing and made it into the shelter the house provided. We turned back and saw that the helo was heading our way. Keith was about at the midpoint of where we had stopped, and blade wash was kicking up dirt, ashes, and dead vegetation. He had his hand up in front of his face to keep his vision clear and the FARC were yelling at him to run. The helo couldn't have been more than seventy-five feet above Keith. In the open door of the cabin, we could all see the gunner. The pilot had briefly brought the helo to a near hover, a bold move given that there were FARC with grenade launchers close by. It was such a strange sight. We could see Keith looking up at the helo, and we could see the gunner looking down at Keith. The gunner finally just shrugged his shoulders and then the helo lurched forward and resumed doing orbits around Keith.

A minute later, Keith was by our side and the FARC had hustled us into a tiny space between the campesino house and the hillside. We stayed wedged in there between the side of the house and the mountainside until the helos cleared the area. The FARC guards dislodged us from our hiding place and led us to the front of the building. On the porch, a woman sat on the ground crying. Her husband stood stiffly off to the side. He had his arms folded and he was rocking back on his heels, eyeing the three of us with disgust and fear. I noticed he was more careful about how he looked at the FARC. He let the disgust drip from his mouth when he spit and left the fear on display.

We could hear gunfire echoing around the hills, and from inside the house the squealing of pigs. One of the guards, a young kid of maybe fifteen, was carrying a .30-caliber Galil, and his face was disfigured by a scar running diagonally from his forehead to his chin. He was fingering a wood-bead necklace and smiling this shit-eating grin like what he was in the middle of was the coolest thing ever.

A few moments later, the helos returned. One was doing orbits directly above the house and we had a classic Mexican standoff. The Colombian military couldn't open fire on our position because they would have killed us. The FARC didn't try to shoot the helo down because the gunner would have returned fire on them. So we were all standing there looking up at them, and they were looking down at us as they hovered overhead.

We were squatting alongside the house, and I could see that there were small openings dug into the slope. Inside of each, a pair of beady eyes stared back at us. Chickens. The Colombian couple who ran the place used the hillside as a chicken coop, and we were playing our own game of chicken right then and there. Who was going to flinch?

The FARC made the next move, pushing us away from one end of the house to the other, where a few bedraggled grapevines clung to a rotting arbor. Each of us had a FARC guard at his side. They led us off, using us as human shields. Once we passed the arbor, we entered a patch of immature coffee plants, about three feet high, and our guards forced us down on our knees and then our bellies with their bodies still interlocked with ours. We crawled among the coffee plants, making our way to the jungle. After a few minutes of crawling, we heard the helos heading off. They didn't return.

As calm and reality sank in, our thoughts turned immediately to our loved ones. We wondered what they would think when they heard the news of our crash. Suddenly so much seemed beyond our control. As a pilot who'd flown more than thirteen thousand hours in a large variety of aircraft, I was always someone who needed to be in control. To me, that's an essential skill for any pilot. You have to tend to all the details, trust only to a certain degree those who maintain, equip, and build your aircraft. Over time, you do learn to let go a bit, but that doesn't mean that you don't run all the checks, keep all the possibilities in your mind, be able to recall at an instant what to do in case of an emergency.

Prompted by the FARC, we moved deeper into the jungle. Only about forty minutes had passed since we first made contact with Colombian soil, and only a few minutes more than that since our engines had fallen silent. I didn't know where the FARC would take us, but I knew there was only so much that I could carry with me. Too many thoughts about the decisions that had led me to Colombia in the first place would weigh me down and make the journey ahead much more difficult. It was as if I was still flying in a damaged plane, and I had to throw out of the cabin anything that I could to lighten the load and conserve fuel. Hopefully I'd make it over the hump to a safe landing on the other side of the mountain. But to be sure, I safely stowed the things—memories of my wife and children—I held most valuable.

I did give myself one last chance to really look back before jettisoning all that baggage. I don't really know why it was that I fell in love with flying. I was born on Cape Cod, loved the sea, and spent much of my time as a kid fishing. I took flying lessons. Given what happened, maybe I should have been a sailor instead. After my first visit to the Caribbean, I knew that was where I wanted to be. I worked all over flying a variety of aircraft, and then I fell in love again. After I visited Peru in the mid-eighties, I was deeply and completely smitten with the country. When I finally got a chance to fly for the U.S. State Department down in Lima in the late eighties, I jumped at it. That led to stints in Peru, Guatemala, Colombia, Ecuador, Venezuela, and Bolivia, back to the U.S., moving from job to job in all kinds of capacities within the aviation industry, with a wife, a stepson, and eventually a second son as my tie-down points.

Something about South America seemed to draw me. I was attracted to nearly everything about it. My Spanish was good, if a bit too formal for the kind of backcountry Spanish most of the FARC spoke, but from the moment of the crash, it proved to be a great aid to our survival. Still I couldn't help but wonder if my love of a place had put my family and me in jeopardy.

Moving toward the jungle, I found myself questioning if I could endure whatever was about to happen. I'd flown all kinds of planes to determine their suitability for different tasks. I sensed we were all about to enroll in the FARC finishing school, enter into a tear-down and rebuild phase of our lives. I wasn't sure how well suited I was for the task of making it through.

The FARC regrouped about half a mile from the ranch building. Sonia, the woman who had been searching the plane, was clearly the leader of the FARC group. Marc, Keith, and I were about in the middle of their column. A guard separated each of us from the other. No one was talking. At first the only noises were our footfalls and the sharp sounds of us crashing through the undergrowth, punctuated by the metallic zing of a machete as it cut through the thick woody vines that hung like curtains from the treetop canopy above. After about twenty minutes, I began to tune in to the other sounds of the woods, hearing an orchestra of insects buzzing amid the incessant rustling of the ground vegetation.

Out of desire and necessity, I trained my eyes either at the ground or straight ahead. I was still feeling the effects of the crash. Every time I tilted my head back, the world would spin. Normally, I would have tried to keep track of the direction we were moving, but the mountain forest was so thick in some areas that little sunlight made it through. Not only did the absence of sun make it hard to determine the direction we were traveling, but we couldn't tell what time it was. I didn't know how many hours we had been marching, but my body was telling me it was quite a few. The FARC guards were constantly on us to keep moving. They wanted to put as many miles between the army and us as possible.

When we finally stopped to take a rest after what had to have been at least five hours of hard marching, Marc and Keith asked the question that had been on all our minds: Where were Sergeant Cruz and Tommy J? We asked the question among ourselves, until the FARC quieted us. Sonia came back to where we were resting. Keith asked her in English, "What happened to our pilot? *Piloto?*" Sonia stared at him blankly and then scratched at her armpit and spat.

She clearly didn't understand English, so I stepped in.

"¿Qué pasó con los otros?"

Sonia answered, her voice expressionless. *"¿El gringo? Lo maté yo mismo."*

I relayed to Marc and Keith that she claimed that she had killed Tommy J herself, and that she would kill us, too. I didn't know whether to believe her or not.

Again, with a chill that we all found disturbing, she said, *"Yo les mataré también."*

We couldn't be sure that Sonia wasn't simply posturing in front of her troops. We also thought she might be falsely adopting the macho attitude typical of Colombian men. It didn't matter. Her telling us that she was going to kill us was enough to make us pause to consider again the possible outcome that had been on all our minds since the crash.

We didn't have long to share our opinions with one another. A FARC guerrilla stepped into the tight circle we'd formed around Sonia. He had Marc's survival vest in his hand, and we could tell he was agitated. One by one, he pulled the items out of the vest and held them up—binoculars, night-vision goggles, our handheld camera—before tossing them to the ground.

At the sight of all this gear, Sonia became seriously agitated. She started saying that we better explain what it all was. When they got to our locator beacon, a bright yellow bit of gear that we could have used to signal our location, we all looked at one another. If the guerrilla had messed with it and turned it on, our exact location was being tracked by folks back home. Even if it wasn't on, if the FARC thought that we'd been transmitting emergency signals, they might execute us then and there. Fortunately, a guard named Farid had disabled the device by removing the batteries. We had a similar reaction when they got to our survival radio and what we called a PRC, which is a combination of a computing device and a transmitter.

If the FARC thought that we had chip implants and we were all being tracked, then this was ample evidence that their suspicions were correct. A contradictory set of emotions and thoughts descended on us like the gathering darkness. The radio, the beacon, and the PRC were our lifelines to the outside world. Without them, we were completely cut off. If we tried to use them in any way, we'd likely be shot immediately. Sonia hammered home that last possibility.

"If you have anything else, I will kill you."

A few minutes later, the FARC had us back up and marching. We forded streams and rivers. The FARC pushed us, telling us we had to keep quiet or they'd kill us. Our feet throbbed and blistered. The moon rose high above the trees, and the temperature plummeted. We stumbled through the darkness without a single light. At one point several hours after full on nightfall, at the point of exhaustion, we stopped on a rocky riverbank. The sound of the running water nearly drowned out the insects and other wildlife. We all sat down and started to rinse our bloodied pulpy feet. The water was cold and it stung the flesh exposed by our blisters. A small group of guerrillas stripped and waded without hesitation into the river.

They urged us to join them. I was still covered in blood, and one of the guerrillas came to me with a tin cup filled with water and began to rinse my head and face. Even the sting of the water in the gash above my eye could barely penetrate my exhaustion. None of us could bring himself to get fully into the river. After a few minutes, they led us a few yards from the water. They pointed to a lean-to-type shack, what they called a *coleta*. It had a thatched roof but no sides. They had prepared a makeshift bed for the three of us. It was so cold and so cramped that we curled up together and fell into a deep collective sleep.

What seemed like only minutes later, the FARC were rousing us. "*¡Vayamos! ¡Vayamos!*"

It was still completely dark. They explained further, "*Tenemos que salir. Los aviones están aquí.*" They pointed to the sky. We could hear the distant sound of airplane motors. We stumbled out of the *coleta* and back down along the riverbank. Clouds had obscured the moon. I didn't think it was possible but it seemed as if it was even darker than before. All of us were stumbling and falling. We were getting our first lesson in jungle threats. The jungle was filled with things that could bite, sting, and otherwise pierce our flesh. Every time we staggered and put a hand out to steady ourselves, we grabbed hold of a vine, tree, or bush that was armored with spines.

We were in enemy territory in every sense of the word.

TWO

Changes in Altitude

February 14, 2003–February 24, 2003

KEITH

Believe it or not, getting awakened in the pitch-black two o'clock darkness of a Colombian mountain-highlands morning wasn't a major
shock to my system. In fact, during that first brief sleep, the opposite
had taken place. The shock had worn off. When we'd been rousted to
get back on the move, the alarm bells going off in my head weren't
enough to stir my body into action.

From my lower back to my right side, I felt an excruciating stiffness
unlike anything I'd experienced before. Every breath was like someone had clamped a bench vise down on my chest and was cranking it
tighter and tighter. The pain was tolerable, but I couldn't deal with the
thought of marching up and down the mountain slopes, each breath
more arduous than the last. In the end, it didn't matter what I could
deal with. They simply pushed us onto our feet and we began to march
through the shadows of the jungle.

In spite of the pain, I had to count my blessings. I always brought a fleece jacket with me on every flight, and when we got to higher altitudes, I'd put it on. I'd had the presence of mind to take it with me when we fled the plane, and on that first overnight march, I really needed it. Even while we were walking, it got ball-shatteringly cold, but with the fleece, I didn't have it as bad as Marc and Tom did. The whole time they shivered uncontrollably, especially when we stopped for a rest.

At one point during a break, we were all sitting in a small cluster on the side of the mountain, trying to catch our breath. Planes were flying overhead, and in between shivers, I used my thumb to probe my side. Gritting my teeth and poking deep, I felt my second and third ribs shifting. I figured that the jagged bits of bone were catching on the cartilage and other soft tissue around them, causing the pain I experienced whenever my lungs filled with air.

One of the guards, a squat little guy named Uriel, was sitting next to me with his girlfriend perched on his lap, and they were looking at me like I was some kind of zoo animal they'd never seen before. I looked away because their staring bothered me, and if I focused on it I might lose control. Tom and Marc were huddled together shivering, and between my pained breaths, I couldn't help but think how uncanny this whole scene was. The night had become crystal-clear, the moonlight was dripping over everything like cake icing, and here we all were clustered up like a pack of monkeys.

Uriel whacked me on the shoulder with the back of his hand and pointed at Marc and Tom. I thought he was going to make some wiseass remark about the two of them trying to keep warm, and I thought of flipping him off, until I saw him wrap his arms around himself, making the signal for "cold." I nodded my head, thinking, *Thatta boy, Einstein, you figured out they're cold. Move on to the bonus round.* Then he did something unexpected: Uriel reached into his backpack and pulled out a sheet. Tom and Marc had zonked out by this time, and Uriel took the sheet and gently wrapped it around the two of them like a mother tucking in her kids. After seeing that, I didn't know what to think. I was in the middle of hell, surrounded by a bunch of people who'd been treating us like animals and could kill me at any moment. Suddenly this guy does something like that. It all seemed like one big contradiction.

That rest stop turned out to be the last one for the night. Pretty soon everybody but the guard on duty and I were all asleep. Though I was exhausted in every way, I couldn't fall asleep. Instead, I was lying there on the hard ground, trying to figure out a plan. As civilian contractors, we didn't have strict rules of engagement or the clear-cut demands of the Uniform Code of Military Justice to guide our actions. If we were still active-duty military, our first obligation would have been to escape, but we weren't military, we were civilians. As such, our objective was survival. Whereas escape might get us killed, so far, being calm and cooperative seemed to satisfy our number one objective of staying alive.

I had my eyes closed and was faking sleep. Every now and then, I'd open one eye, and that guard would be looking right at me, his glare pretty much saying, "Don't think I'm falling asleep." Pretty soon after that, I crashed.

Something must have woken me up, because I remember coming back to reality. I blinked my vision clear, and right in front of my face, in a tiny shaft of moonlight, was a white flower. It was no more than six inches in front of me, so small it looked like a mere detail from an Ansel Adams photograph. At first I thought I was hallucinating. We'd been marching most of the last twenty-four hours, and I'd spent a good part of it looking down. All I saw then was dirt, rock, and dried up leaves. Where the hell did this flower come from?

I'm not the most sentimental guy, but seeing that flower did something to me. I thought about my family and what they would do without me. I told myself that I was going to make it out of there—there was no other option. I'd lost my mom when I was fourteen. I knew what losing a parent at a young age was like. I didn't want my two kids to feel the same anguish of parental loss. That flower gave me the energy I needed to get up that morning. In fact, I felt so much relief that I actually started to question my sanity. What tangible reason, other than this flower, did I have to be so hopeful? I wish that I had picked it and carried it with me, but in a way I did. From then on, I'd always find a way to return to that spot on the ground where, for a brief moment, I'd realized that I would survive.

An hour or so later, just as the sky was showing the first trace of light in the east, we were all back on our feet. Southern Colombia is a mountainous place where the steep cliffs and high valleys are covered in rain-forest vegetation. I knew the geography fairly well from the time I'd spent in-country and the surveillance work I'd done. As nearly as I could surmise, we were in the mountains somewhere between Neiva on the west side and Florencia on the eastern side of the Cordillera Oriental. It was bad, but not as bad as it could have been. The three parallel north/south sets of Cordillera mountain ranges (east, west, and central) are all part of the Andes. I suppose we should have been grateful that our targets for February 13 took us primarily south. If we'd gone farther west in the Cordilleria Central, where the tallest peaks were more than seventeen thousand feet and the lowest passes between them at ten thousand feet, our march, as epic and hellish as it was, would have been even harder.

Given our injuries—Marc was battling a similar back and hip problem to mine, while Tom most likely had a concussion to go along with his head lacerations and broken tooth—even if we had been fully acclimated to the altitude, it still would have been tough going. Add a healthy bit of hunger, lack of real sleep, the enormous stress, and we weren't exactly the von Trapp kids tromping around singing about the hills being alive with the sound of music. Instead, our sound track was the alternating but relentless crunch of feet on the hardpack, the *slurp-suck* sound of the mud, and the heaving gasps of our breaths. This was no picnic, and even when we were on the downhill, our knees, legs, and feet throbbed with pain.

As if walking and breathing weren't hard enough, we were seriously underequipped for the hike at hand. Tom was wearing a pair of cargo pants, a T-shirt, and a pair of nondescript low-cut sneakers. Marc and I had similar clothes on, a pair of chino-type pants and polo shirts. During the day, the clothes weren't a big deal, but as we'd all discovered the night before, the temperature could drop pretty quickly at night. Suddenly having only a short sleeve T-shirt made you realize just how dire the situation was.

Bad as the clothes were, the real problem was footwear. While Tom was wearing a pair of sneakers and I had on some Timberland trail shoes, Marc had on a pair of leather boots that were not the kind of shoes you'd want to go traipsing around the jungle in. They were what Marc called his "mall walking" boots. Slick-as-snot soles without a single bit of tread. Marc was being guarded by Farid, a really young, fit kid who hadn't even grown a full FARC mustache yet, just some faint caterpillar fuzz. He was no caterpillar or butterfly, though. He was a brute, and every time Marc slipped and fell, Farid would grab him by the arm to pull him upright. Farid wasn't polite about it, either; the slower Marc was to get up, the farther he dragged him along.

No matter what we had on our feet, it was as if they were being napalmed with every step. In no time, they were sweaty, and as the grade of the hill changed, our feet slid around inside the shoes—bubbling up blisters, jamming our toes into the tips of the shoe, blackening our nails.

Meanwhile the FARC was clomping along in these rubber rain boots, a black version of the boots the little girl on the Morton Salt label wears. They came to mid calf, and none of the FARC had shoes on underneath them. You could hear this rubbery singing sound as the boots hit their legs and a drumbeat of their heels slapping the soles. After a few hours that second day, we would all have gladly exchanged our footwear for theirs. Not only were their boots waterproof, but they had decent grip, even in the mud. The FARC didn't seem to be slip-sliding nearly as much as we were. Instead they just seemed to watch us as we slid all over the jungle. Marching was hard enough, but having to pick up your own sorry ass after you spilled into the brush of the jungle was even more exhausting.

Making matters worse was that a lot of our marching was in rivers and runoff streams. The algae that clung to those rocks was even slicker than the wet leaves of the jungle, and the water was fast-moving and cold. If any of us had fantasies about falling in and floating away, they were quickly shut down. We were so exhausted we would have drowned. Even if we hadn't been so tired, the streams were so choked with rubble, rocks, deadfall, and other vegetation that we wouldn't have been able to get very far. At a few points, we could hear the sound of what was either a waterfall or a series of rapids. We would not have been able to negotiate either of those. And even if we did manage to slip away from the FARC guerrillas guarding us, we had no idea where we were or what direction to go to find any friendlies—or even if any existed. For the three of us, just putting one foot in front of the other was about the best we could do.

I'm not sure if knowing our destination and for how long we'd be marching would have made things any easier, but we asked the FARC constantly about when we were going to get "there" and where "there" was. Their typical responses were "*un rato más,*" and "we're taking you to rest." This pattern of vague responses infuriated us, but we were quickly learning that our FARC guards were little more than pack animals or slaves to the FARC hierarchy. They were at the very bottom of the information food chain by design. If they couldn't tell us how far or where we were going, it was because they didn't know themselves. Even after a couple of days, we began to doubt that Sonia, the mobile-column leader, was fully aware of where she was taking us. In a way, I guess I should have been flattered by that. As Americans, we were big fish that they'd caught, and we had to be handled with care and the orders had to come from the higher-ups, not from the soldiers on the ground.

The entire time we marched, Sonia was in constant radio communication with the muckety-mucks in the upper ranks of the FARC. What they didn't realize was that each time they switched on the radio, they were threatening to expose our position. The FARC were right to be concerned that U.S. intelligence agencies were listening to them, but they weren't sophisticated enough to understand the different ways those agencies could eavesdrop. While U.S. agencies didn't have a satellite capable of picking up the FARC's actual conversations, they did have the ability to intercept their radio communications. The whole reason we were hightailing it away from the crash site was to put some distance between the army and us, but the Colombian military could track us by intercepting radio communications. Every time Sonia keyed in her FM radio to get additional orders or to report on our status, it was like she was leaving fluorescent blazes along our trail.

To give credit where it's due, as much as it seemed to me that we were just hauling our asses aimlessly around in the jungle, the FARC knew their way around fairly well. Every stream we crossed, and there were a lot of them, and every section of jungle pretty much looked alike. Yet they kept moving, relentlessly pushing to some destination that we couldn't see or hear. I consider myself a decent Boy Scout type of guy, but during those first twenty-four hours, I lost all sense of what direction we were going in. The only thing I knew about our location was that we were climbing higher into the mountains.

The fact that the FARC were jungle rats, expertly navigating a maze of their own making, did not help our hopes for a quick rescue. If some troops were on the ground trailing after us, I had to trust that they were the stealthiest the Colombian Army had. If the FARC detected them, or even if they didn't and we were caught in an ambush, I didn't think our chances of living were good. If any U.S. Special Forces units had been deployed, then I would have increased our odds exponentially, but they still would not have had the sense of the land that the FARC clearly did. I tried not to think of the advantage that any guerrilla operation has over their enemy—local knowledge of the terrain and hideouts.

As we marched we heard several references to someone whose name sent a chill up our spines. I knew that one of our targets that day had been a lab that the FARC used to take the raw coca leaves and process them into the paste that would eventually become rock or powder cocaine. We also knew that the lab was under the control of a high-ranking member of the FARC whose nom de guerre was Mono JoJoy. Mono JoJoy, whose real name was Victor Julio Suárez Rojas, aka Jorge Briceño Suárez, commanded the FARC's Eastern Bloc. Each of the members of the FARC had adopted an alias, and they also had nicknames they used with one another, on top of the code names we assigned them. If it weren't for the nature of the work we were doing, we wouldn't have known what Mono JoJoy's real name was, and with most of the low-ranking guerrillas we'd come into contact with so far, all we knew them by was their alias.

The Eastern Bloc was one of seven major geographic divisions the FARC used to organize their forces. The secretariat or *secretariado* was a seven-member leadership group immediately beneath the commander in chief, Manuel Marulanda. Also a member of the secretariado, Mono JoJoy was primarily responsible for their military operations. Since 1999, he'd been under indictment in the United States on charges of killing three Americans as well as for terrorism and narcotics trafficking—in addition to a laundry list of other charges. Basically, he was a bad dude, someone who had joined the FARC at age twelve and was in his forties at the time of our capture. In that time he must have swallowed so many tons of the radical indoctrination that the Marxist rebel crap spouted out of him at both ends.

The thought that we were potentially being taken to him, combined with the fact that his name was mentioned on our target sheets, put a scare into us. Though Marc had done his best to destroy our papers, there was no guarantee that the FARC hadn't found something. If we were being brought to one of the FARC's high commanders, things didn't look so good for the home team. We'd likely be interrogated, and who knew what kind of torture methods they'd employ. Mono JoJoy was already down for three American deaths; what would three more mean to somebody who'd spent most of his life rising through the ranks of a terrorist organization?

As if the thought of Mono JoJoy weren't enough, I was also troubled by the questions our captors kept asking us, mainly "Why are you working against us?"

We'd reply that we weren't working against them; we were working against the drugs. I wasn't just splitting hairs with them. We had no mission specifically against the FARC. We were there to do drug interdiction work. We never took any direct action against the FARC. When I asked them if they were involved in any way in the drug trafficking going on, some would say yes.

"Well," I'd tell them, "if you're working the drugs, we're working against you. No drugs, no touch you."

Then, one of the smarter, or maybe one of the more brainwashed, among them would say, "We don't do anything with drugs. We just tax. We tax the people in the drug business."

The more they delivered answers like this, the clearer the extent of their indoctrination became. It was like running into a wall, and I was too exhausted to call them out on the obvious lies. A couple of the guerrillas with us were wearing Che T-shirts, and my mind kept returning to the biography of Che I'd been reading on the plane. To them, he was just a face emblazoned on a shirt, a revolutionary image to reinforce their cause. They knew little about who he was and what he actually represented. How they could honestly believe that they were carrying on the ideals of Che Guevara was baffling to me. This was a group that resorted to trafficking drugs, using land mines, recruiting kids, attacking and killing civilians, taking hostages, and demanding ransom for fund-raising and political leverage. A group whose activities had resulted in thousands of deaths and the displacement of many more civilians.

The story of how the FARC had devolved from an idealistic, if violent, organization interested in overturning Colombia's small controlling elite into a group of thuggish terrorists made me sick. When I did ask one of them why they thought we could be legally held, he told me that we had violated their airspace. I couldn't believe it. They were so deluded as to actually believe that they had some kind of sovereign status within Colombia, with actual borders and their own airspace.

It was true that in 1998, former Colombian president Andrés Pastrana had granted the FARC a limited demilitarized zone centered around San Vicente de Caguán—a safe haven of less than twenty thousand square miles in southern Colombia. For years, the FARC had insisted that they wouldn't talk peace unless they had this safe haven, and Pastrana did what he did as an act of good faith, hoping to bring the FARC to the bargaining table to work out a peace accord. However, after receiving the safe haven, they only halfheartedly engaged in negotiations. Instead, they mostly used their demilitarized zone as a place to import arms, export drugs, recruit more minors, and replenish their troops and supplies.

By February of 2002, a full year before we were on the ground with the FARC, Pastrana had called off those talks, putting an end to the demilitarized zone. In fact, the zone we were in, and many other places where the FARC operated, were *highly* militarized. So their imagined status, as a nation with airspace, was even more of a mental apparition, but there was no way to explain any of that to these guys. I could only hope that when we met Mono JoJoy, he'd have a more reasonable explanation for what they were planning to do with us and how they could justify our capture.

In the meantime, I had a lot more slogging to do. The going was not getting any easier, and along with my injuries, there was something wrong with my stomach. I couldn't eat a thing. I was nauseous and a persistent, painful diarrhea was plaguing me. Tom was struggling as much as I was because of his injuries. Marc, being the youngest of us, and the least hurt as far as we could tell, was making better time. Our line was being strung out, and for much of the march into the second day, I couldn't see Marc at all. I knew he was in front of Tom and me, but I didn't know just how far. As night fell on that second day, I had no idea how long it had been since we'd seen him.

We marched until well after dark, stopped alongside a stream, and sat down on a rocky embankment on stones the size of a baby's head. They laid a sheet of black plastic on the rocks, and that's where we slept. In spite of the rocks poking my spine, I passed out pretty fast, but I woke up a while later when the rain came pouring down on top of us. I'd done enough camping in my life to know that rain is a usual part of being outdoors, but it still piled insult on top of insult on top of injury. We moved under one of the guerrillas' tarps to get out of the rain. All night long the sound the rain on the tarp and on the rocks was punctuated by the sound of my guts spilling out of me as I vomited and shat every couple of hours. I couldn't eat, water would run right through me or right back out of me, and I knew on top of my ribs being broken and everything else, I was getting dehydrated.

In the middle of the night I turned to Tom, saying, "I'm real worried right now. I'm at a point physically where I can't make this."

Tom looked at me and he could see in my eyes that I was approaching my breaking point. Neither of us knew what to do. The next morning, we set out again. As before, we marched upriver, battling the frigid water and the slick rocks. After a half hour, we clambered up a bank and came to a road. Ahead of me and above me, I could see a series of steep inclines and switchbacks, but just looking at them, I knew I couldn't do it. I collapsed onto the ground. Tom came up beside me, a crust of blood and scab over his eye. I looked at him, and then at Sonia coming back toward us to check on the cause of the delay.

I lifted my hand a bit to point toward Sonia, and through my cracked and swollen lips I said to Tom, "You tell that bitch for me that she can just shoot me. I don't care. I'm not going any farther. I ain't movin'. I can't. I'm done. I'm out."

Lying in a heap on the ground, somewhere layered beneath my anger, my exhaustion, and my pain, I thought, *I should have grabbed that damned flower.*

MARC

I hated being so far in front of Keith and Tom. I knew there was both physical and emotional strength in numbers, and I was afraid that because I was out in front that I would be taken somewhere ahead of them where I'd be shot or interrogated. I kept thinking about Tommy J and Sergeant Cruz. The FARC had separated them from us and Sonia claimed to have killed them. Was that how the FARC worked—putting their hostages in small groups and then killing them when they weren't in sight of the others?

Farid was pushing me so hard that I had no choice but to keep moving and temporarily leave those thoughts behind on the trail. As much as I disliked how harshly he was grabbing me and pulling me to my feet, what I really hated was that he kept talking to me. I didn't speak much Spanish, but I could recognize a few words and understand his intent. His constant refrain of "*¡Vamos!*" didn't need any translation. It was usually accompanied by a shoulder-socket-tearing jerk on my hand or wrist. As intolerable as that was, it was even worse that he said over and over again that he and I were "*mejores amigos.*" I would nod and say, "*Sí, mejores amigos,*" but I was really thinking that this whole situation was a freak show and this guy was the main attraction.

Maybe it was because we knew that these men and women were

called guerrillas, maybe it was our sick senses of humor, or maybe we were all a product of watching too much American television as kids, but we all immediately thought that we were stuck in *The Planet of the Apes*. I was thrust into the middle of a group whose language I didn't speak and I was being pushed around by a bunch of guys who were about my height but far more stout, and who were about as unrefined a bunch of people as I'd ever seen. Perhaps the most unnerving thing was the staring. Many of them thought I was the most curious sight that they'd ever seen, and every time we stopped, a few of them would cluster around looking at me, their eyes sizing me up like I was a circus attraction. I've always been an open-minded kind of guy, but I felt like I was being backed into a corner and some of my worst impulses were coming out. I could feel a visceral hatred for the FARC—not because of who they were, how they looked, or the language they spoke—but because of what they were doing to us: taking our freedom just because they could. I don't know if Farid was clueless or cruel. Whenever I couldn't go on any more and needed to rest, or when I fell, he started to get in my face and goad me, saying in Spanish, "You can't go on because you are a pussy. I am strong. America is weak."

I'd just stare at him, faking like I couldn't understand what he was saying. He seemed to take more and more pleasure in my pain and weakness as we went along. He'd grab his crotch as he stood over me and point at me: "*¡No tienes huevos!*" He'd laugh and then add, "*Cajones grandes*" while pointing at himself and acting like some caricature of a street thug from a B movie.

Once we'd put a distance between ourselves and the others, Farid seemed to relax a bit—not in his pace, or in his abuse of me—but in his posture. His body language shifted, and he grew more loose-limbed. His face lost some of the lines and creases of worry that had made him appear older, and now he looked like the teenager I suspected he really was. He also began to sing. At first I could only catch a word or two, but after a few hours of hiking and hearing this guy sing the same words over and over again, I could piece together a bit of it. "We love the peace. I am a guerrilla because I love the peace."

When I wasn't being yanked off the ground or listening to Farid spout nonsense, my eyes were focused at the vegetation around me. The dense thicket we traveled through was alive with all kinds of creatures. I'd always enjoyed nature shows on TV, and suddenly I had stepped into one. If it weren't for the circumstances, I would have loved it. There was a greater variety of monkeys than I'd seen at any zoo—most of them different kinds of spider monkeys. Like our captors, they seemed really interested in the new kids in the jungle, and they perched in the trees looking down at us with their enormous grapelike eyes.

Just as the sun was about to set, two guerrillas, or at least guerrilla sympathizers, joined Farid and me. One was a young man, dressed in sweatpants and a T-shirt. He had a campesino hat on—a wide-brimmed woven thing that was a cross between a fedora and a sombrero. The other was a young woman dressed just like the guy, and her eyes were wide with astonishment at the sight of me. They were carrying a small plastic bag filled with white rice and freckled with bits of chicken. The guy used his machete to hack off a couple of palm fronds that we could use as plates. They heaped a pile on two leaves, handed one to Farid and one to me. Sitting down, Farid rounded his body and hunched his shoulders to protect his meal. He began shoveling the food into his mouth with his fingers, his nails black with dirt and so long they had begun to curl.

Even if I hadn't seen Farid wolfing down his food, smacking his lips, and wiping his mouth with the back of his hand, I still wouldn't have had an appetite. I hadn't eaten in nearly forty-eight hours, but the thought of food turned my stomach. The young female guerrilla sat beside me, and I could see the look of concern in her eyes. She put her hands under mine and raised them toward my face. I turned my head and screwed up my face in exaggerated disgust. The food smelled okay, but something was wrong with my stomach. Eventually she just shrugged and dumped my food back in the bag. Between mouthfuls, Farid looked up and waved them on, back down the trail we walked up, presumably to feed the others. Still chewing and licking his lips, Farid got to his feet and pulled me up.

Energized by the first meal that I'd seen him eat since we'd started marching, Farid picked up the pace. I devised a new strategy. Rather than lag behind and deal with Farid's wrath, I'd keep his pace for as long as I could. When I got so winded that I couldn't go on, I would drop to one knee and suck in as much of the thin air as I could. By the time Farid noticed I'd stopped and turned to come get me, I would stand up and start moving toward him. This went on for another hour or so. Full-on darkness was still a ways off, but the sounds of the jungle had switched from the wild and cacophonous to eerie. Along with the insect and wildlife noises, I heard a faint tapping sound—regular as a heartbeat most of the time but with a few pauses. Farid heard it as well, and he put his finger to his lips. As we made our way forward, the sounds grew louder. Farid took his AK-47 off his shoulder and whipped around to quiet me again. He turned and stood with his AK held sideways with the stock perpendicular to the ground, Rambo-gangster style. He continued creeping forward, waving his hand back at me to indicate that I should hold my position. I had no idea what was going on and my mind was racing.

Farid lowered his gun and waved me forward. Peering through the dense bush, I saw another guerrilla slinging his machete to clear another, more overgrown trail. At the head of this new route stood two mules. Farid indicated that I was to get onto one of them, but when I took a step forward, the mule started braying and kicking its back legs at me. The new FARC guerrilla grabbed the mule's rope bridle and tried to quiet him, but the thing was still bucking. Farid picked up a burlap bag that the other guerrilla had left on the ground and placed it over the mule's head. It stilled. I figured the thing got aggressive when it saw someone moving toward it to mount. Farid waved me toward the blinded mule. I edged closer to the mule and finally climbed aboard. It kicked just a bit, but with Farid holding its rein and whispering in its ear, it quickly quieted. Farid jumped on the other mule, and with the sound of the other guerrilla chopping away, we headed up the other trail. When I looked back, it was as if the trail had closed behind us.

I was glad to be off my feet, but riding a saddled mule didn't give me much relief. Every bounce up and down was transferred through my already beat-up feet. We were on a steep incline, but with the mules moving at a good clip, we soon came to a more or less level area of the trail. To my left and to my right was darkness, but ahead of me, through the branches and vines, a dim light faintly shone.

A few moments later we exited the jungle into a large clearing where we were greeted by a breathtaking panorama of mountains spread out across the horizon; each peak cast a silhouette against the violet backdrop of the sky. About a half mile or more away, a little campesino farmhouse sat on a promontory overlooking this vista. An extremely steep switchback trail led up to the farmhouse, and Farid and I paused for a moment, both of us taking in the view. Sitting on the mule, I felt as if I was in a Hollywood western, coming in from a hard day in the mountains rounding up the herd to bring them off pasture for the winter.

When I got to the house, a group of six other guerrillas was there. They were sitting outside around a small fire. They'd driven two small forked sticks into the ground with a metal rod resting in the crotch of each. Suspended above that on the rod was a large pot. One of the guerrillas opened the pot and steam escaped, and the smell of chicken soup wafted across the air. Though I could feel my insides gnawing at themselves, I turned down their offer of food. I was feeling so alien, so dislocated from everything that I'd previously known, and so angry at the situation that I couldn't bring myself to sit down to a meal with them.

The house was divided unequally into two rooms—a larger main area and a storage-closet shed that had a separate door to the outside. Farid pointed to the cramped storage area, no bigger than four feet by ten feet, indicating that this was where I would sleep. That wouldn't have been too bad, except the room was also filled with sacks of rice, bags of black plastic filled with who knew what, and other assorted boxes and packages. When Farid closed the door, the space was overwhelmed by the odor of stale food and decayed flesh. Under normal circumstances, I might have found it hard to sleep, but the next thing I knew, light was filtering through the slits in the wooden walls indicating that morning had come.

The door had no lock on it, so I walked out of the shed. Scattered around the clearing were a few logs and log benches, and I took a seat with my back to the building where most of the FARC were sitting. This was really my first moment of extended time alone, awake, and not preoccupied by thoughts of the march. Into that vacuum came a rush of emotion and thoughts that overpowered me. My mental state reflected the scene in front of me—sharp peaks bathed in sunlight and a steeply carved out valley mottled in shade. As physically high up as I was at that moment, emotionally I had tumbled down that ravinelike cleft.

I found myself thinking of the day I'd left for Colombia to come on this rotation. Before my daughter, Destiney, went off to school that Friday, she'd come into Shane's and my bedroom, where I still lay easing into my morning. Destiney gave me a big kiss and a hug—the kind only a nine-year-old girl could give to make her dad feel so loved. Now, as I sat in a clearing a lifetime away from that moment, I got angry at myself for not having gotten up that morning to spend more time with her. I should have said good-bye to Cody and Joey—my other two kids, whom other people might call my stepsons but who I just thought of as my sons.

All I could think of was Destiney's drawing desk that sat on our screened porch. She would sit for hours at that slant-top desk, painting and drawing. Every time I came back from deployment, she had a new book to show me of colored drawings of various family scenes. I treasured those books and it tore me apart to think about how much time might pass before she presented me with another one. Joey and Cody shared a room, and I visualized them sitting on the floor on the green carpet with the outlines of streets and parking lots "driving" their Hot Wheels cars all around it. Joey's birthday was coming up on the twenty-eighth of February, and I worried about not being there for it. I'd gotten him the Spyder paintball gun he'd been dying to have. I loved wandering around the field where I took the boys to play, and felt bad that we wouldn't be able to try out Joey's new gun.

Everything came back to me in such vivid recollections it was almost as if I could feel the physical presence of them weighing me down. It wasn't that the thought of them was unpleasant; on the contrary, they were the only joy I could find in that otherwise bleak setting. But these thoughts of my kids and my wife made me feel guilty, like somehow I had let them down.

That it appeared as if I'd been brought to this farmhouse to be killed added to that weight. I was never going to see my family again. Not my mom, my dad, my brother. None of them. I'd see them all in heaven, of course, but that wouldn't be for a long, long time. I knew that there were FARC guerrillas near me, and I didn't want to cry in front of them. I tried to hold it all in, but all at once it was as if that weight squeezed everything out of me. I cried until I felt like my whole body was emptied of fluid. I couldn't get the thought out of my head that Tommy J and Sergeant Cruz had been separated from us and that was possibly the end of them. Sonia's cold-blooded, matter-of-fact statement about killing them played again in my head. I kept scanning the clearing, looking to the trailhead where Farid and I had emerged from the jungle. The sunlight was crawling up the ridge opposite me, but still there was no sign of Keith or Tom.

Just when you think you've hit absolute bottom, something comes along to snap you out of it. In the past, that something had taken the form of a prayer or other thought about my faith, my family, or my friends. After I was done crying, I walked toward where the FARC were gathered around the fire and cooking pot. In order to get there, I had to cross a field of empty cellophane saltine cracker wrappers. They were everywhere. One of the big bags in the storeroom I'd slept on sat out in the open with packages of crackers cascading out of it. The FARC guerrillas sat around on the ground stuffing crackers in their mouths. And they weren't doing it a single cracker at a time; they were taking stacks of five crackers and cramming them in there. The sound of their chewing and the sight of crumbs flying everywhere was so ridiculous that I almost forgot about my despairing thoughts.

What also helped was being, for the most part, off my feet and out of my boots. Without the confinement my boots enforced, my feet ran riot. They swelled and throbbed before my eyes like a cartoon thumb struck with a hammer. There were times when I was so fascinated with my feet that I started to feel they'd taken on a life of their own. I was sure the FARC were looking at me as a source of amusement, watching as I stared at my feet. With our shared ridiculousness as an icebreaker, I felt comfortable enough to accept their offer of soup.

I was handed a spoon and an aluminum cup. I sat down on the log bench where I'd had my mini-breakdown just a few minutes before. This time, instead of facing the mountains across the way, I sat looking down the slope toward where I'd emerged from the jungle the previous night. The sun was directly overhead and I had to squint against the bright noon light. The soup was thin and a rainbow of grease, like a small spill of gasoline on a wet driveway, swirled around its surface. I could see parts of chicken sitting on the bottom of the cup. The first sip tasted vaguely of chicken, as if one had recently passed by the pot and left some chicken essence in the air and some had drifted into the broth. It was warm, it was food, and I spooned a few more swallows of it into my mouth. I was busy trying to identify what else was in the cup when something caught my eye.

I looked up and recognized the familiar shapes of Tom and Keith as they bobbed along on some pack animals. I said a quick prayer to Jesus for delivering them to me in apparently no worse shape than when I had left them. It felt like Christmas, and I'd just opened the package that contained exactly what I'd been hoping for.

TOM

Mounting that rise to the campesino house where Marc was, I was relieved about two things: that he was safe and that we were finally at the rest place the FARC had been telling us about. If it is possible to be elated and exhausted all in the same moment, that's what I was at that moment. Even with the aid of the mule I was on and the pony that carried Keith to our reunion point, the journey was still extremely painful. Seeing Marc barefoot lifted my spirits as well. Knowing that he found some relief for his feet made me wonder if I could find the same.

At least my hip wasn't troubling me anymore. The previous day I had been in so much pain that I was reduced to walking with a stiff-legged gait, swinging my leg forward and trying not to use my hip at all. It went on like this for some time, until finally, a young female FARC injected me with some kind of painkiller. I was in such agony, I didn't think twice about dropping my pants for the injection or asking what the medicine was or how many times the needle had been used. Without that shot, I would have asked to be put out of my misery.

Keith was slightly ahead of me, and when he dismounted, Marc was there to meet him. I got down off my mule and gingerly walked toward them. Marc had come toward Keith carrying a small aluminum pot. I saw Keith look at it and shake his head. The pot was passed along to me, and I could see why Keith had refused it. Inside was a thin soup with a pale chicken foot bobbing on the surface. I knew Keith had been complaining about severe stomach distress and he wasn't able to eat. I was sure that sight didn't do much to help. As I brought the broth to my lips, I thought briefly of Mariana's wonderful cooking and the last meal I'd had before the crash. I don't remember much about the soup's taste, but I was glad for the liquids in my system. My wag on it was that I could have just as well been drinking an IV fluid.

We joined the circle of cracker eaters, and Keith managed to eat a few. I ate some, too. During my life, I'd traveled a good bit and been to some out-of-the-way places, but this scene defied belief. A group of adults was sitting around a cooking pot suspended over an open fire, their mouths full of half-eaten crackers and a confetti layer of crumbs outlining each of their positions. We were startled into reality when one of the FARC guerrillas began jumping up and down and pointing at us and then toward the house. He was trying to say something, but the congealed mass of flour in his mouth muffled and distorted his words. Finally, after a bit of swallowing and spitting, he made it clear that he wanted us to be quiet. Several of his guerrilla comrades walked over to the house, where a Sony AM-FM radio was hanging from one of the posts supporting the roof.

"¡Son ustedes! ¡Son ustedes! ¡Son ustedes!"

We all quieted down enough so that we could hear the report on a Colombian radio station about our crash and capture. The details were sketchy. They didn't reveal the exact location of where we'd gone down or what the military was doing to find us. I didn't take much comfort in knowing that we were celebrities in this part of the world. When the FARC heard the radio mention what connected them to us, their response troubled me. They erupted with cheers, acting like the home team had just scored a touchdown at the mere mention of our names.

After things settled down a bit, the weirdness revved up once more. Several yards away, a few of the FARC had gathered around a well and were washing their clothes. The young men had stripped down to the briefest of bikini-type briefs and so had one young woman. I'm not a prude, but their unself-consciousness surprised me a bit, only because it seemed so out of place. Having been all around Latin America, I was used to the region's mores and practices. But the sight of that woman was jarring because it was the picture of innocence in a place and in a set of circumstances that I considered anything but innocent. Of course, all my thoughts of innocence were immediately wiped out when she walked past us to get some food. The other guards, all of them, like her, no more than eighteen years old or so, began hooting and nudging us. "Look! Look! What do you think of that? How do you like her?" It felt more like an outdoor cafeteria at a high school than a temporary prison encampment.

A while later, I saw a little girl riding a pink Barbie pedal car. I understood then that this house didn't belong to the FARC, but to a family. How the hell these people were able to get that car out into the middle of the mountains, and how much it must have cost them in effort and money, was both touching and confusing. Nothing seemed to match with the landscape, and we all sensed it.

"This place is freaking me out. These kids are all in their costumes playing guerrilla." Marc stretched and rolled his head around his shoulders.

"I know exactly what you mean. If it wasn't for the radio, I'd say we'd gone from the information age to the Stone Age," I added.

We hadn't seen Sonia for a while, and after how she had told us about killing Tommy J, I wasn't exactly missing her warm presence. A few minutes later, I saw her coming toward us, moving at her usual pretty good clip. She was making a beeline for Keith, who was sitting on one of the stump seats the campesinos had crudely carved out. I thought that no good could come of this. Either she was going to confront Keith about something, or she was going to take him away somewhere. She had on her face the expression of someone who had been wronged and wanted to be sure that whatever had been done was now made right. I'd seen that look before on my wife's face.

Sonia made a quick change in course and diverted to the well. She came back toward us, carrying a large ceramic bowl filled with water. She set the water bowl in front of Keith and then knelt in front of him. Sonia flicked her mane of hair over her shoulder and untied the laces on Keith's shoes and then pulled the shoes off him completely. I looked at Keith and he seemed as shocked as Marc and I were. We all exchanged glances and shook our heads. Sonia continued to wash Keith's feet and to massage them. Like all of ours, his feet had been wet for the better part of twenty-four hours. They were swollen, wrinkled, and looked like a relief map of the terrain we'd been covering.

We wanted to be sure that we kept the line between "them" and "us" clearly plotted on our charts, so we didn't accept the FARC's offer of letting us sleep in the house—what they called a *finca*—that night. We also knew that the spot that Marc had bunked in the previous night wouldn't hold the three of us. We didn't want to be separated, and none of us wanted to have anything that the others did not. While not being separated was something we discussed, the desire to be treated equally wasn't something we talked about; we just naturally fell into that plan. Without words, we had coalesced into a unit; we were all in this together.

That said, we didn't begrudge anyone when he got something the others didn't. I wasn't upset that Keith had gotten his feet treated as they had. Likewise, I had gotten a pair of the rubber boots, and Keith and Marc hadn't.

We slept on top of a small hay mound, and all through the night, we could hear the campesinos' horses moving around in their little corral just beyond where we slept. They were clearly uneasy about something, and their agitation bothered us, since they could have easily gotten out, come to claim their feed, and stomped on us. In the end, though, sleep won out and we stayed put for the night.

We were awakened in the morning by one of the horses munching on the hay that had been our bed, but it didn't matter. That morning we were back on our march, this time riding the same horses that had annoyed us the night before. It became clear as that day progressed that the FARC's efforts were more coordinated than we'd first thought. After a few hours, we would stop and dismount. Whoever had been guiding would head back down the trail in the direction he'd come from. Another guide, sometimes a civilian, sometimes a guerrilla, would show up. He'd take the lead down the trail. At times we felt like we were the batons that runners in a relay race were handing off to one another. It went on like this for days. Guides arriving and departing, rests coming at intervals of multiple hours, collapsing from exhaustion for the night, and waking up the next morning to do it all over again. With each passing day, we held out hope that we'd meet a FARC member of some importance or in possession of information who could at least give us a better sense of where we were headed, but none arrived.

Finally, several days into our march, we found one FARC who seemed to have some real intelligence. We were stopped at the head of another trail that climbed even higher than the previous ones. The FARC had spread out a sheet of plastic for us to lie down on. That seemed unusual, and we weren't sure what it meant. Briefly, I thought that the sheet would make it easier for them to wrap up our bodies after they'd shot us up. We were lying there when a new FARC guerrilla showed up.

"Hola, me llamo Johnny. Yo soy un médico."

His Spanish was more precise and formal than the campesino Spanish the rest of the Colombians spoke and I didn't have to slash my way through a jungle accent. I assumed that as a medic, Johnny had more formal education than the others.

"Were any of you taking any medication before?"

"I'd been taking medication for my blood pressure," I said.

Johnny nodded and jotted something down in his notebook.

"I will be sure that you get what you need." He actually smiled and wasn't being sarcastic or cruel. "Let me see your head wound." He

cupped my chin in his hand and tilted my head so that he could exam-
ine the gash. "There is no infection yet, but you have been lucky so
far." He seemed to wince at his use of the word *lucky* and stood up
and returned a moment later with hydrogen peroxide and some cotton
balls. As he carefully dabbed at the wound, I watched his pupils dilate
and contract. "This is quite deep." He raised his index finger and asked
me to follow it as he moved it from side to side and closer and farther
away from me, watching my reactions as I had just done with him.

"I will be back," he said.

"Is it more serious than the wound?" I asked.

Johnny turned around and then glanced to the side. "It has been
several days since you hit your head, so it is difficult to say if you had a
concussion. In all likelihood, yes. How is your vision?"

"At times blurry, but I don't have my glasses."

He listed the other symptoms, some of which I had, but they could
have been the result of other things—headache, nausea, but fortunately
no vomiting.

"Excuse me, I will be back."

He returned a while later with some medicine for me and some
gauze for the blisters on our feet. He started treating all our feet.

"How long have you been a medic?" I asked him for Marc.

Johnny shrugged. "For a while now. I was wounded in a battle, now I
have to do this." He didn't sound very happy about his new role.

"A medic is very important."

Johnny paused in wrapping Keith's foot. "Not nearly so important
as a fighter."

"But you must have had a lot of training." Keith paused, "*Mucho
educación.*"

Johnny smiled. "When I was a young man, I wanted to be a doctor.
My family had no money and so I couldn't go to school." He stopped
and shrugged, and in that gesture a whole ruined life was revealed. We
could put it together that it was at this point in his life story that he'd

joined the FARC. I hoped that maybe he hadn't understood our question about his training, so I asked him more specifically how the FARC had trained him to be a medic. As he wrapped Marc's foot, he looked around. "No training. I learned by doing." When he was done with all of our feet, he said, "I hope this helps."

When he was through working on our feet, he walked away, and a few moments later another FARC guerrilla came up to where we sat on the plastic, carrying sets of clothes and pairs of boots for each of us. They provided us with camouflage pants and T-shirts. Keith was considerably larger than most Colombians, and none of the shirts fit him properly. He also couldn't get the boots on because his feet were too large. Even the boots that were too large for Marc, ones he had to wear in spite of them not fitting well, would not accommodate Keith. To make matters worse, Keith was still not able to eat, and he was getting weaker and weaker by the day.

As much as I tried to keep track of the days, it was becoming increasingly difficult. Not only did each day blend into the next because of the ceaseless marching and the constantly changing FARC guards, but we were sleep-deprived and starving. The FARC were pushing us well past our limits.

Ultimately, Keith's more severely damaged body started to go in the opposite direction of mine. I was getting a bit stronger, but without food, Keith was deteriorating. Early on he'd expressed his concern about his ability to continue. Even though a few of the days were spent on horseback, which conserved some energy, he wasn't taking in enough nourishment. He was on the verge of shutting down. Marc and I grew very concerned that if his condition worsened, the FARC would shoot him. We were clearly in a hurry to get away from the army, and if Keith was compromising our ability to escape, well, then we all knew what that might mean.

We continued to hold the pattern we'd developed on that first day, with Marc going on ahead of us. We didn't spend any night separated from him, but he was often well in front of us on the trail. He apologized if that was a problem, but we assured him it wasn't. We knew that Marc setting the pace for us was a good thing. Charging ahead allowed him to get additional breaks, since it meant that he'd cover a good deal of ground quickly and then could rest. This, in turn, meant that his guards weren't as pissed with him for stopping. His style also benefited Keith and me because with him as our "race leader," the overall impression the FARC had was that we were making good time.

Keith felt bad about his inability to be up in the lead. I knew that it was tearing him apart, and that he was afraid that he might be jeopardizing all of us. In truth, I was also grateful that his pace was what it was. At one point during the first week or so of the march, we were sitting together at a rest point. Keith patted me on the shoulder and said, "Thanks for sticking with me."

"Just relax. We'll get through this thing," I said.

At that point in our ordeal, the three of us were so intertwined with one another that it was difficult to tell where one kind of bonding left off and another began. We were also doing what was best for each of us, and as it turned out, this also meant we were doing what was best for all of us.

After a week of marching, we detected a new change among our guards. We'd been with the same group for a few days, and we were all more attuned to their moods. The medic Johnny was among them. The first time I heard one of them mention an airplane, I thought they were talking about one that had flown overhead at some point. When I kept hearing the word *avión*, I asked them what they were talking about. We hadn't seen or heard aircraft for several days. They explained that they were taking us to an airplane.

For the next three days, as we marched along, they would remind us that we were going to an airplane. When we were all gathered for the night, I told Marc and Keith what they'd been saying. We all agreed that this was potentially a very good development. If they were taking us to an airplane, it meant that we were going to be getting on it and going somewhere. We remained hopeful that some agreement was being worked out and that we were going to be released. Why else would we be getting on a plane except to fly to someplace where the exchange could take place?

Over the two days that followed, those constant reminders kept us going. Maybe human beings are capable of making themselves believe just about anything because we kept that one thought firmly in our minds—we were going to an airplane and we were going to be flying off someplace. Even though the track we were on was still climbing higher, it wasn't outside the realm of possibility that the FARC had an airstrip somewhere. Keith and I talked at every chance about the type of plane that could get airborne quickly enough. We'd seen enough large clearings to know that something like a turbocharged Cessna 206 was a likely candidate for an inexpensive, third-world, backwoods aircraft that could take off and land in such spaces.

The day they told us we'd be getting to the plane was one of the most difficult climbs we'd experienced to that point. Part of the time we were marching along a path, traversing the steep mountainside. At other times, we were climbing on all fours, more like rock climbing than hiking, or scrambling among huge boulders and loose fields of stone. As usual, Marc had gone ahead of Keith and me, and this climb was torturous for us both. Finally, the FARC figured out that Keith was not going to go anywhere under his own power. He was grounded.

Rather than just wait for him to regain his strength, the FARC guerrillas put on their own display of strength, cutting down a tree and hanging a hammock on the shortened length of trunk they fashioned as a carrying pole. They loaded Keith into the hammock and then two of them lifted each end of the pole to their shoulders and carried him. He was slung between them like a jungle cat they'd killed and were carrying home as a trophy. The guerrillas had a serious macho thing among them, so they were practically fighting over who was going to take the next turn to carry all 214 pounds of Keith up that incredibly steep pitch to where we'd been told the airplane was waiting. By the time they got to the top, even the strongest of the FARC were exhausted. They basically dumped Keith to the ground and stood with their hands on their knees, their chests heaving. But neither Keith nor I paid much attention. Our eyes were trained on the airplane, or at least what was left of it.

In front of us sat the skeletal remains of a single-engine Cessna. Far from being a working plane, this thing had ceased to function a long time ago. Marc had been there for some time before us, and he walked up to me.

"I know. I know. I can't believe, it either," he said. I didn't have words to respond to him.

Immediately any thoughts we had of being flown to a prisoner exchange evaporated. Looking at that plane, with small-caliber bullet holes riddling one side (clearly not what had brought it to the ground), we couldn't help but think of our own crash and of whoever had been aboard this plane. An overnight bag flapped in the twenty-knot wind. Empty sardine cans lay strewn around the wreckage. The FARC had found still sealed jars of Nescafé instant coffee and were stuffing them in their backpacks. I walked around the seared metal. The smell of decaying flesh was suddenly in my nostrils. I looked inside the cabin. It was empty.

On this exposed ridge at what I guessed had to be well above five thousand feet, the air was frigid. I tried to take it all in. The wreckage. Keith lying on the ground tucked into a fetal position for warmth. Marc, visibly shaken, pale and drawn and lost in his own thoughts of what might have happened to this pilot and crew and what might be happening to us. I hated feeling lucky at that moment, but I did. We were still alive thanks to the skill of Tommy Janis, and now, like the pilot of the wreck before us, he was nowhere to be seen.

I saw a pair of black penny loafers sitting on this wind-scraped hunk of rock. They had to have belonged to someone on board that doomed craft. The pennies were gone. I thought about just how cheap life was to these guerrillas and just how valuable it was to all of us. I'd been driven by the pursuit of the almighty dollar most of my life, but I was just starting to learn that there were a few things more valuable than coin.

THREE

¿Quién Sabe?

February 25, 2003–March 9, 2003

MARC

In some ways, sitting at that windswept crash site was a good thing. The climb to the airplane had taxed our bodies and spirits to their limits. The FARC had made it sound as if this plane was somehow going to help us get free. Now, confronted by the reality, we all felt as though we'd been punched in the gut and had our breath knocked out of us. Whether they were being malicious or just incredibly dense didn't matter. We were learning a valuable lesson the hard way: It was dangerous for us to trust their words.

If there was one positive that we could take from this enormous disappointment, it was that Keith was finally going to get more medical help. Having eaten nothing for the last week and a half except a few crackers, he was at the point when he knew that he could no longer continue. He told Johnny that he was not going any farther, and thank God that Johnny was either sympathetic, worried, or both, because he took Keith seriously. We were in a vulnerable location, where we could be easily spotted from the air, but despite that, they set up a tent for the three of us. We were all shivering so violently that they built a fire, but we were too exhausted to even crawl out of the tent to sit by it.

The only reason we woke up the next morning was that Johnny returned with an IV fluid drip for Keith. I was a little worried about this jungle medic jabbing Keith with a needle, but he seemed to know what he was doing, although it strangely took him another couple of days to stitch up Tom's head wound. After an hour or so of Keith's IV treatment, the bag was empty and we were on the move again with Keith still dangling between two guerrillas in the hammock.

By Tom's count, we had been on this march for eleven days since the plane went down. We still had no idea of where we were going or whether there was a point to this march other than getting us as far away from the Colombian Army as possible. Even if we hadn't been surviving on only a few hours of sleep, those days would have blurred one into another. Our exhaustion was so all-consuming that anytime we stopped marching, even if it was for just a few minutes, we immediately fell asleep. We were all experiencing a kind of vertigo; every image seemed to dance in front of us with dizzying intensity, as if we were viewing everything through troubled water.

Though the FARC continued to provide Keith with IV feedings, beyond that they didn't seem to care much about our mental or physical state. They pushed us relentlessly during the next two weeks, and as they did, our hopes rose and fell. Their answers to our questions about where we were going or when we would be able to rest ranged from "a little while longer" to "pretty soon" to "*¿Quién sabe?*" or "Who knows?"

This last one became more frequent and more frustrating as the days passed. On what would eventually become a twenty-four day march, *¿Quién sabe?* was a tool the FARC wielded almost as frequently as the machetes they used to clear the jungle, with each tool producing a decidedly different effect. The FARC were masters of the machete, slicing and hacking with impressive ferocity or finesse depending upon the situation. From clearing the vines and the gnarled tree trunks in our way to delicately cutting and slicing bamboo shoots to extract water when there was nothing else to drink, their skillful use of their machetes was a testament to how long they had been hiding out in the jungle.

¿Quién sabe?, on the other hand, was more of a blunt instrument, something they used to bludgeon our hopes and flatten our spirits. Each time Keith, Tom, or I asked a question, we gritted our teeth to prepare ourselves for that potentially soul-killing answer. Annoying as it was, those two words didn't discourage us from asking, since nothing could stop us from thinking about home and release.

Evasive as these answers were, we gradually started to gain a better sense of our captors. Most of the foot soldiers marching with us were country boys and girls. Their behavior was crude and disgusting (spitting, openly scratching their crotches—which the men and some of the women did with the same frequency and intensity—nose exploring), but we also felt a measure of sympathy for them. We ran into our own *¿Quién sabe?* when we tried to imagine what these young men and women's lives had been like, how bad the conditions of their existence must have been to make them think that joining the FARC was a step up. A few of them we asked told us the same reason for having joined the guerrillas: "*La violencia.*" They didn't go on to explain what violence had been done to them personally, and we wondered if maybe they meant that they enjoyed being able to inflict damage on other people.

The FARC weren't exactly subtle when it came to the nicknames they gave one another. Lapo had such a prominent lower jaw that he looked like a living caricature. He was named after a jungle animal that was the size of a deer but had the jaw of a moose. Nicuro (Catfish) had wide-set eyes and a droopy mouth. Anthrax had terrible body odor. Bin

Laden had Middle Eastern features. And these young kids didn't think anything of openly referring to one another by these names.

When they weren't calling one another names, the guerrillas were eating sugar, and lots of it. They each carried a block of brown unrefined sugar that they called *panela*. They would break off a bit of it and eat it. They'd also mix Kool-Aid–type drinks from small packets—Royale and Frutino. Sometimes when we'd stop at a stream, one of them would take out a big pot they'd been carrying on their back and mix up the fruit drink. Sometimes they'd add in one, two, or three pounds of sugar, depending on the availability. That began to explain how they were able to move so tirelessly through the jungle. Like us, they weren't eating a lot, but their sugar snacks and drinks were like jungle Gatorade and energy bars.

My initial impression of the FARC as a bunch of Halloween trick-or-treaters was strengthened by this reliance on sugar and the presence of candy among them. Candy was a prized possession and those in charge frequently doled it out as a reward to the underlings. As much as we grew tired of hearing *¿Quién sabe?*, I'm sure that the FARC had to wonder why we kept using the words *bizarre* and *surreal*. To be marching through the jungle, frequently walking past coca fields that we'd likely surveyed from the air, with a bunch of sugar-smacking, lollipop-sucking, brainwashed terrorists had tapped out our vocabularies, so we resorted to using our old reliables.

Even though they were little more than a bunch of teenagers, this group and others like it had wreaked havoc in Colombia, forcing the military to use deadly force against them. I was reminded of just how serious this conflict was a day or so after we left the airplane wreckage. We were taking a fifteen-minute break on a hillside. Suddenly two members of the rear guard—those at the very end of the line—started screaming, "*¡Policía! ¡Policía!*" They ran past us and off into the jungle. The rest of the guerrillas started to panic and talk really loudly. Sonia stepped up and yelled for them all to shut up. They fell silent, and a moment later a FARC guerrilla from a different unit came walking up. He was another of the local guides assigned to help us navigate through the next bit of territory—not a policeman or military guy. So much for what brave warriors the FARC were. Still, their response revealed a more important truth: These guerrillas were being hunted, and many of them had been wounded before. While they looked somewhat laughable to us, they were also extremely volatile. After all, a terrorist organization made up of mostly young men and women isn't anyone's idea of an ideal fighting force. They were undisciplined, and without good discipline, who knew what they might do.

The first time I saw them stand in ranks, military style, it was clear that they saw themselves as an organized disciplined group of fighters. On that particular morning, a FARC commander by the name of Oscar was scheduled to arrive, and we suspected that something was up because the FARC all put their hats on. We didn't know exactly what that meant, but normally they didn't wear them. When Oscar appeared, he obviously was the commander of the Front, which in their organizational hierarchy is basically the platoon that captured us. Their chain of command dictated that Sonia reported to him. Oscar was short even by Colombian standards at about five feet two or so. He was also overweight and carried a belly that swung like a hammock over his belt. The pinkie finger on his right hand was mostly missing, but a stub of bone stuck out of the fleshy nub that remained.

When Oscar called the soldiers together, they were a motley assortment and their ability to form straight lines or stand at attention was more like a Three Stooges routine than a formation. By the time they finally got in a row, the three of us were about to burst out laughing. That morning was one of the few remarkably clear days we'd had in a while, and no sooner had they assembled in their disorder than a plane flew overhead. Oscar began waving and shouting, instructing his people to get back under the jungle canopy and the roof of a crude lean-to type structure they'd built. After the plane was out of earshot, they abandoned the idea of playing soldier for that day.

The FARC made few allowances for gender, and physically, most of the women shamed us. Their ability to march all day was impressive, to say the least. At one point, I asked one of the FARC women if I could pick up her backpack to see how heavy it was. It was so loaded with her gear and food and other supplies for the rest of the unit that I could barely get it off the ground. Keith and I both had daughters, and we were distressed that some of these girls seemed barely older than Keith's Lauren. One young woman struck us as a particularly sad case. She was no more than seventeen or eighteen, and she looked like she belonged on a runway in Paris, not marching through the jungle with a rucksack whose straps would eventually scar her like all the other men and women we'd seen.

Looking at her, we all knew that her youth wasn't going to last—not physically and not spiritually. Many of the FARC women looked far older than their years, and most were in relationships with men much older than themselves. Even in those first three weeks with the FARC, we could see that as much as the FARC preached equality—and in some ways practiced it by having the women carry heavy loads, work equally hard, and take their turns at guard duty—in many ways the women were sexual captives of the FARC men.

The difficult position of the women became fairly clear to us as the march progressed. The day after the group met Oscar, Sonia told Keith that he had to bathe. She knew that with his ribs being broken and in his poor condition, it would be difficult for him to bathe himself, so she called him over to her.

"I have a surprise for you," she said in a tone that none of us had heard before. "You're going to have a great bath."

Three female guerrillas led him down to the stream. Keith lay down on a rock and the three of them helped him strip down to his underwear. They did the same themselves and they proceeded to give him a sponge bath. All Keith could do was lie there with a perplexed look on his face and take in just how bizarre the whole scene was. Afterward he came back up the hill to where I had been resting, when Uriel approached us.

"How did you like that, Kees?" Uriel said, his Colombian accent dropping the *th* sound and making Keith's name sound more like *Kiss.* "It isn't so bad here, is it?"

"Which one do you want?" another guard joined in, pushing a couple of more young female guerrillas toward Keith. "Take this one. Or the other one. A girl will be my gift to you."

"This is all I need," Keith said to me, smiling as he ignored their comments. "I'm in the middle of the jungle getting a sponge bath from three young women. With my luck, aerial recon got a shot of that scene and it'll be splashed all over the front page. Malia sees it and that's the last straw."

It was easy to laugh at the ridiculousness of the situation, but I could detect a little bit of pain seeping around the edges of his joke. As much as we were getting to know more about the FARC, we were also getting to know one another better. Recently Keith had told me that not long before our crash, he and his fiancée, Malia, had just started to work their way through a pretty tough patch in their relationship. Keith wasn't proud of what he'd done, but he'd had an affair with a Colombian flight attendant named Patricia while he was engaged to Malia. He'd confessed everything to Malia, but then learned that Patricia was pregnant with twins. He'd come completely clean and let Malia know that he'd screwed up and that whatever she wanted to do—leave him or work things out—was entirely her call. She'd decided the relationship was worth saving. Now Keith was worried about his kids and leaving Malia at such a tough time in their relationship, but he also had the added anxiety over being the father of yet-to-be-born twins. He said that he was upset with Patricia, initially thinking that she'd purposely gotten pregnant, but he couldn't let that get in the way of feeling and being responsible for the kids he'd fathered.

Although the guards knew nothing of what was going on in Keith's or any of our lives, they cruelly played on our desire to get home. When our energy was flagging and our pace slowed to a crawl, they would relay this message to us through Tom: "If you walk faster, you will see your family in two days."

We had no idea if they were telling the truth, but their claims had the desired effect. We picked up the pace as best we could. Whenever we were together, we'd speculate about whether or not we should believe their words. Our consensus was that it was unlikely that we'd see our families in two days, but maybe that was their way of telling us that we were going somewhere to be released. In our depleted condition—mental, physical, emotional—we were easy targets for that kind of deception. When the two days passed and we were no closer to being with our families, we didn't protest to anyone. We simply chalked it up as a lesson we were learning in Hostage 101.

TOM

Three days after marching from the airplane, we arrived at another *finca*, but unfortunately our second encounter with finca hospitality was only marginally better than our first. This time, instead of sleeping out on a mound of grass on the ground, we were led to a small bedroom. A couple of nasty, dirt-encrusted mattresses were on the floor and all around them were piles of FARC trash, saltine-cracker wrappers, and empty bags of powdered milk. Keith, Marc, and I hardly exchanged a word before we fell onto the mattresses and into a deep, immediate sleep.

When I woke up, I was in a half-dazed, semiaware state for an hour or so. I could hear a lot of voices, and I found myself thinking of the few times when I'd been in South America during a festival. I'd do my sightseeing and go to bed, but the rest of the hard core revelers were still out there. Through my sleep-deprived haze, I could hear them carrying on. This was like that, except it was no party.

A couple of times I raised my head up and looked to the doorway to see a few FARC backlit in the door frame. Each time it seemed the faces were different, the figures posed in a new configuration. I wasn't sure how long we were in the bedroom, but we emerged outside just as the sun was beginning to set. On our march, we'd been accompanied by about sixteen to twenty guerrillas, but at this *finca*, at least sixty guerrillas had gathered. We immediately got the sense that we were a curiosity at worst and celebrities at best. The staring that had marked our first days of captivity resumed as groups FARC guerrillas came to look at us. Some wanted to say a word or two and did so, while the rest just moved their eyes over us as though they were waiting for us to do something.

The *finca*'s kitchen was attached to the house, but instead of having four walls and a roof, it just had a piece of canvas hanging over a few poles to keep the rain off the stove. Alongside the stove sat a large metal tub, big enough for a guy to climb into and bathe. One of the FARC pulled the tub out a ways from the kitchen area while the three of us watched. At first we thought they were going to prepare a bath for us, but a few moments later, we heard the sound of a cow lowing. The cow was led to the tub, and one FARC busied himself with tying the cow's hind legs while another tied its front legs.

The cow, a somewhat thin, haggard-looking animal that seemed to be about as exhausted as we were, just stared at us sleepily. Suddenly a guerrilla put the cow into a headlock and twisted its neck back and to the side, while the other slit the cow's throat with his machete in a single, precise move. The cow's eyes rolled back in its head and it looked completely startled. Unable to keep its balance, the animal toppled over in a heap, and the guerrillas knelt beside it, pressing their hands down on its stomach as blood spurted into a smaller pan they held.

Marc and I looked at each other and then back at the cow, which was taking its last breaths and still looking at us. We didn't say anything. We didn't need to. We both knew that could easily be us at some point.

We stayed at that *finca* for three nights, and I was grateful for the rest. As I took in our surroundings, I was fascinated by the structure of the place. We were seemingly out in the middle of nowhere, and I wondered how anyone could get lumber up there to build anything. I'd been observing the FARC on our march, and a few times when we stopped for a longer rest, they'd taken some smaller trees with a diameter of anywhere between one to three inches. They'd cut those trees into smaller lengths, delimb them, and use the cut lengths as posts to create makeshift shelters. As Marc pointed out, these weren't true *Gilligan's Island*–type huts—with woven sides and palm leaves thatched as roofing. They were nylon tarps or what we called tent tops. The ground was so soft that the guerrillas were able to drive the pointed end of these poles in just about anywhere except the rocky creek or riversides.

Similarly, the ranch house appeared to be made from lumber that was milled on-site. The rough-hewn boards, what they called *tablas*, were actually ripped out of the nearby trees. They didn't have a fancy table saw to do this with; they used a chain saw. I spent part of one afternoon watching the guerrillas as they cut down a jungle tree, stripped off the limbs, and then cut it lengthwise into *tablas*. You could tell that the exterior of the house was made from these rough-hewn *tablas* because the chain saw left distinctive semicircular grooves in the surface. The FARC used these *tablas* to make all kinds of fairly crude pieces of furniture. Platforms to sleep on, tables, chairs, and benches. A few of the guerrillas took advantage of this bit of downtime to use their machetes to fashion fishing poles. I was beginning to think that if you gave a FARC guerrilla a machete and a chain saw, he could build a pretty stout house just about anywhere in that heavily forested jungle.

Their ability to live off this tough land was impressive. We all commented that it was too bad that they were using their skills at construction to such a malicious end. Many of the drug labs the FARC controlled were made out of the same jungle woods and using the same methods. When we'd been in the air above we hadn't been able to tell what they were built of, but being on the ground gave us a different perspective and a new appreciation for the intelligence we couldn't gather from the air.

At times, I found myself slipping into the role of a field observer or an anthropologist. It became my way to escape the reality around me and prevented me from growing even more stressed out than I was. The three of us would talk about our situation, but we could only do that for so long without getting our nerves all in a jangle. We agreed that considering our physical condition, we were actually doing okay. Our strategy of being nonconfrontational had worked. In our minds, goal number one was to survive. Goal number two was not to do anything that betrayed our beliefs. We were captives but that didn't mean that we would behave like criminals. We were going to have to tread a fine line mentally and behaviorally. We weren't guilty of anything, and we could never make it seem to the FARC that we had done anything wrong or that we had intended to.

In those earliest hours, we heard from Sonia and a few others about our imperialist presence and aggression, but it was just FARC party-line propaganda, so we didn't respond. As we heard more anti-American sentiment, we ignored it. The best way to combat those feelings and opinions was by conducting ourselves as honorably as we could. Even though none of us was active-duty military, we were doing work for the Department of Defense and other agencies of the U.S. government. We took seriously the role we were playing to combat narcotics trafficking and as representatives of a country we all loved. None of that would change just because we were being held captive. More than anything, we all had a sense of what was fair and just, and even though we were hostages, we would still demand to be treated fairly and justly. Being tortured, interrogated, or both was still very much on all our minds, and we all agreed that there were lines we simply would not cross.

These lines had become apparent to us a few days earlier as we were climbing down from the airplane. We were negotiating steep terrain, and we noticed that one of the FARC, a slight, delicate woman who could not have been more than sixteen or seventeen, was looking very pale. She wobbled on for a few hours in that state. Suddenly she passed out. Her compatriots just stood around staring at her, and the three of us stepped through the circle of gawkers.

Looking at her on the ground, we could see that she wasn't sweating, which was a sure sign of dehydration, or possibly even heatstroke. We decided that she needed to be cooled immediately. We took off her shirt and loosened her pants to help circulate air around her as best we could. We elevated her feet and gave her water. She had on the usual guerrilla rubber boots, so we pulled them off. That seemed to help. Listening to our suggestion, the FARC began to fan her. All those things were doing the trick, but then she started shivering. Keith still had his fleece jacket with him, so he gave it to her.

In one sense we'd crossed a line. We'd helped one of the FARC by giving this young girl aid and comfort. But we learned then that there was another line that we wouldn't cross. Just because we were being treated inhumanely didn't mean that we had to give up our humanity. All three of us had kids, and both Marc and Keith commented at the time that they were thinking of their daughters, who were respectively nine and fourteen at the time. Looking at this girl was a lot like looking at their own children. How could they have walked away? How could any of us not do the right thing, the thing we would have wanted for us or our own children?

Very early on, Keith said to us that there was the right thing to do and there was the wrong thing to do. There was the easy thing to do and the hard thing to do. We had to do the hard right thing, as much as humanly possible. That was our challenge to ourselves and to one another.

After our three nights of rest at the *finca*, on what I calculated to be the second day of the appropriately named month of March, we set out down the slope and across one of the many mountain streams. We walked for a few hours before making camp for the night. The next day the FARC provided horses for us. We didn't complain about being able to mount up instead of walking. Our route took us upstream. Sometimes the FARC led our horses along the water's edge and sometimes within the stream itself. The streambed was rock-strewn and angled steeply upward. I marveled at the agility of the horses. I was behind a young colt that was following his mother upstream over and around boulders. At several points we moved off the stream unexpectedly, and through the foliage of the banana trees and other vegetation, we could catch glimpses of tumbling and frothing water from sets of rapids.

The path through the mountains was a narrow single track, with a steep drop-off on the downhill side. A number of times, the ground beneath the horses' hooves gave way, causing the horses to lurch to the side or rear up and sending us crashing to the ground. More often than not, the horses regained their balance, but once, my horse fell with me still on it. It happened quickly. One second I was riding along, and the next I was on the ground, with Keith's voice in my ear shouting at me to move. I rolled over just as the horse's massive body collapsed onto the patch of ground where I'd just been.

I probably should have been more concerned about my safety than I was, but I was so grateful not to be on foot that I didn't really care. Not walking gave us more time to heal. Still, each fall from the horses, and we all took more than one, aggravated our injuries and brought back a more intense level of suffering. We weren't eating much, but the FARC were still feeding us a steady diet of hope:

"Negotiations for your release are going on right now."

"You're going to be set free very soon."

"The final details of the negotiation are being worked out."

Each helping of a lie was spiced with "Keep on moving." "You need to hurry." "We must go."

In so many ways, we were victims of our own hope. We wanted to believe what they were telling us so badly. It was as if those fishing poles they made were used to dangle bait in front of us, and we desperately wanted to take it. We'd analyze every little detail. They're wearing hats today. Bosses must be around. Bosses have connections to the higher-ups. The higher-ups would be involved in the negotiations. If a boss is around, maybe he's here to take us to a release/exchange point. Everything became a sign or prediction for the future.

I don't know if any of us really *believed* what we were being told, but we knew that at some point we had to stop allowing our hope to be used *against* us. It was there *for* us and we couldn't let them use it for their ends.

KEITH

One morning, a few days after we'd helped the young girl (who did return my jacket and thank us), Johnny told us to drink up. We were heading over another mountain pass and there would be no water. He wasn't exactly right, but close. We sipped a few drops from some bamboo shoots, and the FARC were able to extract water from some plants that grew in clusters. They had palmlike fronds that were so tightly intertwined that they formed little gutters that collected rainwater.

Being the largest of the bunch was not easy when it came to clothes. What they'd given me barely fit. Worse, the boots they'd provided didn't fit, either, but they insisted I wear them anyway. They knew we were being tracked, and these mountains were filled with what I was used to calling goat trails—paths no wider than a single person that were always muddy enough to leave clear footprints. If the army saw one set of footprints that wasn't like the standard-issue track the rubber boots made, it would have been a big arrow pointing the way to the gringos.

To accommodate my big feet, Johnny cut the toes off of a pair of boots for me so I could march and not be a human locator beacon. It suited their needs but did little for mine. If you've ever done any hiking, you know that having your toes flapping in the breeze out ahead of you is an open invitation for bad stuff to happen. I'm not just talking about stubbing a toe, I'm talking about real bad stuff.

As the days went by I started getting a better idea of what some of those possible bad things were. One night the FARC macheted a small clearing for us to lie down on, and when it was time to sleep, the three of us quickly nodded off. A few seconds later, we heard a woman's scream followed by the sound of boots striking the ground. A young guard named Martín rushed past us with his machete drawn and a panicked, bug-eyed look on his face. For the next thirty seconds or so, we couldn't see a thing, we could only hear the crisp sound of Martín's blade as it rose and fell quickly and without hesitation. He came back, retrieved a long pole, and returned to where he'd been. Using the pole, he jabbed at something on the ground and raised up a snake so big that he struggled to lift the whole thing off the ground. It was about seven feet long and as thick around as my forearm. He carried it all around the camp, showing it off to everyone.

The three of us simply stared in amazement.

"What is it?" Tom asked.

"*Riaca*" was the reply.

I was thinking it was some kind of constrictor, but when we did the international sign for squeezing, they shook their heads and made biting gestures. I looked down at my already ground-up toes and thought that was all I needed, to have my bloodied toes out there like we were chumming for sharks like they had done in *Jaws*. "I think I'm going to need bigger boots," I said.

If huge poisonous snakes weren't enough, we also had to contend with the nasty invisibles infiltrating our bodies. We consumed a lot of water every day, and there was almost always a ready supply of it nearby, but it was also one of the things that was ravaging our digestive systems. When some people who travel to foreign countries fall victim to turista, the little guys causing them problems move on in a few days. In our case, though, the little bug that crawled inside each of us took up residence and did some major housecleaning of our intestinal tracts, ridding them of most everything they found in there and anything we tried to put back in. Trying to keep hydrated was difficult, and we kept getting weaker and weaker.

How much of a toll that was taking on us was something we discovered when we came to a bridge crossing. Just as they'd done with the airplane, the guerrillas had been telling us for at least forty-eight hours that we were coming to a bridge. Listening to them talk about the bridge, you would have thought that the jokers were part of the FARC chamber of commerce or something.

"You have to see this bridge."

"We're coming to the bridge soon."

"Soon we will be at the bridge."

I was glad to hear that there was a bridge for a couple of reasons. First, it meant that we were going to be near civilization. Second, crossing a bridge meant that either we weren't going to have to ford another river or stream or we weren't going to have to descend and then climb up the other side of a ravine. Flat was good but extremely rare.

When Marc, Tom, and I finally exited the thick jungle into a very small clearing, a couple of our guards nodded and pointed ahead of us saying "*puente*" or bridge. We all looked. The scene was like something out of a movie. Indeed there was a ravine ahead of us, but the bridge was not exactly the enormous public-works project I'd been envisioning. Instead, it looked like a replica of the rickety wood-slat suspension bridge from *Romancing the Stone*. No more than eighteen inches wide, the walkway was made out of the *tablas* we'd seen just about everywhere. The *tablas* rested on top of a couple of ropes. Thin wire rose vertically from the slats and another rope ran parallel to the supports under the slats on each side. Together those wires and ropes formed a thin handrail.

Fifty feet below us was a dried riverbed with just a trickle of water and some massive rocks. Slip and fall and you were a splat and not a type of lawyer. The FARC must have sensed our unease because they told us that if the bridge started swaying too much, we should just grab the rope handrail and push it out away from ourselves. That would put tension on all the strung supports to stabilize everything. On a good day, it would have been a sweaty-palm crossing, but given how weak and light-headed we all were, this would be a knee buckler. Only one person could be on the bridge at a time, so it took a while until we all made the crossing.

We each went, and when Tom, the last to cross, made it over, he stood next to me, his face twisted in a knot of anger and disbelief.

"Why would anyone build a bridge out here in the middle of hell and gone? This makes no sense." Marc and I looked at each other, and we were both about to say it, when Tom waved us off, "Don't say it! Don't say it! ¿Quién sabe?"

I felt bad for Tom. He was a pilot first and foremost, and he'd spent his life having to think logically, problem-solve efficiently, and view the world as an orderly and explicable place. He and I had been chewing on the possible answers to what happened that caused the plane we'd seen a few days before to plant itself on the ridgeline of that mountain. Tom's methodical, precise mental ratcheting through the possible options had served him well in the past, but it didn't in our current situation.

Tom and Marc took off ahead of me, and I assumed my place at the back of the line. With about forty FARC guerrillas ahead of me, Tom and Marc disappeared into the jungle, and soon we came to a series of makeshift shelters—slightly more advanced versions of the temporary pole shelters the FARC had built while on the run. The place looked like an old FARC camp, one that had been abandoned in a hurry. There was a series of tent tops already set up, and another group of FARC who weren't with us on the bridge were crossing there as well. They had a kitchen area put together, but what really blew our minds was that in addition to the usual jungle sights and sounds, we could hear a generator and see a television with a small satellite dish. The television was in another little *coleta* building slightly larger than the rest. Inside the TV room was a series of low benches with backs that angled sharply away from the seat. The only activity they looked appropriate for was a dental exam.

When I walked in, Tom and Marc were sitting on one of the benches, resting their elbows on their knees and their heads on their fists. They were staring at the screen. On it was an old black-and-white movie. I took a seat behind them and leaned over the back of their bench.

"What the hell is this?"

Tom turned his head slightly toward me. "We got here. They showed off their TV and asked us what we wanted to watch. We said CNN, of course. They put it on for us, but there was nothing about us. *Crossfire* was on. Talking heads."

"I was watching the crawl," Marc said. "UN inspectors are in Iraq. They just destroyed two Khartoum missiles. Nothing about us. After a couple of minutes, they"—Marc motioned his head toward where the FARC were clustered around the TV laughing—"put this on."

We all shook our heads in confusion. The FARC continued to laugh at the screen and Marc and I asked Tom what was happening. Tom explained that the two men onscreen were in a market stall somewhere in Mexico arguing about the price of tomatoes. Apparently tomato prices were a great source of amusement to terrorists.

"I can't believe they even let us start watching CNN," Marc said. "And then they stop us because they're bored with it. Doesn't any one of them have a clue?"

Marc was absolutely right. CNN could have really helped us cut through some of the FARC bullshit and let us know if there was any truth about their words that our release was just around the corner. Knowing anything for certain would have eliminated *¿Quién sabe?*

As it turned out, Sonia did have a clue. We had nothing better to do than to watch the movie, and after that, we watched something called *Murder of a Wizard* until Sonia came over and told them to shut the thing off. She was clearly pissed that they were letting us watch TV. She ordered a few guerrillas to lead us away from the main camp to a kind of annex, much older and more run-down. There were a few magazines there, old ones, and Tom started leafing through a book.

"This is all about the FARC. Here's some pictures of the top brass—"

He stopped midsentence; we all did.

Suddenly the room filled with the unmistakable sounds of helos coming our way fast and low. The FARC went into scramble mode, and we were in *Full Metal Jacket*. The helos came in right over the top of our camp, and we were once again beatin' feet. So much for our rest period; we were back on the march, trekking through the jungle in the dark. Just when we thought things couldn't get any worse, the sky opened up and a gather-the-critters-two-by-two deluge soaked us. Living in South Georgia and spending a bunch of time in various tropical-like climates, I was used to big rainstorms, but this one was epic.

We marched on for another three days, setting up temporary camps and spending the last night of those three sleeping under a derelict dump truck that was sitting up on concrete blocks. We were freezing our asses off and huddled together for warmth, but the smell of diesel fuel and motor oil made it hard to get a decent night's sleep. The next morning, we could see that we'd stopped just outside a tiny village. On one exterior wall of the little school building was a mural of the most exotic and beautifully colored fish I'd ever seen. The rest of the buildings were run-down and drab, but that school was as vibrant a thing as I'd seen over the last three weeks. It got us thinking about our kids again.

"I hope Shane is putting the right ratio of peanut butter to jelly on Destiney's sandwiches," Marc said. He scratched at the dirt with the heel of his boot. "How could Shane explain any of this to her?"

"I've been thinking the same thing. My little guy is probably wondering why it's taking me so long to get home this time. He gets into his routine just like me and doesn't like it when things get all gummed up and out of sorts," Tom added. I let out a sigh.

"I don't know about you guys, but I got my boy's birthday coming up soon. Never missed a one of them," I said.

We went on for a while talking about birthday gifts, cakes, and pizza parties. For a minute we were out of there and back home. Silence filled the room; the emotional price of talking about home was instantly clear.

We were loaded into a different dump truck, a late-fifties model Ford with a big round cab. The whole lot of us—the FARC and all—were packed into its bed and taken for a crazy drive down a narrow mountain road that led to another village. This one was a bit bigger. One house stood out in our minds. We were told that it belonged to one of the FARC bosses. So much for economic equality; it was clear this was the nicest, most expensive place around, and it was ringed by a barbed-wire fence. We were escorted inside this boss's house, and his wife fed us some soup. I started to eat, but lying on the floor was a McDonald's paper sack. Spilling out of it was the box that had once held a Happy Meal. At that point, I lost it. I went outside and fell to my knees and started crying.

In a situation like that, you never know what's going to trigger something deep inside you. I took Kyle to McDonald's quite a bit and we'd hang out in the restaurant while he ate his Happy Meal. We had a rule. Finish your food then you got to play with the toy. We'd sit and play for a

while and then go on home or finish up whatever errands we were running. Those memories came flooding back, and it was all just too much
thinking of Lauren and Kyle and that I might not ever see them again.

Tom and Marc came out and sat with me for a bit, at first respecting
my need to be alone with all the crap I was feeling.

"It's so weird," Marc said. "To be seeing roads and cars and signs of
civilization. It's like we could just step right back into it, but we can't.
We can't touch any of it."

We stayed silent for a minute. I thanked them both and we went
back into the house to finish eating. After the meal, we marched on
through the center of the town, past the slaughterhouse, empty at that
hour, the hooks and blood drains just waiting patiently. We were walking down the middle of the street and there was no one around. The
houses were all brightly painted in vivid blues, reds, and oranges. Every
house seemed to have flower boxes in the windows with roses or some
other flowers spilling out of them. Yet everything seemed deserted,
shut down. The village square was empty, the church doors closed, the
bell tower silent. At one point, I looked down a narrow avenue off the
main drag and saw a man peering at us around the corner of a building. We kept walking.

Finally the FARC led us past a building where there were some people sitting at crude benches. The smell of tanning solution and leather
was heavy in the air. We stopped for a minute. It was clear the FARC
wanted us to see how industrious these people were; they were making
the leather weapons vests the FARC wore. Instead of being impressed,
the sight had the opposite impact on me. These people were clearly
slaves of the FARC, making who knew what kind of money—if any—to
do their work. None of the workers looked up at us. Word must have
gone around that the three Americans were coming through. Don't
look. Don't touch. On the outskirts of town, we passed by the cemetery.
Even the dead folks knew better than to look up as we shuffled along
kicking up dust devils.

We stopped a click or so outside of town, just pulled up alongside the road, and sat for a few hours. The FARC sent some guys back and they returned with fresh-baked bread and sodas for all of us. A few hours later, a larger group of FARC, about a hundred strong, came down off the hillside and marched us out of there.

Three days later, our twenty-four days of marching came to an end.

FOUR

The Transition

March 2003

TOM

On the last day of our twenty-four-day march, we exited the jungle and found ourselves at a pickup point near a large clearing where a number of ranchers had fenced off the area. We arrived in the late afternoon and were told that we'd be picked up at eight that night. Until then we just had to wait.

As the sun fell, the temperature dropped.

By the time our driver arrived, it was around one in the morning, and we were all freezing. Across the field we could see headlights coming toward us, bucking up and down as the vehicle crossed the rutted ground. Behind the wheel of this Toyota Land Cruiser was a FARC guerrilla wearing a Tommy Hilfiger headband around his shaved head. What an American fashion designer had to do with Marxist doctrine was not something I could figure out. We loaded up in the backseat, and Sonia sat in the front. The driver looked at Sonia and told her to chamber a round in her weapon. He instructed a couple of other guerrillas who were going to ride along on the running boards to do the same.

Then he turned to us with a sleazy smile, "You're surprised? You didn't think the FARC had vehicles, did you?"

The arrogant bandanna boy could drive and was proud of it. We guessed that few of the FARC could, though saying this guy could drive was a bit of an exaggeration. At one in the morning, blackest of night, he tore out of there with the radio blasting and one hand casually flung over the steering wheel. He spent most of his time staring at Sonia and making small talk with her, trying to impress her with his skill and wit. We thought that our first time sitting on comfortable seats in more than three weeks was going to be something close to enjoyable, but it was just another fright-night special of suspension-fracturing ditches, stomach-churning switchbacks, and more FARC nonsense. After an hour, we stopped in the middle of the road. A Toyota pickup with a canvas rubberized tarp hung over a metal-tubing framework pulled out of somewhere and parked alongside us.

We climbed in the back of this new pickup, a different version of the Land Cruiser that was a real mountain bruiser with a stiff suspension. With a jolt, we were off again, bouncing crazily around in the bed, hanging on for dear life. Even with that rough ride, we all dozed off periodically. At one point, just as the sky was starting to bleed across the eastern horizon, we stopped again. Someone ran off into the dark and returned with a mattress that was no more than three inches thick. We scrambled out of the truck bed while our guards arranged the mattress, and when it was set we took off again. What must have been an hour later, we came to the largest, most complex FARC camp we'd seen yet.

It must have been a former maintenance yard, a holdover from the days of the *despeje* or demilitarized zone that former Colombian president Pastrana had created in 1998 to bring the FARC to the bargaining table. While this camp was clearly still up and running, the *despeje* had been lifted in February of 2002, after the FARC carried out a series of terrorist acts. The last straw came when they hijacked a commercial airliner and took Jorge Eduardo Gechem Turbay, a Colombian Liberal Party (PLC) senator and chairman of the peace commission, hostage. Before that, they had attacked several villages and cities, killing scores of civilians, and kidnapped several other government officials including Congresswoman Consuelo González de Perdomo, Congressman Orlando Beltrán Cuellar, Senator Luis Eladio Pérez Bonilla, and Congressman Oscar Tulio Lizcano among many other lawmakers. In their boldest move, they posed as police officers and kidnapped a dozen Colombian legislators. The situation grew so bad that in December of 2001, the Colombian legislature passed a law stating that kidnapped candidates could still run for office even though they weren't present. In the run up to the elections in March of 2002, the FARC kidnapped 840 people in 2001 and 183 persons in the first three months of 2002.

Kidnapping for ransom was a booming business for the FARC, but it wasn't the only terrorist tactic they employed. In an eighteen-month period, the FARC also killed at least four hundred members of the Colombian military, starting in early 2001. Using car bombs and improvised mortars, they wreaked havoc in a way they hadn't done previously. During that same time, three Irish Republican Army members were arrested in Colombia and accused of training the FARC in bomb making.

All of these activities brought an end to the peace talks and the DMZ. Shortly after the talks fell apart in early 2002, the FARC responded by kidnapping Colombian presidential candidate Ingrid Betancourt and several others while they were traveling in guerrilla territory. The heat had been turned up on the FARC ever since, with pressure coming from both domestic and international sources. When Álvaro Uribe ran for president in 2002, his "democratic security" policy was at the heart of his platform. His father had been killed by the FARC and his promise of taking a hard line in dealing with them helped carry him to victory in August of 2002. He took office at a precarious time in Colombia's history, with groups like the FARC seemingly in control of a country whose forty years of civil war was not going to end anytime soon.

Our work was a testament to the fact that the U.S. was heavily invested in ensuring that Colombia achieve some form of political stability. Much of the U.S. funding for Colombia came through something called Plan Colombia, which involved billions of dollars in military, social, and antidrug aid. Without it, the drug traffickers and other criminals would continue to make the country and the region unsafe.

A conservative, Uribe's policies put him at odds with many of the other leaders in the region, especially Hugo Chávez in Venezuela and Ricardo Lagos in Chile, who were far left of center. As Chávez rose to prominence in South America, he used Colombia's ties to the U.S. as a way to gain influence among the fledgling governments in the region. Chávez seized on every opportunity to characterize Uribe as a puppet, who was willing to trade billions of dollars in U.S. aid in exchange for his country's freedom to control its own destiny. In the rhetoric of Chávez, any ally of the U.S. was a potential enemy of South America, regardless of the increased stability U.S. influence might bring to the region and Colombia.

With many South American countries emerging into the light of democratic reforms, battles were being waged to decide who was going to ally with whom. The result of all this was that the FARC's gain also seemed to help Chávez's cause. The longer Colombia's struggle with the FARC went on, the more the country had to rely on U.S. aid, which hurt its standing in South America and gave Chávez more regional leverage.

And now we were thrown into this mix of political kidnapping, murder, foreign tension, and domestic strife. With no peace settlement or negotiations in sight, we didn't know if they considered us a bargaining chip or just some guys to kill to make a statement about their intent to keep the violence going. They'd been exchanging their prisoners for profit the way we'd once returned soda bottles for a deposit. Maybe that was what was about to happen to us.

At this new camp, we were led to a large roofed but wall-less structure where they must have stored their large trucks and road-building equipment. It was the size of a small airplane hangar and in the middle of the floor sat three wood-plank beds, each separated by ten feet. The only other thing in the hangar was a round table on which the slimy FARC set a box of fruit.

Two men walked in wearing neat camouflage uniforms and carrying wooden chairs that they sat down on. At first, all I could focus on were the weapon vests they wore. They each had pistols strapped at each hip, and a rifle was slung over one shoulder. One of the pistols had a billiard ball—an eight ball to be precise—engraved on the handle. They were also wearing scarves the color of the Colombian flag—red, blue, and yellow. Both of them were short and somewhat squat and older than our guards. They had to be close to forty by my best estimation.

We all immediately recognized the one with the pencil-thin mustache—the folds near the corner of both eyes revealed that he was of mixed ancestry—some indigenous and Spanish blood. His name was Fabián Ramírez. In one of our briefings, we'd learned he was the commander of the 14th Front, and one of the men primarily responsible for the drug operations in the Southern Bloc. His real name was José Benito Cabrera Cuevas, and according to our sources, his masterminding of the FARC's cocaine policies meant that he was responsible for hundreds of tons of cocaine making their way to the U.S. and elsewhere. He participated in setting and implementing the FARC's cocaine policies, while directing and controlling the production, manufacture, and distribution of hundreds of tons of cocaine to the United States and the world. His taxes on the drug trade led to millions of dollars being socked away in the FARC's coffers, and his enforcement of the FARC's rules regarding cocaine had put hundreds in their graves. He'd also made a statement following the kidnapping of Ingrid Betancourt that the FARC would take hostage any of the presidential candidates. In addition, he indicated that the government had until the end of 2002 to negotiate for her release before the FARC "did what was convenient."

The other man with Ramírez introduced himself as Burujo. He had a much darker complexion than Ramírez, and he lacked the folds near the corners of the eyes. His voice was soft and quiet, so much so that just to translate properly, I had to incline my head toward him every time he spoke.

At first, their questions were about what we were doing there. They also asked if we were CIA. When we told them we weren't, they both wrinkled their faces in disgust. I didn't care if they believed us or not. I was thinking they could shoot us right there if they wanted to. I was too tired to care. The pair only talked with us for a few minutes. I got the impression they wanted to say more, but another man came walking up to us. He was slightly taller than the others, and he carried himself with a casual arrogance. Along with his camo uniform and the Colombian colors he wore on his shoulder, he had a kaffiyeh—a houndstooth scarf like Yassar Arafat and the PLO wore—wrapped around his neck. Like the others, he was armed, but he had a Browning chrome-plated pistol. He tapped its butt with his fingertips to make sure we all saw his fancy weapon. Burujo and Ramírez had stepped away. They were next to Sonia, who was beaming and standing at taut attention. Clearly this was somebody she wanted to impress and the others respected or feared.

He stood looking at us each in turn, kind of theatrically, I thought. Marc, Keith, and I exchanged glances and rolled our eyes. Then the guy spotted the box of fruit. He walked over to it and took out an apple. I fully expected him to polish it on his uniform for even more dramatic effect, but he didn't. He took a bite out of it, chewed for a few seconds.

"You see what happens when you get involved in a war?" he began. He then continued by accusing us of fighting against the guerrillas.

"We're counternarcotics, nothing more," Marc, Keith and I told him one by one. "We don't fight the guerrillas. We fight the drugs."

Every time we used the word *drugs* or *narcotics,* he flinched a bit.

"Bullshit" was his only response to our telling him the truth.

He went on a political rant. He told us that the Colombian government and the army had been tracking us throughout our twenty-four-day march. He said it didn't matter if they had. The Colombian government couldn't do anything to hurt the FARC because the FARC didn't have a *casa blanca;* instead they had a *casa verde*—their house of green, the jungle. Because they didn't have a headquarters, because they kept on the move constantly, they couldn't be bombed or raided.

By then, I'd figured out who this man was. He was Joaquín Gómez, the leader of the Southern Bloc. Our intel had pegged him as the guy who collected the revenues generated by the FARC's drug-trafficking operations. Ramírez reported to Gómez, so we'd seen the latter's name a few times on our target sheets.

Gómez went on talking, telling us again that the FARC knew that they were being spied on.

"That's right," Keith said.

He raised an eyebrow and looked at Keith. "So, you are saying there is no safe way to communicate."

Keith shrugged. "That's what *you* are telling *us.* That you have no secure phone. Everybody can intercept your communications. The army followed us. They know we're here. They know you're here. You're trapped is what I'm saying. There's nothing you can do."

Gómez said the best way to combat the technology that enabled us to be tracked was to go back in time. We'd already felt that we'd traveled back in time. How much further could they go? Instead of using radio communications, Gómez said, they were going to use messengers to carry handwritten communiques back and forth.

"That's a good plan. That's what I would do," Keith replied, barely able to contain his smirk.

These exchanges with Gómez were hardly an interrogation—more like a simple conversation about our situation. That was both reassuring and disconcerting. What if he was talking so freely with us because he knew we were about to be let go and he was trying to influence our report to the outside? What if he was talking so freely with us because he knew we were about to be executed? Toward the end we told Gómez that he was making a big mistake by holding us captive. He got a bit worked up and said that we were a gift to Uribe because the Colombian Army wanted to kill us and make it look like the FARC had done it. Uribe wanted to make the FARC look bad in the eyes of the world.

We asked Gómez point-blank if the plan was for us to be killed. He repeated his earlier statement: The Colombian military would be the ones who killed us just to damage the reputation of the FARC. The FARC wanted to release us. When they set us free, they would put on a big show. He wanted it to be an international event with ambassadors and journalists from around the world.

We were skeptical about his message, but the significance of our meeting him was undeniable: For the whole of our twenty-four-day march, we had been hoping to get answers. Now we were getting them, and while Gómez was blowing a lot of hot air, at least he was someone with the power to affect our situation. Even though he seemed to be, if not delusional, then definitely exaggerating, we tried to make him understand the situation as we saw it. We laid out a more plausible scenario. By holding three Americans hostage, Americans whose government would not directly negotiate with *terrorists* (he flinched at that word as well), he was simply encouraging the U.S. to further its support for the Colombian government in its efforts against the FARC. That meant more U.S. military support and more money. More equipment and more training. All targeted against him and his compatriots.

We also told him that because he now held Americans captive, the rules of the game were changed. Before we'd been taken hostage, when we or other Americans flying reconnaissance missions had seen FARC guerrillas, we could take no action against them. The only way that we could take direct action against the FARC was if there was an American life in imminent danger. We were now those endangered Americans. The rules of engagement were very different for those employed by the U.S. government to work in Colombia. By holding us, they were opening Pandora's box. Instead of simply working indirectly against the FARC, by interfering with their narco-trafficking, the U.S. could strike directly against them because they were holding American hostages.

To his credit, Gómez agreed with our assessment. In the 1970s and 1980s, a number of FARC members had traveled internationally, many of them to Cuba. The also met with some communist leaders in other parts of the world to be trained and educated. We weren't certain that Joaquín Gómez was one of them, but it was likely. That would explain his more expansive worldview.

But his ego was more powerful than his powers of reasoning. Pastrana's decision to allow the FARC a safe haven or DMZ had given the FARC credibility in their own eyes and in the eyes of others in the region and around the world. Just a year or so before we were captured, Front commanders like Gómez and Ramírez, Mono JoJoy, and the rest of the FARC *secretariado* thought that they were the puppet masters pulling the strings. They had the president of a major Latin American power bowing to their demands. Unfortunately for them, they'd capitalized on their increasing legitimacy not by negotiating but by doing what terrorists do—killing and terrorizing. Not negotiating in good faith had consequences; now they were on the run and paying the price. Instead of safe haven, they were back to tramping around the countryside with the military in hot pursuit. Gómez and the other FARC leaders had been knocked off their imagined pedestal, but with us in his grasp, he had climbed back on it.

With the exception of his brief flashes of anger whenever we mentioned drugs, Gómez was cordial. Keith played up to his ego when he mentioned the Browning Gómez was carrying. He got a big grin on his face and pulled it out to show it off better. Keith took over talking to Gómez directly with the little Spanish he had. Keith tried to tell him something about the weapon's history, and the FARC Front commander led Keith out of the building.

Marc and I were led outside as well. We could see that Keith was in a vehicle with Gómez and a couple of his bodyguards. Burujo and Ramírez were in the front seat of a Toyota Land Cruiser—a silver one this time. Marc was placed in the backseat of that car and I was put in another. A minute or so after Keith's car drove off, we followed.

The young guard watching me chambered a round and kept his gun on me during the five-minute ride to our next stop. No one spoke. In fact, the driver had turned off the radio as soon as we'd gotten under way. We drove down another dirt road until we came to what looked like a more permanent FARC compound. The structures were built much the same as others we'd seen, but instead of nylon tarps for roofs, these had corrugated tin roofs. Around each of the buildings, wooden walkways had been built to keep people out of the mud, with other walkways bisecting the compound and running along the perimeter.

When we entered, we had to walk past another of the wall-less structures. A group of about fifty to sixty FARC guerrillas—low-level types of all ages and both genders—were clustered there. Their stony stares made me feel like I was doing one of those perp walks I'd seen on the television news when a suspect is led past a gauntlet of angry citizens and cops. One guy caught my attention. He was very short and very, very fat with a thick mustache. He reminded me of a Mexican bandit. All he needed was a pair of bandoliers crossed on his chest to complete the look. We were led into a small room that had clear plastic walls partitioning it off from the larger open space.

We took the three plastic patio chairs in the room. Down a ways from us in another room, Sonia was sitting. She was joined by the fat man I'd just noticed. The pair started talking and looking at us. The guards, most of whom had been with us on the march, were as wiped out as we were. Some of them were struggling to keep their eyes open. It was nearing midday and the temperature was climbing. We'd been so used to being in the mountains or under the jungle's canopy that the heat was at first welcome.

We were brought plates of empanadas, fried potato balls, and bananas. After we ate, six new guards, totally unfamiliar to us, came into the room. Instead of sitting, they formed a semicircle in front of us. Like the other FARC we'd seen at this compound, they stared at us, expressionless. Ten minutes later, Burujo, Gómez, and Ramírez came into the room, along with another mini-entourage. We stood up briefly to greet them, but our short conversation was interrupted by a commotion outside the door. A few seconds later, the source of the commotion entered the room. Another FARC upper-echelon commander walked in. He was taller than all the others and thickly built. He wore a red beret with a star on it but was otherwise dressed like the other bloc commander. We could tell he was somebody important within the FARC because Gómez, a man we knew to be the leader of the Southern Bloc and therefore a pretty big deal, jumped up and offered him his chair.

He held out his hand to Keith and then to me. Then a chill ran through me. He hesitated before shaking Marc's hand and his brow furrowed and he stared hard at Marc. He must have been told that I was the one who spoke the best Spanish because he looked at me while gesturing toward Marc.

"Is he American?" he asked.

Marc sensed what was being implied and immediately answered that he was. Marc had a darker complexion than the rest of us, and his dark hair further set him apart from Keith and me. I knew that this man was wondering if Marc was Colombian, mistaking his Portuguese and Italian features for Latin American. I quickly explained Marc's heritage, knowing that if they suspected he was Colombian, he would likely be killed. The FARC leader said something, but I was having a hard time with his accent and the speed of his words. When I sorted things out, I said again—as did Marc—that he was indeed an American.

The FARC leader was introduced to us as Mono JoJoy. As commander of the Central Bloc, Mono JoJoy seemed far too busy to deal with us. After he shook our hands, he turned to Joaquín Gómez and said, "They are not our hostages; we are theirs." This was just another variation on the idea that they were responsible for keeping us alive. According to this theory, the Colombian military was who we really needed to fear because they would kill us for their own gain and to discredit the FARC. By that point, we were tired of hearing that line. We all knew that the opposite was true. If the Colombian military came to rescue us, the FARC would execute us. We didn't bother to dispute Mono JoJoy's ridiculous claim. Even if we had wanted to, we didn't have time.

KEITH

Martín Sombra was the overstuffed empanada of a man we'd earlier seen speaking with Sonia. When Mono JoJoy introduced him to us, he said, "He will take good care of you." We all looked at one another. This guy couldn't even take care of himself, how was he going to care for us? Sombra was no more than five foot three or four, and he seemed nearly as wide as he was tall. Sombra just nodded, and we all watched as Gómez, Ramírez, JoJoy, and their entourage departed. Sonia left with them, too. The only ones who remained were the six guards who fronted us like an execution squad and Sombra.

"Relax, guys," the fat man said to us. "Everything is going to be okay. We're going to set you free. We're going to have good food for you first, and we're going to take you to a place where you can rest."

The food-and-rest part sounded good, but we all knew the parts about being okay and going free were just more bullshit. Sombra was just trying to keep us calm. A calm hostage is easier to take care of and less likely to try an escape. If Sombra thought he was adopting a soothing, buddy-buddy manner, he was way off base. His high-pitched squeaky voice put us all on edge and contrasted sharply to his Porky Pig looks. He sounded like a cross between Mickey Mouse and someone who had been sucking helium out of a balloon. He told us to grab our chairs because we were moving out.

We loaded ourselves and our chairs into the back of another pickup, where we sat with three guards. The truck drove off and wound its way through a series of unmanned guard stations. Though we were no longer marching, our digestive distress hadn't ended and we had Sombra pull over so we could head into a field to do our business. When we came back, Sombra and a guard who'd been introduced to us as Milton were sitting in our chairs in the middle of the road, smoking cigarettes, taking great big drags on them with every breath like they were racing.

They finished and Sombra managed to get back onto his feet like a pregnant woman pushing herself up off a couch.

"I'm going to give you new names," he said, looking us over. He pointed to me and told me my name was Antonio. Tom was Andrés. We couldn't understand what name he was assigning Marc, so Marc said, "I'm Enrique." And so we were the newly christened three amigos. We saw through the bullshit of trying to give us new identities, but we decided to put up with it for now. It was all so transparent and stupid, but essentially harmless since we knew what they were trying to accomplish. If they could break down one small part of our reality—our names—they figured it was going to be easier for them to manipulate us. We ended up flipping that scheme, coming up with our own code names for many of them. That way, if we were talking about them in English, they wouldn't hear any of their names and know they were being talked about. From hour one on, Martín Sombra was Fat Man.

As we drove on, we saw a pile of eighty-pound propane cylinders stacked together. We'd heard that the FARC made them into weapons by cutting off the tapered tops and then slicing the cylinder in half to use the tubes as mortars. They'd pack a charge in one end along with a load of nails and other shrapnel and fire away. Inaccurate as all hell and as a result indiscriminately deadly. Not that collateral damage mattered to them. Seeing those things reminded us that despite how disheveled and disorganized these guerrillas were, they knew how to ruin people's lives.

Our meeting with Mono Jojoy had allowed us to see for ourselves how the hierarchy functioned in this terrorist organization. Though we had been on the jungle floor with our misfit bunch of guards, now we had a better sense for who had been calling the shots in the month since our crash. I'd been observing Sonia as best as I could throughout the march. She spent a lot of time on her shortwave radio in communication with someone—that someone was possibly the Fat Man, but more likely Mono JoJoy. As haphazard as our movements sometimes seemed to be, it was clear that Sonia was being directed to this drop-off point—whether that was from day one or later didn't matter. I saw then that the march, as agonizing as it had been, was also purposeful. The FARC were used to handling hostages and they had a plan in mind for us. I just wished I knew what it was.

After we'd driven less than ten miles, we came to another abandoned camp, a smaller part of the larger compound we'd first entered. Like the area where we'd met with the various FARC bloc leaders, this section had been abandoned. We could see one building, and a small clearing cut into the jungle. We got out of the truck and a guard rushed around with a chair so that Fat Man wouldn't have to stand while he addressed us. Another guy stood right next to him, clearly his second in command.

Fat Man lowered himself into his chair and swept his arm around to indicate everything in this smaller compound. "We do all of this for you."

"All of this" was essentially the one building, what we immediately called our "hooch." It was about sixteen by twenty feet and walled on three sides. The fourth wall was made of chain-link fencing. At least it had a roof, so that if this was where we were going to be bunked, we'd at least be mostly out of the weather. I resented Sombra's thinking we should be appreciative because they'd opened a prison camp for us. Thanks very much. We'll be sure to tip our guards accordingly.

I wanted to cut through the crap, so I rolled out my best Spanish, "¿Quién es el jefe aquí?" I wanted to know who the boss was. We'd met a bunch of different FARC that day and I wanted to know who was directly responsible for us.

Fat Man gave us the party line: There are no bosses. Everyone is equal here. I cut him off and flat-out said, "That's great, but if we need food, who do we talk to."

Sombra jerked his head toward the man standing next to him: "Ferney." His name was pronounced like the words *fair* and *nay* as in negative. We immediately dubbed him the Frenchman, and the immediate impression that he made was that he was a no-nonsense kind of guy. When the Fat Man had been entertaining the other troops earlier and getting them to laugh at his jokes, the Frenchman was the only one who remained stoic. The guy seemed to have no soul at all; he was dead emotionally. It was the Frenchman who led us into our new home away from home.

As we walked up to the building, I knew immediately that this marked the end of our days as kidnapped contract workers and began our life as prisoners. The whole morning had been filled with meetings and conversations about our situation, but now reality was the three-hundred-pound gorilla who sat wherever he wanted. He chose to sit right on us. I felt something deep in the pit of my stomach, a kind of despair that I hadn't ever felt before, even when the march was at its worst. Glancing over at Marc and Tom, I could tell they felt the same way. The place was just depressing. The canopy of jungle foliage and trees didn't allow any sunlight to enter, the building had clearly been there awhile, and the wood was showing signs of rot. When we walked inside, there was nothing on the floor but the unevenly cut and spaced boards on which we'd have to sleep. Some other furniture, again made out of the *tablas* we'd seen before, a couple of chairs, a shelf. A beam, about the size of a flagpole, ran from one end of the structure to the other.

None of us wanted to think about the fact that this tin-roofed shanty was going to be our home for the foreseeable future. We all immediately stepped back out of it onto a patio-like area in front of the chain-link. At one time the patio area (which was really just a dirt/mud area in front of the hooch) had also been fenced in. Postholes and a couple of jagged bits of wood stuck out of the ground. I hoped that they would put that fence back up so that at least we could be outside if we wanted.

One of the guards pointed to a tree nearby and a shelf that was nailed to it. He told us we could put cracker crumbs on the shelves and the monkeys would come to take them. We'd already seen a few monkeys running through our prison camp. We looked at one another. Marc shook his head and said, "Monkey Village." The name stuck. It wasn't really a term of endearment. At one point during the march, we'd come across a troop of monkeys. The FARC were as fascinated by them as we were, but one of the guerrillas warned us to be careful. The monkeys would fling their feces at humans and urinate on them from the tree limbs.

Night was coming on fast. The Frenchman came into our hooch and told us that he wanted the uniforms we'd been wearing. He was going to resupply us. The most any of us got was two uniforms, a T-shirt, two pairs of underwear, two pairs of socks, one sheet, and a mosquito net. Marc was the only one to get another T-shirt. I only had one pair of underwear because they had nothing in my size. They took away our other clothes and we were pretty much geared up. He asked us if we needed anything else. We told him we wanted a radio and reminded him that he'd told us earlier that he would get us one to listen to. We were desperate to know anything from the outside world, especially what was being done on our behalf. The Frenchman assured us that we'd have radios, and he said he'd make sure a rooster would come sing for us. And with that he left.

After the Frenchman left, the door was chained and locked shut. We were given a five-gallon oil jug with the top cut off it to use as our toilet. I think we were all in our own world at that point. We didn't say too much as we spread out over the three platform beds a piece of black plastic they'd also left for us. We lay down underneath our sheets and mosquito nets as the jungle and the knowledge that we were now truly hostages settled over us.

None of us had ever really been locked up until this—not even those times on the march when we slept in a house or other building. It was disturbing to know that you couldn't get up and move around freely when you wanted or needed to. That first night, it turned out, we all needed to. We'd been fed pretty well that day, including some fried meat just before lock up. All of us were still in pretty bad shape digestion-wise, and at some point in the night, that became a problem. We yelled for the guards. We'd been shown a ditch or *zanja* that we were to use as our latrine. It was about twenty feet or so from the hooch. A guard finally showed up, and by this time, I'd been clenching my bowels for so long my leg and butt muscles were quivering. All three of us tried to explain that I needed to be let out of this damn thing immediately.

The guard pointed to our oil container and told me to use that. He wasn't going to let me out. I started yelling, "Let me out! Let me out!," and as I was saying this, I could feel my bowels releasing. If the guard thought I was faking before, his nose and his eyes had ample proof that I really needed to get out of there.

That incident convinced the FARC that there was something seriously wrong with my stomach. I'd started eating a week or so before this, but I was still plagued by whatever bug it was that infected all of us. That next morning the FARC came in and insisted that they were going to perform a procedure on me. Tom translated for me what their intentions were,

"Tell them HELL NO," I said.

"They say all they're going to do is massage your stomach," Tom replied

"Fuck that. Not now. Not ever."

"They say they need to do it. They need to fix your stomach."

I remembered Johnny and some of the good work he'd done on all of us. I wished that he was there, but he wasn't. Finally I gave in. They had me lie on the floor on my back and applied some kind of oil to my stomach. Then two pretty powerful guys began pushing on my stomach, starting at the top and then working their way down toward my navel. The pain was intense. It was as if they thought they could force whatever was in the top of my intestine down and out of me through my colon. They were literally squeezing the shit out of me.

This went on for ten minutes or so. When they stopped I felt better, but only because they'd stopped. Next, two of the stronger guys lifted me up by my feet and dangled me upside down, holding me a few inches off the floor. As I hung there, they lifted me up a bit higher and shook me, dropping me a few inches and then raising me again like a stubborn ketchup bottle. After they were done with the shaking, they took a large bandanna or scarf, and they tied that around my stomach, torquing it so tight I could barely breathe. When they lowered me to the floor again, they said I had to leave what was essentially a kind of tourniquet on my gut for the next twenty-four hours.

After they left, the three of us started talking about their "cure."

"That was almost prehistoric, Keith," Marc said. "Where would you learn something like that?"

"Folk medicine," Tom said, "Not covered by your health plan, but who knows? Maybe it'll do you some good."

"Hey, it hurt like hell, but if nothing else, it proved we are a valuable commodity. If they were going to kill us, why bother to treat me at all?"

"That's true," Tom said. "But they gave me medicine, so why not give you something for your stomach?"

"Maybe what's got my guts all in a knot isn't a bug. Maybe the crash fucked up something internally?"

No matter what was wrong with me, for the next two or three weeks I spent most of my time in our hooch or squatting over the ditch. My family had always talked about folks going from the poorhouse to the shit house; I didn't have either house out there.

My digestive system didn't get much better as the days progressed. Feeling as weak as I did and unable to eat, there wasn't much for me to do but sleep. Several times I woke up alone in the hooch. Still half dazed, I'd hear Tom and Marc talking out front and slowly come to the disgusting realization that I was lying in my own shit. In those moments my only thought was *Could this get any worse?* I was exhausted and miserable. I could do nothing but lie on my back and stare at a beam. Bats were flying around inside the hooch. Ticks would crawl toward me, and get up to my chest before I pushed them away. But they just kept coming back at me. I'd push them away. They'd crawl up me. I'd lie there for an hour until I got the strength to wash myself off.

The only thing that kept me going during those initial days as a prisoner was a spiral-bound notebook and a pen, both of which Ferney had given us along with other basic toiletries—a toothbrush and toothpaste, a razor, laundry soap. Every day, no matter how horrible I felt, I'd think of Lauren, Kyle, the rest of my family, and Malia. I'd write them all a letter. I wouldn't write so much about what was going on in Monkey Village; instead I'd tell them how I felt about them. I'd also write to them about my favorite memories of being with them. I told Lauren about something that happened when she was just nine years old. For a divorced father with custody of two kids, life could be pretty hectic, but a lot of nights Lauren, though only nine, would stand on a plastic milk crate in front of the stove to help make dinner. In this particular memory, she was up there reaching into a cabinet to bring down some macaroni and cheese and a few spices. She added a can of tuna for Kyle and me, and she was so proud of her homemade Tuna Helper. Kyle asked me, "Dad, is she going to burn it?" I told him that no matter what, we were going to eat it, we were going to love it, and we were going to tell her so. It hurt like hell to remember all that and put it down on paper, especially when I wrote that I couldn't wait to get home so she could make it again for us all.

After the first week, I was starting to feel better. Having control of your bowels will do that for you. I wasn't ready to go out and run a marathon, but I could at least participate in more of the regular routine. I was stressed out, and not being physically active made my brain work overtime. With no mental stimulation, my mind was running rampant and that had to be contributing to my physical problems. My mother had taught me a few simple meditation tricks when I was a kid. I tried to focus more on my breathing, counting to six on the inhale and the exhale. That seemed to help calm my nerves.

From the beginning of our stay at Monkey Village, we tried to figure out who was important and whom we might be able to work to our advantage among the FARC. We were there with about thirty guerrillas, an estimate we based on the rotation of the guards. Though we could hear female voices, we never saw any women. The FARC camp was secluded enough from ours that we could see where it was—flashes of movement, the sound of them talking and cooking—but not much else. Marc made an effort to get to know a guerrilla they called Lapo. Fairly soft-spoken and decent, he'd been on our initial march. We asked him to give us the chain of command, and according to him, the Frenchman was the commandant—the lead jailer of the camp. Lapo said that he was number two, and Pollo—who looked like a chicken with his beady eyes, pimply, pebbled skin, and scrawny neck and shoulders—was number three. A day or so later, we asked another guard (who we called the Plumber) the same question. He said the same thing about the Frenchman but flip-flopped Pollo and Lapo. As a result, from that point forward, we referred to Lapo as 2.5.

We liked 2.5. He told us that he had studied in Bogotá before joining the FARC, something he was very proud of. What that meant was that he'd gone through a few early grades of school and learned to read. He was likely a homeless street kid and the FARC offered him a better gig than that—the old three-hots-and-a-cot mentality. To 2.5's credit, in those first few conversations we had with him, we could tell that he had something going for him. Even though our Spanish wasn't the best, a lot of the other FARC we talked to were conversational black holes. They would try, but when it came time for them to express any kind of original thought or opinion, they fell back on the usual FARC rhetoric. All of them had been brainwashed, but a few of them, like Pollo, had been left in the spin cycle too long and it turned them stupid and mean.

Others, like Songster, were pretty easy to get to know. He was only about sixteen or so, a pimple-faced kid who was good-natured most of the time, although he drove Tom insane because he walked around camp singing nonsense songs about elephants and a bunch of other shit. Marc and I couldn't understand what he was singing, so it didn't bother us too much, but Tom wanted to choke him. He was kidding, but he did write in his journal: "Date of first headache in captivity: March 6th, 2003 / Source: Songster." Of course, we had to name him Songster, and we had to put up with him and his warbling. He seemed to be a pretty new recruit, filled with the zeal of the recent convert. He kept engaging us in conversations about politics and spewing the FARC propaganda about American imperialism. Songster said that he was really mad at us because the U.S. still controlled the Panama Canal. We explained that the U.S. gave up control of it in 1999, but he wasn't hearing any of it. For a bit of fun, Marc, Tom, and I engaged him in one of those yes-we-did-no-you-didn't debates until he told us we were just being stupid. He stomped off and didn't talk to us for a few days.

It took a lot of observing and listening to identify and rank all the guards. For the most part, with the exception of the Frenchman and the Fat Man, as near as we could tell, the rest were just grunts. They'd sometimes call one another *Camarada* _____ and use a name, but most of the time it was just *camarada*. The Frenchman was always *commandante*, and in that isolated camp, he wielded the power of God. He was just as stupid and mean as the rest of them, but because he was in charge he was worse because his stupidity and meanness could hurt us more deeply.

MARC

About ten days into our stay at Monkey Village, around the nineteenth or twentieth of March, the three of us were sitting outside in hammocks that the FARC had provided. The hooch was so unbelievably depressing that even lying in a hammock and being bitten by the enormous horseflies out there was an improvement. Hundreds of them would swarm all over and gather on the bottom of our hammocks. They had iridescent green heads and hypodermic-like stingers that could pierce your skin through the hammock's fabric and your clothes, but at least we were out of the mud.

That day, Keith, Tom, and I were sitting outside talking about how strange this entire scene was. The FARC had a toilet, not connected to anything, sitting up on a rise about twenty feet outside our clearing. If that wasn't odd enough, the toilet was also fenced in.

"Why would they put that thing on display?" Tom asked.

"No idea. Check out what I found up there." Keith handed Tom a small wooden knight from a chess set.

Tom turned it over and over in his hand, and with a heavy sigh he asked, "Did you guys have it again last night?"

Keith and I both said yes.

For the first few nights of our imprisonment, each of us had had the same nightmare—what we called the marching dream. They were the most vivid nightmares and each of us could hear the others moving all around their beds. We were dreaming of marching, and our bodies were acting it out as we lay sleeping. We each reported waking from it and being completely surprised that we hadn't moved out of the hooch.

We'd been sitting there, turning over the dreams for a bit, when the Frenchman came in. Normally he stayed out of camp, leaving the day-to-day monitoring to the other guards and only doing an occasional walk by to check on us. The fact that he was coming into our hooch let us know something was up. He pulled Tom aside and I saw Tom's face go pale. Tom licked his lips and came back toward Keith and me.

"We're going to be separated," he began. "We're not to speak to one another, either. If we do, they'll move us even farther apart and we won't ever see one another again."

I'd spent the previous thirty-four days thinking of all the possible terrible things the FARC could do to us, but I hadn't considered this one. This was going to hurt. All we had was one another, and now they wanted to take that from us.

Even as Tom was speaking, I flashed to a conversation the two of us had a few days before. We were both lying in our hammocks looking up at the treetops. The sunlight reflected off the top of them, and that image reminded me of home. Tom was talking about going to work at a Toyota car dealership when we got back. Selling cars seemed pretty safe, he told me. As silly as that conversation sounded, it had taken us out of this place. Being in his own head all day every day was not something that any of us was looking forward to, but it seemed we had no choice.

A few minutes after the Frenchman left, the other guards started to set up our new arrangements. Tom remained in the hooch and Keith and I were once again back in a *coleta* underneath nylon tent tops hung over wooden frameworks. Keith was at one end of the clearing, and I was at the other. I think the FARC knew that our being able to *see* one another but not being able to *speak* to one another was worse than complete separation. With that arrangement, we would be constantly reminded of what was being taken from us.

Before Keith and I were led to our new quarters, the three of us got together. Together we'd formed what we referred to as a "bubble"—a place together that enabled us to endure this madness.

"Look, guys in Nam that were POWs figured out ways to communicate with another. Even in the Hanoi Hilton they managed to put up with some shit that was about as bad as it could get." Keith looked at Tom and me and nodded.

"Whether we're in the same hooch or forty feet apart doesn't matter," I said. "We're still in the bubble. We just need to check on each other everyday. Get ourselves back in it."

Tom said, "We'll figure out some way to get through this. We'll be strong—stronger than them."

The FARC's imposition of silence on us was cruel, and I couldn't see what advantage it had for them. We'd figured out early on that they wanted to keep us calm and in control. Silence and separation would only do the opposite—make us agitated and angry. I had to remind myself that responding to those feelings would not be a good idea. We were sure that the FARC could further separate us and make good on their promise of us never seeing one another again. The FARC were holding hostages all over the country, and the thought of another long march to a different camp was enough of a deterrent to keep us from blatantly disregarding their rules. It didn't make any sense to risk the one thing we had going for us—the three of us and our collective strength.

I knew that I needed to keep to as strict a routine as possible. When Ferney gave us the notebooks upon our arrival, the first thing I did was draw the layout of my family's house. Our house in the Keys was our first home, and we'd bought it about two years before the crash. A typical Florida Keys house, it was elevated on stilts. I had taken drafting classes in high school, so I sketched the floor plan like it was a blueprint. I also sketched in all the furniture in each room. When I woke up every morning, before I went to bed every night, and several times throughout the day, I would look at that line drawing and imagine I was there in my house. I would visualize what my family would be doing at that exact moment in time.

The depression that had been lingering in the shadows those first few weeks in Monkey Village set in after the separation. Everything was so foreign. The food was different, the people were different, the language was different, being outside and subject to the whims of Mother Nature was equal parts fascinating and terrifying. But of all that, not being able to talk to Tom and Keith was by far the hardest part. I had a difficult time communicating with the guards. The particular dialect most of the FARC spoke only vaguely resembled the textbook Spanish I'd been learning. Ultimately it didn't matter, since after the second or third day of the silence, we were told that we couldn't speak to the guards, either.

The boredom became all-consuming. I could only write in my journal for so long, could only reread what I'd read so many times. The AM-FM radios the Frenchman had promised to us never showed up. I had twenty-four hours a day to fill up with some kind of activity, and given that there weren't many activities to do, my logical choice was to shorten the day as much as I could. That meant that I would stay in bed in the morning as long as I could. We had no electricity in the camp, so the length of our day was determined by the sun. Keith and Tom got up when the sun rose, but I frequently stayed in bed for several hours after that, skipping breakfast entirely. From the grumbles I heard from Tom and Keith and from what I'd experienced firsthand, I wasn't missing much. Soup and an *arepa*—a fried bit of cornmeal—on most days.

I wasn't a big coffee drinker, so I let Tom and Keith take my portion of either the coffee they brought out or the hot chocolate they gave us.

I knew that by staying in my hooch I was missing out on one thing. The guards brought the food to one point, where they left the pots so we could serve ourselves. If we all gathered there at the same time, the guards didn't mind. That was an opportunity for us to at least be near one another and to whisper a few words of encouragement or even nonsense. Anything to keep the connection going. I had to weigh my desire for that contact against my desire to shorten the day. There were other opportunities during the day to engage in limited attempts at socializing, so in the mornings I opted to sleep in as long as I could. I did enjoy hearing Tom and Keith grousing about the fish heads in their soup some days, but I definitely wouldn't have enjoyed having to deal with that soup. I took some satisfaction in knowing that my not participating in breakfast in the jungle would guarantee that Keith's coffee habit did not go unmet.

Even before captivity Tom was an early riser who hated the heat. At Monkey Village he'd get up at sunrise and then lie in his hammock. The flies weren't out at that hour and that way so he could get about an hour of insect-free peace. He would have spent more time in his building and out of the heat, but there was a rat's nest in the beams supporting the tin roof and it rained down a constant stream of droppings, twigs, and leaves. He tried to keep his place as clean and orderly as he could, but the amount of effort and the results he could achieve with the jungle broom he was provided with didn't measure up.

When I'd been at home in Florida, every now and then I'd watch a nature show with my kids, but watching nature on the Discovery Channel and living in it full-time were two very different things. The FARC had pigs, actually they were peccaries, that would come around to eat whatever scraps were left from our meals. I didn't mind them too much, but their squealing, when added to the rest of the incessant jungle noises of insects, birds, and monkeys, made it hard to forget where I was. The guards were as bored as we were, and they sometimes treated the pigs like pets, scratching their bellies and giving them nicknames like Niña. *Niña* means "girl," so the guards weren't the most imaginative people in the world; they were like kids naming their dog Dog.

Given all of the juvenile traits they'd displayed during the march, I wasn't surprised to see the FARC playing with peashooters. Actually, we admired their peashooters and copied them. One of the plants in the area produced shoots that were easily hollowed out. It also produced seeds, so it offered both weapon and ammunition. One of the guards would doze off (they also took shifts in pairs) and the other would shoot him. Sometimes they'd shoot at us, and we'd return fire.

The FARC were almost fanatical yo-yo players as well. One of the cereal grains they were supplied with had included a yo-yo. While they didn't play with the yo-yos all the time, if a guerrilla had one, a few of the others would gather around. It was both funny and sad simultaneously. They were trying to teach one another how to use a yo-yo and their efforts were hilarious and heartbreaking. I mostly laughed, but later on, when it was getting to be dark and things were quieting down, I could feel my sadness settling down on my shoulders. I'd think briefly about the guards and know that they were so impoverished as kids that a yo-yo was something they could only dream about. That made me think of my own kids. They were well provided for, but they were missing a vital part of their lives—me.

Whatever enjoyment we got from peashooters and yo-yos, and it was very little, didn't last. On the march, we had so much to occupy our minds—just the relatively simple act of walking took so much concentration because of the harsh terrain. I can't say that I would have preferred to keep walking, but I realized in Monkey Village that as much as we were fleeing from the Colombian military, we were also running from the reality that we were captives. Now the truth was unavoidable. The facts of our situation set in, and set in hard.

I don't know if it was for that reason or because I knew that it was important to stay physically active, but I walked a lot to ease the boredom and relieve my mounting anxiety. I could only pace back and forth across the small clearing we had, a distance of thirty yards or so, but that constituted the greatest portion of our world. All we could see beyond that were banana and palm tress and tangled masses of undergrowth.

A friend of mine once told me that he couldn't take his kids to the zoo. It made him too sad. He knew a lot about animals, and he told me that zoo animals exhibited what was called "zoo behaviors." He said that as a result of their captivity, lions and tigers, for example, would pace relentlessly back and forth in their cages or enclosures. You would never see them do that in the wild, he told me. I didn't really understand what he meant at the time, but in Monkey Village I got a firsthand lesson in what he meant, as I found myself empathizing with every zoo animal I'd seen.

Still, my walking burned off some of my nervous energy and allowed me to explore my new world as much as possible. I thought of each of the members of my family and placed a picture in my head of each of them as I walked. I prayed daily, which also helped me some. I was raised Catholic, and though I'd drifted away from the Church, I retained a firm belief in God. I had never wanted to be a priest or a monk, but I was gaining some appreciation for what a life of quiet, solitude, and faith must be like. Some small parts of it I liked, but I hated living in my own head exclusively. It got too crowded in there.

The first time I saw an enormous campaign of ants on the march, I immediately thought the phenomenon was just like my mental state. The FARC called it the *ronda,* and it was like something out of *National Geographic,* a massive swarm of ants—as large as a twenty-foot-long football-shaped area rug—moving along in a mass so thick you couldn't

see the ground. After we saw the *ronda* a second time, we picked up on
the signs that it was approaching. The birds would fly in ahead of it, low
to the ground, in anticipation of the feast that was to come. Next we'd
see the other crawling insects—spiders, tarantulas, crickets—and even
amphibians like frogs and salamanders fleeing from the approaching
ants. The birds would land and gorge themselves. Everything would
move on once the ants passed through our little camp.

Those ants were like my darkest thoughts of being executed or killed
in a rescue attempt. Those thoughts in turn stirred up my other fears
and worries. There were just too many for them to ever disappear completely. A lot of those fears were, of course, centered around my family,
especially my kids. Along with worrying about my own safety, I feared
for them. What if Destiney was in a school bus accident? What if Cody
or Joey got hurt playing baseball or another sport? What if one of them
drowned while swimming? The list could go on and on, and I had to
figure out some way to keep that swarm of thoughts from marching
across my mind.

At night, I was defenseless against the onslaught. In addition to the
marching nightmare, my sleep was troubled by what I called the reverse
dream. In it, the reality of our situation would penetrate any defenses I
put up, and the "bubble" we had put up as well. Those dreams were so
vivid that even after I woke up from them, I had a hard time sorting out
if I was dreaming that I was awake and my dream was my real life or
vice versa. In one, we were marching through the jungle and we came
upon a large trench. One of the guerrillas told me to stop and to kneel
alongside it. He put a pistol to my head and pulled the trigger. I'd wake
up sweating and thrashing under my mosquito net and the thought
that I'd never see my wife and kids again was suffocating me.

A few times when I was walking, I'd imagine that I wouldn't see
my family for a very long time. When I was released, Destiney was
going to be a woman and not my little girl. I would see my family's
life going by in fast-forward, and I wouldn't be anywhere in the tape.

I'd run through the list of things I'd miss out on—dance recitals, school dances, her learning to drive, graduating from high school, first crushes and heartbreaks—all the stuff that makes up a life. Even the most pleasant memories—our recent family vacation to Disneyland or watching *The Little Mermaid* with Destiney—became painful to replay in my head, but I was like a kid with a loose tooth probing it with his tongue and tugging at it with his fingers. I wasn't trying to torture myself with the past but I couldn't shut my mind off, either. I couldn't control when things would come to me. One minute I was there in the jungles of Colombia, held hostage by terrorists, lying in a makeshift shelter thinking of family and home, and then suddenly the lyrics to the *Blues Clues* theme song would run through my head:

"Sit down in your thinking chair and think, think, think . . ."

This happy little jingle would just tear me to pieces. I wrote about these things in my journal all the time; I just poured my heart and soul onto the paper. Sometimes, when I wasn't feeling so bad, I'd reread what I'd written and realize that I was in a very desperate state. I was so emotional, so sensitive to everything, fragile, and on the verge of being broken. I was glad for those moments when I could see myself clearly enough to recognize what was happening to me. I'd resolve to be better, pray for strength, and inevitably something would happen on those days when I'd just about reached the edge that would pull me back from utter despair.

I continued to pray to God to get me the hell out of there. I did the usual thing and told Him that I would reform myself, become a better person, a better Christian, do whatever it was that He wanted me to do. Thy will be done, but please let Thy will be what I want more than anything else in the world—to see my family again. I received no great revelations. I didn't hear the voice of God telling me that I would be fine. Instead, I'd look across the camp and Keith would give me a thumbs-up. I'd see Tom sitting in his hammock reading one of the FARC newsletters, and as if he sensed my eyes on him, he'd look up and give me a nod and a smile. I knew they were hurting as badly as I was. To see them struggling with what I could only imagine to be similar thoughts and doubts as mine and not be able to speak to them was as cruel a form of torture as I'd ever experienced. But even though we couldn't speak openly, the fact that we were sharing this experience with one another helped ease the pain.

In those first weeks at Monkey Village, I was being tested; we all were. And one morning, I felt like I was being rewarded, if not for acing the test, then at least for passing it. I was pacing back and forth, and I saw a butterfly fluttering very low to the ground. It was just fluttering past me, and it caught my eye because it was the most beautiful butterfly I'd ever seen. It had transparent wings that were outlined in a deep red with two pink spots on the back of each wing. The spots were Barbie pink—Destiney's favorite color. I immediately thought of her and named this butterfly Destiney's butterfly. Every time I would see it, I would immediately be filled with such a mix of emotions. I would think of my daughter. That butterfly was a sign. It had to be. I knew there was some significance to that butterfly flying past me just when I'd doubted whether I could make it through.

I was in the process of undergoing a great change. If I was going to survive this, I would have to draw on resources that I wasn't completely sure I had. The transition from being on the march would require a new set of skills. The challenges here were far more mental, emotional, and spiritual than they had been in the mountains. We had descended from the highest point to the lowlands, topographically and emotionally. It was hard to believe that the agony of our feet and legs could be made to seem slight when compared to what was going on in our hearts and minds.

One day I just got tired of all the negative thoughts and emotions I was having. I'd gone over a lot of my life, looked at decisions I'd made, actions I'd taken, and just beaten myself up over all the could-haves, should-haves, and would-haves that make up a life. I sat down with my journal and decided that I was going to lay out a new vision of myself, something I called my PLO—personal life outline. I identified five points in my life where I saw some weakness, some areas that needed improving. I laid out those five points and a plan for bettering myself in those areas. I created a code system so that if the notebook was ever taken away to be read by the FARC (something Sombra told us at the very beginning would happen—but we were "free" to write whatever we wanted), they wouldn't be able to decipher my plan. I decided that:

1. I wanted to be a stronger spiritual leader for my family.
2. I wanted to be stronger in the face of distraction or temptation.
3. I wanted to become the best father I could to my children.
4. I wanted to become the best husband to my wife that I could.
5. I wanted to become the most decent, honest, and fair person in my everyday dealings with other people.

Beneath each of these, I listed a series of subpoints. Doing this helped me keep my mind occupied; it also gave me a project to work on and goals to be achieved. The project was me, of course, but given that all the FARC really wanted us to do was to continue breathing, it was better than nothing. That plan also helped alleviate some of the massive guilt I was feeling. I had put my family into a bad situation, something I never wanted to do. I was causing them pain, and that hurt far more than anything that was being done to me. Since I couldn't fix this for them, I had to figure out a way to do something that would benefit them, and me, in the long term.

It also seemed as if change was in the air as well as on my mind. We could hear chain saws and hammering in the distance. The FARC seemed especially busy as we approached our third week in Monkey Village. The display toilet was carried off. The next day, the one-thousand-liter cistern they used to store water in was moved. Sombra, who only checked on us once a week, showed up out of the blue.

He didn't have any real news, but he asked us to make a list of all the things we wanted.

"You need a VCR, put it on the list," Sombra said.

We were attuned enough and adjusted enough to prison-camp life that we knew to ignore the Fat Man's blowhard exaggerations of what he could get us. So we listed things like sheets, blankets, a few more towels, nonextravagant creature comforts. We asked for radios—*again*.

We'd also noticed that aircraft were once again overhead near our camp. Change was definitely in the air, but we didn't know yet what that meant.

FIVE

Settling In

April 2003—June 2003

TOM

About a week after we'd first heard the sound of chain saws in the far distance, the Frenchman asked me to let Keith and Marc know that we would be moving. Handing me three burlap bags, he said we'd be marching in the middle of the night and would need to have our things together.

That next morning, sometime after midnight, we were awakened and led out. The moon had already gone down, and we were in total darkness save for the flashlights the FARC used. We marched for what seemed to be twenty minutes. When we stopped, I initially thought we were just going to rest for a bit, but in the faint starlight light, I saw that we'd arrived at another camp. My heart fell. Even from a distance, I could see the newly downed and chain-saw-milled posts and boards of our new prison. They were the color of bone against the dark backdrop of the jungle. I didn't need anyone to tell me that this was not good; I felt it in the pit of my stomach, a sensation similar to flying through an air pocket and losing altitude.

I'd been struggling throughout the march and in the three weeks at Monkey Village. We all talked about guilt, and mine was just a variant on what Keith and Marc were feeling. I kept replaying the conversation I had with my wife the night before the crash. What if I had decided that enough was enough and I wanted to stop the vagabond life and live in my dream house in Florida? What would have been so bad about that? Well, I hadn't and now I was a hostage. Meanwhile, she was an immigrant to the U.S. How would she handle being alone in a country that wasn't truly her own? She spoke English, but it wasn't her first language. And then there was my son. At forty-nine, I was a father of a young boy of only five. Was Tommy going to grow up without a father? I hadn't really gotten to enjoy much time with him because of my schedule and traveling. The last time I saw him I had taken him to the bus stop for his ride to kindergarten. I could tell he was nervous, but he climbed aboard and got a seat near the window. When the bus lurched off, he started waving. He didn't stop the whole time the bus was visible. All I'd done since we arrived at Monkey Village was lie in my hammock and try to force the image of him waving good-bye to me out of my mind.

When we arrived at this newly constructed camp, those feelings only intensified. I'd been hoping for a release, and instead I'd gotten a longer sentence. I knew that the FARC wouldn't have gone to the time and effort to build a new camp if they intended to release us anytime soon. The Frenchman led us past a hastily built fence into a round clearing that was about fifty feet in diameter. Three structures stood in the clearing—one larger than the other two. The biggest of the three was in the far corner and that was where we were led. It was made from the usual *tablas,* and it had a small covered porch area and a door with a chain-link window. Like the previous one in Monkey Village, this structure was large enough to accommodate the three of us, and in fact, this one was divided into three rooms. We all assumed that the three of us were going to be housed in it, but when Keith and Marc stepped onto the porch, their guard, Pollo, said, "No. No," and led them off to the other buildings. Each of them had a separate building that was no more than six or seven feet long and the same distance wide. They were basically square boxes encased in chain-link fencing. It was clear to me that they were originally intended to be used for storage, but somehow, through the chain of command, an order had been issued stating that the three of us were going to be separated as much as possible.

When we were shown the bathroom facility, we got an even stronger sense that we were in here for the long haul. Instead of a hastily dug and quickly filled slit trench, the FARC had built an actual outhouse with a manual flush system. As glad as we might have been for that small comfort and convenience, knowing that the ceramic toilet they'd once had on display was now to be used just added months to what we assumed would be the length of our stay. I'd been optimistically telling myself that we'd be held for three weeks. Well, the three weeks had long since passed during the twenty-four-day march and at Monkey Village, and now we'd been moved to what seemed to be a permanent site. The camp was in better condition, we all had raised platform beds to keep us out of the mud, but none of that mattered.

That first night, I experienced what must have been an acute anxiety attack. When the guards had wrapped the chain through the door and snapped the lock shut, it was as if they'd wrapped it around my neck. My heart raced, I sweated, and the racking dry heaves that turned my guts inside out were so violent and loud that Keith and Marc could hear them. They shouted for the guards, trying to reason with them in their minimal Spanish to unlock my door. I made it through the first night, but there was little improvement the next day. I felt guilty that the hooch I had was bigger than Keith and Marc's. Keith was tall enough that he couldn't lie completely straight in his without hitting his head or his feet on the wall. I wasn't claustrophobic, but I couldn't imagine what it was like to be in those coffinlike shacks. I began to dread nightfall and the sound of the chains being fed through the holes in our doors; the ratcheting metallic clink and the click of the lock were like being water-tortured.

I slept fitfully, if at all, and in the morning, all my pent-up anxiety needed to be let out somehow. I'd wake at first light and the guard would open my hooch to let me out. I'd walk a loop around the perimeter of the camp. Every day it seemed to rain at least a bit, and the track I made grew gradually muddier and muddier. I started with 60 laps and increased that to 150, walking in circle after circle after circle. I was sure that Keith and Marc were getting sick to death of the sucking sound of my boots in the muck and mire, but I had to do something physical. My thoughts were racing out of control. I couldn't get out of my mind the idea that we were going to be there for six years. I'd take one step and I'd hear the word *six* in my head. I'd take another step and hear the word *years*. I'd repeat those words and imagine I was tromping them into the mud, but they'd just keep rising back up like a hand wanting to pull me down beneath the surface.

We still couldn't speak to one another, and even though Keith and Marc were in such close proximity to me, the isolation was really upsetting. About three or four days into what we referred to as "the New Camp," I hit a bottom that I didn't even know existed. I thought I'd made firm contact with this dark runway before, but I fell even deeper. Even though during the day we were allowed to move freely about our enclosure, that day I chose to sit off in a corner of the camp on a *tablas* bench. For a long time, I sat there questioning my ability to make it through this, until Keith walked past me and dropped a small scrap of paper on the ground within my line of sight. I waited until he was back at the far end of the clearing near Marc. I unfolded it and read, "We are not forgotten. People are looking for us. One day at a time. We will go home."

The skies didn't suddenly brighten and I didn't feel like dancing, but it was a start. I looked over at Keith and Marc and they both nodded at me. It was like they were driving their point home, nailing that scrap of paper on the wall so that it could serve as a constant reminder of what I needed to stay focused on. I'm not a spiritual guy. Religion for me begins and ends with a period. But I knew at that moment that I had to start believing in something, mostly myself and my ability to endure this. That note was like someone opening the door of the cockpit and telling me to get back into the pilot's seat. This was a whole new aircraft, a whole new way of piloting. I didn't have any of my old maps or charts, but I did have a couple of guys who were going to help me figure out a course. I'd have to learn how to fly the bird, but I had plenty of experience at doing that.

Keith's note also made me realize something else. Part of my stress during this time was because I was the one who spoke the language. I was the one responsible for doing most of the communicating. Knowing that my ability to speak and understand Spanish was crucial to the survival of all of us, I was putting too much pressure on myself as I focused on how my actions affected Keith and Marc—not just me.

I was also anxious because of Keith's condition. Keith was by far the most physically imposing of us and he was also one of the brashest, most confident people I'd ever met. As a former Marine, he had more survival training experience than the rest of us. To see him injured and laid low by his stomach issues was frightening in this respect—if he was hurting that bad, what did that mean for Marc and me? If the march had taken a toll on Keith and Marc, two men far younger than I was, what did that mean for me and my health? Mission one was to endure and get home. What if I didn't have the skills it took? While Keith's health seemed to be improving, he wasn't nearly as physically active as he'd been before. I'd known him as a guy who was full of life and energy, seldom able to just sit still. In Monkey Village and in the first days at the New Camp, he seemed to be spending a lot of time in his hooch alone. His note let me know that if he was weaker physically than he'd ever been, he was probably more mentally strong.

Seeing Keith's note, I realized that we all had different and necessary skills to succeed. Figuring out how to use those skills to survive captivity was what we now needed to concentrate on. We were applying old skills in a new environment. That was going to take time and trial and error. I had never been a very patient guy and my walking around in furious circles was proof of that.

I learned something about patience and how to get through the day from Marc. I'd always been a guy who liked a set routine. That was one reason why each morning I walked the camp. I was also very meticulous about caring for the few possessions I had—part of my pilot's training specifically and my temperament generally. I liked to do things as quickly and efficiently as possible. The FARC did not. There seemed to be very little in the way of orderliness to what they did. I was impressed with their construction abilities, even though the structures they built were hastily erected and somewhat slipshod. I knew that in most cases what they built was temporary, but I was always a believer that if you were going to do something, it was worth doing it right and making it last.

Though Marc didn't realize it at the time, he turned into my teacher. Each morning he would wake up and scrub clean all his possessions with an old toothbrush. What we had didn't amount to much. The clothes we wore, our spare clothes, our boots, the plastic lawn chairs we'd sat on in the back of the pickup truck, and a few other odds and ends. In our other life, we probably could have scrubbed all that spotless with that toothbrush in an hour, but Marc could occupy himself for an hour just getting the mud out of the treads on the sole of his boots. He'd sit there with a look of deep concentration on his face, rarely even looking up from his work.

I began to copy him. I thought that if I could just slow down like

Marc and really take my time doing things, I wouldn't be so anxious. I could get some control over my thoughts and my emotions. I began to see a pattern emerging in my life. As a pilot, I had been constantly on the move. My job was all about going somewhere. I'd moved around the country and the world; I was seldom still. The march was horrific, but I did have those moments when I marveled at how I was able to keep *going*. Now I had no place to go. I had to sit idle, which was hard, but Marc's example really helped me.

At one point early on, Marc had talked about watching spiders weave their webs and how he could sit for hours to watch the spinning. While at first I couldn't do that, I did spend hours tying fisherman's knots with a string. Back home, I'd always anticipated problems and devised strategies to fix them, but in captivity, I didn't have any real objects to do that with. I began to make lists of things that needed to be done to our newly purchased house, going through the house system by system—electrical, plumbing, structural—and deciding the necessary steps. As time went on, I'd do the same thing with other objects that were familiar and important to me. I'd ridden motorcycles on and off for my whole adult life. I mentally took one apart and reassembled it, piece by piece, every nut, bolt, washer, flange, housing, circlip, switch, and wire. I'd think about whether a part was aluminum, steel, plastic, or rubber, or whether it was milled, anodized, cast, or plated and what that meant in terms of what tools to use on it or what solvents could be used to safely clean it. When I got through with that, I'd narrow my focus down even more intently. For each nut and bolt, I'd picture in my mind what kind of thread it had (coarse or fine) and what its pitch was. When I was done with the motorcycle rebuilding and maintenance, I would start working on a plane.

I was definitely a work in progress. I still worried about my health, and in particular my blood pressure. The FARC seemed to be of the opinion that if they gave you medicine for something once, it meant the problem was gone and you were cured. After the supply of pills that

Johnny had given me was gone, I had to ask again and again for more. Our medic was the guard Pollo. He would tell me that he wasn't going to get me any more of the medicine. I'd have to complain to the Frenchman and he would have to talk to Sombra. Of course, that meant that Pollo would get in trouble for not doing his job—keeping us alive.

A month into life at the New Camp, I developed an eye infection. My eye was red and puffy and itched and oozed a discharge. I'd had conjunctivitis before and knew it was a nuisance but treatable. I asked for eyedrops. Pollo brought them and administered them to me. *Once!* I tried to be patient and explain to him that an infection needed to be treated with a course of antibiotics. A onetime application wasn't a miracle cure. He administered it again for a couple of days and then stopped again. Pollo was also the one who locked us up at night, so he was no favorite of any of us. The fourth night of the eyedrops, Pollo showed up and locked Keith and Marc in their boxes. He came to my hooch, and I was expecting him to put the drops in my eyes and then lock up. Instead he locked the chain and started to walk away.

"Give me the damn medicine," I yelled.

He stopped and walked up to the chain-link window, his dark beady eyes even darker and more sinister.

"I don't want to waste the medicine on you," he replied.

I lost it. I started screaming and cursing, while Pollo was returning fire. We shouted at each other for a few minutes. I was sure the Frenchman and the other guerrillas could hear us, and I was waiting for someone with some sense to come to sort things out. Pollo walked away into the darkness and no one came. I was so angry I was shaking.

Pollo's arbitrary behavior pissed me off, but his walking away brought to real life a dread fear that I'd been having since we'd been captured. I walked around a lot of the time with this sense that there was a black hole nearby that I was going to disappear in. Being ignored was like being told I didn't exist. Being told that he didn't want to give me the drug I needed was like being told I didn't matter.

In truth, this argument with Pollo was just one in a series of unsettling things that had put me on edge. The FARC kept seven white pigs across the creek from us. Sometimes they would cross the creek to our side. Some of the FARC would yell and scream at the pigs to get them back across to their side. We didn't think much of it, but later we heard the bloodcurdling sound of a pig screaming. The FARC had apparently decided to castrate one of the domesticated pigs, but were botching the job or doing it in the most inhumane manner possible. The pig's screams went on for forty-five minutes, shattering whatever calm any of us had managed to find for ourselves.

Even worse, a few days before the pig castration, we were in our boxes when we heard a single gunshot and a woman's piercing scream. We heard the FARC scrambling around and a whole lot of commotion and yelling and sobbing. No one would tell us what had happened, but it was clear that someone had been shot. Was it a guerrilla? A hostage from another group? (We'd heard rumors that there were other camps similar to ours scattered around our zone.) Were executions starting? Had the FARC purposely killed one of their own? In the absence of any information, our thoughts and speculations ran wild.

To say the least, my nerves were already frayed when Pollo showed up and refused to give me my medicine. None of us expected the FARC to treat us with kid gloves or hand out special privileges. We simply asked that they treat us humanely and decently. That was how we were treating them and we expected that it be returned in kind.

KEITH

Stress does different things to different people. I'd seen it in all kinds of situations on the job, with my family, driving down the street. Tom, Marc, and I all had to choose how we were going to deal with our confinement. I think having to stay flat on my back in the hooch made my choice a bit easier and kept the monkey on my back under control.

I knew that at some point, I was going to have to dig pretty deep, so I figured why not reach inside and see what I had right away?

In the jungle, I needed to set my bullshit detector on "self" and strip away the many layers that had built up during my precaptivity days. I knew that the standard operating procedure of before was not the SOP that would get us through this. Course corrections were the order of the day and it was going to take some time to get our bearings before we started to plot out where we needed to head next. I tried to look at the silence as one of those right, hard things, something that had to be done, even if it added to my stress. I'd gotten through the brutal boot camp at Parris Island when I was in the Marines, and found the mental discipline that we leathernecks had to develop or risk getting booted from the corps. I'd also spent hundreds of hours tearing down and rebuilding various aircraft and aircraft systems in my time in the Marines and as a reservist. Knowing that what you were doing could make the difference between a flight crew and others onboard living and dying, you refined your ability to focus and to shut out distractions.

The mind is a funny thing, but the longer I lay there, the more I learned I could control my thoughts as long as I filtered out the distractions. Maybe it was the messed-up physical condition that allowed me to just lie so still for so long, but having some time to reflect was good for me. When I was a kid or even later as an adult, if I had a problem, I'd go off by myself into the woods or wherever else I could be alone to sort things out. My hooch became my sanctuary, even though I could barely fit in it.

A lot of this reflection centered around the thing that had gotten me into this mess—my job. Tom and I had several conversations about this during the march. We both loved our jobs and what they enabled us to do for our families, but there was no way around the truth: If it weren't for the money, we wouldn't have been in Colombia. We were making good coin, and that was important to us—what it bought us, what it meant to our egos, what it might mean down the line for our kids and our retirement. I wasn't so much interested in being a hero with a capital *H* as I was in being a hero to my family and in my own mind by bringing down some big bucks. Call me shallow. Call me greedy. Call me what you want. I didn't care. I still don't, really. All I was doing was living the American Dream.

Both of my parents were academics, Ph.D.s. Very, very smart and loving folks who busted their asses but didn't, in my mind, reap the financial rewards they might have. My father was a director of a vocational education center and my stepmom worked in administration there. They did good, important work and they told me there were other ways that you could be rewarded besides a salary.

I stored that as good advice and went down my own road, but now I was rethinking things. Humping through the jungles and mountains of Colombia, my guts twisted in a knot, I had said to Tom, "When we get out of here, there's no way I'm going back to work like we were doing. No way." Tom agreed.

Stretched out on the floor, I knew I'd messed up things for my family, and I vowed to never do that again. Other things were more important than the number of digits in a bank account or on a paycheck. I'd tell myself I could cut some spending here, cut some there. We'd be okay. I didn't need to make that kind of money. I could be happy without it. I'd gotten a pretty nasty wake up call, but that was only the start for me.

I went back to a lesson my father had taught me, a lesson as old school as it gets, but it helped. He was a big believer in the "T list"—put your positives on the right and your negatives on the left of the vertical line. As much as I focused on painful memories, regrets, and the guilt I felt about what I was putting my family through, I also thought about some of the good things. I was proud of being a good father to my kids. It wasn't easy being a single dad, and Malia had come on board like a second mom to Lauren and Kyle. I wasn't the best husband, fiancé, or boyfriend, but I was a good dad. My relationship with Patricia, the

Colombian flight attendant I'd had an affair with, was an example of an experience falling on both sides of the plus and minus line. I was upset with Patricia and me for her getting pregnant, but I was also glad to be a dad again. I was upset with myself for all the pain my affair caused Malia, but I was glad that our bond was tight enough that we were working things out. I had to figure out some strategy to stop getting in the way of my own success by doing something dumb and selfish.

While my mind wandered through this jungle of thoughts, I felt some of the same anxiety that Tom and Marc did, but I dealt with it differently. I was able to relax, and inside the cramped confines of my hooch, I could just vegetate. A while back, my dad had given me some audiotapes by a guy named Dr. Wayne Dyer. I'd listened to them and picked up a few things about the mind-body connection. I'd think about things and try to imagine what was going to happen to us in the next few months; I tried to anticipate as best I could what the wazoo FARC had up the sleeves of their grimy little Che T-shirts.

I continued my study of the guards and the other guerrillas. One cat I couldn't figure out at all was Milton. He seemed to be Sombra's right-hand man. We almost always saw the two of them together, but there was something odd about the pair. The Fat Man was fat obviously, but he was pretty slick with the language, tried to joke quite a bit, and always made promises he wouldn't keep. Milton, on the other hand, was a blank but damned ugly slate. We weren't sure if a real thought passed between the guy's ears. As it turned out, a bullet had passed through that same neighborhood once, and now Milton was the Fat Man's little toady or even his little mascot. Everywhere Sombra went, there was Milton. He'd just stare vacantly and nod in agreement with whatever the Fat Man said.

It was sad in a way, knowing the guy had been wounded, but we figured there had to be more to him than met the eye.

In the New Camp we continued to exploit a weakness in the guards that we'd first noticed in Monkey Village: nicotine. Periodically, we were given cigarettes, but we didn't really take up smoking. For us, they were currency. Most of the guerrillas were seriously addicted to smoking. Advantage: Americans. We saw the way nearly all the guerrillas were puffing away on the things and figured that we could parlay that into some sweet deals for ourselves. Like most things, cigarettes came into camp sporadically, and because of this, we were able to wheel and deal with our stockpiles of smokes. Even if we couldn't buy any material goods, we could at least make a down payment on some goodwill with some of our more susceptible captors.

One of them was a guy named Smiley. He was a young, good-natured kid, very animated and emotional. When he was first guarding us, it was like he had a crush on us—his first Americans. He was one of the first guerrillas I really reached out to as we were figuring out our *Hogan's Heroes* thing—how to get the guards to do things for us. I could tell that Smiley had a brain, that he was more of a freethinker and willing to take risks for us. One day, about six weeks or so into our stay at the New Camp, Smiley came up behind my hooch. Back there, he was blocked from view by anyone except me. He looked like he was about to cry and laugh and shit his pants all at the same time. He was smiling and flapping his hands in imitation of a bird, meaning we were being set free. I could tell he was genuinely happy for us. No one was that good of an actor.

Risking the guards banging down on us, I ran to Tom and Marc. "Listen to what I've gotten from Smiley. He seems to think we're going to get released."

"What do you mean?" Marc said. "How does he know?"

"I'm not sure. I've got to find out more, but my Spanish isn't good enough. All he could do was gesture and hold out his arms like an airplane's wings."

"I'll talk to him as soon as I can," Tom whispered, and broke off when another guard took notice of us and headed our way. The day after Smiley gave me the bird-airplane signal, Tom asked him where he heard that we were being released. The look on Smiley's face changed, and his expression turned panicky.

"They'll kill me. They'll kill me," he said as he shook his head.

We were hoping he'd let us know what Colombian radio station he'd heard the news on, but his response was the next best thing. We now had two bits of evidence to prop up our hopes of being released. To add to that, a day or so later, the Frenchman came to Tom all businesslike and told him that he needed all our civilian clothing sizes: shirts, pants, socks, shoes. We were thrilled by this, thinking that if we were getting *civilian* clothes, it could only mean one thing—release. For the next couple of days, Tom had a real spring in his mud-clomping step, Marc was the cat who ate the canary, and I was already mentally ordering my first meal at my favorite barbecue shack in South Georgia.

To confirm our suspicions, we'd been hearing a whole lot of aircraft activity for a few days and the frequency of the flyovers only increased. The suspense was killing us, and three or four days after Smiley's revelation, the Frenchman came into our camp. On our behalf, Tom was all over him asking questions about what the FARC's plans were for us. Normally the Frenchman would take those questions head-on and fling a bunch of bullshit at us. This time he was really evasive and not promising anything. He said that maybe we would be there for years.

I didn't put too much stock in what he said. The Frenchman probably never knew when he was telling a lie or telling the truth. A few days later, Pollo opened our hooches so we could get breakfast. Usually Marc was out of his hooch pretty quickly and I was the one lagging behind. But on this morning, I didn't see him and got a whiff of something in the air. Even though we weren't supposed to, Tom and I walked into Marc's hooch.

He was sitting on the bed, staring absently at the ground. We could tell immediately that the floor had dropped out from underneath him. We sat down on either side of him and put our arms around him and asked him what was going on. He couldn't even lift his chin up. Then the tears started. My arm was still around his shoulders and it started twitching up and down with Marc's heaving shoulders. There was nothing else we could do or say at that point except sit there with him.

After a few minutes, he told us that what the Frenchman had said about being there for a long time had just leveled him. He'd also had a dream that night. He was with his father and Destiney. Destiney was in his lap and Marc was looking at her braids. He said it was so real. He could smell the Johnson's baby shampoo in her hair, see where each strand of hair was knotted in her braids. And that was when he woke up. He wasn't with his daughter; instead he was in a box in the jungle in Colombia.

We stayed with Marc as long as we could before the guards pushed us out of there.

A night or two later, the three of us were standing at a spot in our clearing where we could see through the trees. The guards would let us stand there, and since we were a pretty good distance from their station, they couldn't hear us if we whispered. We were all just checking in on one another. I looked up, and the sun was going down, and Marc pointed to the sky. A bit of rainbow was arcing across the opening.

"Maybe it's a sign," Tom said.

We'd all been looking for signs and indications just about everywhere; I supposed this one was as good as any. I looked at Marc, and I could see he was deep in thought, whether it was about what Tom had said or something else I couldn't say, but he seemed at peace. I wasn't about to step into those calm waters and disturb them. I just stood there enjoying the moment of communion with them.

From the beginning, we developed a shorthand way of checking in with one another to see what mental state we were each in on any particular day. If you were in your bubble, that was a good thing. You were safe, secured, and protected. If you were out of the bubble, you were agitated and anxious. I liked the metaphor because I visualized it as a level—the tool a carpenter uses to measure if a board or an entire wall of building was plumb—straight up and down—or level on the horizontal plane. If a small air bubble suspended in liquid is between two lines on the small cylinder, then whatever you are checking is level either vertically or horizontally. I liked that image because it allowed for the individual difference among the three of us. When I was flat on my back, that meant I was in my bubble. If Tom and Marc were up and around and busy with their walking or their cleaning, it meant they were in their bubbles.

We hadn't forgotten about Smiley's revelation, but a few days had passed since our conversation with the Frenchman about our future. Tom followed up briefly with the Frenchman and asked him that if the order was given for our release, how long would it take until we were actually let go?

"Eight days" was his only response.

When Tom reported that information back to us, we were all puzzled and impressed. Why eight days? Why not a week? Did the guy have it down to that exact number because a plan was already in place? The Frenchman's precise answer combined with the continued increase in aircraft activity upped our anticipation level. We could hear a plane—we weren't sure if it was a Grand Caravan like we'd flown (and thus our sister ship from California Microwave) or if it was a King Air run by another group out of Bogotá. The planes were essentially boxing in our location, flying in a pattern similar to what we did over our target zones and narrowing it down through a series of turns.

That was a good thing and a bad thing. We knew that a recon plane would be looking for us on the ground. The jungles of Colombia are vast, and our small clearing could easily blend into the surrounding vegetation. We weren't just a needle in jungle haystack, we were the eye of the needle—a tiny empty space in a vast carpet of green and therefore very easy to miss. The comfort in all of this was that the presence of these aircraft near our location verified our assumption that we were being tracked and people were looking for us.

The bad news was that the thought of rescue still troubled us big-time. The one-thousand-liter plastic cistern the FARC used for water was a veritable bull's-eye of a target. It was about ten feet wide, black, and was raised off the ground about twelve feet so that gravity could feed the water out a valve. Our planes were equipped with infrared sensors, so the water in that tank would be like a flashing light signaling any intelligence airplane that flew overhead. If the aerial guys were able to pin down our location, it meant the Colombian military could come in and attempt an ambush rescue operation. We were convinced we could easily die in that kind of action—especially at night, when we would be in our boxes and easy to gun down. We'd talked about what we would do in case of such a rescue attempt, but our success at getting out of there was dependent on being out of the boxes, which meant during daylight hours. Any successful raid would likely come at night and that wasn't good for the home team.

A week after Smiley gave us the word and about sixty-five days into our stay in the New Camp, we were all locked up for the night when we heard a new sound: jet engines coming in low and fast. And I mean low, just barely over the tops of the trees. I couldn't be sure if they were U.S.-made A-37s or Israeli-manufactured Kfirs, but it didn't matter—they were fighter jets and their low approach meant only one thing—we were going to get rained on in the form of high explosives. Marc and I both started to yell at the guards to get us out of those boxes. We did not want to be sitting ducks. I hit the deck, trying to take whatever cover I could for what I knew was coming.

The terror was unlike anything I'd felt before. We had no place to run to, nothing of any substance to get under or behind to protect ourselves, and we were about to be strafed by bombs and bullets. The FARC might have just as well staked us out spread-eagle in the clearing in chains with giant arrows pointing to us. Their only response was "Don't worry. Everything is fine."

When the jets circled back not a minute later, the first bomb hit. The initial impact sounded like thunder, and it was followed by a split second of silence. All the ambient jungle noise that was so incessant—the sound of insects, birds, monkeys—stopped for the briefest of moments. And then the concussion from the explosion came rippling through the leaves of the trees and underbrush like a giant creature tearing through the underbrush. The bombs were hitting within a kilometer of us, and the thunderous *crump* of their impact with the ground could be heard and felt.

The three of us were screaming to be let out of our boxes, and we heard only a single voice say, "Don't worry. The Frenchman is asleep. You should be, too." That was followed by the sound of a guard puking his guts out with fear.

I stood up and crept over to the edge of my hooch. The boards had a tiny gap in them, and I could see the Frenchman huddled right next to my hooch with a couple of other guards. They'd abandoned their camp, which was about twenty or so yards from ours, and taken cover behind our hooch. I couldn't see the rest of the forty or so FARC who were nearby and assumed they'd either gotten hit or had fled into the jungle.

The jets did several bombing runs, and after they departed, we heard the sound of OV–10 Broncos. I'd flown in them in the Marine Corps and these Broncos were the workhorse of the Colombian Air Force. We could hear heavy machine-gun fire ranging from .30 caliber to .50 caliber peppering the area. That was accompanied by the sound of Fantasma gunships circling for a long time overhead, hoping to pick off any FARC stupid enough to show themselves. For the next half hour, we heard the drone of the engines and the sporadic sound of gunfire.

When they finally flew off, we filled our lungs with a deep breath and began a session of whining, screaming, and yelling. Having the good guys nearly take you out in a bombing run doesn't make for happy campers. We vented our spleens all that night and into the next day.

We did it knowing that we had to get it out of our system. The FARC received their fair share of our anger along with the Colombian military. That said, Tom, Marc, and I understood that we had not been the focus. We trusted that the Colombians did not know that we were in a camp nearby their targets.

On one level, we understood the game. The FARC used the presence of the *secuestrados*, the hostages, as a way to try to tie the hands of the Colombian government. In that sense, we were human shields. The FARC hoped that by holding hostages in various locations along with or nearby their units, the military wouldn't attack for fear of killing or injuring hostages. We'd just had close-up evidence that the Colombian military wasn't going to let the FARC employ that strategy with impunity. We understood that the government couldn't let the FARC get the upper hand, couldn't just freeze all their military action. If they stopped bombing FARC targets, they wouldn't be an effective fighting force and the FARC insurgency would gain more traction.

In the aftermath of the bombings, Tom said something that we all had to agree with. We were on the back side of the power curve as hostages. We were being sacrificed. We had no idea how many casualties they took as a result of that attack, but as a rule, when the FARC took a hit, we would take a hit, too. On this occasion, we were lucky. We hated being bombed, but we took satisfaction in knowing that the FARC had incurred damages and were on the losing side of this; even though it nearly cost us our lives, it was cause for celebration. We also hated the idea that simply by holding us as hostages, the FARC could claim some sort of victory. As hostages or prisoners, there wasn't a lot that we could directly do to defeat the FARC ourselves. There were things we could do in small ways—like not believing any of their Marxist propaganda bullshit and by conducting ourselves in ways that countered their opinion of us as imperialist pigs.

In the end, we chalked this one up as a victory—one that scared the bejesus out of us and pissed us off—but a victory nonetheless. Winning in captivity took on a new dimension, and understanding that was crucial to our adjustment.

MARC

Three days after the bombing raid, the Frenchman told us to pack our stuff. We were moving out. With the Frenchman's request for our civilian clothes sizes still fresh in our minds, we figured our release was at hand. We'd been held captive for approximately thirteen weeks, and we'd crashed on the thirteenth of February. I wasn't superstitious but noticed the coincidence in my journal. Keith had been saying that he wanted to be home for Kyle's birthday on May 20, and as we gathered our things together Tom said to him, "It looks like you're going to make that birthday celebration after all. Maybe a couple of days late, but close enough, considering."

We had only forty-five minutes to pack. While at the New Camp, we'd been given a few more personal items—flashlights whose lenses we had to shroud with leaves to keep them from being too bright and working as signal devices, a nylon tent top, and all our toiletries and soap. We stowed our entire lives in the new backpacks we'd been issued. We marched out, retracing on foot the route we'd taken after we'd first arrived following the twenty-four-day march. We walked past the larger compound and saw Sombra sitting in a truck. We all hoped that, as bad a driver as Sombra was, he was taking us to some point where we'd be released. He looked at us and said, "Guys, you have to step in the same footprints as you cross this road. We can't leave too many tracks."

With that in mind, we marched off into the jungle. We were in a column of about forty guerrillas and we noticed their livestock was with them. Upon seeing the animals, we all realized that if we were being marched out with that many FARC and all of their supplies including livestock, the likelihood of our being led to a release point was not good at all. We spent that night sleeping on black plastic on the ground with our new tent tops suspended over us on short sticks. When we woke up in the morning I heard Tom and Keith talking and laughing.

"Would you look at that, Marc?" Tom said. He pointed to where Keith had been lying a few seconds before.

"Oh my God." I stared down at the ground and saw that overnight, a swarm of termites had invaded Keith's space—so many in fact that when Keith stood up, he left an empty space in the shape of his body with the rest of the surrounding ground covered in termites, the mere sight of which caused us to start laughing.

As it turned out, we all were going to need a sense of humor because we spent several weeks living in a dank, foggy mist. We'd been at this temporary camp for several days when the Frenchman came to speak with Tom. They walked off to one side, and I couldn't hear what they were saying. I saw Tom's shoulders slump and he raised his hands as if pleading, so I knew the news was not good. At first I thought we were in trouble for talking, but when Tom came and told us what was really going on, I was devastated. Orders had come in that we were to be placed in chains.

Being locked in the boxes at Monkey Village and the New Camp was horrible. Being told not to speak to one another was worse. Now the thought of having chains around our necks full time was an unimaginable blow to our new and fragile resolve to get through this experience. Our chains weren't there yet, so in place of them the FARC used polyester cord. They fashioned a kind of harness that fit around our shoulders and then tied a choker knot on the loop that went around our necks. If they needed to, they could pull on the end of the cord to choke us. The first time that harness was placed on me, I had to just shut my eyes and pray to keep myself from violently shuddering and vomiting. To be treated like a dog or other animal was bad enough, but to have the FARC tell us that this was for our own good, that the Colombian military was around and would try to kill us, so we needed to be controlled better, and all that other shit just angered me even more.

With the introduction of these restraints, things had gone from brutal to inhumane. Sleeping on the ground with just one or two threadbare cotton sheets to keep us "warm," a sheet of black plastic as a mattress, a bug net to keep the insects off of us, and a nylon tent top as the roof over our heads was barely tolerable. But to be tied up? After the first day of being tied while marching, we learned that it was going to be our life for a while. Eventually we stopped marching. We simply rough-camped in the bush. We didn't make a clearing, we didn't build any platform beds or any structures, we made do in the mud. Worse, our harnesses stayed on and the ends were tied off to a tree or bush or post. As a result, we spent most of our time in what passed for our beds, lying beneath our nylon camouflaged tent tops. The only time we were outside we sat in the rain tied to a post. Any thoughts of being released were buried in the mud along with everything we had to our names.

As much as we tried to keep to our routines, and stay positive, it simply wasn't possible. Our nerves were frayed and now, without any real physical activity to speak of to help us blow off steam—Tom couldn't walk his laps, I couldn't spend hours cleaning things—we took out some of our frustration on one another. None of us was surprised by this. We had been together with very few exceptions from mid-February to May. I defy anyone to get along 100 percent of the time with anyone—not your wife, your twin sister or brother, your best friend—for that amount of time without there being some tension between you. Take three people who were, essentially, not strangers but coworkers, and put them in the situation we were in and under the conditions we existed in and see what happens.

Much of the problems stemmed from the fact that, in what we started to refer to as the Mud Camp, we were in much more of a confined space than we had been at either Monkey Village or the New Camp. We weren't just in the same area, we were right on top of one another. Americans have a pretty large personal space we like to keep around ourselves, and ours had been reduced greatly. Rubbing up against one another physically and emotionally was bound to cause friction. We'd seen some of that in the New Camp even when we weren't so close together.

One recurring issue at the Mud Camp revolved around the pigs. The FARC had placed a little garbage dump near Tom's hooch so that it was away from their camp, and at night, some of the camp pigs would root around in the trash—particularly around five in the morning, at first light. This would wake up Tom, who would then shout at them to quiet down. Tom didn't realize that his shouting was louder than the pigs, loud enough to wake up Keith and me. Keith was very direct in asking Tom to stop his yelling, which in turn pissed Tom off. He'd tell Keith to shut up, and they would part ways angry at each other. We didn't have a lot to think about during the day, so the two of them would stew all day about what was said and the next day the pig fight would start all over again.

It didn't go like that every day, but it seemed there was always something little that was setting one of us off. Just like people everywhere, you put up with something annoying for a while, but you store away that anger or resentment for later use. You don't realize that you're stockpiling things, but you are. All of us were or had been married, and we all knew that fighting fair meant sticking to the issue at hand, but whenever we were upset about something, some slight we'd stored up would be taken out in the heat of the moment, growing out of proportion until it stank like a spoiled piece of meat.

Part of the reason why Tom and Keith got on each other's nerves more than I got on theirs was a difference in personality. Tom was a reserved guy, a true Yankee in temperament, while Keith was louder and assertive, a self-proclaimed southern backwoods redneck. Under the best of circumstances, they wouldn't have gotten on well all the time. Tom hated tension in the camp, just hated it. He knew it added to our collective anxiety, and so when he found himself getting sucked into an argument or tiff, it made him feel even worse.

I wasn't immune to these run-ins or feeling the effects of them. We
had to learn to accommodate certain things. Though we were able to
bathe regularly, wearing rubber boots all day produced a foot odor in
Keith and me that could have killed a cat and made small children cry.
Tom had to put up with that, but he did for the most part because it was
something we couldn't really control. But sitting six inches away from
someone while eating every meal for a couple of months, you get tired
of their openmouthed chewing or even the sound of their lips smacking when they first open them to take a bite. In that confined space,
everything was intensified.

Tom and Keith admitted that in some ways they were like oil and
water, and as a result they were less tolerant of each other and each
other's idiosyncrasies than they were of me and mine. As it turned out,
the one thing they could always talk about was a subject that I often
grew tired of: airplanes. Both of them were airplane fanatics. If they
could, they would have talked about airplanes twenty-four hours a day,
seven days a week (and at times I felt like they were). Normally I could
have just walked away when a conversation wasn't to my liking, but I
had nowhere to go. It was enough to make me scream, and sometimes
I did.

In spite of all this, most of the time we were as thick as thieves. The
Mud Camp's conditions, the cords and harnesses, the severe blow to
our hopes of a quick release, all combined to really rub us all raw. Even
when those disputes were at their worst, we were becoming close as
brothers. We were seeing the guards as even more of an adversary than
before. With the cords around our necks and being tied up, we became
more dependent on them. We hated that and they hated that. If you had
to pee, you needed a guard to come and untie you and take you to the
trench. Sometimes they didn't feel like letting you go, so they wouldn't.
For an adult to have to plead with someone to let you relieve yourself
was incredibly demeaning. It seemed to be the FARC's intent to drag
us down as low as they could.

Pretty much everything contributed to our misery in the Mud Camp. From late May through the summer, we were in the rainy season. Everything was soaking wet and muddy. When we went to bathe in the nearby creek, we had to pass by the kitchen or what the FARC called the *rancho*. Water was obviously needed for cooking, so the rancho was often placed as close to the creek as possible. That made sense. What didn't make sense was the FARC throwing all their garbage in the water right where we were to bathe and wash our clothes. We would be wading in the river in a floating stew of onion skins, vegetable tops, and animals parts, and that was supposed to pass for a bathing area.

Toward the very end of our stay at the Mud Camp, Pollo came into our area and tossed nine bars of soap on the ground. These blue bars were very valuable to everyone. Though they were intended to be used as laundry soap, they were mild enough and more plentiful than the bath soap we used to clean ourselves and nearly everything else we had.

"Where you're going, this is hard to find," Pollo said cryptically.

His words frightened us. If we were heading deeper into the jungle and farther from whatever supply lines the FARC had, it meant our release was even more remote than we'd thought. We'd also heard some bombing activity, not as close to us as previously, but hearing it had put Tom in a poor mood. He said that he had gotten it into his mind, and he didn't know exactly why, that there would be a fifteen-day cease-fire prior to our release. When the bombs fell, it added an additional fifteen days to his sentence. Keith knew that Pollo's indication about a possible release in time for his son's birthday on May 20 was just so much more of the usual FARC lies that we'd fallen victim to again.

A few days later, we learned that we were going to be on the move again. We did the best we could to tell ourselves that the move was a good thing—but we were poking at the ashes of a fire that had long since gone out. We moved out overnight, and even though the march was only a few hours, we were in agony. The nearly five weeks at the Mud Camp of being tied up and not allowed to move freely had taken

their toll. It was only when we'd been forced to march that we understood just how much our physical condition had deteriorated. Wherever they were taking us, we were hoping that it wouldn't be far. After a
four-hour slog, we camped along a river for three nights, before aluminum river canoes showed up to whisk us away, deeper into the jungle
than we'd ever been.

SIX

Proof of Life

July 2003–September 2003

KEITH

I never would have guessed that knowing how many bars of soap I had at my disposal would have such an influence on my outlook. When Pollo dumped those things at our feet and told us they'd be in short supply, he might as well have been dumping our hearts onto the ground. As quickly as we scrambled to pick up those blue bars, I knew we'd have to be just as fast at picking ourselves up if we were going to make it back to higher emotional ground. A day or so later, Ferney dropped off more razors, toothpaste, and toothbrushes. Message received, sir: We were going away for a long time to a place or places where resupply was going to be tough. As much as we'd been able in the past to spin a spiderweb of hope out of the most insignificant of things—hat vs. hatless guards, being near a road, changes in the guards' shift patterns—there was no denying this new reality.

To give you a better idea of how much our inactivity affected our previous reality, we could barely scrub our clothes for more than a minute or two without being winded. Though it only lasted a few hours, we were grateful to be loaded into boats for the next part of our trek. The FARC had a number of twenty-foot-long aluminum river canoes. Seated on slat benches, we took off down a tree-choked stream, though it was hard to tell if it was an actual stream or if the rainy season had simply flooded the whole area. At times, there was so much vegetation clogging the water that our canoe trip wasn't much different from hiking through the jungle. The boats were made by a company called Duroboat and those things lived up to their name. Our boat driver would gun that Yamaha forty-horse engine and drive that thing like a bulldozer as he plowed through the debris.

Sometimes we'd have to go so close to the water's banks that we had to duck under the low-hanging branches and then endure a rain of insects, spiders, and other creepy-crawlies as they shook loose from their perches. We'd long since gotten used to being stung or bitten, and though I would swell up like a balloon every time the wasps got me, I was never worse for the wear.

Despite the insects, this three-day boat trip was a real treat. We'd been living under confinement in the jungle for about six months, and during that time, we weren't just under the FARC's umbrella, we were under the flora and fauna's umbrella as well. As down as we were about the prospect of another release going by the wayside, being out in even the limited space of the water was a literal breath of fresh air. Even better was when we reached the more open areas where the boat could maneuver freely and the sun shone on our pale white skin.

With blue July sky above us, and even bluer skies on the horizon, the boat trip felt a little bit like a vacation. Being under a jungle canopy for any length of time has a very depressing effect on you. We noticed the difference even when we were on a march and came into a clearing. It was like a spot of sun on an otherwise rainy day. You'd enter it and feel a sudden boost of energy; you'd exit it and feel that energy just drain away.

Unlike when we were marching, we were doing a lot of our moving during daylight hours. We'd travel most of the morning and usually quit in early afternoon. Even when we were in open areas, the FARC didn't seem to be as on edge as they had previously. None of the guerrillas scanned the skies for planes; none of them watched the banks for signs of Colombian military activity. Marc, Tom, and I were still in our harnesses and ropes, but the guards eased up on the no-talking rule. The three of us didn't abuse the privilege, but one of our main topics of discussion was how openly we were being moved—we knew that we were close to "civilization" a few times because we could hear other boats navigating tributaries to our left and right.

We could only draw two logical conclusions for the change in our movement: The first was that the FARC had agreed to some kind of deal on us and had gotten the DMZ they were always asking for—thus, we could travel without fear of being detected. The second was that somehow the FARC had gotten intel from the Colombian military that had informed them that this was a cool zone. The second seemed more unlikely. We hadn't seen much in the way of tactical competence from the FARC up until then, so why would we assume that they were able to engage in any kind of covert operations at higher levels.

All through the boat ride, we were still in travel mode—just sleeping on the ground, sometimes for a single night and sometimes for more. On July 23, 130 days into our captivity, the Fat Man walked into one of these temporary camps with his Santa Claus aura. He sat down at a barlike table the FARC had carried with them and hastily set up in a few minutes near our campsite. We immediately sensed something was up. Sombra had two switches—badass and nice guy—but that day he seemed different. He reached into his shirt pocket and showed us that he had lollipops. He signaled for Tom to come and sit with him on the same bench. Sombra was in his speechifying mood, so Marc and I could hear what he was saying.

"Tomorrow we will once again demonstrate our strength and unity to all the world. They will understand our commitment to our cause and see how just we are."

Tom decided to play along. "You love the peace, I know. But what does that have to do with us?"

"An international press will be here tomorrow to speak with all of you."

"International press?"

"Yes, a well-known journalist and others will speak with you." Sombra paused for dramatic effect. "I need to know your clothes sizes. You must look good for your visitors. You will have a chance to clean up."

Tom turned to us while Sombra sat and held the lollipops in his hand like a kid's doctor waiting to deliver an inoculation. "He seems to be saying that this is a big deal. Besides talking about the journalist, he used the term *prueba de vida*—proof of life."

We'd heard the term before, but we were wondering exactly how the Fat Man and his cronies conducted such a thing. We knew the basics, that we'd be photographed or videotaped with some dated document, a newspaper usually from the day of the proof of life, to show everyone that we were still alive. We didn't have much time for who, what, when, where, or why questions. A couple of guards came in holding their hands up like just-scrubbed surgeons going into an operating theater. They had scissors in them, and we were clearly the objects of their intentions. The rest of the guards gathered around to watch us get our haircuts. After that, we were brought big bowls of rice and canned tuna. We were clearly being worked. They wanted us to be happy and full-bellied for this proof of life meeting.

We took advantage of the situation by talking openly.

"What else did he say? Did he let us know how the proof of life was going to go down?" I asked.

"He said that we would send a communication to our families and that would fuel an interchange. He didn't give me any more details than that."

Marc scratched at his neck, trying to rid himself of newly cut hairs, "Why would they go through all this trouble to let people know we're alive if they weren't going to release us? They must have worked some deal."

"I wonder if the journalist is from CNN? Christiane Amanpour does a whole bunch of their international stuff," I added.

Tom said, "I don't care who they send, just that this proof of life gets back to our families."

Marc smiled and shook his head. "I know. Shane and my mom are going to see this and they're going to be excited. Can you imagine sitting at home and seeing our faces come up on-screen? After all this time. They have to have known that we were alive, right?"

Marc returned to a question that had been on all our minds for so long. We knew the military had seen us alive that first day when the helo gunner and I had made eye contact. Without any proof of life since then, did any of them wonder if the FARC had executed us? I had to push that thought away.

"Somebody in our government has been in touch with them, Marc. They know we're out here. We aren't forgotten. This proof of life is probably a demand from somebody through channels that lead to D.C. They know, bro."

Following a mostly sleepless night, Sombra retrieved us the next morning. We'd been told to prepare for an overnight stay, so we packed light. The Frenchman, Milton, Smiley, and a couple of other guards accompanied us. At one point, we had to stop for refueling on a small island. Sombra walked off with Ferney and we were left with Milton and another guard. They started talking and eventually the news leaked out to us that Colin Powell, the God-bless-him-four-star-general secretary of state of the United States of America, had just been in Colombia on our behalf. We were all completely jacked up to hear that.

Immediately our brains' motors spun up and we were wondering who else besides the press might show up at our proof of life. We thought of the U.S. ambassador to Colombia at the time, Anne Patterson, other possible State Department officials, maybe even representatives of Northrop Grumman. We also talked about what Colombian officials might be there—Interior and Justice Minister Fernando Londoño and others.

Once back on the boat, we were handed blindfolds and a lame apology from Sombra for the "necessity." A short while later, they placed us under black plastic, but the smell of gas under there was making us all sick. We raised hell until they lifted the plastic and let us remain visible the rest of the way. After a four- to six-hour boat ride, we were led off the boats by our harnesses and up an incline. The sounds of the jungle and the boat motor were replaced by the noises of passing cars and human voices. We were placed in some kind of vehicle—likely the back of one of their Toyota Land Cruiser trucks—and driven off. We could feel the breeze on our faces and hear the hum of civilization all around us. When we stopped, we were helped out of the truck, and a guard took each of us by his harness and cord. They led us along a wooden boardwalk, and as we walked, chatter from a crowd gathered and the roar of a portable generator rose up around us.

I assumed that we were being taken somewhere like a hotel room or someplace else for the *prueba de vida,* but when we were sat down in chairs and our blindfolds were removed, I saw that we were in another small twelve-by-twelve room made of *tablas.* Just as we had been when we met Gómez, Ramírez, and Mono JoJoy, we were now zoo animals. A whole group of FARC we'd never seen before passed by the open door of the room we were in and they were staring at us. Most of them put on a big macho display of anger directed at the gringos until the Frenchman and the Fat Man put an end to viewing hours and led us to another small room with *tablas* supported on sawhorses. So much for nice beds and a turndown service at night.

In an adjoining room, there was a large plastic water barrel. Because we'd been communing with the pigs at the Mud Camp, their indiscriminate pissing and shitting in the mud at our swimming area made us wary of water of any kind. We pulled the top and couldn't believe what we were seeing—the bottom of the barrel—for once literally instead of figuratively. We'd been so used to drinking and bathing in cloudy brown water that the sight of the bottom of that barrel through the crystal-clear water had us staring like we were reading the formula for turning lead into gold. It was so pristine we were tempted not to use it all, but hygiene and vanity won out.

After our baths, we were fed french fries and asked if there was anything else we needed. I'd developed some kind of jungle rash and I asked for medicine to treat it. To my surprise, I received it—the entire tube and not just a single treatment. We bedded down on a platform resting on sawhorses, and with the exception of a rat living up in the rafters, we were pretty much left alone the whole evening. Outside, we could hear the FARC conducting some kind of meeting. They sang their "We Love the Peace" song and the "Legalization Is the Solution" chant while speakers addressed the crowd on some aspect of FARC-ness. We estimated that about thirty to forty guerrillas were there, and the general tone of the place was much more orderly and military-like than it had been with the field units. They all had on the same uniforms, they were more disciplined about wearing their hats, and they seemed to be better squared away generally than the guys we'd been with in the jungle.

The Fat Man seemed a bit on edge and we saw all kinds of activity going on in the room next to ours, where they were setting up for the proof of life. We also smelled some kind of Pine-Sol like cleaner, and figured they were really going all out for us. That was when Sombra told us that the great and magnificent Mono JoJoy would soon be joining us once again.

Sombra said that he wanted me to know that he had seen a picture of my son. I was stunned. Didn't he mean sons? Patricia was pregnant with twins, what had happened? Did I misunderstand what he said? Sombra shrugged when I asked for details. Marc and Tom tried to assure me there was some mistake, but I couldn't shake the feeling that something was wrong. Twenty or so minutes later, Mono JoJoy walked in, accompanied by a guerrilla we'd never seen before. Mono JoJoy started speaking to us, and at that point it became clear that the other man with him was his interpreter/translator. The only thing was, it seemed like the guy was so nervous about everything that he could barely converse in Spanish let alone English.

In the middle of this mini Tower-of-Babel moment, I spotted a woman in a FARC uniform standing in the background. She clearly wasn't Colombian, and she stood out immediately. Her high, prominent cheekbones had been made sharper by what I figured must have been a diet similar to ours. Her skin was pale compared to the other guerrillas, her nose and cheeks were red-tinged from exposure to the sun and elements. Light brown hair framed her oval face, and even the harsh conditions she must have lived under couldn't hide the fact that she was a very attractive young woman who looked extremely out of place in a FARC uniform.

She stepped forward and started a conversation with me in accented but perfectly constructed English, and I knew we had our translator. There was something odd about this whole situation and her entry into it. I couldn't place her accent or get her to tell us who she was. All I could do was ask her to serve as our translator with the FARC. I said that she spoke far better English than the man with Mono JoJoy, and since he had no objections, she stepped in.

Just as she began to translate, a civilian, who could speak English as well, walked in carrying a video camera and it was clear he was taping.

"My name is Jorge Enrique Botero," he said, addressing the three of us. Before we could get any questions out, he turned to Marc. "I have a message for you from your mother."

MARC

I wasn't sure what to expect from the proof of life, but when Botero uttered those words, I realized just how hard this was going to be.

After telling me that he had a message from my mother, Botero immediately turned his back on me and stepped to the other side of the table. I was stunned by what he had said and I couldn't figure out why he hadn't given me the message. The last thing I expected out of this Proof of Life (POL) was to hear from anyone in my family. I willed myself to focus on what was going on.

Mono JoJoy started telling us that we were being held because we had violated the FARC's national sovereignty. We'd heard this lame explanation before and found it laughable—a terrorist organization is not a sovereign nation. JoJoy went on, with the young woman translating for him.

"From the moment you crashed," he said, "you are part of the group of prisoners of war. Our mission is to keep you alive to do the exchange of prisoners."

That was the clearest statement of their intent we'd had since all this began, but it also wiped out any hope of a unilateral release—something we'd been told would happen from the time we were on the twenty-four-day march. At that point, Keith stepped in and spoke up for all of us, hoping to get more clarification.

"If Colombian president Uribe refuses to negotiate," he said, "if he doesn't go along with the idea of prisoner exchange, then we could be here for five or ten years. How are you going to get us out of here?"

"Negotiations will begin." JoJoy responded. "We don't know when.

Our commander in chief, Manuel Marulanda, ordered us that you could send a sign of life to your families. Because of this, a Colombian journalist is here. Is that okay with you?"

We all said yes, but we were disappointed that JoJoy hadn't fully answered our question. Keith asked him again how we could possibly get out of there. JoJoy used the Spanish word for exchange—*canje*—which meant us being exchanged for FARC prisoners held in Colombian jails, and *dinero*—or money. By the time Tom got all this translated, it was clear that our session with JoJoy was almost over. We wanted to ask him about the ransom; having that as an option was an enormous relief. Tom stepped up for us and asked Mono JoJoy to clarify what he meant about *monetario*.

"*Humanitario. Humanitario,*" the translator replied. There would be no ransom. No release. Just some kind of exchange.

Mono JoJoy stood and we all shook hands again and said, "*Respectos.*" I wasn't feeling any kind of respect for him, but the proof of life mattered more than my feelings. The same was true of how we felt about the journalist who would interview us. We didn't know Botero at all, but the fact that he was allowed into the FARC camp and his chummy demeanor didn't sit well with us. We knew in some ways we were being used by him, but we also wanted to let our families know that we were okay—even if he wasn't from the States or from CNN.

Before we got to make our statements to our families, Botero wanted to ask us some questions. Alfredo, a FARC higher-up, let us know that he was going to sit in on all this. Botero was having trouble with his camera lens fogging up, so we took a brief break and he handed us a couple of printouts, a *Newsweek* magazine, and a paperback copy of John Grisham's *The Street Lawyer*.

Keith started reading the printout of an article he'd been handed. It was off the Internet and was a story about us on MSNBC.

"Oh, man. This is not good," he said suddenly. He tried to explain what he'd read to Tom, but the camera started rolling again. Tom, who'd also been reading something that Botero gave him, said, "We've invaded Iraq." Before he could fill us in any more, Botero was ready.

The first question that Alfredo asked was, "Who hired you?" Keith began by explaining what he'd read: Northrop Grumman was no longer dealing with the reconnaissance contract that had brought us to the country. The contract had been awarded to a company called CIAO. None of us had ever heard of it, but we were incredulous that someone who was contracted to do intelligence operations would called themselves CIAO. This initials confusion would only make things harder for us.

Sure enough, the next question Alfredo asked was, "Are you working for the CIA?"

"No. No," we all said.

Keith still had the document in his hand, so Tom and I let him take over, "This says that a company called CIAO. That's ciao—C-I-A-O not C-I-A." I wasn't sure if we convinced them or just muddied the waters even more.

The session moved from topic to topic, with Keith asking most of the questions, trying to find out as much as he could about our situation. In the back-and-forth, Botero confirmed something we'd suspected since February 13: Tommy Janis had been executed along with our host-nation rider, Sergeant Cruz. Botero asked us if we had any message for the family of the Colombian, and Keith gave them the rough outline of our time spent with him on the day of the crash. We expressed all our condolences to the family, but our minds were more on Tommy J than with Cruz. We'd all held out some small hope that he had been taken hostage and separated from us, however, we weren't surprised to hear that his body had been recovered. Tommy J was ex-military and ex–Special Forces and we were pretty sure that he had tried to escape, fulfilling the duty he had been sworn to do while in the service. He'd also said to Tom on one occasion that if he were ever taken hostage, he would do whatever it took to get out of there. We didn't need any kind of official report to confirm our suspicions.

With Botero behind the camera, the bad news kept coming. We learned that shortly after our plane had gone down, another American plane had crashed. About a month after our engine failure, the second Grand Caravan in the fleet had crashed on takeoff, killing all three on board. These guys were heading out to look for us, and they died. Ralph Ponticelli was probably the one that we were closest with, and when we learned that he had died, Tom and I both started to well up with tears. Learning that Tommy Schmidt and Butch Oliver had also lost their lives made us feel even worse.

Botero must have planned all these revelations in order to elicit some emotion from us, and he succeeded. Tom was so upset about Ralph's death that he grabbed the copy of the day's *Miami Herald* they had intended to use in the POL to shield his face from the camera. Botero zoomed in tighter, framing Tom in a close-up. Tragedy makes good TV, but this was just piling it on.

I'd been thinking about my mother's message and wondering if it was a letter, a cassette tape, or something else. Botero took out a videotape, put it in his camera, and wired up a small monitor for me to view the video. After seeing him use Ralph's death to capture Tom at his most vulnerable, I was determined not to become a part of Botero's propaganda scheme. Despite how I was feeling about hearing a voice from home, I told myself I wasn't going to cry when I watched the message. It helped that Botero messed something up and started playing it without sound, forcing him to rewind it before giving me the headset.

The setup was simple. My mom was at home, sitting on the couch with the camera steady in front of her. Gradually the camera panned over to a photo of me in my air force uniform that she had on a shelf. When she finally spoke, her voice was a measured calm, like she was making an effort not to show just how upset she was.

"I just want to tell you that I love you very much. I hope you come home soon, safe and alive—and also your colleagues. There are hundreds of people praying for you and I just need you to come home because I miss you so much and I worry about you. Please stay strong. You'll be home soon. I love you."

I sat there as stone-faced as I could, biting my lip to keep it from quivering, clenching my jaw to keep it from chattering. A variety of emotions were churning inside of me. I was ecstatic to see a familiar face and hear a familiar voice, but I was broken up to see that face in so much pain. I was angry with the FARC for putting me in that position, guilt-ridden for having done this to my loved ones.

I hated that this journalist was manipulating us, but I tried to remember something Keith had said to us earlier, before we'd even gone on camera. We were all gathered in the room where we slept, and we decided that we had to go along with what the FARC were having us do—not for them, but for our families. They'd dressed us up and put us in our best clothes and given us haircuts and fed us well so that we'd look as happy and healthy as possible. After Mono JoJoy had left and we regrouped in the room, Keith said that we each needed to look good for our families. He was straightening Tom's collar as he said it and he went on to say that we needed to be strong for them so that they wouldn't worry. We had to let them know we were fine and being treated well (even though we weren't). That was our only job today. That was what we had to do to the best of our abilities. Call that manipulation if you want, but we were doing it out of compassion, not to hurt or deceive.

After viewing my mom's message, we took another break. We went out onto the porch, and for the first time we weren't blindfolded when we were outside the building. I walked up to the young, pale-skinned woman who had been translating, who was standing on a slice of ground nearby. My mind was so scattered by everything we were hearing that I just needed confirmation of some part of it.

"Do you think that we're going to live through this?" I asked her.

She was smoking a cigarette and took a casual drag before exhaling. She grimaced and kind of shook her head. And then said, "I don't know. It depends on what your government does."

"What do you mean?"

"Well, the government has troops right now here in Colombia, and they're training to do a rescue."

I paused, waiting for her to continue. When she did, she had a puzzled look on her face. "You didn't hear about the other hostages?"

I told her we had no radios, had no way of getting news about anything. She stubbed out her cigarette on a porch post. She shrugged and matter-of-factly told me that there was a group of hostages that the government had recently tried to rescue. Among them was the former governor of one of the departments, she thought Antioquia, and a former defense minister named Echeverri. When the military came in, the FARC killed both of them along with ten other military hostages. Her words echoed her previous statement, and other things we'd heard from the FARC in the jungle: "Rescue comes. We kill everybody."

She wasn't being overly dramatic, but her understated, matter-of-fact tone had the desired effect. I told Tom and Keith what I'd learned, and they were as shaken as I was. We were called back inside, and before Botero could ask his first question, Keith turned to Alfredo.

"During a rescue, what is your mission?" he asked. "Isn't it to kill us?"

It would have been too much to expect to have Alfredo man up and say yes. Instead he gave us the usual response, "No. During a rescue, if you're killed, it will be by Colombian military bullets. It won't be our fingers that pull the trigger."

His words completely contradicted what the female translator had said. As cold-blooded as she was about the deaths of innocents, I at least had some respect for her telling the truth. But after Alfredo's statement, it became clear that she also had been taking a great deal of pleasure in frightening me.

Botero followed that exchange with this question: "What do you think when you hear the word *rescue*?"

We'd just heard five minutes before about a group of hostages being obliterated, so what could our response be? We all said essentially the same things, but I think that Keith put it the most eloquently when he said, "Enough lives have been lost in our accident and its aftermath. We've lost four colleagues, and a fifth man who was completely inno-cent. I don't want to die. None of us want to die. I am sick of death. Life is the only victory and I pray for a diplomatic solution."

After a few more questions from Botero, we took another break. The translator got into a discussion with one of us—this time it was Keith. I edged over to them when I heard her say something about Cuba and the U.S. embargo.

"The reason," she said, "that the U.S. instituted the trade blockade was because if the U.S. lifted it, everyone in the U.S. would flee there."

Keith looked at her.

"Have you ever been to Cuba?" he asked. "Because I have. My first girlfriend was Cuban. My sister in-law is Cuban. I was raised in Florida in a heavily Cuban neighborhood."

The translator said nothing and took a drag on her cigarette. I could see that she was getting irritated with him and his ability to stand up to her.

"What's your relationship with Cuba?" he continued. "What color is you passport? Your accent seems a bit Cuban American, am I wrong?"

She didn't respond to any of these questions. She had enough and she walked away without a word.

Keith looked at me and said, "What's with this city guerrilla girl any-way?"

He was right. She was definitely a wannabe revolutionary. Though she was dressed in camouflage pants, they were clearly non–standard issue. They rode low on her hips and were tailored. She also wore what we'd come to know in Colombia as an *ombligo*—a shirt that exposed her belly button and was held up by thin spaghetti straps. She'd also mentioned that she had heard about our capture when she was in Bogotá—most likely shopping for her outfit.

In the end, speculating about the translator was the least of our problems. Tom, Keith, and I were suffering from information overload. We'd all been figuratively and at times literally living in boxes for the previous six months. We hadn't heard any news except for a few bits of rumor—we were going to be released—from the guards. As much as that day was supposed to be a proof of life, it had turned out to be a proof of death—Tommy J, Sergeant Cruz, Ralph Ponticelli, Tommy Schmidt, and Butch Oliver, along with the other Colombian hostages who were massacred. Throughout the day, I suffered from one of the worst headaches I'd ever had—from the stress, the news of death, my mother's video—it was all too much. We hadn't spoken openly for the last few months, but now words had invaded every pore, infiltrating our brains until they hurt.

Botero asked us more questions; sometimes we could understand his broken English, other times the young woman translated for him. His inquiries ran the gamut from what we missed most (family) to what our daily routine was like (boring). We knew that our families might see the video, and we did our best to put a positive spin on everything. At every opportunity, we told them that we were well; we were healthy; we were being treated humanely. None of it was true, but it was what we needed our families to hear.

I told Botero about the diagram of my house that I drew on page thirteen of my journal and how each morning and each night I went into each room and said something to each of my family members as they went about their days in those rooms. If I didn't survive, I wanted them to have a record of something that I did to keep them close to me, to know how they helped me keep going when things were very, very tough.

As much as I was guarded about the responses I gave Botero, it was difficult to factor in every part of the equation when answering his questions. We had so many different perspectives to consider. Ultimately, I hoped that two messages were clear: I wanted to live. I wanted to be back with my family. When it came time for me to address them directly in the video, I was glad that I had decided not to prepare any remarks. I wanted to speak from the heart, and when talking about them earlier in the Q&A session, I'd choked up quite a bit. Keith and Tom were always there to put a hand on my arm or around my shoulders, but I didn't want them to have to do that. I wanted to do what my mother had said—to be strong. My mother's words still hung in the air around me. I wanted to tell my mother how proud I was of her. I didn't know how she did it, how she managed to record that video and get it into the right hands so that I could see it. The fact that her voice had penetrated that thick, humid, gloomy jungle amazed me and awed me.

In part, what I said was this:

"Mom, I got your message and I thank you for doing what you had to do to get that message to me. I love you, too. I want you to know that I am being strong. I'm not being hurt or tortured. I'm just waiting to come home.

"Shane. I love you. I've been waiting to tell you that I think about you every day. Just wait for me, baby.

"Joey, Cody, Destiney. I love you guys. I'm just waiting to come home. Just wait for me. I'm waiting to get back to you. I love you.

"That's it."

TOM

For nearly all of our captivity, I had been hoping to get news of any kind. For a while I had been saying that we had all been taken out of the information age and pushed back into the Stone Age. When we finally learned some news, it was nearly all bad. Learning that our country was at war with another group of terrorists was the best thing we'd heard. I didn't want any Americans to die, but knowing that we were fighting against a regime that had done so much damage to the very people it was supposed to protect and had harbored terrorists, it was a necessary sacrifice. Given that we were being held by guerrillas had only hardened my stance against wiping out anyone who denied the rights and liberties of others.

When the POL activity was over, I had a chance to analyze everything that happened. I was pleased that we had had an opportunity to communicate messages to our families. I was glad that we'd gotten some reading materials and learned a few things about the outside world. I was hopeful, but as always, that hope had come with the caveat of bad news.

Death was very much on all our minds. I'd wanted to break out of the isolation we'd all been experiencing, but learning about the deaths of others was not what I had been hoping for. Receiving confirmation of Tommy J's death was tough enough, but the additional deaths of Ralph, Tommy Schmidt, and Butch were bad. I'd been around long enough to know pilots and crew members who had died in aircraft accidents. That potential threat was always a part of the job, but this was the first time I'd experienced other people's loss of life due to them trying to help me. That didn't sit well with any of us. The irony that we were being videotaped to prove we were alive, only to learn of other people's deaths, was a bitter pill to swallow. Add in the fact that someone whose intentions you suspected had been sticking a camera in your face to capture your reaction, and this hard situation became exponentially more difficult.

I didn't want my family to worry about me, and who knew what Botero planned to do with the image of me learning that good friends had died. I sensed almost immediately that Botero or others would use our words to advance their agenda and set up another opportunity to propagandize. Weighing that knowledge against our desire to reassure our families created a lot of anxiety in us all.

After it was said and done, I also wasn't certain that our POL would even reach our families. We'd been led to believe that an international journalist was going to be there, and instead this Colombian showed up. Botero didn't have any credentials. He didn't have a film crew with him.

As far as we knew, he could have been some guy the FARC used to act as a journalist. Botero had told us that two journalists in Los Angeles were working to track down our families so that they could be provided with our messages, but that wasn't the most precise answer to our questions about how the video would be used. Maybe they wanted to do the proof of life just to calm us all down, to make us think that our release was near. We all knew that happy prisoners were easier to control.

My skepticism was reinforced when the taping was wrapped up and we were waiting to return to our bunk room. I found a piece of paper on the floor. I looked it over and saw that it was a letter from a hostage—not one of of us—and it was addressed to his family. I didn't feel comfortable reading it, so I didn't, but it made me angry to think that one of the many FARC upper-echelon guys who'd been there with us, or even Botero, had likely failed to deliver on a promise to another prisoner. That could easily have been a letter from me to Mariana.

I was proud of us and how we'd conducted ourselves throughout the day. We'd refuted every one of their bogus claims about what our mission had been. Whenever any of us got choked by emotion, the others stepped up and offered support and comfort. We all spoke from the heart and stuck to our plan to be as reassuring as possible. I had been given a pair of reading glasses to use temporarily. I made it appear as though I'd been administered a miracle cure. I could now read, whereas before I was nearly blind. I hoped the FARC got the message via word and action. I needed glasses.

When it came time for us to speak to our families, I tried to be as thoughtful and deliberate as I could. I was glad that I'd been able to hear Keith's words. He said a lot of what I wanted to say, particularly when he was asked what he missed. He was pretty choked up, and seeing him that way got to me.

"I'm kind of a hard-ass. I apologize," he'd said in his statement. "The two things that get me in the heart are my two children and my fiancée. When I feel sometimes like not going on, I think in my mind of my eleven-year-old son, Kyle—I'm sorry I missed your birthday—and my fourteen-year-old daughter, Lauren, and Malia, my fiancée. And I think of what they'd want me to do. And I think what they'd most want me to do is to come home."

Keith went on to talk about his mother dying when he was fourteen and how bad he felt about not being there for his family. I was forty-three years old when I had my son, Tommy, with Mariana. The thought of him having to grow up without a father was too much to bear. I wasn't sure why, but he and I had an incredible bond. From the moment he was out of the womb, he was a daddy's boy. I reveled in our special connection but worried about how he was doing in my absence. My stepson, Santiago, was old enough that I knew that he'd be okay. The littlest ones always suffered the most. Like Keith, I'd also lost my mother when I was a teen. I knew something about grieving and getting on. I, too, could identify with Keith's statements to his kids during his proof of life:

"If I can come home, that's great. If not, keep living. Keep your chin up. Keep going." Keith's twins had to weigh heavily on his mind.

When it was my turn, I expressed similar sentiments. I stuck with the plan of letting my family know that I was in good shape physically and that I was being treated well. I let my wife know that I loved her and missed her. I told Tommy and my stepson, Santiago, that I would be back and was eager to see them. Everything I said felt anticlimactic. I was so burned out mentally that I wanted to keep things brief and to the point. I hoped that whatever images of me they saw would convey what I was feeling. Seeing was believing; if it was proof that I was still alive that the FARC wanted me to provide, then that was what I was going to give them—little more. The less the FARC had to use to help them, the better.

Making sense was not the order of the day, obviously, and at times I struggled with accomplishing that simple task. Like Marc, I had an epic headache that day. On one of the breaks, I was given some ibuprofen, but that didn't help. The fan in the room was supposed to cool the room but it just pushed the stale air around, buzzing incessantly until it was in my head.

That night, as I replayed the day's events over in my head, I wished that I'd had a chance to clarify at least one point. When I was asked about my response to the word *rescue,* I wanted to make a distinction clear. I was afraid that after everything I'd seen that day, the message would get muddled. I wanted to be able to come out and say clearly that while I thought there was a danger to a rescue attempt, my feelings only applied to a Colombian military rescue. In my mind, when I heard the word rescue I thought of freedom and America. When I heard the word *rescate* I thought of massacre and death. At that point, I didn't really trust that the Colombian military had sufficient training in hostage rescue operations. I couldn't really say all that on the video since by saying it, I would have frightened my wife and kids. I knew that the U.S. military had far more experience in hostage rescue operations, had far more advanced intelligence systems, weaponry, and tactics to rescue us. I didn't want to leave whoever saw Botero's video with the impression that we were against being rescued. Lying there that night in our little room propped up on our sawhorse bed, I wondered about just how flimsy the whole event had really been.

The boat ride back to our previous camp was uneventful. Every one seemed much more relaxed. We didn't have our blindfolds on for as much of the ride as we did on the way to the POL. We'd spent so much time rehashing everything we'd heard and learned that Marc, Keith, and I didn't do a whole lot of talking, other than to point out some of the wildlife we spotted. I was particularly interested in the caimans after living in Florida for a while and hearing all kinds of stories about what pests gators could be. It felt good to be on the water and moving, though if I had my choice, I would have preferred to have been on a plane bound for home and not back to my tent top and a muddy patch of jungle.

When we arrived back at our camp, the change in attitude among our guards was noticeable. Everyone seemed a lot more jovial. The pressure was off, I suppose. Even the most serious guards, the ones who never smiled, waved at us and grinned as if we were movie stars. They all took pleasure in knowing that in even the smallest way, by being the guy who locked us up at night, for example, they'd contributed to the FARC's success. That humanized them a bit—people everywhere like to attach themselves to a success regardless of how much they really contributed. Only when I reminded myself that these people who were holding us hostage had killed some of my friends did I resent our reception. Despite what Mono JoJoy contended, when it came down to it, the FARC were primarily killers.

With just a few more hours of separation from the event, I was able to process the POL experience in different ways. I was glad for the Colin Powell news, and I was glad that I'd heard some of the FARC discussing a possible UN intervention. How reasonable either of those two possibilities sounded to me varied by the hour. My interpretation of the events shifted with the sun, and I knew I wasn't going to find lasting relief or true comfort. At that moment I chose to believe that these were positive signs.

The morning after we returned to what we called the Second Mud Camp, we all took a chance that our imposed silence was over. We gathered outside my hooch. With more time since the POL, our points of view had clarified.

"The thing I can't get out of my mind is those other hostages being killed," Marc said. "Can you imagine that? You hear a helo and the next thing you know you're rounded up and shot dead like a dog?"

"We've got to be careful of helos. You've seen it before, though. We can pick up on them being in the area before these guys." Keith reminded me that we did have that distinct advantage.

"Even a few minutes of head start are going to make a big difference," I told Marc.

"Tom's exactly right. If the execution order comes, we want to be as far away or in the best defensive position we can be in. The threat level has been upped, that's for sure," Keith said.

"I'm going to need your help a bit with this, guys," I said. Marc and Keith nodded. They knew that after years of flying and being around running engines and the high-pitched wind noise, my hearing wasn't as acute as theirs.

The proof of life had made one thing clear: In the event of a rescue, we needed to get ourselves as far away from the FARC as possible so they couldn't gun us down. Having the three of us as early-warning devices—Keith had brought Marc up to speed so that he could detect the difference between a U.S. Blackhawk helicopter and a Huey UH-1 by this time—was a small but significant victory over the FARC, one of the few advantages we were able to hold over them. Most of them had never been airborne, so their ability to perform the kind of instant threat analysis that we were able to do was severely compromised. If any attack or rescue attempt came, we'd at least have a couple minutes head start on the FARC. It wasn't much, but in what could potentially be a game of seconds, it was an edge. Gradually they learned that if the three of us had our eyes or our ears focused skyward, they should come to us and ask what was literally "up." To maintain our control, we would respond by telling them things that suited our needs, and they never knew the difference between what was real and what we fabricated.

Since our arrival at the Second Mud Camp, the skies had been clear of aircraft. That unsettled us a bit. We liked the idea of aircraft being above us—especially the planes. Planes made us feel comfortable; their presence meant that someone was up there watching us or looking for us. We knew that the "they" up there weren't the FARC. A week or so after the proof of life, as July turned into August, the planes returned. We hoped their arrival had something to do with the proof-of-life messages being delivered. In particular, we had one that did large orbits around us. We couldn't ID it confidently, but we knew it was up there at high altitude, circling around our position at what seemed to be thirty-minute intervals. Pre– and post–proof of life, the equation was the same: Planes were good and helos were bad. For most of the time in the Second Mud Camp, the helos were not nearby.

That didn't mean we stopped jumping out of our hooches at the first indication of air activity. I'd see the guerrillas standing in the clearing with their ears cocked looking a little bit like a couple of hunting dogs on point. We established an informal kind of threat-level assessment. If the Fantasmas—the gunships—were in the immediate area, we knew to get out of our hooches and to be prepared to run. If it was a fixed-wing intel bird, like our high-flying friend, we could relax.

Perhaps the most positive immediate impact of the POL was that it put an end to the rules regarding our communal silence. During the POL, we asked to be allowed to speak again, and while Ferney never made an official proclamation, the silence and separation rules were eased and then eliminated. The guards no longer harassed us to stop speaking, and even began to engage us in conversation more. The same was true of our restraints. We still had to wear them, but we no longer had to tie ourselves to a branch.

Freer to move about and to speak to one another, we spent a lot of our time at the Second Mud Camp obtaining an oftentimes painful education in botany, ornithology, and entomology. We were constantly being bitten by something. If it wasn't the *tábanos* (horseflies), *monta blancas* (gnatlike pests), *jejenes* (no-see-ums with a vicious bite), it was the tarantulas and scorpions and their ant foot soldiers, the *yanaves* or *congas*. We began to refer to getting up in the night to urinate as Russian roulette. You never knew what was going to be in your boots when you put them on in the dark. In addition, wasps were a constant threat, and the worst was when you were being attacked and fled the path. If you lost your balance and put your hand out to steady yourself on a tree trunk, you had better hope you didn't have the misfortune of coming in contact with the *barras santas* (holy bar) tree and the stinging ants of the same name. Holy shit would have been a better name for that pair of irritants, whose stings were like electric shocks.

I would not have earned a very good grade in ornithology. The toucans, parrots, and macaws kept their distance, so it was difficult to enjoy them in detail. Marc's descriptions and his ability to mimic all three species' calls were amazing, right down to the clicking of their beaks as they closed their mouths at the end of the call. As sad as the toucan's call was, the howler monkey and another type whose name we didn't know made the toucan seem almost pleasant. If we didn't know any better, we would have sworn that sumo wrestlers were sparring outside our camp.

Very few of the FARC took any interest in the natural world. It seemed as if they divided everything into opposing categories: edible/inedible, poisonous/not poisonous, very dangerous/deadly. Given their circumstances, those seemed to be important distinctions to make. Though by the time we left the Second Mud Camp, we had been with the FARC for nearly nine months, we were still amazed by some of their behaviors. When eating rice and beans, we sometimes offered them a spoon. They would shake their heads and continue to eat by hand. When they spouted their propaganda and told us that by taking over the country they would end corruption, we asked them how they could do that when they were stealing from one another all the time? Their version of a better Colombia was everyone having an apartment and a television. When we asked them how they would bring that about, what specific actions they would take, they fell silent.

Being able to talk again and becoming more savvy captives coincided. Having the reading materials we'd received at the POL certainly helped. We read and reread all that we had. We had also taken the copy of John Grisham's *The Street Lawyer* with us as a gift from Botero. That was the only place, besides in our conversations with one another, that we were able to find any semblance of logic, anything that resembled the world that we had left behind, any kind of people with whom we could relate. Keith and Marc passed the book back and forth to devour over the course of the first few days we had it. Without reading glasses, I couldn't read, so Keith and Marc took turns reading to me. Almost as soon as we'd finished the book, we started to read it again. It provided a nice escape from jungle life and we were able to immerse ourselves temporarily in the world of a high-powered Washington, D.C., law firm. We enjoyed reading about Michael Brock's decision to drop out of the fast lane and work to help those with little or no money. I think we were all glad to add Michael Brock to our short list of people who could reason clearly, communicate effectively, and be trusted to do the right thing—even if he was a lawyer.

A couple of months after the POL, Mono JoJoy made another appearance, announcing this time that we were going to be placed in yet another camp—only this time we wouldn't be by ourselves, we'd be with the political prisoners. We had a pretty good idea of who would be there—we'd read all about the various kidnappings of major politicians and candidates before we'd been taken hostage. We never thought that all the FARC's high-value prisoners would be put together in the same place, and we were excited about the possibilities this development represented. We were eager to meet with them. Suddenly, after months of only having one another, we'd have many more people to interact with. Suddenly we'd be thrust back into some semblance of a society.

In spite of the uncertainties involved, we were all convinced that this political camp would bring nothing but good into our lives. More people, less boredom, more freedoms. As usual, we were surprised by how wrong we were.

SEVEN

Caribe

October 2003–December 2003

MARC

On October 20 of 2003, we approached the political prisoners' camp with real anticipation. It didn't take long for that feeling to be replaced by dread. In front of us stood a large compound completely surrounded by chain-link fence topped with barbed wire. Spaced at intervals around this rectangle stood six elevated guard shacks, manned by guards with automatic weapons. Inside the perimeter fence, a second chain-link fence completed another rectangle. Within that enclosure was a large structure, as big as a two-car garage. We all stopped and looked at this brutal reality: For the first time, we were in a compound that reminded us of the photos we'd seen of actual POW camps—not the neat and clean camps from Hollywood like in *The Great Escape* or *Stalag 17*, but a dingy, used version of them.

Sombra urged us on and paraded us around the perimeter of the compound, still outside the main fence. As we walked along the first wall, inside the compound we saw a group of people dressed in civilian clothes, idly swinging in hammocks. They looked our way but made no effort to approach. Farther along, we saw a courtyard and another building. A group of men were standing in that open space looking out at us. Music and the buzz and hum of conversation came from inside the building. We continued our walk around the perimeter until we reached the front gate, where a desk and chair sat along with two impassive sentries.

As we stood waiting for Sombra to give the order for the gate to be opened, one of the prisoners, dressed in somewhat ragged civilian clothes like the others, approached us. He had hair down to his waist and a full beard, both of which made him look like a Colombian version of Robinson Crusoe. He greeted us in Spanish with a polite, *"Buenos días."*

A large group of prisoners—there must have been about twenty of them—came out of the building and jogged over to the fence. Like the man who greeted us, they were all dressed in worn-down civilian clothes.

"How long have you been here?" I asked in Spanish.

"Some of us four years. Some five. Some of us six," one of them answered in decent but heavily accented English.

I felt my stomach curdle. The group was in a bad way. One of them had a nasty rash that covered nearly his entire back, others were missing teeth, and some were going bald and stood slightly stooped over. My first thought was how bad I felt for them. Then I realized that I could end up like that, too.

We assumed that we were going to be imprisoned with this group, but Sombra said, *"Vámonos,"* and continued to lead his prized possessions around the outside of the camp. A smaller, fenced-in enclosure sat to one side, and quite a few chains hung from it. They weren't around the prisoners' necks, but they still screamed out to us that this was a prison camp. Sombra led us back around to the gate. We were waiting to go inside when a woman, fairly slight and with long wavy hair trailing after her, bustled up with a group of maybe five or six others in her wake. We followed Sombra through the main gate and saw that the woman and the group with her were in another smaller, fenced-off enclosure.

Just as we were about to be let into this smaller space, we heard the woman say to one of the men in Spanish, "There is no room in here. What are we going to do? We can't take them in here. This isn't going to work. We have to tell them."

"Ingrid, we do for them what we did for you. We welcome them in," the man responded.

We didn't need to hear her name spoken to know that the woman who didn't want us in her part of the camp was Ingrid Betancourt. Almost a year and a week before the day that we had crashed, Betancourt had been captured by the FARC. Keith had told me once that the day after she was taken, as a favor to our host nation, he had been the mission commander on a flight over the spot where she'd been kidnapped. They didn't expect to find her, but they did an aerial reconnaissance of the area. Keith remembered finding it odd at the time that a U.S. subcontractor had been tapped to do the search and not the Colombian military.

I'd heard the news of her being taken while I was still in the States. Since I was applying for jobs in Colombia at almost the same time she was taken, anything that had to do with Colombia interested me. Later, when I was first living in Bogotá, I saw an enormous billboard with a photo of her with the slogan, FREE INGRID beneath it while driving through the city. When you see someone's likeness on a billboard, it is kind of hard to forget that face.

Ingrid Betancourt was a French-Colombian politician, who had been a Colombian senator and was a candidate for president in 2002 for the Oxygen Green Party she had founded. Shortly after the Colombian government revoked the FARC's DMZ, Betancourt went on a campaign trip to that area, despite the government's and the military's insistence that she not travel to such a dangerous spot. While in the contested lands, she was stopped at a FARC checkpoint and taken prisoner. She was from a prominent family and her first husband was a fellow student from a prestigious school she'd attended in Paris. He worked in the French diplomatic corps and Ingrid had traveled widely as a result.

Based on how she greeted us, she didn't seem very diplomatic herself. Ignoring what her fellow captive said to her, she approached Sombra and repeated her concerns about space while adding others. What surprised me most was that she seemed to issue an order to Sombra when she used the command form of the verb *to put,* saying, "*Póngalos en alguna parte más.*" Even if I hadn't been picking up more Spanish, I would have been able to detect that she wasn't making a request, but issuing a command. She wanted us put in some other part of the camp. Her tone was sharp, and I could see the look of disgust on Sombra's face. He told her that we were educated guys and that we were staying there.

For some reason, Sombra seemed to cave in to Ingrid's pressure and allowed her to lead him inside the building the political hostages had just exited so that they could discuss the situation further. We could hear two women's voices, Ingrid's and another woman's, and they were giving Sombra hell. After a few minutes of back-and-forth, he came out of the building and stomped past us without a word.

The three of us were a bit stunned. This wasn't the greeting we'd expected, and we'd basically been rejected sight unseen. We stood in the doorway and peered into the building where Sombra and Ingrid had been arguing. The place was a palatial mansion compared to anything we'd been in before. Even if they added three new beds, it seemed there would be plenty of room for everyone to fit. We lingered there like unwelcome relatives who'd dropped in for a surprise visit. I was trying to be open-minded and give them the benefit of the doubt. I wondered if I would have responded the same way and thought of this place as "my" house and the newcomers as uninvited guests. I hoped not and I hoped that after the initial shock of seeing us (we'd been told we were moving to their camp but I didn't know if they had been told about us as well), they'd get over it and welcome us.

There were a total of seven Colombian prisoners and they were whispering together, breaking into small groups, and discussing things some more.

"Well," Keith said, turning to us with an exasperated look, "I guess this is better than them coming over here and sniffing us."

I recalled a conversation that Keith and I had had in the previous camp. Keith had been talking about hunting, dogs, and wildlife in general. We got on the subject of dominance and submissiveness in dogs, their pack mentality, and pecking orders in the animal kingdom. I knew that Keith was interpreting this as a display of dominance, but I couldn't figure out why he saw things as he did. We were pretty used to being together as a trio. If someone else had come into our group, it would have taken some time to adjust. We had only been at the camp for a few minutes, perhaps they just needed some time to adjust.

After a short debate with one another, they came and greeted us. This time they seemed genuinely happy to meet us, even Ingrid, who said to me in her precise English, "We're happy you're here. And do you know what we are going to do tonight? We are going to have a party. And we're going to dance."

She smiled and walked away, and I was left trying to figure out what had just happened and why this woman had so suddenly and drastically changed her attitude toward us. I chalked up the oddness of the greeting to the shock of them having their routine disrupted, but I still wasn't comfortable with the idea that their first reaction had been to shun us. We were all eager to have more people to talk to, and having someone else who spoke English was especially appealing to Keith and me. We were also thrilled to see that they had radios, which meant contact with the outside world. Several of them had small transistor radios and there was also a larger multiband AM-FM radio they referred to as a *panalón* or panel radio.

"Your families are both doing well, Keith and Marc. We have heard from them on the radio," Ingrid told the two of us.

Tom was off speaking to the other politicals while Ingrid explained how it was that our families had been able to get any information to her. "Because there are so many hostages in Colombia, several radio stations allow family members and friends to send messages to them. They then play them over the air. Generally at night or in the early hours of the morning." She shrugged her shoulders and smiled. "Hostages are not good business and don't attract advertisers, so they must do this at odd hours."

"Doesn't matter to me. I'd stay up twenty four/seven to hear from them."

Ingrid nodded. "And your efforts would be rewarded. Your mother has been all over the airwaves. We hear her messages all the time. Clearly she loves you very much. My mother is the same."

She went on to tell us that each of our families wanted us to know that they were okay and that our company was taking good care of them. Hearing those words was a tremendous relief for all of us, as we had talked about and worried over whether the company was taking care of our families since we'd first crashed. To have someone independently and without our asking tell us that they were being provided for was a welcome bit of news.

Still, there was more anxiety than joy in the air. It was like the proof of life all over again—a lot of information was coming at us quickly. Ingrid and the others were all talking at once, but we stayed focused on her because with her we didn't need Tom to translate. She introduced us to a somewhat short but dignified-looking man named Luis Eladio Pérez, whom they all called Lucho. He looped his arm around her waist and joined in the conversation like we were at a cocktail party.

The two of them filled us in on the news that they'd been hearing about the FARC and the possibility of peace talks, hostage exchanges, and releases. We trusted them since they were Colombians, politicians, and knew the culture and all the players. Both Lucho and Ingrid seemed certain that Ingrid's release was just around the corner. In fact, she believed that the whole reason the camp we were in was built was that the FARC knew she was about to be released. They wanted her to see all the prominent hostages so that she could verify that we were alive and well.

"Can you believe that?" Keith said as Ingrid walked away. He looked like he'd taken a bite of a rotten piece of fruit. "The frickin' princess thinks that the FARC built this castle for her alone. How arrogant is that?"

It did seem odd that she would believe that about herself. I knew that she was just one of hundreds and hundreds of Colombians being held captive. That her capture had even been newsworthy in the U.S. made me think that she was one of the most prominent captives there. It didn't matter to me; she'd obviously thought about how she'd first greeted us and made an about-face. She'd delivered good news and that was what I was focusing on. But she'd rubbed Keith the wrong way. He was big on hostages treating one another with as much dignity and respect as possible to offset how badly the FARC were treating us, but I was willing to let her reaction go as surprise and move on.

After that brief flurry of interaction, we were given some time to settle in, but no sooner had we put our things down on the benches than one of the other women approached us again. She'd introduced herself earlier as Clara Rojas, and now she wanted to discuss a bath schedule. Clara was very slight, almost fragile-looking, and her bright but nervous smile seemed to flicker on and off like a neon sign with little relation to what was being said. Clara had been Ingrid's campaign manager and had been with Ingrid when the FARC had taken her. Because Clara was speaking in Spanish, I couldn't really understand what she was saying, but she seemed really agitated. From what I could gather, it seemed like every other sentence began with the word *Ingrid*.

When Clara stopped talking, Tom explained that Ingrid and Lucho had pretty much decided what the bathing schedule was going to be—the rest of us just had to fill in the other slots. This fit with what we'd already sensed and could see in the arrangement of our living quarters. We were coming into their previously established territory and we were going to have to fit in where we could. If the outside area seemed to be dominated by Ingrid and Lucho, at least the building was large enough to house the ten of us easily, and it was equally divided.

Tom was invaluable in helping us to understand the dynamic at work here. Even before arriving at what we named Camp Caribe—because of the piranha-like fish that were abundant in the nearby water—Tom had explained to us that Colombians had a definite love-hate relationship with Americans. We were in their country, and now we had "invaded" their prison camp. For most of their lives, Colombians had heard that the best things in the world came from the U.S. According to Tom, many Colombians considered Disney World and Miami a prime vacation spot and the center of commerce and finance respectively. Tom believed that many Colombians, particularly of the upper class like Ingrid and Lucho, resented America's idealized position as the land of opportunity being rammed down their throats. They'd grown tired of some seeing the U.S. as an example of the biggest and the best but had a grudging respect for it.

Knowing all this and understanding that in several different ways we were outsiders, we needed to tread carefully and let things sort themselves out. We had been successful in dealing with the FARC by doing nothing but behaving as respectfully and humanely as we possibly could. We saw no reason to change our approach, especially since we were dealing with fellow prisoners and not our enemy. I didn't think that any of us had an especially strong sense of fairness and justice, but compared to some of the Colombians in that group of seven, it seemed like we did.

Moving into a place where people had been together for a while proved to be an interesting experience—almost like being the new kid at school and having to figure out who the cool kids were, who was friends with whom, and all of that. It took some time to get to know everyone, and it seemed like each of the three of us, as was normal, had conflicting views of everyone. I was immediately suspicious when one of the Colombian men, Orlando, came to us late the next day to tell us that there'd been some dispute over where we were going to sleep. We thought it had all been settled, but Orlando told Tom that Clara was trying to get the FARC to give us a triple-decker bunk bed to save space for everyone else. We didn't know whether to believe him, since we hadn't heard Clara say anything like that to us. Orlando seemed to want to throw Clara under the bus, but for what purpose? Immediately I made a mental note to myself to watch this guy.

Not every one of the politicals presented such a mystery to us. Consuelo González de Perdomo was one of those who seemed to share our view of how we should have been treating one another. Consuelo was a first-year congresswoman who was abducted in 2001 while on her way to the capital. She told us that she had represented Neiva, a rural district in Colombia, and she had been a schoolteacher before turning to politics. Ironically, she came from a leftist family and probably held the most anti-American views of any of our new bunkmates. Despite that, she treated us well. Consuelo was extremely religious and a devoted mother, who talked a great deal about her babies and cried every time she spoke of them. At first, I assumed that she had small children, but it was only when we got to know each other a bit better that I found out they were both in their twenties. She didn't moan and wail and make a spectacle of herself when she cried, she was always very dignified—except when it came time to play *banco russo* (Russian bank) the card game she taught us and took great pride in whipping our asses at.

When we first met her, Keith, Tom, and I sensed that she was someone we could trust to deal fairly with us. She also had a lilting, singing quality to her voice. It didn't matter what she was saying, it all sounded beautiful. Her religious beliefs contributed to her kind nature and fair treatment of us, but it was also just who she was. Her husband was a dairy farmer and a real hardworking, self-made guy. As a result of her upbringing and values, we all identified with her as she did with us.

A day or two after our arrival, we got to spend more time with Jorge Eduardo Gerchen Turbay and Gloria Polanco. They were clearly very close to each other. It was Jorge's abduction during the FARC's hijacking of an Aires Airlines commercial jet in February 2002 that had caused then Colombian president Pastrana to cancel peace talks, end the DMZ, and intensify efforts against the FARC. Because he was a well-respected career politician, Jorge's kidnapping resulted in a massive search for him. Keith pointed out that in comparison to the initial efforts to find Ingrid, the Colombians had pulled out all the stops in their search for the man who asked that we call him Jorge. We could understand why he was so well regarded from the moment we met him. Soft-spoken, he was extremely dignified and gracious, but though he had only a year or two on Tom, he looked much older. Life in the jungle was not something a man of his background and standing was prepared for. His thick wavy hair had turned gray and that more than likely added to the impression of his being older, but he generally seemed in poor health and walked gingerly, obviously troubled by back pain.

Gloria, meanwhile, doted on him, cared for him, and ministered to his needs with real devotion. We all admired her for that, especially given what she had been through herself. Her husband, Jaime Lozada, had been the governor of Huila, one of Colombia's thirty-two departments. They were living in Neiva, the department's capital (a department is similar to a state in America), when the FARC targeted their apartment building and took multiple hostages in July of 2001. The FARC used explosives to destroy the door to their apartment, but Jaime Lozada was not at home when the raid occurred. In his place, they took Gloria and two of her sons, Jaime Felipe and Juan Sebastian, hostage. Afterward, the FARC openly asked for ransom for the two boys, who were both teenagers.

In much the same way that Gloria cared for Jorge, it seemed to us that Lucho did for Ingrid. Under different circumstances, there would have been a lot to like and admire about Lucho. He was a career politician, starting off at the age of twenty-five as the ambassador to Paraguay. He left Colombia's diplomatic corps and had been the governor of the Nariño department and then a senator. He was on what he called a "political push," campaigning in the south of the country when the FARC stole his truck. With one of his bodyguards, he went to a FARC stronghold to negotiate to get the truck back. They kidnapped him and kept his truck. With his thin, angular features and a dusting of gray in his Vandyke beard, Lucho looked somewhat wolfish, and his clear, intelligent eyes added to the perception that he was always watchful and wary.

Despite the status of these politicians, we weren't intimidated by them. As politicians, they would have insights into our situation that might prove very helpful. We were definitely strangers in a strange land, and it was good to know that despite our rough start, they could potentially help us survive this ordeal. But with these personalities came new risks. Whereas before, we just had to worry about the dynamics among the guards, now there was a whole new set of connections of which we had to become aware. If our rocky beginning at Camp Caribe taught us anything, it was that the name of the game now was knowing whom to trust.

KEITH

Before my mother passed away, she taught me a lot of things about life and people. One of the expressions she used came back to me the first day we were in with the politicians: "How you start is how you finish." My mother meant that in terms of starting a task and being prepared to follow through with it, but she also meant it in terms of relationships. You shouldn't be quick to judge people, but in the end you often found out that how people first presented themselves to you was pretty accurate and indicative of how you'd ultimately interact with them when all was said and done.

I'm no genius, and I claim no special skill when it comes to figuring people out, but even I could see what was up with Camp Caribe almost immediately.

I had to give Ingrid credit for being big enough to come to me the morning of our third day there and tell me that she had once again gone to the FARC, asking for us to be taken out of their section. I was pissed and told her so, but I was mostly upset because I had already learned from one of the more reliable guards that Ingrid had sent notes to Sombra telling him that we were CIA agents and she wanted us out of there for that reason. Along with Lucho, she also sent another note claiming that we had microchips in our blood and the FARC needed to be careful as a result of our being so closely tracked.

I couldn't believe that fellow prisoners would put us in such danger. They were both senators and in the eyes of the FARC extremely valuable bargaining chips. More than that, they were educated. The simpletons holding us prisoner knew that Lucho and Ingrid were smart and could easily have believed them. We could have been executed because she wanted more space in the camp for herself. It was reckless and irresponsible and I was so angry I could hardly see straight. Thanks to Marc and Tom, who were both willing to listen to me rant and provide me with some perspective, I was able to contain my rage at that moment.

Later in the day, Marc, Tom, and I agreed to meet with all of the political prisoners to discuss the new arrangements. It was clear to everybody that putting the three of us into the mix had raised tensions around camp. Nobody wanted that, so we agreed to sit down in the hooch and have an honest talk about the situation and what we might be able to do to remedy the problems. Lucho took the lead in the meeting. "It is important to sort out any difficulties immediately. We will each take our turn expressing our feelings about how everyone is behaving. We will all know how we each feel and there will be no secrets."

What followed was a few minutes of general griping about us, none of which was true. What how we smelled or if we wore underwear had to do with anything I couldn't figure out. I just let them whine and get it out of their systems. I was only half listening when, unprovoked, Lucho started shouting. *"¡No hay putas aquí! ¡No hay putas aquí!"* I'd heard the word *putas* before, and I sat there confused about why he was going on about whores. Tom was trying to translate, but Lucho was so upset and yelling so loud that we couldn't hear Tom.

I turned to Ingrid and asked her what he was saying and she said, "He's defending me." I couldn't figure out what he was defending her from, and the only answer that made any sense was that he thought the three of us had nothing on our minds but getting in the pants of these female politicians.

I'd seen enough of Lucho walking around marking his territory to know that he was really protective of Ingrid. The man was insecure about his standing in the pack, we came in as outsiders, and he needed to defend his territory. That was, if not fine with me, then at least understandable. He perceived us as a threat. What I couldn't understand was his apparent view that we were a trio of lowlifes who viewed the presence of women in the camp as an open invitation for sex. Worse, I was being lectured on morality by a guy who was married and whom the three of us had seen being openly affectionate toward Ingrid. I wasn't going to put up with that, so I walked out.

Later on, Marc and I had a chance to talk about what took place. As usual, Marc was more even-tempered than I was, and he helped to calm me down some. He said it hurt him to think that people believed such rotten things about him when he had done nothing but think of his wife and how much he missed her. We were both offended by the assumptions that had been made and the words that Lucho had said, but neither one of us could figure out what had made him shout "There are no whores here!" in the first place. Maybe it was just some of his Latin macho gone wild. Maybe it was just defensive. Either way, there was something about it that just didn't add up.

The more Marc and I talked, the more I realized that what Lucho and Ingrid were doing wasn't just the product of their own imaginations. I remembered a conversation that we had had with Smiley prior to coming to the political camp. We hadn't been told yet where we were going, but Smiley couldn't help himself. He told us that he wasn't supposed to say anything to us, but he kept on whispering, "Hey, there's going to be *viejas*," which means old ladies (as in how some people refer to their mate as their old lady or old man regardless of their age). He said that there were four of them and we could have sex with them. We had no idea what he was talking about or why he would tell us that. We also remembered that on the boat ride to the camp, Sombra had warned us about Ingrid. He'd come right out and said that we shouldn't trust her and that she was a snake.

As I recalled Smiley's and Sombra's words, some of the pieces started to fit together. We sometimes saw Sombra as stupid. I'd seen signs of that in abundance, but I also saw signs, a lot less frequently, that he could be cagey and manipulative. I figured that if Sombra, through his guard Smiley, had planted a seed in our heads that we were going someplace where there were women who'd have sex with us, the Colombians might have been fed a similar line of bullshit about us. Sombra was trying to play both ends against the middle and divide us. I'd read about some of the tactics the Nazis used in their concentration camps, and the idea of divide and conquer was as old as the Roman hills. A camp in which people fought against one another was an easier camp to control. If we were all unified, then we would have been more of a threat to them and not to one another. It was classic prison-camp psychological warfare and we were victims of it.

Even though I'd figured some of what was going on, I wasn't ready to dismiss all the petty behavior of camp as simply a product of FARC mind games. That would have been giving the FARC way too much credit. Sombra may have been intentionally stirring things up, but that didn't explain all the selfish bullshit I saw around us—people fighting over water, space, and the other scant resources we had. The three of us had been living in mud for the last two months and hating every minute of it. By comparison, this place, as horrific as it was, was like staying at the Four Seasons, and yet, with all the bickering, at times I found myself missing the mud and the isolation.

It didn't help that Marc, Tom, and I were struggling in our friendship. We always said that being held captive together forced the three of us into an arranged marriage. In Camp Caribe, it was like our marriage had been suddenly dropped into the middle of a polygamist sect, so that while we were going through this tense period with the politicals, the three of us were also divided. In part it was the same language barrier that had always been difficult playing itself out on a larger scale now that there were more personalities. Because of Tom's Spanish, he could interact with everyone else on a level that Marc and I could not. Tom really enjoyed being with the others, and unable to speak for ourselves, we felt left out. Since we were taken hostage, Marc and I had relied on Tom to keep us in the loop about what was going on, and we didn't think of our need to understand as an extra burden on him. By this point in our "marriage," it was like we'd fallen into a habit of each of us having specific household tasks. Simply put, Marc and I took Tom's ability to translate for granted, and we probably stopped asking him to do it and stopped thanking him when he did.

Of course, I wasn't thinking about it in those terms at the time. Instead I was thinking about how on the boat ride to the political camp, Tom had been taking a break from doing a lot of translating. It seemed to me that he spent a lot of his time talking to Sombra and the two of them were sharing some laughs. I didn't like that. I didn't want to socialize and be a buddy with Sombra, and I didn't want Tom to, either. He wasn't doing anything but being Tom—a gregarious kind of guy—but his approach to things was different from mine. The FARC was our enemy and we used the guards to gain an advantage, nothing more. Tom hadn't crossed any lines or done anything he shouldn't have, but episodes like the boat ride made language an easy target for my anger and frustration. I hated having to rely on him to do one of the most fundamental things that makes us human—communicate with others. It was as if I had a broken leg and had to have someone bring me my food. I was still hurting and wondering about the fate of the twins.

My resentment only got worse the longer we were at Camp Caribe. I saw how Tom was interacting with the Colombians. He was doing nothing but being himself and enjoying their company, but as with his jokes with Sombra on the boat, it worried me. Sombra's warning to us about Ingrid may have been a ploy, but based on what I had witnessed in my brief interactions with her, I didn't need him to tell me that she was a snake. I'd seen what some people might call her charm and her charisma, but I'd also seen how she'd gone from pissed-off bitch to welcoming hostess in the span of just a couple of minutes. I knew she wasn't crazy; she was smart. She was a politician. I sensed that she saw no advantage in continuing to openly confront us. When the decision came down that we were staying in that part of the camp no matter what she said or how much she whined, she had to switch gears. The woman was shrewd.

On top of my suspicions about Ingrid, I knew that in dealing with people in captivity, whether it was the guards or the politicals, knowledge was currency, knowledge was power. Having to constantly ask what someone had just said, knowing that I couldn't understand, and knowing that other people knew I couldn't understand was tough. We'd walked into a situation where we were already outnumbered. I hadn't anticipated an adversarial nature to our relationship with our fellow prisoners, but Ingrid and Lucho had made it clear from the beginning that there was us and there was them. They believed they had a home-field advantage because they'd been in the camp longer and it was their country; I wanted to change that.

When I shared my reservations with Tom and told him to be careful, he got upset with me. He thought I was telling him what to think and how to conduct himself. Tom and I had butted heads a few times before, and I knew that he was a smart guy who sensed that wherever there are people there are going to be power struggles. As such, he tried to dismiss my concerns with his knowledge of the Colombian culture. It was true that Tom had spent a lot more time in Latin America than I had. He understood the culture and the class dynamics better than I did. He tried to explain to me that in Colombia, the upper class had a way of dealing with other people from different classes. But I just shut down to those answers. I didn't want to hear it. I was an American, and I was going to act like an American no matter where in the world I was, and that was that. I could see Tom growing defensive, thinking that my stubbornness was unproductive, but we were both doing what we had to do to make it. We were just doing it different ways, yet we couldn't see that in the heat of the moment.

There was a clear pecking order, with Ingrid and Lucho on top, Gloria and Jorge next in line, and the other three—Clara, Consuelo, and Orlando, a guy I hit it off with immediately—as outsiders of that clique. To me, Orlando "Big Cat" Beltrán was a politician through and through, but a more generous one. On our first morning with them, he saw that I only had a T-shirt that was too tight and rapidly disintegrating. He pulled a pile of new and barely used clothes from underneath his bed and dug through his supply until he found a T-shirt that might fit me.

He handed it to me and said, "*Mejor.*" I couldn't disagree; anything was better than what I had.

Orlando was a congressman who had also been taken hostage in 2001. He was a big guy, nearly six feet tall, broad-shouldered, and thick through the chest and arms. He earned his nickname for the graceful way he moved and his stealthy manner. I didn't ask him how he'd accumulated all the clothes he had, but I had a pretty good idea. From our first conversations, it was clear that Orlando was a mover and a shaker—the kind of guy who loved making deals and always had his eye on what he could do next.

In time, I figured out that Orlando was the "single guy" among the politicians. Like Lucho and Ingrid, Jorge and Gloria spent most of their time with each other. It was clear that as much as she was a kind of nurse for him, their feelings for each other went far deeper. I understood what Tom had been saying about different values and cultural norms, but when you see someone kissing and caressing someone else, see them showering together and generally acting like a couple, you make certain assumptions about the nature of their relationship.

We didn't see Clara or Consuelo engaging in any of those behaviors with any of the men, and we didn't see either of them sleeping next to or sometimes in the same "bed" as a man the way we did with Lucho and Ingrid and Gloria and Jorge. While none of us was about to stare and gape at what went on at night, we assumed what the nature of those "couples" relationships was. We were fine with that, knowing that they were all consenting adults. What we didn't like was when those relationships turned into power plays to control some aspect of our lives. Live and let live and all that, but don't tread on me.

For that reason, Orlando, like Marc, Tom and me, seemed to be slightly on the outside of their circle. There was some class resentment toward him, since like Consuelo, he was not born into the upper class. He was street-smart, a definite wheeler-dealer, man-of-the-people type, but he could hang with the others in any kind of political discussion. Like us, he kept his eyes and ears open and was quick with his analysis of situations and circumstances.

I didn't think that Marc, Tom, and I had any kind of hierarchy among us, but when we were introduced into this new mix, I sensed that we were in real danger of getting the short end of the stick at every turn. I decided to exert myself more to bring things to a better balance. As the largest guy among us and as the one with the loudest voice and most forceful personality, I could be perceived as being the alpha male. That was a position I enjoyed. I remember once early on, Tom and I were talking and he said to me while pointing at my fist—"I never want to be on the wrong end of that." I told him not to worry. No matter what. No matter how upset I got with him or Marc or anyone else, I wouldn't attack them physically. I'd defend myself when attacked, but I wouldn't go after anybody. Like me, Tom had read about prison camps in Germany and he knew some things about hierarchies. We'd all worked in companies and organizations, so we were familiar with the game playing that could go on, and we had to be on the lookout for it—especially with all these new players in the lineup.

Add into this volatile chemistry of personalities and interests the fact that we were living in such close quarters, and it was a wonder that there weren't physical confrontations every day. At home, if I was upset with someone and I really needed to get it out of my system, I could hop on my motorcycle, jump in the car, go for walk, do whatever it took to get some space between him or her and me. In a jungle prison, we had nowhere to go—or at least not very far.

After I confronted Tom with my assessment of these people and his attitude, we didn't really speak for the next couple of days. It was just our way of putting distance between ourselves. Marc did his best to not take sides, and he was clearly upset by all the stress. I didn't appreciate him not seeing things my way, and I'm pretty sure that Tom felt the same. None of us were saints by any stretch, and we certainly were not Buddhist monks who maintained our serenity at all times. We were people put in a shitty situation, and we sometimes behaved like shits.

In the days after Tom and I had our little spat, we continued to battle with Ingrid over territory and witness her unbelievable sense of privilege. On the day the FARC delivered mattresses to us, she got pissed off because the one they wanted her to have was baby blue and that color would show mud too easily. We were stunned. We'd been sleeping on bare ground, on boards, or on palm fronds for almost a year and this woman was doing a "Princess and the Pea" act.

Later that day Tom was out of the hooch in the open area looking for a place to hang his hammock. He found a spot near the corner of the hooch and tied it off. I could see Ingrid and Lucho sitting on their bench in the part of the yard that they'd staked a claim on. Tom was now in "their" space. The two of them got this look on their faces and they started talking and giving the stink eye to Tom. Instead of going up to him and dealing with it directly, they went inside the hooch. They came out with the sheets from their beds and hung them out on the clothesline so that they were flapping in Tom's face.

I had been sitting with Marc watching this develop, and I told Marc, "I know that the three of us haven't been getting along. This has been a tough stretch here, bro, but we've got to stick together on this one."

Ingrid and Lucho knew what was going on among the three of us. They sensed weakness, and Tom had waltzed into trouble like the sheep who'd been separated from his flock. They figured he was easy pickings at that point, and sure enough, they descended on him, with Ingrid telling him that he should have gotten Lucho's approval before putting up his hammock. Tom, being the good guy that he was and trying to get along with everyone, started to reason with them.

No matter what was going on between us, Marc and I needed to be there for Tom. Stepping in, we explained to Ingrid and Lucho that no one had to ask permission to put up a hammock anywhere—especially from the two people who had claimed more than half of the limited open area we had as their own. We weren't raising our voices much, just doing what Tom was doing—trying to be reasonable. Ingrid and Lucho created such a ruckus that Rogelio, one of the FARC guards that the three of us couldn't stand, came in and intervened. He got them to quiet down and then he basically took our side and finished up by saying that Ingrid needed to learn to respect other people. It was a big moment; all of the politicals were watching this go down, and in our brief time there, it was the first instance we'd seen Ingrid being put in her place by a guard.

I'd like to say that the three of us hugged and made up, but we didn't. Things improved among us but we didn't need to say anything. The point was clear. We were brothers. We fought like brothers, and we had one another's backs like brothers do. I'd also like to say that Ingrid and Lucho did learn to respect us more and to climb down from their high horses, but that didn't happen, either. It was in their nature. They were politicians and they'd been spouting their own praises for so long they had begun to believe everything they said about themselves.

In some ways, they were on the campaign trail and we were the voters. They would tell us whatever they thought we wanted to hear and had no trouble lying. At that first meeting, when we were supposed to talk about how to improve our prison life, Ingrid flatly denied telling anyone she wanted us out of the camp, even though we had heard her say as much with our own ears. In just about every conversation, it seemed like Lucho worked in a statement of his belief that Ingrid would become the president of Colombia when she was released.

"Is that coffee warm?" he would ask. "Well, when Ingrid is president soon after her release, everyone's coffee will be ever warm."

The two of them spent their days plotting and planning a new Colombia together. Despite the drama, gossip, and backstabbing that seemed to follow Ingrid around, I had to admit the woman could get things done that benefited us all. The hooch only had a windowless door and a tiny cutout in one wall. When Ingrid complained about the fact that it was so dark and dismal in the hooch, the FARC came out with chain saws. I think they thought they were doing this to spite her, but it turned out to be great for us all. They cut out an enormous picture window in one of the walls. We enjoyed the extra light and air. If Ingrid's political party was the Oxygen Green Party, then I at least supported one plank in its platform.

In the end, those first weeks at Camp Caribe taught us that we all had to be quick on our feet. On any given day, you didn't know what side of someone was going to come out—conciliatory, friendly, two-faced, political, or just plain nasty. I guess it's true whenever you have a group of people together. Allegiances are going to be formed, friendships tested, decisions made and sometimes regretted. Mostly, though, judgments were formed, and while they weren't cut in stone and impressions altered, I kept coming back to what my mom had told me. I was a long way from home, but the same rules still applied.

TOM

I wasn't immune from the bickering, and I saw some of the unfairness that was going on. We each have our own lines and our own tolerances for people and circumstances. I responded when I had felt a line had been crossed. I'd hoped to find intelligent, good-hearted, and communicative people at Caribe and for the most part that's what I'd found. If we could have stepped back and looked at things from the perspective of "are you better off today than you were before?," I think that we might have been able to get along better.

So what if the manual-flush toilet system the FARC had improvised— you had to pour a bucket of water into the porcelain bowl—often clogged? That was still better than having to squat in the bush. So what if Ingrid or someone else hogged the space where we could keep our toiletries? I was just grateful we were at least able to take showers—cold, muddy showers, but at least we were able to stand on boards instead of tromping around in the mud. We had a spot in the bathroom building where we could scrub our clothes and that beat the hell out of mucking around with the pigs and their churned-up and floating filth. We were given boiled water, so Keith's and Marc's guts weren't being wrenched as often. We weren't marching. We weren't in restraints. We weren't under orders to be silent. We had access to books and other reading material—about a dozen different volumes. We had a chance to learn more about our situation because of the radios and the collective information and insights of a larger group of people. I was sleeping on a mattress for the first time in months and actually making it through most of the night and not waking up in agony.

As a captive, you have to develop your own methods to do the most important thing: survive. That's what I wanted to do. My to-do list for the day always started with one of the things that Keith had listed for us all early on. Take it a day at a time and get through it. I knew that it couldn't possibly be as simple as that given that my day involved interacting with a large group of people with different agendas and attitudes than mine. I did try to keep it to the basics, however. And as I looked at it, as much as I enjoyed Ingrid's company, and as much as she was a great conversationalist and a charming and charismatic woman, she wanted something from me that I wasn't going to give—control. She wanted power over all of us, and I felt like I already had one boss—the FARC—and I didn't need another. The FARC were feeding and clothing me. They were keeping the rain off me. As a result, I didn't need or want another boss among the prisoners. That meant Marc and Keith and the rest of the Colombians along with Ingrid. I was fine with us helping one another out and getting by as best we could, but no one else was going to control me.

As the weeks and months passed at Caribe, I came to see it as far too simplistic and illogical to look at our situation from a *sequestrados colombianos vs. sequestrados gringos* perspective. First, we all had a common enemy in the FARC. Second, whenever we made a judgment about a person's behavior, or whenever we decided on a course of action, based on nationality, we weren't just being narrow-minded but were missing the point entirely. Those kinds of emotional responses were counterproductive. We needed to be thinking in terms of what was fair, what was decent, and what would help us all to get through the hell we were in. Our judgments and decisions often did fall along national lines and loyalties, but not always.

The one area where I can say with some certainty that the *sequestrados colombianos* had a distinct advantage over us was in dealing with the guards. I didn't believe that the guards showed any kind of favoritism toward the politicals, but the politicals were used to dealing with their own people. They knew better how to work with them or in some cases manipulate them. Orlando, for example, employed a number of campesinos in some of his private business enterprises, and because of his roots, he was used to dealing with people from the lower classes of Colombian society. As a result, he was able to interact and manage them in a way that we couldn't.

Going into Camp Caribe, we'd assumed that, given the FARC's aim to liberate the lower classes and radically reorder Colombian society, they would be more resentful toward them. However, the opposite seemed to be true. Some of the guards showed deference to these well-educated and powerful Colombian men and women, which in turn enabled the politicals to gain more in the way of supplies. Whenever clothes came into the camp, it seemed as if one of the politicals was always called over to receive them. Keith continually fought to get clothes that fit him. When T-shirts large enough for him did come in, Gloria and Ingrid made sure to get them for themselves because they liked to sleep in them. We would not have minded if the politicals had been fairer in distributing what came in, but they weren't. Because of that unfair distribution setup, our provisions usually suffered.

Similarly we'd been promised radios since the first days of our captivity. There were plenty of them in camp and we were glad for this, regardless of who owned them. Listening to the radio became an important ritual in our lives, the one thing above all else that united the ten of us. No matter how bad things were going in the camp, no matter what the petty disputes were, the unstated rule was that you did whatever you could to notify whoever was getting a message from his or her family on the air. We had only been in camp a day or two when we were all sitting and listening to the program *Radio Difusora*. It was an evening message program, and we were all in the hooch. At that hour it was dark enough to get good reception on the AM band but not dark enough to use our precious supply of candles. As we sat there in the fading light of the day, Marc's mother's voice came out clear and strong. She told him that she missed him and loved him and that he should keep the faith. She added that people were "in a commotion" about us being in the jungle. She went on to tell Keith and me individually that our families were okay and that we were going to be okay. We all felt wonderful, and took her words about the "commotion" as a positive sign.

Unfortunately, November of 2003 brought news via the radio that let us know we might not make it out for a long time—if ever. President Uribe announced that he was no longer going to negotiate to get any hostages out; the only option, he said, was rescue. In his statement, Uribe repeated something he'd apparently said back in May regarding the hostages the FARC had killed during the failed rescue operation. He would only support rescue operations, and hostages would be released by *fuego y sangre*—fire and blood. Those words sent a chill through all of us, and set off a discussion.

Jorge said, "I have heard these words, or ones like them, before from Uribe. I have not forgotten them in the months since he uttered them, 'The failure to rescue many of the hostages,' said Uribe, 'cannot be attributed to the lack of political will, but to the lack of technical assis-

tance and sophisticated equipment. That is what we need to crush terrorism in Colombia.' " Jorge sat back, obviously feeling as though he'd
been crushed.

"Uribe's words echo my thoughts exactly," I told the others. "Without the right combination of expertise and equipment, a rescue would
be a danger to us all."

Gloria said, "Uribe has other motives. He wants to appear to be
strong so the people will reelect him. I'm not convinced he has all our
interests at heart—"

Lucho cut her off. "That's it exactly. He wants your Congress"—he
pointed at Marc, Keith, and me in turn as though Congress were truly
ours and we were responsible for its actions—"to enact legislation that
would provide him with even more sophisticated and expensive tools
for his military. That way he can control the people by demonstrating
his might—a surrogate might since it is not his own."

"Are you talking about things like the Predator?" Keith asked.
"Unmanned drones may not put people like us in danger, but I don't
think you can ever replace us with whatever the latest widget is."

I had to explain what Keith meant by widget and added that I agreed.
Maybe I was a dinosaur, but I would have rather seen the U.S. give the
Colombians better training in how to fight the insurgency than outfit
them with the latest toy from the catalog. The conversation continued
along those lines.

Uribe also mentioned that he hoped Predators could be used in rescue operations and specifically referenced the three of us as a way to
sway President Bush and the democrats in the U.S. Congress. Orlando
and Consuelo told us that there had been a lot of debate recently in the
U.S. Congress about the viability of Plan Colombia and the $700 mil-
lion in aid it provided to Colombia. In spite of the doubts, Congress had
approved the money that kept our drug interdiction program in the air
and even expanded the scope of the operation to allow for surveillance
to search for and track arms shipments in the country. The bad news

was that the more heat the FARC felt, the more it trickled down to us, and obviously rescue operations meant that we were in danger of being executed. In fact, a few days after we heard Uribe's remarks, the FARC issued a communiqué that stated they would execute prisoners in the event of a rescue operation.

We felt like insignificant pawns in an enormous chess match involving the U.S. and Colombia. Along with that, Colombia's regional politics always played a part in our safety. The politicals filled us in on the activities of an organization we'd heard of but had not really paid much attention to—the Group of Friends. The U.S., Brazil, Chile, Spain, Mexico, and Portugal all sent representatives to that body. Those representatives had been meeting with representatives of the Organization of American States (OAS) to see what could be done about what our Colombian politicians referred to as the "Venezuelan issue." Venezuelan president Hugo Chávez had not attended several scheduled bargaining sessions to help resolve several matters in the region. The politicals all seemed as concerned about Chávez and his role as we were about President Bush and Congress.

Marc, Keith, and I talked among ourselves about Chávez and the role Venezuela might have been playing in Colombia and how that affected us. The military-type clothing we received all had "Made in Venezuela" labels sewn into them, and we suspected that the FARC were receiving other additional supplies from Venezuela as well. While we couldn't say for certain that the Venezuelan government was providing all this for the FARC's use, the facts certainly seemed to point in that direction. Chávez stood to gain from the FARC's conflict with Colombia. The more Uribe was tied up fighting terrorists in his own country, the less he was challenging Chávez for regional military supremacy and influence.

Furthermore, it was clear that the FARC had a shared affection for Chávez. We had to endure a lot of propagandizing from the FARC, and they had spoken openly about their admiration for Chávez. In the eyes of the FARC, Chávez stood up to America and the other countries in the region. They compared him to Simón Bolívar, an iconic figure in South American history who helped defeat the Spanish imperialists and free the lands that today comprise Venezuela, Colombia, Ecuador, Peru, Panama, and Bolivia. In Chávez, the FARC saw someone who might be able to restore "Gran Colombia," the nation made up of the newly independent countries over which Bolívar had first presided. The FARC had their own delusions of grandeur regarding how they were going to transform Colombia. It seemed almost laughable that they idolized someone who seemed to be equally delusional.

The fact that we had to consider the volatile figure of Chávez when exploring the complex dynamic at work only underscored our doubts about a speedy release and reinforced our concerns about a Colombian rescue attempt. After the November statement, we devised several escape plans from Camp Caribe in the event of a rescue and the FARC's anticipated deadly response. Behind the bathroom, we discovered a small gap between the bottom of the fence and the ground. It was between two posts, so we could easily maneuver the slack and crawl out beneath it. In case of a rescue attempt, that was option number one. We also brainstormed other ideas and Keith suggested that the large black water barrels that each held a thousand liters would be ideal hiding spots if we couldn't make it to the fence. We knew that being proactive was even more important than staying informed. With our ability to make an early identification of various aircraft, we felt a little more secure knowing that we had a plan of escape in place.

The weeks after November's dismal news were difficult at the camp, and Thanksgiving Day 2003 was not an easy one for any of us—particularly Keith. He knew that all of his family was gathered in Florida having an enormous cookout and he wasn't there with them. For Marc, the first Christmas was bad. We heard Christmas songs on the radio and Keith and I could see Marc visibly deflating before our eyes. Not being with his kids menaced him. For all of us, though, the birthdays of our children were the worst. We knew each of them, and as those days approached—May 23 for Keith's son, Kyle, and September 17 for his daughter, Lauren; November 20 for Marc's daughter, Destiney; July 8 for Cody and February 28 for Joey; March 3 for my son, Tommy and June 21 for my stepson, Santiago—it seemed as if there was always some news we heard that gave us hope that we'd make them.

It wasn't until after Christmas that we got another radio message from some of our family members. We were up early as usual, listening a little after five on a Sunday morning. Consuelo had her radio on and she called us over. As soon as Marc heard his wife Shane's voice, he burst into tears. He was sitting on Consuelo's bed crying and then Keith got a message from his son, Kyle, and his fiancée, Malia. He started to cry. When I heard my wife's voice for the first time on the radio, the air rushed out of my lungs. I couldn't breathe and my vision narrowed.

"Please, Tom, know that I miss you greatly. And, please don't do anything that will endanger your life, we need you back home with us."

Mariana was quite aware that I could get a little mouthy and was sending me the message to hold my tongue and count to ten before I spoke. I had to walk away when she was through. Keith and Marc and Consuelo were all wrapped up together in their group, and I couldn't join them. I was feeling a level of emotion that I had never before experienced in my life. I had to just go off alone; those feelings were not something I could really share with anyone at that point.

Only someone who has endured that kind of forced separation can understand the combination of absolute elation and devastation that you feel at a moment like that. Hearing a voice you knew so well coming to you in the depths of the jungle was almost as if that person suddenly materialized in front of you—not just as a voice but as a palpable, physical presence. Those sound waves didn't just vibrate your eardrums; they touched your whole body. The hair on our arms would stand on end and it really was as if that person was touching you. I'd seen in movies when jailed prisoners were visited by their loves and were separated by glass. I couldn't understand why the actors put their hands on the glass. It wasn't like those people could actually feel each other's fingertips. When I started to receive those messages I understood just how capable an instrument our bodies are. They could tune in to signals in a way I'd never understood before.

Those messages were few and far between, but depending on their content, they could either sustain or cripple you for days after. Keith was elated to hear from Kyle the first time, but a few days after receiving that message from home, he told us that he was troubled by something that his fiancée, Malia, had *not* said. She hadn't told him that she loved him. As we did with any input we received, we turned this over again and again, analyzing each word and every possible interpretation. In the weeks after he received that message, I'd sometimes see Keith in his hammock, sitting by himself, and I knew that he was chewing on that message and what had been left out. As hard as we tried to be there for one another, there were moments when we knew to keep our distance, that we could only get so close to someone else's grief or worry. Marc had a similar experience with his wife and things that she didn't say. We came to realize that it was the people closest to us who could inflict the most pain but could also bring us the most joy as well.

We all hated seeing one another down, especially if it had to do with home and the absence of messages. That just ripped into each of us and twisted our guts, whether it was happening to us personally or we were witnessing it happen to our brother. As much as Marc, Keith, and I were hurt by the more immediate slings and arrows from the other prisoners, that amounted to a whole lot of petty nonsense. It was the pain of home that the three of us felt more acutely than anything else.

EIGHT

Broken Bones and Broken Bonds

January 2004–September 2004

KEITH

After Marc, Tom, and I had been at Caribe for a couple of months, everyone at the camp settled in to something faintly resembling a functioning family. Despite all the human drama, the three of us came to see that there were certain advantages that Camp Caribe had to offer. For one thing, we now had books and learning we could escape into.

My excitement about the books wasn't so much because I was looking to get lost in another world as it was because I was trying to develop what I considered to be another essential survival skill. I knew that Tom was doing a good job on a tough assignment—translating for us all—but I felt like I needed to better understand firsthand what was going on and being said. I also wanted to be able to express myself better. I knew that my loud speaking voice and physical size made it easy for someone to think I was bullying them when I was just saying hello. Gloria had a Spanish–English dictionary and she was kind enough to loan it to me. Every day I would take the dictionary and split off from the group to read it. The plot didn't have much going for it, but I liked all the characters.

Orlando's English was about as good as my Spanish, and most of our initial conversations were more like grunt-and-gesture exercises. I guess we were the two cavemen there who had discovered fire but wanted to move on to the wheel and stop drawing pictures on the wall. At night, after the sun went down, Orlando and I would just sit and toss words back and forth like we were playing catch. Eventually, we started to have more or less formal lessons where we would help each other out.

One thing that held us back a bit was that Gloria was very protective of her dictionary. If I kept it too long, I had to pay Gloria the librarian a late fee in cigarettes. Unfortunately for her, I was learning enough Spanish to understand from Orlando that Gloria's dictionary was not really "hers." One morning Orlando and Consuelo saw me paying my fine. When I sat down with them to start the lesson, they both said to me, *"Mal hecho. Mal hecho."* I knew what that meant since *badly done* was one of the expressions they used to correct me. They went on to explain that I didn't need to pay Gloria a fine. The FARC had handed the dictionary to her, but it was for the whole group. Though it was a public dictionary, she put her name in it and considered it her own—penmanship being nine-tenths of the law I guess. She tried to tell us that the FARC gave it to her and told her she was responsible for it, so she wanted to be sure nothing bad happened to it. We bickered about it for a bit, but eventually I resigned myself to paying the fine. In some ways, I felt like a chump, but that was better than having a daily confrontation. In the end, I understood that when you have so little, everything you "own" takes on huge importance.

In addition to Gloria's book and the lessons with Orlando and Consuelo, I got ahold of a simply worded book on the Panama Canal that had been translated into Spanish from English. It was perfect for me to develop my beginner's Spanish. I would borrow the dictionary, grab the book, and read for forty-five minutes a day using the dictionary to help me. Every day at nine-thirty, I would study. Everything seemed fine, and no one had a problem with my little routine. Then, one morning, I went to get the dictionary and it was gone. Ingrid had it. So I spoke to Gloria and Jorge about setting up a schedule so that we could all have fair access to the dictionary. The thing that got to me, of course, was that Ingrid was perfectly fluent in Spanish and English and didn't really need the dictionary. The FARC had built a small writing desk, and naturally Ingrid, and her shadow, Lucho, used it almost exclusively. She sat at the writing desk with the book serving as a paperweight essentially.

Her not really needing or using it was part of a larger pattern of entitlement that she displayed at all times. Books were so valuable to us all, and Ingrid, Lucho, and Clara in particular had a number of books stored under their beds that they refused to share. The three of us wanted to set up a system, like a library for honest adults, where all the books we had collectively could be set out and people could borrow them on the honor system. Our idea got shot down.

"Oh, we're not reading them now, but we want to in the future" was the response we were always met with. I got it. Even in camp there were the haves and have-nots. Marc and I used to say that we lived in the ghetto. We had the crappiest part of the hooch, while Ingrid and Lucho lived uptown in the best neighborhood.

If I hadn't seen the military prisoners behaving differently, I might have been able to give the politicians some slack. The military and police guys behaved so much better than the politicians did—from Colonel Mendieta, the highest-ranking guy in their camp, all the way down. They had a copy of a magazine that published a bestseller list for books. They gave the list to the FARC, asked for all the books on the list, and amazingly, they got all of them. They had a really nice collection of books, and anytime one of us sent a note over to their camp asking for a book, they sent it over. No questions. No hassles. Of course, their generosity had to be taken advantage of. The politicals borrowed more books than they could possibly read. When a note came back from the military guys asking that a particular book be returned, Ingrid and Lucho would get it and read it. "No. No. No. We can't let that book go back. We haven't gotten to it yet."

Those guys even helped us out with our lessons. They sent over a copy of *How to Speak and Write English,* a great little basic instructional book that I used to teach Orlando and Consuelo. It was interesting teaching the two of them. Orlando was making better progress because he didn't care if he made a mistake; Consuelo could not allow herself to be anything but perfect. If she didn't know an answer, she wouldn't guess. Because of Orlando's humble background, he didn't have the social-class pressure of keeping up appearances to slow him down.

I learned Spanish much faster than my counterparts did English mostly because I was immersed in Spanish all day every day. I was drowning in Spanish and it was really a case of sink or swim. At first I had the vocabulary but not the grammar. In time, I learned to conjugate verbs and get all the verb tenses straight. Consuelo was the verb mistress and an enormous help in refining me so I could make a proper debut in Colombian high society someday.

For the most part, we managed to form some kind of livable arrangement during the first few months we were all together. On the whole, we all tolerated one another, enjoyed playing card games, and engaged in our language instruction the rest of the time. One exception to all this was Clara. Early on, we noticed that Clara, who seemed to be the most affected by captivity, started to isolate herself much of the time. We also witnessed an odd transformation of her body. Her arms and legs grew thin but her torso became larger. Pretty soon it was obvious to us all—Clara Rojas was pregnant.

None of us said anything, but one day not long after she began to show, the three of us were sitting with several of the other politicals. Clara came up to us and seemed really nervous and excited. She had a way of twitching and fluttering her limbs as she spoke, and that day, her nervous energy was on full tilt.

"I have something to tell you all that is very important and I hope you will listen to me carefully so you will have shared with me this important news that I have chosen now to tell you." She barely paused before lunging headlong into the next sentence. "I am very pleased to announce to you all that I am pregnant with a child and I will be giving birth in four to five months. I ask that you respect my privacy such as it is under these conditions and not ask me any questions about this subject. Thank you in advance and please respect my wishes." She nodded and blinked and walked away toward Ingrid and Lucho's little setup.

We all sat there like we'd just been at a very hastily put together press conference and someone's representative had read a statement denying some allegations of wrongdoing but wasn't going to answer any questions to clear up the matter. Clara had to know what we were all thinking and wondering about, and her desire to keep that matter private would have been fine under normal circumstances, but these weren't normal circumstances, and even under normal circumstances, everyone would have wanted the question answered: Who was the father?

Later, Marc, Tom, and I were sitting by Tom's hammock spot when Marc said, "It's got to be one of the politicals. Who else has she been around?"

"The guerrillas is all I can figure." Tom swung the pendulum in the other direction. "Clara wasn't around the other male politicals at a point when it would make sense chronologically that one of them was the father."

"It doesn't matter to me who it is just so long as folks know who it *wasn't*," I said. "Word of this is going to get out and I don't want this pregnancy linked to me in any way. I can't have that happen."

"I agree," Marc said. "We can't have our wives or fiancées wondering about what is going on out here. This is all tough enough without having to worry about what our wives are going to think when the news comes out. And trust me, it will come out."

"Well, I know it wasn't one of us, but that won't do us much good unless someone else steps up and vouches for us. Preferably Clara." Tom nailed it on the head. None of us had been around her long enough to have been the one to impregnate her. We were curious out of natural human inquisitiveness but also to protect our asses. I was engaged to one woman and assuming Sombra had made a mistake, I was the father of twins with another; all the other guys in our camp were married. We were wondering what our women would think when they heard that a hostage was pregnant. Maybe I was just a little more sensitive to possible accusations and assumptions because of my personal life.

The whole conversation made me return to Malia's message and why she had seemed so distant. Telling me that "we all can't wait for you to get back up here to South Georgia" made it sound as if I'd gone north for the summer like some retiree. If I had any chance with the woman I'd spent the last six years of my life with, the woman whom I'd taken this job for so I could provide us both with a big house we'd planned to build, then a "miss ya" wasn't going to cut it.

I figured that Malia had likely changed her mind. I'd told her when I confessed to her about my affair with Patricia and her pregnancy that she didn't have to stand by me, that I'd understand if she bolted and wouldn't blame her if she did. Instead she told me she loved me and that we could work things out. My being kidnapped wasn't anything either of us could have foreseen or prevented, but if she'd changed her mind because of what happened before I was kidnapped, I could understand that. What I couldn't understand was if she decided that because I had been kidnapped, she now had an excuse to do the easy thing.

To make matters even more confusing for me, shortly before Clara

Marc with his kids, Joey *(left)* and Cody *(right)*, a year before the crash. The separation from his kids during the twenty-eight-day rotations in Colombia had been difficult, but Marc felt the job was important in order to provide for his family.

(Left to right) Cody, Joey, and Marc's daughter, Destiney. Destiney was only nine when Marc's plane went down.

Tom had flown planes all over South America before the crash. As the one fluent Spanish speaker among us, Tom quickly became our translator.

Tom with his son, Tommy. From the moment Tommy was born, Tom felt a close connection to him. Tommy was only five when his father became a hostage of the FARC.

Keith with Lauren and Kyle. Being a single father was never easy, but Keith had always taken pride in being there for his kids.

Lauren and Kyle with Keith's father and his stepmother. After the plane went down, there was little about home that Keith knew for sure, but he could count on his parents to be there for his kids.

This shot of Lauren and Kyle was taken not long after Keith went down in the crash.

This picture of our California Microwave group was taken a few weeks before our plane went down, while Marc was on his home shift. Tom is in the top row, second from the left, and Keith is in the top row, fifth from the left. Tommy Janis, the hero of our flight who skillfully brought us to the ground in one piece, is in the top row wearing the yellow shirt. Also pictured here are Ralph Ponticelli (third from the left in the green hat) and Tommy Schmidt (first row, third from the left), two terrific coworkers who died when their plane crashed while searching for us.

The Colombian countryside terrain ranges from lowland plains to mountainous jungles. While it was bad that our plane went down in the mountains, we were lucky that we weren't near the country's highest peaks. As hard as our initial twenty-four-day march was, it would have been impossible had we been dealing with higher mountain passes.

As true jungle rats, the FARC were incredibly skilled at getting the raw materials they needed to survive from their surroundings. With just a machete, most of them could make tables, chairs, or a bed like the one in this photo.

While there were some nights that we slept on the ground and some nights that we slept on *tablas*, this photo is a good representation of another type of bed we had. We frequently used palm fronds to soften the bedding and provide a slight cushion. The frame itself is made out of young trees cut apart with machetes.

The beds pictured here are typical of FARC sleeping arrangements. Because they were able to forage for raw materials as much as they wanted, the FARC often set up their bedding in a more convenient (and comfortable) way.

This is a pathway leading to a meeting area at an abandoned FARC camp. With the rainy season taking up much of the year, the FARC commonly make walkways using and from nearby rivers and trees. Over time we learned to read their construction habits to help us figure out how long we would be staying at a given camp. The more construction that occurred, the longer our stay might be.

The food serving area pictured here is a bit fancier than what we were accustomed to. On the far left of the lower shelf, there is a block of sugar that the FARC called *panela*. The FARC frequently carried these with them for general cooking as well as for boosts of energy during the marches.

These are the kind of boots that everyone (FARC included) wore. Because Keith couldn't find any that fit him in the days immediately following the crash and the FARC didn't want his big footprints creating a trail behind us, they cut off the toes of a pair of boots and forced him to wear them. He had to walk through the jungle with his toes dangling out of the front.

Some of the FARC's standard weaponry—an FN FAL battle rifle, a Remington Nylon 66 .22 for hunting, an H&K G3 carbine, and a handheld multiple grenade launcher. Even though we did build relationships with some of the guards, their guns were a constant reminder of the threat they posed and their true loyalties.

The jungle canopy was so tightly knit that we very rarely got direct sunlight or clear views of the sky. As a result we always had to rely on our ears to detect when planes or helos were heading our way.

In all of the camps, cigarettes like these were our currency with the guards. We used them to get everything from extra bath supplies to radios to information about what the FARC higher-ups had in store for us.

Radios like this one were our lifelines to the outside world, and gaining access to them was a beautiful thing. Whether it was studying the news or waiting for messages from our loved ones, we couldn't get enough of the radios. The initials LJ engraved into the front stand for the name of the guard that Marc got this radio from.

This was Marc's jungle sewing kit. Because we got new clothes from the FARC so infrequently and the clothes we did get rarely fit us properly, we each had to become much better with a needle and thread.

We lived in fear that any rescue attempt by the Colombian government would result in the FARC trying to execute us. We each had a go kit of supplies prepared so that we could make a break for it at the first sound of incoming helos. This one contains a mirror, toilet paper, a fishing line and hook, a lighter that has a small LED light at the bottom, and a razor blade.

This is the chess set that took Marc about a year to whittle. After he finished it in December 2005, we played marathon games, with Tom usually emerging victorious The board was made out of an old cardboard box and we signed the bottom with our names and the message "Three Americans taken hostage February 13, 2003. Still alive 10 December 2005."

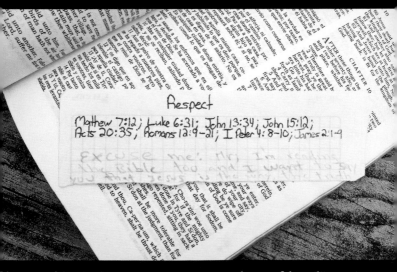

This copy of the New Testament was given to Marc by one of the military prisoners, Sergeant Lasso. It had passages written in English side by side with passages in Spanish, which helped Marc learn the language.

Sunday, 12 February 2006 - Day 1097

1:30~ Three years of suffering, it shows. I was checking myself carefully in the mirror this morning. I was looking at the changes that have taken place over these three years. I've lost alot of hair ~~~~~~~~~~~~ and on my hair line. Alot of the hair on the sides has turned grey. Wrinkles are starting to form around my eyes, mouth and on my forehead. My teeth are in bad shape, with several chips and visible calcylous along the gumline. Their not as white as they used to be, and gums don't look very good. My gums have been hurting lately. Physically I've lost alot of weight, adding to the daunt appearance in my face. I have several stretch marks on my sides and on the inside of my thighs. I have much more muscle tone and muscle mass, the only positive change I saw. My finger nails are full of grooves, ridges, and holes. I have fungus on my toe nails. I have an outbreak of a pimply looking rash on my back. But the most impressive change is in my eyes. I have black rings around each eye, their bloodshot and look sunken in. And there is something else about them thats different, but I don't know how to describe it, their just different. When I look at my face in the mirror I see a person who doesn't look healthy, especially in the eyes.

A few days after my last entry I was told Pajalo and Mono are dead. On the 25th of January we left camp and marched on a dirt road, then a mule trail for two days. On the way we met up with a gaurd named Earnesto who seems to be our guide. Our new camp, is located near the mule trail, and our section of camp is close to the guards section. Normally we aren't loaded so close to them. Our beds are made of logs and dirt. They haven't fenced us in yet, but Milton has threatened to do it several times. He's been coming over and threatening us because we broke a branch on a tree or a plant is knocked over. Usually the damage is something we didn't even do or had to do to put our tents up. The other

We were each given writing materials when we arrived at our first camp, Monkey Village. Writing was one of the few things that helped keep us going throughout our time in captivity. This page from Marc's journal describes the day before our third anniversary in captivity.

During the spring of 2008, the Blackhawk activity around us increased significantly. Every day it seemed like they were up there, and their presence always elicited a reaction from the FARC. It felt like the helos were herding us, but it wasn't until after our rescue that we understood what they'd been up to.

We took this picture with Colombian General Montoya on the plane ride following our rescue. General Montoya played a crucial role in orchestrating Operation Jaque, which freed us.

In the hours after the rescue, we flew out of Bogotá bound for San Antonio, Texas. This shot of us was taken right after we landed in San Antonio.

Marc's and Tom's first steps back on American soil, July 2, 2008.

The folks at BAMC treated us incredibly and they were very well equipped to handle our reintegration. We began by going on small trips away from the base for burgers, which was where this shot was taken.

Another one of our day trips was to the local Harley dealership in San Antonio, where we started dreaming about the Freedom Ride all over again.

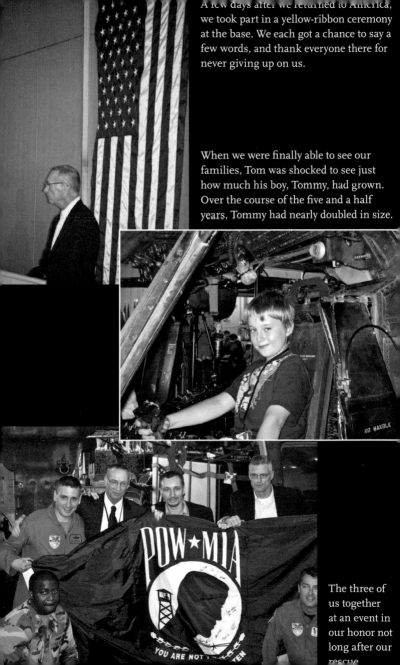

A few days after we returned to America, we took part in a yellow-ribbon ceremony at the base. We each got a chance to say a few words, and thank everyone there for never giving up on us.

When we were finally able to see our families, Tom was shocked to see just how much his boy, Tommy, had grown. Over the course of the five and a half years, Tommy had nearly doubled in size.

The three of us together at an event in our honor not long after our rescue.

Keith's son, Kyle, went from being a boy when we crashed to being a tall young man by the time we were rescued. The little kid Keith had left behind was now taller than he was. Meanwhile, his daughter, Lauren, who'd been fourteen at the time of the crash, had also blossomed and was now in college.

In spite of everything, Patricia stood by Keith and sent him messages over the radio throughout his captivity. While in the jungle, Keith got word out to her by way of a released hostage that he wanted to make their family work.

Keith's family, together at last: *(left to right)* Patricia, Kyle, Keith with Keith Jr. and Nick, and Lauren.

Marc with Destiney, Joey, and Cody on July 4, 2008, two days after the rescue. Marc's little girl, Destiney, was no longer a little girl; now a fifteen-year-old, she was almost a woman.

Marc with his family: *(left to right)* his stepsister, Corina; his stepmother, Monique; his mother; his brother; and his father. Marc's mom was so instrumental in raising awareness about our situation in America and abroad. Her constant messages in the jungle were a boost to us all, and after we were freed, Colombia made her an honorary citizen.

After we returned, Harley-Davidson did their part to get the Freedom Ride going by generously giving us each a new bike. The Freedom Ride will happen soon enough

had made her announcement, I was sitting in the hooch when I heard Lucho yelling, "Keith. Keith. Come over here. It's Patricia. They're going to play a message from her to you."

I had one of those brain-cramp moments when I thought he must be nuts, but then I saw him waving his radio. While I'd heard that one report about my "son" being okay, not knowing more left a huge hole in my universe. But at some point over the last several months, Patricia had taken it upon herself to start sending messages to me. I tore over there and skidded to a stop like a cartoon character. I held the radio to my ear. I was breathing hard, but it wasn't because of the short run. Hearing the voice of anyone I'd known before was reason to be excited. After a few commercials and some announcements, I heard the voice that had thrilled me the first time I heard it on an Avianca flight from Bogotá to Panama.

"Keith, this is Patricia. I want you to know that I love you. I hate it that I don't know if you are able to hear me or not. The boys, Nicholas and Keith, are doing well, but they need you. Nick has three teeth and Keith has two—"

I had to put the radio down then. Everyone was looking at me, and I was just so torn up, I didn't know what to do. It was an enormous relief that both of the boys were alive. On top of that, to hear this woman whom I'd basically told to move on with her life. A woman whom I'd told not to count on me to be any part of the children's lives other than financially supporting them. To hear that same woman professing her love for me was too much. It just didn't make sense. I'd known and been with Malia for six years, but I'd dated Patricia for only six months. If my fiancée didn't seem to be standing by me, why the hell would Patricia?

In light of this message, it became even more important for Clara to tell people that I wasn't the father and neither were Marc or Tom. Orlando agreed with us that Clara should tell people we weren't the father, but the rest of the group said that it was a private matter. In some ways, I could understand their position about wanting to keep this piece of news quiet. If word got out about this kind of thing going on, then the two pairs—Ingrid and Lucho and Gloria and Jorge—were vulnerable. When we first arrived, I knew that the four of them were close, but as the months went on it was obvious that both pairs had become couples in every sense of the word.

As the initial shock of her announcement wore off, the will of the couples won out, and Clara remained silent about the identity of the father. Whatever had happened, I assumed there was something more complicated going on, but as her pregnancy progressed she still refused to give up the father. The mystery remained in place.

When April rolled around, she was escorted from camp to give birth. While she was gone, we speculated about the whole thing, and the longer she was gone, the more we figured that the little bird was a lot cagier than we thought. On the surface it looked like her pregnancy had gotten her released, but that didn't seem like something the FARC would do. It was too decent a gesture for them; however, after four weeks of her absence, we couldn't come up with a better explanation. If she'd gotten away, then we were happy for her. That gave us all hope. If she had just been relocated, we were happy for ourselves. If any one of us had been taken out of the mix, I would have said the same thing. Marc always said we were like rats in an experiment, and if one rat was out of the cage, it gave the rest of us more room.

One day near the beginning of May, Marc and I were exercising. I was on the stepper, and when I rose up a few inches, I could see out into the clearing. A convoy of FARC was heading our way. A small phalanx of guards, and a few others, flanked Clara. I didn't have to shout to anyone, because the military group had seen her and were shouting her name. As she came to the gate, we could see that she was holding a baby wrapped up in a thin cotton sheet. Clara smiled sheepishly, and ducked under the arm of the guard who held the gate open for her, and with that, she was back in Camp Caribe.

Everyone rushed out to see her, and the ladies, naturally, elbowed their way to the front to take a look at her new child, Emanuel. Consuelo was one of the first to greet her, and her squeals of delight over seeing the baby were nice sounds to hear. We'd been surrounded by death and threats for so long, any sign of life was a big deal. The sea of onlookers parted so that Clara could go to the hooch to sit down.

Clara gingerly sat herself down, and beads of sweat pearled her hairline. Her skin, normally a less yellowish caramel color, was washed out and the lines around her eyes and the bags beneath them, though folded over and empty, still stood out. She began her story by telling us that she had gone to a separate section of the FARC camp.

Before she could go on, the baby let out a yowl and one of the FARC guards double-timed his way toward us, a look of panic on his face. Clara clutched the baby to her chest, muffling the sound, but doing nothing to still its squirming. His arm was wrapped in a makeshift bandage. Emanuel was a healthy-looking baby, but his arm was visibly broken, bent at an unnatural angle and swollen. With his cries rising up, I got the sense that none of this was going smoothly.

"After two weeks and no labor, they came to me to tell me that they were going to perform a C-section. Milton, the older man, was the one who would do the operation."

At the mere mention of his name in connection to surgery, looks of horror stretched across Marc's and Tom's faces. Milton—the guard we thought of as a mascot or as simpleminded—was one of the soldiers who'd operated on her. Taking in the sight of mother and baby, we could see the results of Milton's work. Whatever attempts the FARC made to repair the damage—we could all imagine Milton simply yanking the baby out as though tossing a vine out of the way—hadn't been successful.

"By that time, I wanted the baby out of me. They gave me some kind of drug to block the pain, but I was still awake. It is all a tangle of images, but I know that at one point Milton told me that there was some difficulty and the baby needed to be extracted." She paused to collect herself and look down at the small child. "He increased the size of the incision, going down well below my navel, while the other guerrillas rushed in to brush the flies away. I could hear them buzzing and saw a cloud of them swarming over the fresh blood."

The description was almost too much to listen to. The fact that it had actually happened made me feel disgusted again.

"I felt him tugging at my insides, and I could see him lay my intestines on my belly. He said something about them moving in his hands like earthworms. I heard the baby's cries, and I knew that something was not good, that Emanuel was not well. Seeing Milton's face as he held the baby and then rushed off and away from me—" Clara's tears and Emanuel's bandaged arm told us the rest.

Because of his injury but also because of his infancy, Emanuel continued to cry a lot, which created a lot of concern among the FARC. Recently there had been some helo flybys, and if the kid was making a lot of noise, he was putting the guerrillas at risk. Their response, of course, was to drug him up, but even with those drugs, the little guy cried most of the time from the obvious pain he was in. When he wasn't crying he seemed to just stare vacantly. I knew from personal experience that newborns didn't do a whole lot, but this was different. The kid barely responded to any stimulus at all.

We had all seen a lot of bad things in our captivity, but this was just sick. Clara's baby did not belong in the jungle. The kid needed to be in a hospital somewhere getting legitimate medical care. In a rare showing of unification and outrage, the entire camp quickly organized a meeting. Lucho and Ingrid started things off, with the former senator taking the lead,

"We all agree that Clara and Emanuel should not be forced to live under these conditions. This is inhumane at best and a potentially lethal threat to the baby at worst. The FARC must be made to know that we will not tolerate this." I'd heard Lucho worked up before about one thing or another, but he was sincerely pissed off and there was no faking the blood that rose to his cheeks and the indignation that burned in his eyes.

"Together, we can put the pressure on them that we need to get them to do the right thing for the baby's sake and for Clara's." Ingrid was no less stirred up, but her quiet tone of certainty and a resolute firmness struck me as different from Lucho's more theatrical display.

Consuelo continued the thread: "We can say whatever we want, but we need to do something to let the FARC know that we will not tolerate this. They will not be moved by reason."

Simultaneously several people mentioned a hunger strike, and we each agreed. I'd seen some pretty selfish behavior out of everyone in that camp, the three of us included, but I could see that there was no doubting that we were all in this fight on the same side. To get the kid the medical attention he needed, we would starve ourselves. As bad as our food was, we all understood the larger point. In their own way, the FARC tried to keep us healthy. The hunger strike would hit Sombra and his guards where it hurt.

"It is agreed that we will not eat today nor at any point hereafter until our demands are met." Lucho looked at each of us in turn and we either nodded or said yes.

After we'd broken up our meeting, Tom said, "It's not like passing on the stuff they usually feed us is that big of a deal."

I knew that Tom was purposely downplaying our sacrifice. Yeah, the food wasn't great, and we'd all survived starvation rations before on marches, but this was different. None of us knew what it would be like to purposely go without food and what it might do to us. I was determined to do the right thing—we all were—but a whole unknown had been laid out in front of us. When one of the guards came to bring us our food pot, none of us got up to get it. We all went about our business and ignored the order to retrieve it.

The FARC came in the next day and escorted Clara and the baby out of the camp, but a while later, Clara came back without Emanuel. She was a mess from crying and screaming.

"What did they do to you?" Gloria asked.

Clara sank to her knees and then sat on the ground.

Orlando sat down beside her and put his arm around her. They sat there for a minute, with Clara's body racked by heaving sobs. We could tell she was saying something, and then Orlando relayed her words to us: "The FARC have done part of what we asked—they removed Emanuel from our section of the camp. But they are going to keep him with a few of the female guerrillas who are going to care for him. Clara will be allowed to see him a few minutes a day."

"How the fuck can they do that?" I asked.

Orlando looked at me and shrugged. "Because they can. Because they believe that if he is not kept quiet, he poses a serious risk to us all."

We were between a rock and hard place. If we said or did anything else, the FARC would have just taken Emanuel somewhere else and Clara wouldn't have gotten to see her child at all. As much as we wanted to believe we could accomplish what we'd hoped for, Sombra had trumped our hand. In the end, we decided that it wasn't worth making our point if it was going to harm Clara's chances of seeing her kid.

As the days went on, our disappointment with the results of the hunger strike was replaced by a feeling of complete helplessness. The FARC set up a closely monitored schedule so that Clara could have forty-five minutes a day with her son. She lived for those moments, and the rest of the time she wailed and screamed at the guards to be allowed to see him. Gloria, Consuelo, and Ingrid tried to console her, but she was so devastated that there was little they could do.

During the day, Clara would stand at the fence shrieking in agony. When people tried to console her she'd tell them to leave her alone. At night, we would hear the haunting sound of Clara singing lullabies as loud as she could to her absent child. For every day of those first few weeks after Emanuel was taken from her, it seemed like Clara was on the edge of emotional collapse. None of us knew how to behave at those times—not just toward Clara, but toward one another. After the failure of our hunger strike, we felt hopeless and incapable of doing anything for her. Never one of the stronger people in camp, Clara grew weaker and weaker, and it seemed to us that she was hanging on to the ragged edge of our little society. Seeing her in agony raised specters of our own issues of anxiety and loss.

The pain of separation from our kids was one that the three of us knew all too well, but we couldn't imagine what it was like for Clara to know that her newborn child was just a few yards away. Over the course of the next four months, the FARC would not relent and Clara and her son were essentially kept apart. We watched to see how the boy's arm would mend, but we were all concerned that a more important bond had been broken.

TOM

While Clara's situation united all ten of us on certain fronts, it didn't stop fissures from forming for all sorts of reasons. As the months rolled by at Caribe, we found that one of the most frequent sources of contention was food. If there was one thing you could always count on to sow conflict in the group, it was food. Because the FARC had limited supplies most of the time, food had always been an issue for us—even before we arrived at Caribe. On the occasions when there was enough to eat, it wasn't particularly tasty, and compared to the FARC, we were probably picky eaters. We knew better than they did that food didn't have to be just rice and beans and the worst cuts of meat imaginable.

When we came to the political camp, our concerns about food shifted. It wasn't just that we had to deal with the quality of food, we had to deal with another issue—competition for food. At first, we'd tried to be courteous and set an example, going to the end of the line at mealtime and waiting to be served last. Consuelo was very good about taking her place back there with us, but we quickly learned that no good deed goes unpunished. Those in front didn't consider the needs of those at the back. Frequently, we'd have to ask the guards for more because the food ran out before we got a chance to serve ourselves. We eventually learned not to be so polite and stopped always being the last in line, but we didn't do what had been done to us. We only took portions that would allow everyone to have equal amounts of food. We tried to alternate getting in the front of the line, the middle of the line, and the back of the line, but the problems persisted. It got to the point that the FARC noticed what was going on and intervened, doling out the portions themselves to make sure that everyone got an equal amount. That worked out better, but it also made me sad to think that a group of adults needed to be treated like children.

The food was often awful and sometimes inedible, but we still needed some form of nourishment. (Sometimes I wondered if people taking more than their share and leaving the end-of-the-liners with very little or no food was an act of kindness.) The FARC didn't waste anything, and their version of chicken soup included the heads, the feet, and the beaks. It quickly became a running joke about Marc and the chicken heads, since it always seemed like he got a chicken head in his soup.

The chickens weren't just in the soup; they were everywhere. Camp Caribe could easily have been called Camp Tyson. The military guys had captured and bred chickens. They kept some in a coop and others were walking around free. Marc became obsessed with the idea of abducting a chicken for the egg ransom. The smell of eggs cooking was enough to make an otherwise grown and law-abiding man resort to such criminal behavior. The military guys were kind enough to share their eggs with us every now and then, but Marc was too industrious (and too hungry) a guy to rely on handouts. One of the chickens seemed to like the relative chicken-free quiet of our camp, so she came over to visit quite a bit. Marc set his sights on her as the beginning of his chicken empire.

When she came into our side of the camp, his eyes lit up. He'd run around grabbing any unused *tablas,* vines, clothing, or anything he could get his hands on to seal up the little breaches in the fence where a chicken could squeeze through. He knew that, regular as clockwork at around noon, this chicken would lay an egg. All he needed was that one egg and he'd be on his way to becoming a chicken mogul. No matter what Marc did to block the hole in the fence, the chicken would invariably find some other place else to escape. Once outside our enclosure, she would lay her egg tantalizingly out of reach. Marc was often so busy trying to plug one hole in the fence that he didn't notice that the chicken was gone. We all took great pleasure in seeing him turn around to discover that his chicken had escaped again. His face would go from expectant to crestfallen in about the time it took for us to go from observing to laughing.

Marc wasn't the only one who was taken with animals. A few stray cats hung around camp. They weren't feral cats but domesticated ones who would run off to wherever they could find food. We fed them a bit; mostly, though, they feasted on the rats and mice that ate our food supplies. Because they performed a valuable service, the FARC let them be. The Colombians had very different attitudes toward these animals than we Americans did. Consuelo was appalled that we would pick up the cat and set it in our lap to pet it. She would shake her head, put her hand up to block the sight of the cat from her eyes, and say, *"Ah, Dios mio."* She would no sooner finish questioning how we could touch a filthy cat when she would pick up a chicken, put it in her lap, and pet and kiss it. As Keith would say, "And we're the dirty Americans."

In spite of the food conflicts with the other prisoners, the months continued to roll by. While we were able to share laughs and stories with them from time to time, one thing we did not share was our escape plan. The three of us didn't talk about it much, but the hole behind the bathroom was ever present in our minds. We were always on the alert for aircraft activity. We had all put together what we called our "go kits," a mesh bag of essentials that we would take with us in case of an escape or rescue attempt. The go kits were our best case scenario situation. If we had the time and we were prepared enough in advance, we'd grab them and go. We all knew where we had to go in the event of an attack or rescue. The question that remained was whether we'd ever be forced to use it.

One night at about six-thirty, we were all sitting outside and talking. At one point, Marc held up his hand to silence us and said, "I think that's a plane."

Keith cocked his head in his familiar bloodhound-dog look as he narrowed his eyes. "That's a Blackhawk. More than one of them."

When we'd speculated about escape-and-attack scenarios in the past, we talked mostly about the fixed-wing aircraft that we saw. Helos were another matter. We really didn't know how the FARC would react to a helo incursion into our area, but hearing them that night, we knew we didn't have time to grab our go kits. It was the first time in our captivity that we'd heard helos and this was no rehearsal. It was what we'd been planning for. We had to act. We had no idea if the FARC would wait to see what the helos did or if they would simply execute us on the spot.

The helos were low and fast approaching. My heart raced as the sounds of the choppers grew closer, starting to consume the entire camp. The FARC began to scramble.

"Follow me, guys," Marc said, gesturing with his flashlight. Marc hurriedly walked toward the bathroom, looking around furtively to see if anyone was watching him. He made his way to the small gap in the fence. The darkness swelled around us, and without my glasses it was even harder for me to see. Marc moved to the hole, and Keith and I stood back. Lifting his head up to the sky, Keith listened to the helos and suddenly hesitated.

"Marc!" Keith whispered as loud as he could. "Marc, stay back. Don't go out yet."

But the sounds were too loud and Keith's whisper too faint.

"Marc?" I said. "Marc?" I felt the question tearing at my clenched throat. Yelling would have attracted too much attention. I could hear the other hostages scrambling around and their anguished chatter was like a spotlight fixing the point in the camp where they were hiding.

I stared into the darkness in the direction I assumed Marc had taken.

"Damn it," Keith said, letting out a heavy sigh and turning to me. "I don't think those Blackhawks are here to extract us."

I paused to listen to the rotors.

"You're right," I replied. I remembered hearing on the radio that President Uribe was going to be appearing at a forward air base in our vicinity. Most likely the helos were doing security for that event. They were just patrolling. We were not going anywhere. But with Marc out there and alone in the jungle, with nothing but a flashlight, what was going to happen to him? We'd always said that a solo escape was the most risky.

With this realization, our situation became even more grave. Marc had demonstrated that he could get out and avoid detection. Now the question was could he get back in without being noticed. If the FARC got even a hint of his escape, it could mean chains for all of us, or worse, death for Marc. At the very least they'd seal the hole in the fence and we'd need a new escape route. Our backs were against the wall.

Keith and I didn't want to draw any attention to the area where he was going to reenter, so we drifted off toward the others, who were in a panic. Keith and I tried to calm them, and as we spoke it became even clearer that our assumption was correct. The helos were passing by.

In the darkness, I heard Orlando ask, "Where is Marc?"

Keith replied, "He's back in the hooch. Let's just stay here for a bit, give the FARC a chance to do their thing and check out the situation. Too much movement is going to keep them on edge."

Keith and I did exactly the opposite of what he said. We edged back over toward our living quarters, where Marc was nowhere to be seen.

"This is not good," Keith said under his breath.

"I'm sure he's okay," I replied as much to reassure Keith as myself. "The guards have scrambled around the perimeter, but they aren't going out beyond the yard."

"You're right, but the sooner he gets back in here, the easier it will be for me to breathe."

A few minutes went by and Marc was still nowhere to be found. We paced around the hooch, anxiety on the tips of our tongues. We didn't hear any shots or yelling, but we also had no idea where Marc could be. We walked over to the bathroom building, careful to see that no one was watching. We didn't want to draw attention to the spot where we expected to see Marc.

"We should move back out of here," Keith said after a few more minutes with no sign of Marc. I could hear the tension in his voice. I knew that the longer Marc was gone, the more time the guards had to assemble and get more organized. We could hear their voices in the distance, but to that point, we'd not heard them walking on the perimeter pathway. We stood near the hooch.

When Marc finally appeared around the corner of the bathroom, he strolled over as casually as he could. The front of his clothes were dirt-stained and a layer of sweat lined his face. But he was back in one piece.

Marc had made it all the way to the tree line, roughly thirty yards beyond the fence, before realizing the helos were not a part of any rescue effort. He'd escaped, but his timing couldn't have been worse. He knew that he needed to get back inside the camp quickly. Immediately he fell to the ground and Marine-crawled back to the fence, but it was there that he ran into a problem. The escape plan had been designed to exit not to reenter. When he was on the inside, he pushed the fence out away from the camp, creating enough space to get under it. Now that he was on the outside, he pulled the fence toward him and there was no more give in it. He couldn't maneuver the fence in any way to lift the bottom up so that he could crawl under it. To make matters worse, the terrain sloped up a bit in that spot, reducing the clearance in the chain-link even more.

Just as he reached the fence, he could hear the sound of a guard's boots approaching on the walkway. He only had a few seconds to react. He pushed the fence back toward the compound and it grudgingly began to give way. Readjusting his grip, he gave it a more forceful push, opening up just enough room for him to squeeze his body between the ends of the fence and the dirt of the ground. He was back inside. He was safe.

It was only then that he realized his mistake: He'd dropped his flashlight. He looked back cautiously and saw it lying in the grass. If he tried to reach for the light, there was a chance the guard might see him. The sound of the boots got louder as the guard drew near. If he left the light there, the guard might see it or he might not, there was no guarantee, but if he went back for it, there was no way the guard would miss him.

He didn't have much time to act. Hesitantly he drew back into the shadows behind the bathroom, leaving the flashlight on the ground. The guard passed by and Marc went unnoticed. Cautiously he retrieved the light and returned to the hooch.

As Marc stood before us now, he was exhausted. The adrenaline that had been pumping through him had finally slowed. With each passing moment, he relaxed a bit more. Suddenly Keith turned to him with a grin.

"You ain't no chicken, are you? Your bird would have gotten back in here with no problem." At the mere mention of Marc's chicken, we all cracked a smile and laughed for the first time in a bit. Keith put his hand on Marc's shoulder. "Glad you made it back, bro."

The FARC confiscated all the flashlights following that night, and we were relieved that nothing more had been sacrificed. At least this way we knew that our plan would work. Next time, and we were sure there would be one, we had no intention of sneaking back in. Still we'd have to be more careful in the future about jumping the gun. Our advance warning from the sound of the aircraft had given us a head start, but it had also caused us to get ahead of ourselves. In many ways, everything had gone according to our plan. We'd anticipated the helos more quickly than the FARC had and the delay of a few minutes had proven crucial. The FARC personnel had responded once they heard helos coming our way, but it had taken them a few minutes to get organized. By the time they were all assembled, minutes had passed, and we'd already figured out that the helos were no longer a threat.

Two weeks later, we had another chance to test our plan. That time, we heard more than two Blackhawks bearing down on our position. We scrambled as we'd discussed, but so did the rest of the hostages. We all found ourselves standing behind the bathroom. Access to the fence was impossible. The three of us drifted away from the area, using the cord we had tied from our hooch to the bathroom. We needed to be able to get to the bathroom at night, but without our flashlights, the cord was the only viable solution. Whether we had access to our escape point or not didn't really seem to matter. The FARC responded far more quickly than they had the first time. They stood on their walkway. They spaced themselves five yards apart and had their weapons at the ready. We assumed all they needed was the order to shoot us.

We retreated into our hooch. We were all upset and very much frightened for our lives. We could hear the helos approaching, and I wondered at what point the FARC would receive the order to open fire on us. To think that we'd all put up with so much and then be gunned down just before a rescue attempt. I wondered if the FARC would get my journals to my family. I was glad that I'd written so much for them. I would have liked to have the chance to speak to my wife and my boy one more time. I would never have had the time to put into words as much as I had put down on paper. I thought of the messages we'd all received and how much they mattered to us. I couldn't imagine what it would be like to be on the other end of this. How would I have felt if I was at home and a knock at the door came and a stranger said, "We regret to inform you . . ."

When the FARC sent an execution squad into our compound, those imaginings seemed more real. One guard was assigned to each of us, and they stood at the opening to our hooch waiting for the order. Keith and Marc were nearest to the exit and the gate where Ferney stood. I could see the veins standing out on Keith's temples and forehead in the light cast by the FARC's flashlights. A guard called to Ferney, "Are we going to shoot them." I couldn't recognize the voice, and at that point it didn't seem to matter who had said it. There wasn't going to be any chance for revenge.

Keith broke out of the pack and approached Ferney. "Don't gun us down like a pack of cowards. If you're going to shoot me, do it straight up. Just look me in the eye and then do it."

None of us could believe how angry he sounded. Orlando went out to pull him back in. I noticed that Marc was missing. I saw a shadowy figure standing on the chin-up bar. A moment later I heard the sound of footsteps on the tin roof and then the sound of Marc landing on the ground.

Consuelo was crying and we all tried to calm her and comfort her. The worst thing was, we heard the FARC giggling. Whenever we heard them do that, we knew they were nervous. Having a group of nervous guerrillas armed and ready to gun you down when the order came was not something I ever thought I'd have to deal with in my life, but I was strangely calm. I really had no control over the situation. What was going to happen was out of my hands. Normally, I hated that feeling, but we'd been struggling with control issues for so long in that camp, I'd come to understand better how to deal with things.

When the helos flew off and the order came to stand down, we all stood in stunned silence while the guards filed out. There would be no rescue that night, just the lingering effects of another confirmation of the FARC's deadly policy. They had told us that they had no intention of killing us, but their word was broken as easily as the lie was given.

MARC

In the days after that second helo incident, it was hard to look at our guards as we had done before, even the ones we had developed decent relationships with. Whatever connection we'd made with them had definitely been severed. Seeing just how close they'd come to pulling the trigger was eye-opening. It reminded us that no matter what, we could never count on them to do what was right. We didn't bother to discuss the situation with them. We knew what their answer would be. Instead of *¿Quién sabe?* they would have said, "We were only following orders."

I tried to put myself in their shoes. I didn't know how I would have felt if I was told that my assignment was to take care of and to protect something (in this case someone) who was supposedly of great value to our cause. Would I have been able to pull the trigger when ordered? Would I have objected because I saw the illogic of the command or because of the humanitarian issues involved? I didn't like thinking about the fact that neither of these questions occurred to our guards.

After the second helo attack, the FARC sorted through our gear again. This time they didn't want flashlights—since they'd already taken them—instead they wanted our radios. Seizing these was just another way to increase security on us. The politicals had a number of radios in camp, including Consuelo's large panel radio with shortwave capability. Giving them up would be hard. We needed to know that there was a world outside of the fencing that enclosed us. We needed to listen to the message programs in hope that we would hear from a loved one.

In addition, we had become heavily reliant on the radios because of the news reports. In June of 2004, we had been with the Colombians for sixteen months, when we learned via radio that President Uribe and the U.S. government had implemented a new plan to confront the FARC in southern Colombia. Named Plan Patriota (Plan Patriot), the program was heavily funded by the U.S. government, and it involved the U.S. actively training Colombian soldiers as special jungle commandos. According to the radio reports we heard, Plan Patriota was the most aggressive effort the Colombian military had ever engaged in to deal with the FARC, involving a substantial offensive against the guerrillas in southern Colombia.

Some of the sources in Colombia claimed that Plan Patriota took the disguise off of the U.S.'s efforts to cripple the drug trade. Whereas the stated aim of Plan Colombia—the strategy that had brought us and California Microwave into Colombia in first place—was to wipe out the drug trade, many Colombians, including a number of the politicians in our camp, had always believed it was merely a front for taking on the FARC.

Plan Patriota was designed to succeed where Plan Colombia had failed: wiping out the FARC. We had no idea how long Plan Patriota had been in effect, but a number of the Colombian radio commentators believed that with Plan Patriota, the U.S. and Colombian governments had decided to drop the pretense of drug interdiction and engage the FARC more directly. This raised the ire of some of the politicals at Caribe, but none of us wanted to debate them on the issue of U.S. aid to Colombia. What we did want to debate was how this would affect our chances of being rescued, freed, or executed. The news that more troops were on the ground and intent on capturing or killing the FARC was a mixed blessing. While we knew this heightened engagement of the FARC was the hard right thing for the governments to do, the offensive increased our chances of being killed.

Radios kept us connected to all of these developments as they unfolded, helping us stay ahead of the news as much as possible. Knowing that the jungle commandos were U.S.-trained was a good thing; if U.S. Special Forces were on the ground in Colombia, it would be the best thing. We needed to know who was coming after us so that we could plan our response appropriately. If the FARC was going to execute us during a rescue attempt, the radios were crucial to our survival.

The day the FARC came to seize the radios, I was standing by Orlando. 2.5 showed up in our hooch, and Gloria and Consuelo gave him the four radios they had. I looked over to the back of the hooch, and I saw Ingrid putting one of the small transistor radios in her boot. She saw me and pointed to her boot to indicate that she had it hidden. Keith and Orlando also saw what Ingrid had done. 2.5, meanwhile, glared at Keith.

"Does Ingrid have a radio?" he asked.

Keith met 2.5's steady gaze.

"No, sir," he said without skipping a beat. "She does not."

Orlando said the same thing when asked. 2.5 shrugged and walked out.

At first I wondered why Ingrid would risk getting caught hiding a radio. It was either courageous or an act of selfishness, as though she believed that out of all of us, she deserved to continue to have a radio. I'd seen so many things in the months we'd been in that camp that it was difficult to treat any individual action as an isolated case. I was willing to wait this one out to see how things developed. I didn't have to wait long.

Keith had stood up for Ingrid by lying to 2.5. I knew he did that for all of us and not just for her. Her lone radio would be a true lifeline for us all. Unfortunately, within days of the radios being taken, that lifeline was cut off. Before, we had listened to the radios openly, but after the seizure, that was no longer possible. Ingrid had to be very careful about when and where she listened. We all expected her to fill us in on what she heard about developments within Colombia and relay any messages she heard from our family members, but she didn't do either of those things.

Her behavior was a shock to all of us. Because he'd put himself at risk by lying for her, Keith was probably the most upset among the three of us. He saw Ingrid's actions as just another power play, an attempt to use the radio to control us. If she wanted to bestow a favor on one of us by passing along a message, we'd be grateful and more likely to do something for her in return. I didn't want to be that cynical about her motivations or anyone else's, but even if I viewed this act on its own, it was hard to come up with any other plausible explanation.

To add insult to injury, keeping us in radio silence took serious effort on her part. She had to go out of her way to do it. We were in such close quarters and with the same people all the time that it was difficult, if not impossible, to hide anything. A lot of our barriers or boundaries had already been broken down. The three of us were so familiar with the sight of one another squatting down to move our bowels that it didn't even register in our minds that this was something unusual, that in our lives before, it would have taken extraordinary circumstances for us to have even contemplated doing it.

Sleeping in a small room with ten other people, eating with them every day, you developed a kind of casual and forced intimacy that I had only experienced before in boot camp. If you spoke with someone, you were almost always within earshot of others. If you whispered or wandered off to a secluded part of the enclosure with that person, you might as well have been setting off alarm bells or firing a signal flair into the sky to let everyone else know you were sharing some business.

In a way, Camp Caribe was a kind of boot camp. We were being tested physically and mentally. We were being stripped down and laid bare, torn apart so that new selves could emerge. Keith had noticed this process taking place in himself and the three of us. He said that "character will out." In other words, captivity would reveal the essential nature of us all. The jungle would strip away all layers of camouflage. Now, in the case of Ingrid and the radio, it appeared that was exactly what was happening.

Keith complained about Ingrid's selfishness to anyone who would listen, and Orlando was in complete agreement with him. For everything that Keith said, Orlando added another log to the fire, riling Keith up and saying that we couldn't let her get away with it. While Keith's motivations were almost always clear, Orlando seemed to instigate things for other reasons, always working to get the best deal. The more he stoked Keith up, the more I questioned how all of this was going to play out.

Eventually, Keith and Orlando decided that the best course of action was for all of us to confront Ingrid and demand that she share information with us. Lucho and Ingrid were in their part of the hooch, and we assumed Orlando went inside to ask her to join the rest of us outside for a discussion. When she came out, she was livid—so angry, she was shaking. She sat down on a chair and crossed her legs. One leg was bouncing, and when she tried to light her cigarette, she could barely keep the match lit she was moving so dramatically. Looking her straight in the eye, Keith told her that unless she started sharing the information from the radio with the rest of us, he was going to have to turn her in.

She returned his stare and for a moment neither of them spoke. This particular strategy was one we'd discussed before approaching Ingrid. It was a bluff, but we'd decided it was a bluff worth making. We had no intention of following through on the threat. We were all hostages and had to stick together, but since Ingrid was the one part of the group who refused to abide by this, she believed we were capable of turning her in. That she and the other politicians didn't share our sense of camaraderie was sky-written across the heavens when Ingrid spoke.

"Instead of worrying about me and my radio, you should be concerned about Consuelo," she said, her voice cracking. "After all, Consuelo was the one who had the large panel radio. How do you think she got it?" The only way she could have, Ingrid was insinuating, was by cooperating with the FARC.

A part of me had to admire Ingrid for her quick thinking. Her response had nothing to do with the situation at hand. It was a misdirection, and it wasn't fair of her to accuse Consuelo of conspiring with our enemy. After all, she had already given it up. It was a low blow no matter how you looked at it, and everyone was up in arms.

Just as tempers began to rise, Orlando, who'd been silent until that point, stepped in and much to everyone's surprise began to defend Ingrid, telling her how he was upset at "their" accusations and that he'd tried to defend her. At first I was a bit stunned by Orlando playing both ends against the middle so obviously. I'd seen him do it in much more subtle ways before, but this was as overt as they came. A few minutes before defending Ingrid, he had been the one urging us all on to confront her, saying how unfair her action had been to us all. Now he seemed to have forgotten that altogether.

Keith couldn't believe what he'd heard. He asked Orlando to step to the side so that he could talk to him. Keith's Spanish wasn't great, but his simple and astonished question—"¿Qué pasa?"—didn't need any interpretation. I couldn't hear what Orlando's explanation was, but Keith came back over to where Ingrid was sitting and repeated what he'd said earlier. Then he told her he was so disgusted that he couldn't even be near her at that point. He walked away, shaking his head and muttering.

I stuck around just long enough to see Orlando convince Ingrid that it was in her best interest to give him the radio. Suddenly all the pieces fell into place. Orlando, the ace wheeler-dealer, had won the pot. He'd wanted the radio from the beginning and had leveraged our legitimate outrage to get it. A part of me stood back and surveyed this situation with some admiration for Orlando. He got what he wanted—the radio and the power that went with it. He managed to still look good in Ingrid's eyes by defending her and offering a seemingly reasonable solution to the problem. Keith looked like the bad guy because he was angry, and I was sure in Ingrid's mind she thought he was demanding possession of the radio and not access to information. Orlando walked away looking like the good guy in everyone's eyes and in possession of the thing he wanted most.

In the end, little turns like this were what Caribe was all about. Small power plays, people competing for control. I felt like I was sitting in on a master class in the art of negotiation and power politics. I liked Orlando all right, but this incident highlighted that he was a master manipulator. I'd seen him get other people angry at one another. At various times he'd told us that Ingrid was writing letters to Sombra telling him that we were CIA agents or that we were dangerous and negative influences on camp life. When Clara was removed from camp to give birth, he told us that Ingrid was writing letters to her to encourage her to name Tom as the father of her baby. He'd planted a seed that we were dirty, smelly Americans who didn't wear underwear, had rashes that would infect everyone in the camp, and were generally unhygienic. By nature, he was an instigator. I knew that he and Keith were close, so I mostly kept my perceptions to myself. Keith was usually an amazing judge of character, but in the case of Orlando, he seemed to have a bit of a blind spot—something he could have easily said (and did) about Tom and me.

I did have Orlando's skills at manipulation to thank for confusing me even more about all the relationships among the prisoners and the guards. Not much more than a month or two into our time at Caribe, one of the lead guards, Fabio, came into our compound, followed by another guard carrying a small TV, a VCR, and a generator. They set the equipment up and inserted a video into the VCR. It was a proof of life video of the twenty-eight military hostages in the adjacent compound, and some of the politicians in ours—Orlando, Consuelo, Jorge, and Gloria. Like ours, their proof of life had also been produced by Jorge Enrique Botero. After the video was over, he inserted another tape. The first shots to appear were from a car driving through my mother's neighborhood. I recognized the area immediately, and Fabio quickly turned the video off. We knew it was our proof of life, and we pleaded with Fabio to let us see it. Orlando helped us, convincing Fabio that everything would be fine if we saw it, and that we wouldn't tell anyone. Fabio relented.

The three of us were all seated in front of the little TV, with Keith on my right side. Consuelo was sitting next to me on my left, and Ingrid was sitting next to Consuelo. When the video continued, we saw scenes of our family members. All three of us were extremely emotional by the first sight of our family members in such a long time. We were all choked up and had tears in our eyes. I saw my mother's message again, but then I saw Shane. As soon as I saw her I burst into tears right there in front of everyone. I was watching my wife on that little TV, trying to concentrate with all my might, and find some type of mental telepathic force within me so that I could transport myself from that jail to my living room where I saw Shane seated and upset on our sofa. But I didn't have that power, so I continued to watch the video, sobbing and hoping to see my children. Then I felt someone consoling me, caressing the back of my head. When the scene of my wife ended, I looked to my left, expecting to see Consuelo comforting me. But it wasn't Consuelo, it was Ingrid. I looked into her eyes, and I could see pain. It was my pain, she was feeling my pain, and I could see that her empathy was real. I wondered again who this woman really was, how she could be capable of such generosity and such selfishness.

This whole display made me wonder how much I could trust what was being told to me. My Spanish was getting better, but I could easily have misunderstood something or been flat out lied to. I chose to believe that everyone was being honest with me about news like Plan Patriota and other items that affected my fate. I knew that no one would mess with messages from home. If there was one thing that was sacred to us all, it was those messages. We knew that we had to be very careful in assessing the truthfulness of anything the FARC told us; I didn't want to have to do the same with what we heard from the other hostages.

Something told me that I had to up my Spanish skills more quickly. During our time in the political camp, I finally took to reading a book I'd been given in camp: the Spanish-language edition of *Harry Potter and the Sorcerer's Stone*. This book became my gateway to increased literacy. Like nearly everyone on the planet, I had heard of the books and the films that followed their publication. I hadn't read them, but after I got the book at Caribe, I carried it around thinking that since it was a kids' book, it might prove helpful in learning the language better.

I read the book and kept my journal with me. It seemed as if on every page I was coming across fifteen or so words that I was unfamiliar with. I'd jot those words down in my notebook and look them up later in Gloria's dictionary. Sometimes I read aloud to Tom and he helped me get through, but not surprisingly some words didn't seem to translate. As Tom read with me, we were both sucked into the world J. K. Rowling had created. I'd started out reading it with an agenda—to learn more Spanish in order to cut through some of the clouds of deception and doubt that our communication with the politicians had produced. I ended up almost completely forgetting about all that and just enjoying the story.

In early September of 2004, I learned via radio that my mother was in Colombia. By then, Orlando and Ingrid had worked out a system to share the radio. I found out that one of the reasons why Ingrid wanted a radio in her possession was that she received messages from her mother nearly every day the programs were broadcast. She was extremely close to her mother, and her mother's devotion to her was clear from the frequency of the messages. When I heard this, I felt a little bad about the whole radio ordeal. My mom and Ingrid's mom were a lot alike in their desire to stay in contact with their children. I heard messages from my mom far more frequently than anyone else among the three of us.

When I learned that my mom was in Colombia, part of me was afraid because it wasn't a particularly safe place for her to be. At the same time, though, I was thrilled just to know that she was that much closer to me and proud that she'd come to Colombia to meet with people in the government and family members of other hostages. The

Colombian media made a big deal out of her weeklong visit, and after hearing the news, Ingrid immediately told me. She seemed genuinely happy for me, and when she invited me to share her radio during the early-morning/overnight message programs, I was taken aback. Just hearing her words, I realized that this wasn't the same Ingrid I'd spent the last ten months with. Instead of a selfish, domineering woman, she seemed to be a bit kinder, with less of an edge. Still, I was suspicious of her offer and wondered what she might want from me in return for this favor.

If she was using bait to lure me in, then she chose the perfect one. Who could resist the opportunity to hear their mother's voice? Because we had to keep the volume low, we sat right next to each other, with our heads inclined and the radio pressed to both of our ears. We sat that way for hours the first night, and while I didn't get a message from my mother, Ingrid got one from hers. At the first sound of her mother's voice, Ingrid's breath caught, as though she was choking on air. We were so close together that I heard her gulp as she tried to stifle a tear. My Spanish still wasn't good enough to understand the message, but I was happier that way. I didn't want to know what had been said. Ingrid, however, whispered the details in my ear anyway. For the rest of the night we sat there smiling together, sitting in the dark listening to the rest of the show, each of us in that little cocoon of radio voices and silence.

It wasn't until the next day that I really stopped and thought about how emotionally intimate that moment had been. I'd shared similar experiences with Keith and Tom when we relayed messages or related painful stories from our past. On the surface, that night with Ingrid seemed no different from these, but at the same time I could tell it was different. Tom, Keith, and I had no choice but to share those moments with one another. We were all we had those first months together. With Ingrid, I thought I knew her and she did some things that I questioned.

Other people I trusted had far less respect for her, or in Keith's case, no respect at all. I remembered what Keith had said about character gradually revealing itself. I knew that he had already tried and convicted Ingrid for her crimes against the rest of us. But maybe she was not the person we thought she was. Maybe Ingrid was a far more complicated and multidimensional person than she'd allowed us to believe.

That one night didn't completely alter my opinion of her. A few hours sharing a radio wasn't going to undo months of selfishness and haughty pride. Just as we'd all been thrown by her ability to switch from wanting us to be kept out of the camp one moment to telling us that we should have a party to celebrate our arrival the next, I wasn't sure which Ingrid Betancourt was the real one—if, in fact, there was a real genuine Ingrid in there anywhere.

Over the remainder of the week my mother was in Colombia, Ingrid and I sat huddled together listening to the show. Each night I heard nothing from my mom, and Ingrid could tell I was disappointed. When the message portion of the program was over, she would pat my arm and try to console me. Finally, late on the last night that my mother was in Colombia, a Saturday, the announcer spoke her name. By that point, Ingrid and I were both drowsy; sitting in the absolute dark in the quiet hours of the morning, it was sometimes hard to stay awake through the whole program. Our heads had been pressed together for so long that my neck was aching and my back had long since gone tight.

All those aches disappeared the moment I heard my mother say my name. Her voice brought me back from the brink of sleep, and all at once I was sitting in a jungle hooch somewhere in southern Colombia with a woman I knew but didn't know. My eyes welled with tears and my breath shortened. Ingrid must have sensed my emotion. She slid her hand into my mine and held it, running her thumb along the top of mine. My mother's message was brief, but by the time she was finished, I'd forgotten every word. I asked Ingrid to repeat what my mother had said. She told me that my mother loved me. She missed me. She wanted me to be strong.

I bit down hard on my lip. In her retelling, Ingrid had produced the same emotions in me, as if I were hearing the original message all over again. I felt like my mother was right there with me and the gut-gnawing homesickness of it all nearly knocked me over. I asked Ingrid to tell me again what my mother said. She patiently repeated her words a second time. Finally, still not satisfied but knowing that what Ingrid had done for me was enough, I sat with her and listened until the program ended and the soft static faded as Ingrid lowered the volume completely.

I went to bed and lay there unable to sleep. The excitement of hearing my mother's voice was still like an electric shock coursing through my body. I remembered going into the confessional at St. Paul's Church when I was a kid. I had to kneel down and speak into a small rectangle meshed with wire. There I examined my conscience and let the priest know all the ways that I had sinned. Somehow hearing that message with Ingrid that night brought back that memory in sharp detail. I could smell the tang of the leather kneeler and the wood-spice fragrance of the incense from the just-concluded Stations of the Cross ritual and the sweet smell of the beeswax candles. I could hear the sound of the priest sliding the divider and see the wedge of light playing across the ledge where I rested my elbows, and my hands folded in prayer.

I hadn't gone to confession in many years. I'd kept my faith in God but not in the Catholic Church. I'd prayed every day in captivity for guidance and for my safe return. That night, I included one more person in my prayers. I told God that I was sorry that I'd chosen to see the bad in someone and thanked him for shedding that small wedge of light on a person in whom, until then, I'd only seen darkness.

For a few days after I'd gotten my mother's message, I would ask Ingrid again to repeat the words she'd heard. She always smiled and told me that it was fine that I'd asked. She said she understood, and I was glad that she did.

NINE

Ruin and Recovery

September 2004–May 2005

TOM

If President Uribe's objective with his Plan Patriota was to flush out the FARC and get them on the run in order to wipe them out, then his efforts nearly did the same to us. On September 28, 2004, after eleven months with the politicals, we fled Camp Caribe.

None of us was comfortable knowing that our fate was so closely linked with the FARC's. The inside perspective of the politicals helped us see that a new phase in the FARC-Colombian conflict was beginning. Uribe's government had lost all patience with the guerrillas, demanding action on a new scale. Uribe no longer believed in the FARC's ability to negotiate fairly and honorably, and now he would make the FARC pay a price for their misguided overestimation of themselves and their power.

How the FARC treated us was often a reflection of how they were being treated themselves, and our hasty departure from Camp Caribe didn't bode well. We knew that based on all the activity around us, we had to leave the area, but the speed with which we left came as a surprise. We were given little information about what was going on, and while that itself was not a strange thing, it was odd given the scope of the moving required. All they told us was to pack up and get ready to leave. Everyone was heading out—all the politicals, all the military guys, the three of us, and all the FARC, even Sombra. They wouldn't say how long we'd be gone or whether we'd return.

The brutality of the forty days we marched after we abandoned Camp Caribe rivaled anything we'd been through before. For the first several months at the camp, we had done a good job of getting ourselves into decent physical condition, but since June 2004 when Plan Patriota was first announced, the FARC fed us so little that we were weak even before we started the march. Existing on what we called cow-guts soup—because of its foul smell and the disgusting bits of cow that floated on the thickly congealed fat layer—and a few spoonfuls of rice or beans had taken its toll on us.

In addition, the three of us were marching with many more possessions than we'd carried back in October of 2003. We had all accumulated so many things that we couldn't possibly take it all. Though we left a lot behind, we took what we considered necessary. I attached my mattress to my *equipo*. I thought that having a comfortable place to sleep made all the difference in my attitude and ability to manage. I was wrong. Trying to maneuver through the jungle with that large roll on my back required me to do hundreds of squats as I bent under vines and downed trees. I soon abandoned it and quite a few other things to lighten my carriage. Everyone else did the same, and the longer we marched, the more we reduced our loads to the essentials.

If we were grateful for anything, it was the lessons of generosity and perseverance the military prisoners displayed. They insisted on giving whatever they could to help us, even though we weren't allowed to speak with them. For several days, we set up a temporary camp just

a few kilometers from Camp Caribe, where the three of us found ourselves next to the military prisoners. I met a young man and former
policeman named Jhon Jairo Dúran. He was in his midthirties, though
he looked much younger with his closely cropped thick dark hair. He'd
been kidnapped six years earlier and his deep faith seemed to sustain
him and inform all the choices he made about how to conduct himself.
I don't know why he chose to risk talking to me, but he gave me a cotton sheet and a lined parkalike jacket. I tried to gesture to him that I
would be okay without, but he wouldn't listen. He gave me some rope
and string, and they, too, proved vital on that forced march.

Everyone had it bad, including the FARC. Once again we saw the
lower-level FARC guerrillas being treated like pack animals. They carried heavy propane cylinders, cookstoves, and large bags of food. They
ferried one load ahead, returned, and then set out again with another
heavy load. They repeated the process over and over again. Our young
friend The Songster had his own gear and Ingrid's—she was too weak
from what she claimed was a bout with dysentery—as well as a large
cooking pot strapped to his back. He'd wobble and fall down. Keith
would help him back to his feet. Eventually, Ingrid could not walk at all.
She was placed in a hammock like Keith had been on our first march.
The FARC weren't too happy about having to carry her, and at every
opportunity they accidentally swung her against the many spiny trees
that grew near the creeks.

Like most people, I've complained at one time or another of hunger
pains or said I was "starving." Until this march, I hadn't really experienced either of those. Knee-buckling pain, similar to severe muscle
cramps, raked our stomachs. We were so weak that our heads spun and
our vision blurred and narrowed. Marc and I both had extreme pain
in our knees and my legs swelled to the point that my kneecaps were
a tiny bump of bone anchored in a sea of tissue. Keith's back injuries
continued to plague him, but he seldom complained. He said that he

took much of his inspiration from the military prisoners, who were chained together by the neck throughout the march. Their rigorous physical training helped them, but no one had it easy.

Everyone did the best they could to help the others, but the FARC were suffering as badly as we were and they took out their frustrations on us. At one point, Clara, who was carrying her own backpack and doing the best she could, fell in the mud, losing one of her boots in the process. Emanuel was being carried by several female guerrillas, and now she struggled in this deep stew of mud and prickly vegetation by herself. I stepped out of line and went to help her. We each had a guard in front of us and in back of us. They both yelled at me, *"¡Vámonos! ¡Vámonos!"*

I continued to move toward Clara. "I'm going to help her. She can't get up." As I bent down to lift her up, I heard the sounds of rounds being chambered in their AK-47s. Ignoring my wife's plea that I not do anything to endanger myself, I shouted at them, "Go ahead. Shoot me. You don't have the balls or the orders to shoot me, so go ahead."

I finished helping Clara get to her feet while the two guerrillas glared at me.

Several days before, we'd had a group of six Blackhawk helos fly overhead and the guards had done what we'd come to expect—they surrounded us with their weapons drawn. I was getting tired of that, and even though I knew they were as stressed as we were and likely to snap, I couldn't put up with their total lack of humanity. Unlike the previous encounter, when we had been in relatively good shape, we were beaten down and vulnerable. I half expected someone to make a run for it. Fortunately, the helos stayed away, and after a tense few minutes of standing there with a circle of terrorists with their weapons drawn taking a bead on us all, they ended up yelling at us to *"vámonos."*

I was especially angry because we noticed that when we did get our meager amount of food, the guards doled it out to us, making sure that there was some left for themselves. They were under direct orders not to do that. If we had complained, we would have simply angered them even more and who knew what they might have done to us as a result.

Their breakdown in discipline was something that Keith had anticipated for months. He told Marc and me time and time again that these men and women of the FARC weren't true soldiers and when things got tough we had to be careful. We were all being pushed beyond our limits and we lashed out at the guards with increasing frequency.

In contrast to the FARC's breakdown in restraint, and in defiance of their cruelty, the military prisoners conducted themselves in a way that awed us. One of them, Julian, suffered from a painful condition. He had what appeared to be a large blood blister that ran up his legs and groin and into his torso. It looked like a river on a relief map. After the first two weeks, the guards had either lifted or were too tired to enforce the ban on speaking with the military guys. Julian told us that as a policeman, he had taken a bullet to the head during an altercation in Bogotá. Mono, a FARC guard, told us that he'd been present at the battle when Julian was captured. Julian had fought valiantly and had killed a number of guerrillas.

After a few weeks of the deprivation we faced, Julian fell while we were marching. His guards yelled at him to keep going, and he did. He couldn't stand, but he crawled, using his hands and his one good leg while dragging the other behind him. He knew that if he held up the march, the rest of us would suffer. To see him crawling while another prisoner was carried in a hammock was a sight more painful than our hunger. After we came to a camp, Jhon Jairo demonstrated the kind of humanity that the FARC did not. He went to Guillermo, the camp medic, and pleaded with him to take off Julian's chains. Out of respect for Julian and Jhon Jiaro, Guillermo agreed; Julian walked and crawled for the rest of the forty days unchained.

As was always true, for every FARC good deed, there was also a bad one. Keith needed Guillermo's help after we had negotiated a rope-assisted river crossing, during which Keith had stepped on a spiny tree and its nettles embedded themselves under the nail of his big toe. Instead of administering any kind of painkiller or even cleaning the area, Guillermo took a scalpel and began hacking at Keith's foot, essentially slashing and pulling up the nail to get at what was buried beneath it. While he was working on Keith he was muttering about how weak Americans were. Another FARC guard, Cereal Boy, was standing nearby watching. He knew that Guillermo was purposely making things more painful for Keith, and standing behind Guillermo so the medic couldn't see him, he mouthed words of encouragement to Keith. For some reason, Guillermo didn't like Keith and later insisted that he be chained to another prisoner for a day's march.

We were truly at our breaking point on that march. When we were offered a few bites of box turtle feet, we ate them. When we finally reached a resupply point, we were handed one pack of cigarettes apiece and a single block of *panela*. Our systems were so depleted that when we ate the raw sugar, it was like we had mainlined it directly to our adrenal glands. After eating half the block one night and a good part of what was left the next morning, for the first part of that day's march I was supercharged.

As the march progressed, the hundred or more FARC escorting us had whittled down their numbers as well as our original number of thirty-eight hostages. The first to leave after about two weeks were Ingrid and Lucho and eight of the military prisoners along with many FARC. Ten days later, four other prisoners along with Consuelo and Gloria (who were both stalwarts throughout the march), Clara, Alan, Jorge, and Orlando were separated off. Finally, after another seven days, ten others departed, leaving our group with the three of us and five military prisoners—Javier Rodríguez, Jhon Jairo Durán, Erasmo Romero, Julian Guevera, and Julio Caesar Buitrago.

As we had been learning all along, we all found a way to get through each day. Our bodies were growing weaker, but we found some reserve of strength somewhere. Keith found his in defiance—he refused to let the FARC win. Marc found his in his faith, beginning every day with a prayer. I called upon the old reliable that kept us going always—family and a return to our homeland. At one point, I stumbled, fell, and lay there in the mud thinking that it would be easy to just stay where I was, but I didn't. I picked myself up and kept putting one foot in front of the other. From knee-high mud through neck-deep water and up-and-down *cansa-perros*—hills that were high enough to tire out dogs—into shivering nights when our bodies were so depleted of calories that we could not stay warm, we stretched the limits of what we thought we could endure.

For all of us, getting back to our own country and the freedoms we enjoyed there played a crucial role in our perseverance. Keith and Marc told me that one of the ways they got through the day was by focusing on a specific fantasy. Those fantasies usually revolved around the simple pleasures of their lives back home with family. Whether it was a day spent at the beach, at a ballpark watching a youth league game, or dinner at the kids' favorite spot, we didn't think about anything wild or elaborate.

Each of us believed that freedom and a return to our way of life was the most powerful motivation we had when the going seemed impossible. Wanting to be out from under the thumb of people who oppressed us and denied us our rights was the most basic desire we had. It was an almost primal urge, ingrained in us after years and years of being able to do just that—exert our free will. That's what we wanted for ourselves and that's what we as a country wanted for other people as well. Many of the FARC asked us what the U.S. was like, and when we told them that the United States was about freedom, they couldn't believe that our answer could be that simple. The guerrillas took a lot from us, but they could never get their minds or their hands around the idea that what we valued most was our freedom. As long as we were capable of drawing on what it was we had in our hearts and memories, we would endure.

KEITH

It was a good thing that after thirty-nine days of hell, the FARC loaded the eight of us into a boat. By that time I was sick and tired of seeing that fat son of a bitch Sombra walking without an *equipo* while his latest mama, Spider Woman, busted her hump like the rest of us. Whenever we stopped, a couple of other female guerrillas would flutter around him, making sure he had water, that his boots were free of stones, and that his blubbery thighs weren't chafing too badly. I imagined the last of those, just as I imagined those flabby thighs creating enough friction to barbecue his balls. At one rest point, the Fat Man's minions rushed to set up a little bench for him so he wouldn't have to put his lard ass on the ground and they did their usual ministering to his needs. I sat nearby staring at him, thinking of *Animal Farm* and the pig Napoleon saying, "All animals are equal, some animals are more equal than others." I would have loved to be able to treat Sombra with an equal amount of cruelty he dished out to us.

Before we got on the boat, we sat alongside a river, all of us drifting off into a semisleep. From a distance, the sound of cantina music and a few disco songs carried downriver. I knew I wasn't dreaming because I'd never let a note of disco penetrate my consciousness. Later, when darkness fell, we finally began our boat trip. We cruised past that bar. It was little more than a few rectangles of light on the shore that slid down at odd angles and reflected on the river, but we hadn't seen a sign of civilization like that since the proof of life more than a year earlier. Cigarettes glowing in our hands, we cruised upriver under a night sky freckled with stars, and when we were all out of smokes, we huddled together under a sheet of black plastic, trying to contain our collective warmth.

Shortly after first light we pulled up to shore near a rotted walkway that led from the water to a clearing. In that clearing an old FARC camp stood like a crumbling skeleton. One of the buildings had been bombed and several other of the wooden structures were being reclaimed by the jungle. In the midst of this was an actual concrete building with a tin roof. We were led inside, and as we walked on the dirty cement floors and past two small surgical suites, we realized that we were in the remains of an old hospital. All around us tables still sat flanked by monitors and other equipment. Everything was covered in several years' worth of dust. Whoever had occupied this hospital was long gone, but we didn't have time to speculate about what had happened to them. It seemed like gravity's pull was much stronger inside those walls, and we were all asleep before we hit the floor.

For the next week, we rested and ate. We had beef, carrots, beets, and other vegetables for the first time in more than a year. Our bodies were so unused to having anything solid or substantial in them that they treated the food like an invader and shot it out almost as fast as we could put it in. When we weren't eating we were lying down or sleeping. Only rarely were we allowed to wander outside the hollowed-out hospital. We counted it a treat to be allowed to walk escorted by guards through the half-dozen rooms that made up the small medical site. In my mind, the place seemed haunted by the patients long gone. Like so many things about the landscape there, you just had to accept this wreckage without question. Whoever had made this hospital a priority had long since moved on. Now all that was left were a handful of old pieces of equipment and our voices bouncing off the walls.

About halfway through the week, the five remaining military guys were told to pack up and were led off by Ferney. We were sorry to see them go, but we wouldn't miss the Frenchman a bit. Milton, the guy we had assumed was Sombra's pet or mascot, was left in charge of us. The guards seemed far more relaxed than they had been. I think they were as grateful as we were that the madness of the forty-day march was over.

At the end of those seven days, we took a brief boat trip and then a truck ride into the Macarena Mountains. Along the way, we came to a decent-size town, Santo Domingo, that consisted of maybe eighty buildings or so, and immediately we all grew incredibly excited. A few days before we headed out of the hospital, two guards, Rogelio and Costeño, told us that they'd heard a rumor that a ransom was being paid for us and we were going to be released. This information fit in with what we'd heard on the forty-day march—that the Colombian government had unilaterally released forty-five prisoners. We figured this might have something to do with us. Why would the Colombians after all this time let their FARC prisoners go if they weren't sure that the other side would reciprocate? Now that we were in an actual town, the pieces seemed to be falling into place. Why else would we be near a town, in the population, unless we were being released? Towns meant roads and transportation, telephones and electricity to power their laptops, easier communications with their Front and bloc leaders.

Another possibility came from something else we'd heard. The Colombian military had captured two FARC leaders—Simón Trinidad and a woman named Sonia (not our first captor but another woman with the same name). Trinidad was the son of wealthy traditional landowners who'd gone bad. His parents were leftists themselves, but Trinidad had gone really far left. He was captured in Ecuador in January of 2004 and had been extradited to Colombia almost immediately. While we'd been with the politcals, we'd heard that the U.S. was hoping to get him extradited to the States to stand trial there. Marc, Tom, and I agreed that this wouldn't be a good thing for us—it would piss off the FARC and maybe they'd take their anger out on Americans—but it was a good thing for our country and the world to have this guy put away. We knew that the U.S. government didn't negotiate with terrorists.

As much as it sucked to know that, we also understood it was a good policy. We briefly considered a scenario in which the U.S. government would trade Trinidad or Sonia or both for us, but we knew that was just big pie-in-the-sky-thinking.

All of our optimism disappeared when our truck didn't even stop in Santo Domingo. Instead we simply headed up into the mountains. We were packed in the back of a Land Cruiser pickup, twenty of us crammed into a canvas-covered six-foot truck bed. With each rut we rocked over, a little more of our collective hope leaked out of me. Marc and I looked over at each other. We'd each been sandwiched between female guards; one of them, Tatiana, had fallen asleep with her head on my shoulder and the other, Mona, had done the same on Marc's. We both wished that we could have rested that easily, but with visions of our release growing smaller, this strange physical proximity to our enemy sickened me.

We spent three weeks at a temporary camp in the mountains. We were still near enough to Santo Domingo that we were adequately resupplied—we even had foam mattresses. We received new boots, new *toldillo* or bug nets, and some new clothes. The fattening up process continued, and Milton even started hunting for food to supplement our rations. One day we saw him walking through camp dragging two monkeys by their tails—one of which was still breathing, while the other had a live baby clinging to her. We looked away in disgust. For most of my life I'd been around hunting. I knew a humane kill from an inhumane one, but Milton didn't seem to care. Later that night, when we ate fried *marimba,* those thoughts about the ethics of hunting were swallowed up along with a healthy portion of monkey meat. No matter where it came from, it was still meat that we needed.

Taking the moral high ground in that situation made no sense, and only Marc seemed to have any qualms about eating it. A few days later, Milton took down a deer. Marc and I had had a series of discussions about hunting, and he was in the Bambi camp—that the cute and fluffy deserved to live free and fearless. That was before he found out that cute and fluffy can be tasty and nutritious. His look of trepidation turned into glee when he bit into his first hunk of venison cooked over an open flame.

Milton seemed far more interested in hunting than he did in monitoring things around camp. Back on the march, the military prisoners had told us that we'd be lucky if we ever had Milton as our *comandante*. We only knew Milton for his blank stare and his lackey demeanor. They said he was basically a decent, simple guy who liked being out in the jungle. There were two things Milton seemed to know how to do—hunt and beg for cigarettes. If you talked to him about the weather, how the streams ran downhill, or about hunting, he was right there with you. Vary from that script and Milton didn't stammer or make shit up. He'd just go quiet and then walk away.

The FARC had camped a ways downhill from us and they trekked uphill at intervals throughout the day to bring us food or to switch guard assignments. We got to know some of the guards better in this setup. Eliécer (Bird Man) was a decent guy in his midthirties. He took his FARC name, Jorge Eliécer Gaitán, after a populist left-wing politician from the early to middle part of the twentieth century. He was assassinated in 1948 and his death led to *la violencia*, one of the bloodiest periods of political unrest in Colombian history.

The Eliécer we knew was anything but violent, but he was certainly a victim of it. He'd been with the FARC for quite a while, and we could tell that he had been brainwashed. When we first met him, he said, "All Americans are gangsters and criminals. We have been warned not to trust you. You have no morals."

"Eliécer," I said, "we're the first Americans you've ever met. How do you know what we're all like?"

"This is what I've been told and it's what I believe. I've seen what your government has done to my people."

Though we tried reasoning with him, he continued to resist our words. One night several months later, he came up to me and wanted to talk.

"I was wounded in a battle." He rubbed the back of his head. "I was hit with a bullet here."

"You're a lucky man to be alive, Eliécer. Very lucky," I said.

"It doesn't feel lucky to me," he said. "I would like to be one of you."

"One of us?" Marc asked. "A hostage? Are you serious?"

"Not a hostage, but one of you. An American."

"I thought we were all just a bunch of immoral cutthroats—losers, bad guys ruining Colombia."

Eliécer's expression was sheepish, but he looked me in the eye and said, "I was wrong. I believed what I was told, but now I believe what I see. You're good men. I see how you treat one another. I don't think you'd do some of the things we do to each other."

"What do you mean?" I asked.

Eliécer looked away and blew out a sigh, "I no longer have a girlfriend. She is with someone else."

"That's a tough thing," I said. "The women here can be pretty brutal."

"Because of my injury"—he tapped his head—"I sometimes can't—" He took his hand from his head and tapped his crotch. "No erection."

I was surprised that he would make an admission like that but felt bad for him. I looked at Marc, who said, "Maybe if you exercised or something. Got rid of some of the stress."

Eliécer shook his head. "It won't do any good." With that, he walked away.

I felt bad for him, because in that environment, with the guerrillas living in such close quarters, I knew that he was lying there at night, badly injured, feeling like shit about his manhood, and he had to hear his ex-girlfriend getting the wood laid to her by her new lover.

We'd heard someone in the camp making really strange noises at night, just screaming in agony. I knew then that was Eliécer. He said that particularly when there was a full moon, he couldn't sleep and then the pain was the worst. The guy needed some medicine to control whatever was wrong with him as a result of his brain injury. The FARC wouldn't get it to him all the time. In every other outfit in the world, a guy in Eliécer's condition would have been released from active duty, but the FARC didn't give a shit. He was in for life, and as a big guy, he had to carry a heavy mortar around on those marches. He was one of a group that Tom often referred to as the pack mules. We hated seeing those guys just getting abused.

Eliécer wasn't the only guy who revealed things to us. Two of the guards who opened up to us quite a bit were young kids, Cereal Boy and the Plumber. The latter told us that the shots that we had heard fired when we were in the New Camp and the woman's scream that followed were the result of a FARC guard's suicide. He'd been the clown who laughed every time Marc fell down on our first march. The human in me felt bad that he found it necessary to inhale a round from his AK-47, but the hostage in me, the patriot in me, thought one fewer is not a bad thing.

The problem was, though, that for every one that was gone, there were still whole bunches around. In that temporary camp, we were plagued by ticks, tiny little bloodsuckers about the size of a pinhead. The ticks got in places on us that had never seen daylight. They worked their way into our skin, and if we had let them stay there long enough, they would have sucked the life out of us. They had one purpose and one purpose only in life. They were FARC bugs.

As Christmas Day 2004 rolled around, we didn't have a whole lot to celebrate except having one another on our side in this battle. Christmas Eve 2004 we found ourselves sitting on a hillside in Colombia talking about what the day should have been like while we heard the

FARC having a little celebration of their own. The wind was up and whipping us that night, and we all sat hugging our own legs to keep warm.

We heard footsteps behind us, and turned around to find Eliécer standing there.

"Why aren't you at the party?" I asked.

"I was there. I just wanted to come to wish you all a good Christmas."

He stepped in front of us and offered his hand. I extended mine, and Eliécer took it in both of his large callused hands. He nodded formally and said, "Merry Christmas, Keith. I'm sorry that you won't be with your family."

I thanked him and asked him about his own.

"I don't want to think about them tonight. I want to choose to think about other things."

He continued down the line, wishing Marc and Tom well just as he had me.

"Eliécer's a smart guy," I said as we watched him walk away. "He's figured out what freedom means out here. I'm glad he realizes he has some choice about what to think about."

MARC

In addition to overseeing our imprisonment, Milton was also responsible for managing a work detail. Ever since we'd arrived at this temporary camp, we'd heard the sound of chain saws in the distance. We saw FARC guards carrying what looked like building supplies from as far away as a quarter of a mile. Whatever it was that they were building, we had a feeling we'd be heading there soon.

After our second Christmas in captivity and New Year's 2005 had come and gone, the camp that Milton's group had been working on was finally ready for its inhabitants. As we walked uphill toward our new space, a dry wind was blowing and leaves skittered along the steeply sloped terrain. The sun was warm but the air cool. To rid myself of my post-Christmas blues, I closed my eyes, and I was back in Connecticut enjoying an Indian-summer day in New England. In my imagination, I could smell the twin scents of leafy decay and a distant fire. Destiney was squealing with delight as she sat in a pile of leaves and tossed them skyward. They tumbled back down, and rested on the pink hood that covered her curly hair. She smiled and revealed a gap in her top row of teeth, a reminder to Shane and me that the tooth fairy needed to make a stop. Joey and Cody stood nearby, bunches of leaves in their hands, ready to attack their mom and me. I licked my lips and I could taste the last bit of sweetness from the caramel apple I'd just eaten.

That vision, pleasant as it was, was not enough to hold off the reality that stood before us: Perched on the hillside was what appeared to be a very large birdcage constructed out of a few posts supporting a cube of barbed wire. If Camp Caribe had a prisoner-of-war detention-camp aura, then this rustic wood-and-wire hooch was something out of a Halloween house of horrors. I knew, but did not want to believe, that anyone could expect a single human being, let alone three of them, to live in that figment of someone's demented imagination brought to life on a scarred patch of land in Colombia. I thought of the fact that we were in the Macarena Mountains and the silly dance craze of the same name that briefly had America's in its grasp—this thing had to be someone's idea of a joke.

Milton escorted us to the gate, and when we refused to go in, he nudged us inside with the butt of his AK-47. It was approximately eighteen by eighteen by eight, topped with barbed wire and black plastic sheeting. The guards set our foam mattresses down. We kept our *equipos* on our backs, not so subtly signaling our intention to, as Keith would say, "beat feet" out of there. We asked Milton what the deal was, and at first, instead of saying anything, he bared his teeth and made a clawing motion.

"*Tigres,*" he said. He went on to explain that big jungle cats could climb over most any fence. "They come in. They eat you."

Keith and Tom started laughing at him. Milton grew furious and stormed out. We knew that there were jungle cats in Colombia—the FARC had even killed a jaguar that had invaded one of our camps during the forty-day march. But to claim that predators were the reason they built this torture chamber was just ridiculous.

We spread our mattresses on the floor. Keith was in the middle and Tom and I flanked him. We had about six inches between us, and a roughly six-by-twelve area at our feet. We decided that keeping the beds in one area instead of spreading them out around the room maximized the limited space we had. Going from the high of anticipating our release to being housed in a barbed-wire cube was a real punch in the gut. Faced with no choice, we settled in.

As with previous camps, we had no idea how long we were going to be there, but we based our assumptions on the formula that the amount of effort to build it equaled the longer period of time we were going to remain there. It wasn't always an accurate equation, since any intense heat from aircraft usually put us back on the move. Still, we figured at the very least we would mark the start of our third year in captivity in our new birdcage. Even though we had far less space than we'd ever had and we were once again reduced to calling for a guard to let us out every time we needed to use the *chaunto* or slit trench to defecate or the pit hole to urinate, we got by with the coping skills we'd picked up along the way. It seemed as if the more adverse the conditions, the better we all got along. Part of the reason for this was the realization that if we'd been in pressure cookers before, we were now in a vacuum-sealed can. It was in none of our interests to cause trouble.

We also drew on the lessons we'd learned from our captivity thus far. Twentysomething months in, we were veterans of several hard marches and had just come off a tension-filled stay in Camp Caribe. With all this under our belts, we wanted life in the birdcage to be as stress-free as possible. The only time we were allowed outside our enclosure was when we bathed, and the water we were able to use for drinking and cleaning was a substantial improvement over the chocolate water we'd had in the lowlands. If things got tense, as they were bound to, we at least had a means to cool off, scrub clean, and not carry that tension into the next day.

For that reason, we also produced our own miniature versions of exercise equipment. Keith gathered sawdust and chips from the FARC's construction project and made a softer pad on which he ran in place for thirty minutes. I had a pull-up bar, and while at first I struggled to hoist myself up to my chin, gradually I was able to do multiple repetitions. I hadn't forgotten my idea of improving myself physically that I had developed all the way back at the New Camp, and our recent forced march had seen me shed, by my estimation, forty of the excess pounds that had my precrash weight at 190. I'd shed the weight, but I needed to put on muscle, and as the number of pull-ups increased, I could see the results and that motivated me further.

Tom did a bit of exercising, but without the ability to do his laps, he spent more time in his hammock doing his various "projects." Instead of motorcycle repair or airplane assembly, he tackled a house-building project. He also amassed a financial empire, beginning with resort hotels and establishing himself as a real estate mogul who could trump Trump.

We were also fortunate that gaining the trust of the guards began to pay dividends for us. The Plumber became the "getter" of this group of FARC. If you needed something, he would be able to get it for you. The currency in all the camps was cigarettes, and making deals for various supplies had occupied a lot of time when we were in Camp Caribe. Now that we were back to just the three of us and our sense of competition was duller, our economy took a serious nosedive. Fortunately, the Plumber had a radio that he was willing to lend us. At the hospital Tom had scrounged a roll of insulated copper wire that we were able to use as an antenna. We strung that all around the inside and outside of our hooch. The wire on the outside looked like our clothesline, so no one ever questioned us about it.

We resumed listening to the message shows, and Keith and I switched off nights. Tom's hearing wasn't good enough for him to listen to the shows at the necessary low volume to avoid detection. With the antennae wire hooked up to it and the sun down, we were able to pull in decent reception. We had all come to an agreement. Because the programs were on late at night into the early morning, we agreed that if a message came in for someone who wasn't awake, the listener's responsibility was to get the message in full and not risk missing any of it by running to wake up the intended recipient. That was crucial at that camp because we weren't supposed to have a radio and shouting about a message was a dead giveaway.

One Saturday night, I was on the radio when I heard the announcer say that they had a reporter from MTV news who had a message for one of the three Americans. He didn't say which of us, so I had to wait. It was well after midnight, and I was half dozing and half listening. When I heard the MTV reporter's voice, I immediately sprang up. At first, he was speaking in Spanish. My Harry Potter Spanish still wasn't great, so I struggled to get everything straight in my head. Then he switched to English. He said that he had talked to Lauren and Kyle and that Keith shouldn't worry. They were doing fine under the circumstances. He went on for a minute or so telling Keith that he hoped that he was still alive and well. He couldn't understand why people would do these things to one another and that he was deeply sorry for what had happened. He wanted the FARC to let the hostages go. He'd been traveling all around Colombia trying to get this message to Keith, and everywhere he went, people said the same thing—let the hostages free.

Lauren's voice came over the radio. I concentrated on what she was saying as she filled Keith in on Kyle and her. Her "we miss you" was heartfelt and touching. She loved him so much and couldn't wait to see him again. When she was through, I ran over everything in my mind. Our agreement was that we should wait until the morning to pass the message along, but this was like Christmas morning and I couldn't wait. I crawled next to Keith's bed and shook his shoulder to wake him. The jungle quieted, almost as if it wanted to hear what Lauren had to say. I whispered in his ear everything that I could remember of the message.

When I was through, Keith clasped his hand around the back of my neck and whispered, "Thank you, bro."

My eyes were brimming with tears. I was so happy for Keith and so happy that I'd been able to help bring him that gift. I knew that Lauren's message was special. Keith had always said that if there was anyone he could count on to come through for him, it was she. I also knew that the last message Keith had gotten was during our first weeks at Camp Caribe. The hit-and-miss nature of getting the messages aside, more than a year without any contact was a long time no matter how you looked at it.

For days after that, Keith's pleasure was visible. Every time he thought of Lauren's message, it was as if he'd gotten a sudden jolt of energy throughout his system. Keith had what he referred to as his library of memories and he put that one on a prominent, easy-to-access shelf. Every day he would walk into that library and select a pleasant place, person, or event to revisit—from his childhood, from his life with his kids, moments with his siblings and parents. I got the feeling that Lauren's message was one he checked out regularly.

The same was true of me. I was deeply touched by Lauren's message, and knowing that it had come to one of the three of us was the same as if it had been for me. The fact that I'd done something to help my friend was a powerful thing. I returned to those moments and those sensations often.

Whether by plan or coincidence, at times it seemed as if the FARC were diabolically clever. Just when we hit a high, they did something to knock us back down. A few nights later, we heard on the news that the U.S. had made arrangements with Colombia to have Simón Trinidad extradited there to eventually stand trial. President Uribe announced that if the FARC didn't want this to happen, they needed to release all their prisoners immediately. We knew that was never going to occur anytime soon. The only response that we heard from the FARC was a rumor, but one that was believable enough to send us hurtling downhill from the Lauren high: The FARC were going to hold all the hostages for the same length of time as the sentence Trinidad received. We didn't know the formal charges against him, but it seemed possible that he could receive a life sentence.

A week after the Trinidad news, Mono, who had become one of the more decent guards, came to us with an offer. He told us that he had been wandering in the jungle and came across an abandoned camp where he found a few Spanish-language magazines. Keith said that we would love to have them. With the exception of Tom's copy of *The General in His Labyrinth* by Gabriel García Márquez, we had shed all of our reading materials on the forty-day march. (In another gesture of kindness, Cereal Boy had found the copy of the book that Tom had discarded on the march and returned it to him when the march was over.) Mono said that he would get them for us so long as we promised to keep them hidden.

That we didn't rat him out after he brought us the magazines built up Mono's confidence in us. He began to open up to us, telling us his life story. He'd started out as a cow thief, then he joined the militia before becoming a full-fledged guerrilla. Mono was a bright kid and handsome, with definite European features. He was also completely into the macho thing and wore his rifle everywhere he went. He spoke with an obviously deliberate, lowered tone to his voice. It was funny and sad at the same time, like a kid playing a man in a high school play.

One evening when Mono was on guard duty, we were talking about the FARC policy of kidnapping and hostage taking as a political tool. We explained to him that if they really believed they were involved in a civil war, then those actions violated the Geneva Conventions. We went on to say that all it did was earn them ill will in their country and around the world. Mono didn't put up an argument. Instead he told us that for a while his duty assignment was in the kidnapping and ransoming units. They referred to those victims as economic hostages. He told us that the FARC had a law, law 001, which stated that if a person had more than a certain amount of money and didn't pay their "taxes" to the FARC, they would take that person hostage. The FARC would hold that person until someone paid the negotiated ransom. If the family wouldn't pay, then the hostage had to be executed.

"Mono," I said to him, "you're a bright guy. How could you think that a law that says you should kill other people is justified?"

Mono paused. "There are those who take and those who get taken from."

"Have you ever been a part of an execution?" Tom asked.

Mono sat up a bit straighter. "I have seen them. I've done one."

Keith asked, "How did you do it?"

"The prisoner was tied up and led to a space where a hole had been dug. As soon as the prisoner saw the hole, he cried. They always cry. I told the prisoner to get into the hole, but just as prisoners always cried, they always refused to do as ordered." Mono sounded as if he couldn't understand why the person he had to execute would do either of those things—cry or refuse an order, delaying death. "When I finally got the man into the hole, I put the gun to the prisoner's head and pulled the trigger. Then I buried the man."

We all sat in silence for a few moments. "How did that make you feel?" I asked.

"I really didn't want to do it," Mono said, lighting a cigarette, "but my comrades were all watching, and if I didn't do it, I would be ashamed. I had to do it in the spirit of the revolution or they would kill me."

We liked Mono and we liked what he could do for us, but the cold indifference of that story revealed, if not his true nature, then what he had been transformed into by the FARC. We didn't say a lot to Mono. We hadn't thought of him as a killer, but he was. I added to my library a sobering reality—new, unbearably grim images of ways I could possibly die.

To combat those fears, I sat and watched the Plumber whittling a piece of wood while guarding us. He used his knife to transform the stick into a cylinder and then into a spinning top. I'd taken a variety of shop classes and thought I was pretty decent at working with my hands. I asked him if he could get me a piece of wood; whittling and carving seemed like good ways to keep my mind occupied. The next day he brought me a piece of wood and his knife. He asked me to whittle it into a cylinder. He supervised the operation and was pleased with my work and I was happy to have something to do.

I didn't think that my skills were good enough yet to work on a detailed scale, so I asked the Plumber for a short log—about a foot in length. We'd asked for a chess game and never gotten one, so I decided to carve a pawn. I needed something simple that I could carve and a pawn wasn't that much different from the cylinder I'd made for the Plumber. I spent the day whittling and carving. After I returned the knife at the end of the day, I showed it to Tom and Keith. They looked at me. They looked at my project. Keith just shook his head, and when I looked objectively at what I'd done, I could see that my pawn looked more like a primitive fertility idol than a chess piece.

Using my rusty drafting skills, I drew out my vision of a pawn. My drawing was to scale, but I wasn't completely satisfied. In one of the magazines Mono had stolen for us, there was an article about a brilliant young Russian woman. She was supersmart but also a beautiful model. She was going to be in Colombia. One photo of her showed her sitting in front of a chess set. I decided to copy the style of those pawns. I did my drawing and then began carving. Over the course of the following two days, I finished my first chess piece. I showed it to Tom and Keith and got no wisecracks, just the answer I'd wanted, "Now that's a pawn."

Over the next three months, I carved more. I tried not to think of the significance of carving chess pieces, in particular pawns, but I was reminded of that irony while I was working on my fifth one. There had been somewhat limited aircraft activity throughout our stay in the birdcage. One night, about five months into life at the birdcage, an aircraft came into our airspace and began circling our location. We received word to evacuate the camp and head up the hill. In the dead of night, we heard several people shouting, *"¡Ningunas luces! ¡Ningunas luces!"* No lights. It didn't make sense to any of us that we were heading to a high point. If the aircraft had any infrared gear on board, they'd pick up our heat signals so much easier if we were in a clearing—especially if we all huddled up. But the FARC had no idea what they were doing, and their confusion was evident. They were insistent that we remain in the clearing, and so, forced to hold our position, the three of us spread out as best we could.

In the distance, we could hear the heavy thump of high-caliber gunfire, but it was too far away to be directed at us. The familiar sound of a Fantasma gunship tracking and flying orbits around a target rang out. We heard a supply truck driving and then the sound of its motor was replaced by the screaming of the Fantasma and its guns. The noises were in the distance, but they weren't getting closer. It seemed that luckily for us the pilots had located a different target than our camp.

Once the Fantasma broke off, we headed down the hill and talked some more about the attack. We were glad that we hadn't heard Black-hawks. What we'd survived wasn't a much-feared rescue attempt; the

Colombians had made no effort as far as we knew to put men on the ground. But now our eyes had been opened to a new risk that we added to our ever-growing list: being mistakenly caught in a gunship raid.

Milton decided that the attack was too close for comfort and gave orders for us to pack up. We headed out that same night, and walking down the hill into the jungle, none of us turned back for a last look at our barbed-wire cage.

TEN

Getting Healthy

May 2005–November 2005

KEITH

After two weeks of marching and setting up temporary camps, in mid-May of 2005, we came to another abandoned FARC camp. We could tell that this one dated back to the FARC's glory days simply because it was still standing. When the FARC had their DMZ, they weren't constantly on the run, so their camps were more or less permanent settlements. The camp was just a variation on what we'd seen over the years—a kitchen was dug out and topped by a tin roof, the other buildings were constructed of *tablas*, most were open-sided or at least partially so. They had constructed more than the usual number of benches and low tables and things. Unlike Caribe, there were no guard towers or a fence, and that always made any camp feel less threatening. That was soon to change.

After we'd left the barbed wire camp, Milton had sent a small group back to dismantle everything. He was under orders to leave no trace of our presence. Milton became increasingly fanatic about our doing everything possible to make it difficult for the Colombian military to track us. He seemed to have no qualms about stomping around in the jungle hunting, but if any of us snapped a twig, broke a branch, or otherwise made a sound or left some indication that we had been through the area, he would yell and threaten us. Meanwhile, Milton didn't stop long enough to realize that shooting a couple of monkeys and dragging their corpses through the jungle was going to leave a trail.

As vigilant as he was about obeying orders not to leave a trace, he also lacked follow-through, and this was one time when we were grateful for the general slothfulness of the FARC. The work detail that had gone back to dismantle our previous camp had taken apart our barbed-wire hell cage, but they were too lazy to bring the rolls of barbed wire back with them to our new camp. As a result, our hooch was made of wood again and so was the fence they put up to enclose us. Though we had only a little more space than at the previous camp, not being caged in barbed wire was good for us mentally and materially—we each had torn holes in just about everything we had—clothes, hammocks, plastic sheets, and tent tops—in brushes against that braided steel.

Though the absence of barbed wire was helpful, Milton once again placed our wooden hooch on a slope. That may not sound like a big deal, but it was. None of us enjoyed sleeping on an angle, not to mention the fact that when it rained, water would rush downhill and flood the hooch. As we usually did when dealing with the idiocy and arbitrary cruelty of the FARC, we overcame it. In the first couple of weeks after our arrival, we hauled in enough dirt to level our small area. That made it much easier for us to walk around and to exercise. We asked our guards for shovels, and they provided them. When Milton found out about our little excavation and landscaping project, he was pissed—at us and at his guys for helping us. If the entire camp wasn't supposed to be leaving any trace, a big patch of dirt large enough to accommodate three sleeping spots and three men would definitely alert the government it was us who had been there.

This was just one of several instances we witnessed when the underlying tension between Milton and the guards started to boil to the surface. There was a definite crack being exposed and we moved to exploit it as best we could. Like us, a number of the FARC saw Milton for what he was—a simpleton and a petty tyrant. He wasn't the only one obsessed with hunting, but he was the only one who seemed to think that the fewer supplies we had, the better. Every now and then the Front commander Efren would show up to find out what our group needed. Milton would reply, "Nothing." When he did that we could see the low-level guys beginning to fume. There was a laundry list of necessities and extras they would have loved to have. Maybe Milton thought that traveling light was a good thing because the heat on us meant we were going to be on the move a lot. What he didn't realize, or didn't seem to care about, was that an army travels on its stomach. If he had kept his guys happy and better fed and outfitted, they would have been more loyal to him.

That said, there was never the potential for mass mutiny, but there were several occasions when a guerrilla opened up and said something that explicitly revealed the level of discontent among the ranks. At first, those complaints were just general remarks. One guerrilla explained his feelings by tapping his foot and saying, "Milton commands with his foot and not his head." He meant that two ways: First, Milton had his boot up his guys' asses all the time. He was a strict but random disciplinarian who played big-time favorites. That upset his guys more than anything else. Second, all these marches and temporary camps were getting to them. Rather than think strategically, Milton just seemed to have them and us running around all over. There may have been a strategy, but they couldn't see it; and given the fact that he was not renowned for his intelligence, chances were he couldn't see it, either.

Grunts in every outfit feel like they're not being told what is going on and the brass has no clue. If you're a good leader and your guys respect and trust you, then that's not much of an issue. There will always be a few malcontents no matter what. But as far as we could tell, there was widespread questioning of purpose and a dislike for this duty. On the forty-day jaunt after Caribe, we saw that the guerrillas didn't like the forced marches any more than we did. Now that seed of discontent had blossomed.

Like all the rest of the older FARC leaders, Milton had a young woman as his partner. Natalia was a short and squat girl who seemed to do little except tend to Milton's needs. A number of times guards grumbled to us and we overhead them complaining to one another: Natalia gets the best shampoo, candy, and clothes. Natalia does none of the work. She was the laziest. She got the best hours for guard duty. What the FARC grunts didn't seem to understand—but what we picked up on immediately—was that the guy who was officially the number two man in these camps really wasn't. It was always the leader's woman who unofficially assumed the role. She was the one who handled most of the communications with the radio; she was the one who really managed the day-to-day operations of the camp's cooking and provisioning. She had people under her, the *economista,* who did the work supplying the kitchen, and the *racionista,* who was in charge of distributing the food. Natalia oversaw those positions, and if nobody had respect for the boss, then they weren't going to have respect for the boss's girlfriend. Natalia didn't help her cause by being a bitch with a nasty tongue and an I'm-cool-and-you're-not attitude.

There were definite cliques among the guerrillas. Our "friendly" guards—the Plumber, Mono, and Alfonso—also had women and they were the power couples out there. At some points, morale deteriorated among the FARC to the point that those three talked openly with us about their plan to kill Natalia. They wanted to drown her and say that either she was bathing and drowned or that she wandered off and a big

cat must have gotten her. As appalled as we were by the idea of murder (my one-less-is-a-good-thing principle still held even though I was
appalled), we couldn't believe that they were willing to tell us about it.
They finally settled on a plan to drag her off to a deep part of the river
and tie her up and put stones around her to keep her body from floating to the surface. We knew that the FARC had little regard for human
life, and this murder plot just reinforced that idea in capital letters and
underlined it.

More important, we also knew that we could exploit this rift to our
advantage and we did. Sometimes, however, we did set aside strategic
advantages in the name of humanity. Eliécer was one such case.

One day, he was sitting nearby on guard duty and he said to us: "You
know, you guys, I'm not in agreement with this."

We looked at him and said, "What?," wondering if he was telling us
ahead of time about some decision that had been handed down regarding our fate. Were we going to be shot or something?

He dug at the ground with the heel of his boot.

"I don't believe that we should take hostages. I know this is wrong.
I'm sorry. A number of the other guys, they also don't believe in kidnapping, but there's nothing any of us can do about it. We have no
choice. If we dissent or do anything to oppose the orders from above,
we'll be killed."

We paused for a moment to chew on his words. While guards often
made passing remarks about not liking our imprisonment, they very
rarely seemed as genuine as Eliécer. He didn't say it, but we understood
this much as well: He was willing to do whatever he could to help us as
long as it didn't get him killed or in trouble.

Eliécer broke the silence.

"Keith, I don't want to be here anymore."

Marc and I looked at each other to confirm that we were thinking
the same thing. This guy wasn't talking about deserting; he was talking about offing himself. Here was one of the only decent humans

in this place and he was talking about killing himself. That was what the FARC did to its own, that was its gift to its members. If you had a conscience, it seemed your only option out of the madness was to end it all. Eliécer had a strong enough sense of self to know that what they were doing was wrong. He recognized that he was being abused and asked to do inhumane things to others. Unfortunately for him, he was also smart enough to realize that there were few choices left for him. He'd been trapped for so long, he could no longer fathom the idea of freedom. What made things worse was that he'd probably never even known it to begin with. He was essentially a slave, and the fact that he'd realized this made his life that much harder.

My one-less-is-a-good-thing rule was completely out the window at that point. I walked to the fence.

"What are you talking about? Look at us. I mean, look at our future and what it holds for us. You'll never see us want to give up living."

Hearing yourself saying words out loud that you didn't even want to think was tough—that he had a better chance of getting out of there than we did, that he just had to make the choice to go. We were worried about him, and for the next few nights we listened to hear if he was in a bad way. A few days later, he was on duty to bring us our morning coffee and food. He looked like shit. His eyes were bloodshot and red-rimmed like he'd been on a two-day alcohol bender, and the bags under his eyes seemed big enough to pull his entire body down.

The next time we got a chance to speak, he said a lot of the same things. He was tired of being worked like a dog. He just wanted to be released or sent to a farm where he could do work that didn't kill him. He just couldn't take it anymore. For the rest of our stay there, it went like that. With each day that passed, we worried even more about the guy. He didn't get much better, but he was at least able to keep slogging away. I hoped he would be able to hold out until some other option presented itself.

Another guy whom we connected with over Milton's oppressiveness was Cereal Boy. He was one of the more educated guys out there. He could read and write and he taught some of the others the same skills. Of all the FARC we dealt with, he was the most inquisitive. One morning he was on guard duty and sat reading a Spanish-language magazine called *Most Interesting*. He started asking us about the U.S. space program and in particular about the Apollo missions. As we talked, it came out that he didn't believe that the U.S. had sent men to the moon. I had been raised in South Florida and Tom lived near Cape Canaveral. We tried to explain to Cereal Boy what a rocket was, how large the ones used for moon missions were, what kind of fuel they used as a propellant, how satellites worked and helped to transmit signals, as well as all the things you could see at the museum there. I told him that I'd seen actual rocks from the moon, and he just stared at me in disbelief, saying I couldn't have.

Marc, Tom, and I must have talked for close to an hour, with all three of us trying to get him to understand the basic ideas behind the space program. He was completely blown away. To his credit, he was trying to learn. He loved listening to the radio and kept a notebook with him and took notes all the time. He liked history and would write down all kinds of dates and trivia. He would come up to us and ask questions like, "Is it true Theodore Roosevelt wrote a book on naval history when he was in college?" or "Did you know John F. Kennedy swam twice a day in a pool in the White House?"

I'd try to think of topics related to his questions, and it was good for me to exercise my brain in that way. Trying to remember other details and facts was like lifting mental weights. We were talking about diplomacy one day, and thinking of his question about Roosevelt, I told him about America's Great White Fleet. I detailed the story of how Roosevelt issued an order sending a United States Navy battle fleet—four battleships and their escorts—around the world. Their hulls were painted white to show our neutrality, but it also demonstrated to everyone our growing American military power and blue-water navy capability.

Roosevelt wanted to let other nations know that we would stay out of their business, but if someone crossed a line, we could be there.

With this story, the class switched from history to current events, as Cereal Boy started talking about how we were interventionists. Just as it was easier for him to say we didn't go to the moon, it was easier for him to believe what had been pumped into his head by the FARC. I tried to explain to him that the world was a lot more complicated than that, and while I couldn't undo all of the FARC's hard work with my facts, at least Cereal Boy was willing to acknowledge a point of view that was different from the FARC's. That was more than you could say for most of our guards.

One reason why some of the guerrillas felt more comfortable than ever before in talking to us was that we were farther away from their camp than normal. A fairly steep little ravine separated us—it was about fourteen feet deep and the FARC had to build a small log bridge to span it. We were a few hundred yards away from them, so you really had to look long and hard to see into our camp and vice versa. This was just another example of Milton's stupidity and the FARC's overall laziness and lack of oversight.

In spite of the distance, our growing associations with the guards didn't go unnoticed by Milton himself. A few months into our stay at this camp—what we called the Exercise Camp—Mono came up to me and said, "I just want you to know that if I ever said anything bad about you, I did it because I had to."

With a little bit of information from the other guards, we were able to figure out that Milton had held a meeting with his crew to discuss the prisoner situation. He accused some of his guys of respecting us more than they did him. We knew that a small number of them did and that even those who didn't respect us more had little respect for their leader. In order to cover their asses, these guys had to say bad things about us in the meeting. Some of our camp intel channels closed up for a bit, but at least no one ratted us out about the radio the Plumber had given us back at the original birdcage. They all seemed to be happy to believe that the thick six-gauge wire we had running around our beds, out the roof of our hooch, and around our little "yard" was really just clothesline—red, insulated copper-wire clothesline.

Milton's official number two was Rogelio, who was also disliked by the other guards and whom the three of us decided was just nuts. One of the more volatile personalities we had to contend with, Rogelio was the *racionista,* so if you wanted anything, you had to ask him for it. There was no pattern to his behavior and no reliable pattern of logic for which requests he would grant and which he would deny. One week you might ask him if it was possible to have more noodles at dinner and you'd be met with the response: "No. Starve. I don't care." The next day a cow might have been slaughtered, and before lunchtime, Rogelio would bring you big steaks that he'd cooked himself.

If the fact that he acted bat-shit crazy most of the time wasn't enough, he was also hard to communicate with in general. He talked about 250 words a minute in the most garbled Spanish any of us had ever heard and he had the annoying habit of sucking his teeth all the time. Combine the three—talking way too fast, being a mush mouth, and sucking his teeth—and you've got somebody who's hard to talk to in any language. Throw into that mix eyes like a windup toy dog and a high-pitched screech of a laugh and you've got one seriously messed-up dude to deal with.

Marc and Tom would split every time Rogelio came around, so it was left to me to deal with him. I figured the guy was the number two, he was the one who provided us with whatever it was we needed, so it was worth putting up with him. In a lot of ways, it was like being nice to the weird kid in school and letting him sit at your lunch table one time.

In the aftermath of his crackdown on the guards for talking to us, Milton instituted a policy whereby a guard had to escort us to wherever we wanted to go outside of our enclosure—including to the bathroom trenches. Nobody liked the policy, including the FARC. It meant that one of them had to trek the couple of hundred yards to their camp and back. Rogelio was the one most responsible for us, so he was always nearby whenever we had to answer one of nature's calls.

It wasn't anyone's ideal, but we tolerated it. Just one more bit of insanity that we had to put up with if we wanted to keep our security level status quo. We'd made too many inroads to have everything shut down completely, so we did what we could to avoid kicking up too much dust.

MARC

After we left the barbed-wire birdcage and were heading toward our current camp, we had to walk along another of the winding mountain roads that the FARC had gouged into the countryside. All along this particular road, we saw junk scattered at various intervals. Most of the piles had been there for quite a while—they were dust-covered and anything organic had rotted and decayed. Down below the piles the jungle thickened and the paths that led into that particular section of vegetation and trees disappeared in the dense foliage.

Tom named this particular route the Road of Misery. He pointed out that each pile was likely left from a FARC camp that once held hostages like us. Or it was from a drug lab. Or kidnap victims had been held there just before Mono or someone like him ended those captives' lives. It was hard not to feel sad, especially when we thought of the hundreds and hundreds of hostages in Colombia. We knew we weren't the only ones on the march on that day or at that hour. It was a sobering thought, but it also made us want to do whatever we could to be sure that we didn't end up discarded and mourned.

As we'd shown during the helo incidents in Caribe and at the birdcage, if we were going to escape the FARC or survive a rescue and the FARC's deadly response to it, we had to have the mental and physical strength to execute our own plan for surviving. Planning was the one aspect of escape and survival that we felt confident of. We knew that circumstances and the way other people responded to them were for the most part out of our control. What we could control, and what we needed to have command of, was our minds and bodies. We needed the physical strength to be able to move quickly and possibly defend ourselves. We never considered overpowering the guards as a group, but if we were in a situation in which we had to engage one of them in order to escape or avoid execution, it was best to be prepared. Also, if we did manage to escape on our own or in the middle of a rescue, we would have to survive in the jungle and be as strong as possible physically to get to someplace where we could then be rescued.

With this in mind, we branded our current camp the Exercise Camp. When we arrived there, we were in better shape than we had been immediately after the forty-day march, but that wasn't saying much. We had been so depleted during that bit of hell that even the relatively small amount of exercise we were able to do in the barbed-wire cage had improved our fitness level. We were nowhere near where we wanted to be or needed to be.

To compensate, we set up our own little jungle gym—carrying over some of the basic ideas we'd had at the barbed-wire cage. Creating a pull-up bar was always the easiest task. All we needed was a piece of wood long enough to span two trees with low branches. We could also put a branch between two parts of the hooch that would support our weight. With the help of guards who were willing to give us the tools and supplies we needed, we also built a double-step that we could walk or run up and down on to improve our cardiovascular fitness. Milton was going nutty complaining about us wearing a path that could be detected, so our walking regimen had to be curtailed a little bit. The stepper was a tougher workout, and Tom and I both had knee pain, so stairs weren't the best thing for us—at least at the beginning.

I found that the more I used the stepper and the stronger the muscles in my legs became, the less my knees hurt. I also used the physical training as a way to give structure to the day, to pass some time, and to relieve stress. We all talked about how after exercise we experienced the rush of endorphins that some people refer to as the runner's high.

I used to talk all the time about us being like lab rats in a maze. Well, those same lab rats, when they weren't being used in experiments, lived their lives in small cages. So did we. I didn't realize until captivity how important and freeing it was just to walk out of my house, get in the car, and go to work. I didn't understand that at my previous intel job, getting up and going to the watercooler, the restroom, the break room, or anywhere else provided me with a little change in the routine and some exercise. Movement meant freedom, and if we had been shackled physically and completely prevented from moving except when the FARC allowed us to, I don't know how I could have endured it. As it was, we went far more places and ranged more freely in our minds than we did physically. We talked about those moments when we were so engaged in a conversation or were each taking on a task in our minds or revisiting a memory. At those times, we were beyond the walls of the hooch. At those times, we were free.

Exercise did that for us as well. We each had our own routines and sometimes we worked out together and sometimes we did our own thing, but at the Exercise Camp, we all focused on our physical fitness in a way we hadn't before. If the forty-day march had done nothing else for us, it made us realize that we never wanted to be in that weakened condition again. None of us wanted to repeat the agony of having every single footstep be an act of torture. As it is for anybody starting to work out, it was hard at first to get motivated, but once we got going on it for a while, we started to really look forward to getting up in the morning to work out. It also helped that we started to set goals for ourselves. Tom got into lifting weights more than at any other time in his life. Keith got into the stepping thing, and started out by saying he wanted to do thirty minutes a day. Once he reached that level and was able to achieve that goal regularly and easily, he upped it to thirty-five. By the time we left the Exercise Camp, he was doing fifty minutes a day pretty regularly.

The other good thing about setting up our gym was that it was a definite do-it-yourself project—a Jungle Depot special. We had to build the bench we used for bench pressing. Of course, we needed to borrow tools and materials from the guerrillas, but we did all the work ourselves. That activity gave us exercise, a sense of accomplishment, and a purpose each day. When it came time to build the barbells for the bench press, squats, and military press, we all pitched in. It felt good not to be the lone carver. We took a fairly stout log, one that was six inches or so around, and whittled away at it so that the bar was down to about an inch around and the ends were still the original diameter. It took us a week or two to accomplish this, but we all chipped in. Again, we sometimes worked alone on it, and sometimes we worked together, but they were "our" weights. When we got stronger and wanted a heavier barbell, we did the same thing with a larger log. We jokingly called it our *Flintstones* gym, but we also took pride in having done it ourselves.

None of us had ever been a gym rat before, but we figured out a good approach to working out. One day I would focus on my upper body with pushing exercises—bench press, military press, and push-ups. The next day it would still be upper body, but pulling exercises like curls and pull-ups. The day after that was the lower body, with squats and abdominal work like sit-ups and crunches. We all set goals for ourselves and these were something crucial to staying positive. We had only one long-term goal—of getting home again, but we also needed to keep focused on the everyday and the short term as well.

This didn't apply just to our physical work but to our mental and emotional efforts. Writing in journals still occupied some of our time, as did learning Spanish and reading. Sergeant César Augusto Lasso had given me a Bible while at Caribe, and my goal was to read it from start to finish. It was a Gideon Bible, the New Testament only, and half of the books were in English and half were in Spanish. From the moment I got it, I read a few passages every day. Keith started to read it along with me. I found strength and freedom in that book and in those stories as well.

Before I was taken hostage, sometimes my faith felt like a burden. I thought of it in terms of things that I had to do (go to church) and restrictions (don't lie or swear) instead of what it could do for me and what it allowed me to do. At the Exercise Camp, I really came to see just how my faith had allowed me to grow stronger. I wouldn't have been able to find the resolve and determination to exercise my body if it hadn't been for all the work I was doing on my soul at the same time. My prayers and daily Bible reading gave me the mental strength I needed to keep pushing myself.

Part of our mental planning at the Exercise Camp involved doing what was necessary to avoid being placed in chains. We'd seen how the military prisoners had to endure that indignity and that physical strain. We were continually aware of the risk chains held during an attack or rescue attempt. The time it might take during a rescue attempt to untangle a chain or maneuver around an obstacle could be enough to keep us from meeting our goal of surviving to return home. One of the main reasons why we preached to ourselves that it was okay to put up with some of the garbage from the FARC in exchange for earning their confidence was so that the chains would never come out.

Besides chains, the other thing that the FARC could do to punish us was to increase the amount of security on us. None of us wanted that. In the case of a rescue, and if the FARC came after us to execute us, the fewer number of guards we had around us, the better.

The fact that some of the guerrillas were providing us with information was also important to how we prepared ourselves for any possible rescue or escape situation. Through them, we learned that the Exercise Camp was very near the town of Santo Domingo in the Vista

Hermosa municipality of the Meta department. We'd passed by Santo Domingo once before and now we knew we were on the east side of the Andes, very near the center of the country. Based on what we'd heard on Colombian radio, the department's capital, Villavicencio, was a haven for refugees fleeing the FARC and the conflict. Though none of us was certain where the capital was in terms of location, we at least had a definite destination in mind, and that was a lot more than we'd ever had before. From the intelligence reports we read when we were flying missions, we knew that vast areas of Colombia were FARC controlled. If we did escape, we needed to be sure that we wouldn't fall right back into the hands of our enemy.

We'd already seen how all these concerns were tied together. Throughout our time at the Exercise Camp, there were nearly nightly flyovers by the Fantasmas. One day in May of 2005, we heard the distinctive sound of a Fantasma approaching.

"Here we go again," Keith said.

"It's roundup time." Tom grabbed a few of his things and we all stood waiting for the guards to lead us out. We were herded down the steep slope of the ravine into what we assumed was a safe hiding spot. We couldn't be spotted easily in the ravine, but escape from the FARC in case of a rescue was next to impossible. Scrambling up that rock-strewn ravine would have been next to impossible no matter how hard we were working out.

"Let's check out the action." I nodded toward the Plumber, who was nearby with a radio scanner.

We were all hunkered down with our backs resting on the walls of the ravine, kind of like I'd seen GIs doing in a fox hole. The Plumber didn't mind us listening to the radio transmissions he was able to intercept.

We sat there for a minute listening to the Fantasma pilot reporting back to his command center.

"These guys are sounding more and more professional every time,"

Keith said, and tossed a small rock against the opposite-side wall. A few loose stones cascaded down.

"Just a routine mission," Tom said. "Sounds like just another day at the office."

We continued listening as the pilot reported his coordinates. Then something changed in the pitch of his voice and the speed of his words. He was excited about something, but trying to keep command of his voice.

"He's talking to somebody else now," I said. "He's not going back to command."

A few seconds later, we could hear above us what was going on. A Kfir jet was approaching.

"This is a whole 'nother ball game now." Keith stood to try to scan the sky above us, but all we were able to see was a relatively small slice.

"He's guiding him in. They better get their coordinates right," Tom said, an edge was in his voice because the Fantasma pilot was leading his Kfir into a bombing zone. We had no idea what the target was going to be, but they were definitely close to us, and it only took a few seconds' delay or a slight miscommunication for those bombs to miss their intended target by a quarter mile or more.

We looked at the Plumber and Tom said, "You're going to feel what we're talking about in a minute."

The Plumber frowned. We liked to show him and the other guards that we understood what was going on in the skies better than they did. A few seconds later, we felt the impact and heard the distinctive *crump* of a bomb making contact with the ground. That was followed by the explosion.

My heart was beating faster, but more in excitement than in fear. Knowing that the Colombian military pilots were nearby and doing damage to one FARC installation or another was a reason to feel good.

"Let's hope they're making good drops," Keith said. "I hate to think about innocents getting rained on."

I tuned in again to what was being said over the radio, and I felt, if not pride, then certainly satisfaction as the coordinated efforts of the two crews produced the desired results. At the tail end of the bombing, we heard the pilot of the Kfir state that they had destroyed the bridge. We were glad that the target wasn't another group of FARC. We still thought about the other hostages and their welfare.

"Good to know they're safe," I said.

"Let's hope so," Tom added.

Sitting there and praying that night, I realized that I wasn't as afraid as I had been before. I understood the risks and the options we had. I knew I had been preparing myself as best I could—mind, body, and spirit—for what might come. I took a lot of comfort in that.

I also came to understand that most of the FARC didn't have our ability to assess situations and devise plans. We sensed that with every-thing that was happening—daily and nightly flyovers, bombing runs, the general discontent between Milton and his guerrillas—some of them—not just Eliécer—wanted their freedom as much as we did. One evening the Plumber was on duty and he was talking about some of these issues very indirectly.

Keith looked at Tom and me and said, "Hey, guys. What do you think? I may ask the Plumber straight what he thinks about escaping."

We agreed that the risk to us was low, so Keith asked him, "Would you be willing to get us out of here if we told you we could help you?"

"Yes." The Plumber's face lit up and then darkened just as quickly. He paused. "Tell me more about what I've heard. Is the U.S. serious about providing a reward if we surrender ourselves?"

"That's what I've heard," Tom said. "They can help you with visas, put you in witness protection. No one would hurt you."

"What about my family?" the Plumber asked.

Keith shrugged. "I don't know everything there is to know about immigration, but if you were to help us get free, all kinds of doors would open for you."

The offer was legitimate as far as we knew and a lot of the guerrillas talked about it.

We were feeling pretty good about the Plumber's willingness until we heard his plan. "We would have to kill everyone else in the camp. That's the only way. If any of them survive, we would be tracked down and I would be killed."

Tom, Keith, and I exchanged glances. Keith's face said it all. The guy didn't really have a "plan" or a strategy. We didn't have a problem with that morally, but we did have a problem with it strategically. The Plumber had one AK-47. There were nineteen other FARC guerrillas with us. Earlier in our captivity, we had learned from our more friendly guerrillas that if we tried to escape and no FARC got hurt, they were under direct orders to track us down and return us, but not to kill us. However, if we tried to escape, killed a guard in the process, and then got taken again, we'd be executed.

Fortunately, once the Plumber admitted that he was willing to escape, we could use this information to our advantage. The Plumber also told us which guards we could trust and which ones we couldn't. We weren't going to waste our time or energy trying to manage the ones we couldn't trust.

Milton was a guy we could always trust *not* to do the right thing. After one of the more serious Fantasma attacks—the helos came in during daylight and fired more aggressively and with more planes than ever before—we got out of the ravine. Milton was freaking out. He'd been wounded in an air assault once before, so he was especially frightened by airplanes. He had us all just run deeper into the jungle. We took no supplies; later, Milton sent some of his guerrillas back to our camp to retrieve things.

Two weeks after this, Milton ordered us back to the site of the Exercise Camp; we were too far from water, and he wanted to make life a little easier on everyone. When we got back, we saw that Milton had done something he'd promised he'd do to us if we didn't respect him and his guerrillas. He made our enclosure smaller. All the work we'd done creating a more level area was undone, but as soon as we moved back in, we started leveling it off again. With our smaller area and our stronger bodies, it took a lot less time to get the job done.

TOM

It seemed as if at every camp, there was a particular species of pest we had to deal with. Rogelio was one of them at the Exercise Camp. What was of more concern to us was that after two years of being in the jungle, we had all been afflicted with some kind of jungle illness or condition. Over time these all built up to take a collective toll on us.

Walking through the jungle, it was easy to get a cut or scratch. In the barbed-wire cage, we were constantly getting scratched up. It was there that Keith and I both developed leishmaniasis, a fairly common jungle disease, and though it makes you look like a leper, it isn't life-threatening—so long as you get treated. It's caused by a parasite that certain jungle flies carry. Those flies are attracted to open wounds; they transmit the parasite when they bite you, and you later develop open sores or ulcers that spread in size. Untreated, the sores continue to spread and multiply and can eventually endanger internal organs. Several months into our stay at the Exercise Camp, shortly after Eliécer had talked about suicide, I developed sores on my foot and hand, while Keith had one on his elbow.

In addition to being the *racionista,* Rogelio was, in defiance of all logic and common sense, our medic. He was a borderline sociopath, but he was the one we had to see to be checked out. He immediately told Keith he had "leish" and they started him on a course of treatment. He received intramuscular injections forty to fifty times to help clear it up. The FARC had easy access to a drug called glucantime since it was a fairly common problem.

Despite the fact that I had a spreading sore on my foot that looked exactly like Keith's, Rogelio and the "consulting physicians" decided I didn't have leish. I didn't get the injections and the sore spread and grew deeper and deeper. They just thought I had some rash and gave me antibiotics. Back at Caribe, we had heard from the military guys that it sometimes took as many as two hundred to three hundred doses of the injection to get rid of the stuff. Knowing this, I began to get worried and made more demands for the proper treatment. Those complaints fell on stupid ears. Finally, after the sore on my foot grew to the size of a silver dollar, I got the proper injections. Rogelio wasn't about to give in completely and do the right thing. Whenever he felt like it, he withheld the medication.

Going back a ways, Rogelio and I were on pretty bad terms. His ignorance got to me and I wasn't afraid to expose it. He was one of the FARC whom I would question a lot of the time when he spouted off propaganda, and that made things pretty adversarial. I'd press him, asking how they were going to take over the country. I'd tell him that they'd been at it for almost forty years, how could he think that they'd succeed now, when their numbers were dwindling? I also got to him by pointing out that sitting in the jungle holding us captive didn't seem to be doing much to advance their cause. He'd say something else that was crazy or unintelligible, suck his teeth, and twitch his eyes.

Because of the contentious dynamic between us, when I pressed him on the issue of the medicine, he pushed back. It started a cycle in which Keith would intervene, using his good relationship with Rogelio as leverage to get me what I needed. I'd then get my medicine until Rogelio decided to mess me up again. Things went on like this for a while, and during one argument, he even turned to Keith and said, pointing to me, "I don't care if the old man dies or not." I knew he meant it and I knew I felt the same way about him.

I didn't like Keith having to deal with Rogelio for me, but it seemed the only way to get him to cooperate. I'd had to deal with the same thing with my blood-pressure medications, and having this guy mess with my health was not something I could tolerate. I refused to let them think I was just going to lie down and allow them to control my health. The guard we had earlier in our captivity—the one called Smiley—had a bad case of leish and I saw what it did to him. It spread into a gaping wound. I was not going to let that happen to me. Finally, we worked out an arrangement so that I could get the injections I needed. Rogelio didn't want to deal with me and I didn't want to deal with him, so Keith gave me the injections.

Around the same time that I was battling Rogelio over the leish treatment, we came into contact with another jungle affliction, one that has no equivalent word in English: *chuchorros*. We were never sure what caused them. They were painful open sores that swelled and oozed pus. The sore was just the surface symptom. Somewhere deeper in your tissue, some kind of inflammation spread and you swelled up. It was like the wound on your skin was the cone of a volcano and that deeper inflammation in your flesh was the volcano's core. The *chuchorros* produced a deep, stinging pain. The only way to get rid of them was to squeeze the surrounding flesh. In some ways, the cure was worse than the pain of the infection or whatever caused the buildup of pus.

Of course, Rogelio was also in charge of alleviating *chuchorros*. The first time I saw one on someone it was Keith; it looked like he'd taken a .38-caliber round in the arm. The hole was perfectly shaped like an entry wound. When Rogelio came around and Keith pointed it out to him, Rogelio knew exactly what to do. With all his might, he squeezed the swollen flesh around the hole. His eyes were tearing with the strain and he was gasping for air—and he was the one doing the cure. After a few minutes of pushing and pressing, what looked like a cross between a slug and a slug—a bullet and the insect—popped out of the open wound. Rogelio wasn't done. He said that he had to get "the mother."

He pressed some more. Eventually a hard marble like a ball of hardened pus also came out.

Rogelio pronounced Keith fixed. The FARC didn't have any kind of ointments or liquids at that time, so they took the antidiarrhea medication they had and ground it into a powder, poured it into the wound, and slapped some tape over it. It seemed to us that Rogelio took particular pleasure in being the "popper," and perhaps for this reason, when Marc and I developed *chuchorros,* we didn't go to him. He didn't like either of us very much and we imagined that if he had worked so hard on Keith, he would really put it to us.

During our time at the Exercise Camp, we also came into contact with an ailment we'd encountered earlier in our captivity, something called a *nuche.* Again, we hadn't heard the word before and assumed it was part of a Colombian dialect and not something we'd find in a Spanish dictionary. A *nuche* was like a worm or a larva that was left by a certain type of fly. Similar to the *chuchorros,* except it didn't have a hard marblelike mother as its source. We assumed that whatever caused the swelling and wound was transmitted by a fly.

Nuche also produced a gunshot-type wound, around which the flesh would swell a bit and harden into a shape like a mushroom cap. The first time it happened to me I assumed it was just a pimple or an ingrown hair. When it grew in size and oozed a yellowish discharge for quite a while, I knew I had to get it checked out. This was back when we were with Sombra, who identified it and told me that he had a jungle cure for it. He asked me if I wanted him to use it. I figured if they'd been dealing with the problem for a while, he should know what he was doing, so I agreed to let Sombra treat me.

I sat in a chair and he sat next to me, lighting a cigarette as if we were gathered together for a chat. He took long lung-filling drags on it before exhaling into his cupped hand. He repeated that action until the cigarette was done and a dingy yellow smudge of nicotine was left in the palm of his hand. He rolled that around a bit until he had made a kind of paste, which he then rubbed into the wound. Taping it up, he told me to come back the next day.

When I did, he removed the tape and looked things over. He asked if I was ready and told me that if anything started to really hurt, he would back off. Sombra lit a cigarette and brought the lit end close to the wound. He put it as close as he could without burning me. He asked another guard to squeeze the area. In a few seconds, the guard held a translucent worm about an inch long and a quarter inch in diameter in his palm. The worm had been eating my flesh until the nicotine in the cigarette had made it sick, caused it to stop chewing, and forced it to release its jaws. The squeezing part was obvious.

When I got another *nuche* at the Exercise Camp, we replicated Sombra's cure, only with a little more care and attention paid to sterilizing the area. Keith served as the extractor. At one point, I had three *nuches* at a single time. He got them all out, but he squeezed with such force that one of them shot out of me; never to be found. After that, Keith became the expert in *nuche* removal, and we joked that one day he could hang out his shingle in Colombia and make good money.

As the months passed at the Exercise Camp, my issues with Rogelio spread beyond my health and his propagandizing. As much as I disliked Rogelio for the way he treated us, I disliked him even more because of his treatment of a girl named Vanessa, whom he was with. She was a very young woman who had no self-esteem. That was the only reason I could figure out for why she was with as despicable a character as Rogelio. What really puzzled me was that she was the only one of the FARC in camp who'd completed high school. Seeing her waste her life in the jungle with the FARC and with Rogelio really got to me.

The FARC had control over every aspect of the guerrillas' lives— including what passed for romantic relationships. Though we saw a lot of promiscuity and swapping of mates—you have to keep in mind that these were mostly teenagers and young adults in their early twenties—none of their official pairing off could be done without the approval of their superiors. If they wanted to be a couple, they had to get approval. The FARC weren't interested in increasing their numbers through childbirth. The women were given contraceptive pills, and if a woman did get pregnant, she would have to abort the fetus—no questions asked. This didn't stop the FARC guerrillas from engaging openly and frequently in sex. That, the FARC *comandantes* couldn't control, but in all other ways they allowed the guerrillas little freedom with their love lives.

Becoming closer to many of the guards at the Exercise Camp helped us to see how the FARC's tight restrictions on its foot soldiers set off a chain reaction that impacted us. Because they had so little command of their own lives and made so few choices for themselves, we were just about the only things that they could actually control. Even though they were never able to control us completely, the need to assert themselves over us had a lot to do with their cruel and arbitrary treatment. Knowing this didn't justify their actions, of course, but it did help explain them. It was easy, both literally and figuratively, to put myself in the boots of those low-level FARC every now and then. I didn't have to walk a mile in their shoes because I'd already done probably hundreds of miles in the ones they grudgingly supplied me. Even though the FARC refused to give me glasses for so long, I could see them clearly for what they were.

It was no secret that among the three of us, I was the most difficult for the FARC to deal with, and that was okay with me. If the only way I could confront their need to control me was by being standoffish, I was comfortable with it. We each had our different ways of coping with Keith's proverbial shitheads. Sometimes the way I engaged them came back to bite me, but I got back at them, as I knew I would in the end. I wasn't going to give in completely, and neither were Keith and Marc. I made my decision to cooperate with them on my terms, but we all went along with them in the larger sense because this would ultimately be a victory for us. We'd survive.

It was precisely this kind of big-picture thinking that evaded the FARC. Sometimes when we were trading with the guards, they'd take advantage of us in one way or another. There was always a steep learning curve for us as far as that went, but it was always easier to learn from our mistakes than to make a big fuss. The guards knew when they were giving you the short end of the stick on deals, and their guilt motivated them to help us in other ways. When we were on marches and in real need of something, like plastic bags to keep our gear dry in a torrential downpour, one of the guards would usually come through for all of us, including me. I think they just liked the idea of being able to exert some kind of power over us that was good for once.

If my being led astray in deals made them more likely to help us all out when it really mattered, then it was a sacrifice worth making. If my being on bad terms with most of the FARC meant that they would treat Keith or Marc better, then whatever I suffered didn't matter. If the FARC didn't want to give me my share of food or supplies, it was not a problem. The three of us had an unstated and never-violated policy of sharing everything as equally as possible. If my role was to be the bad guy, the old guy whom they didn't care if he lived or died, then so be it. In the long run, the more confidence they had in Marc and Keith, the better for all three of us. By being the focus of their anger and ill will, I could sometimes distract them. I knew how far to push things so that they never brought the heavy hammer down on me or the three of us. I guess in my own way I was just another jungle pest, hoping to get under their skin and eat away at their flesh a bit.

What the FARC never really understood was that we seldom did anything without a reason that benefited us. Even our more visceral reactions, raw and impulsive as they were, still retained something calculated and measured. At one time or another, we all lost our control when dealing with the cruel and unfair actions of the FARC, but we never lost sight of our goal: getting our freedom back.

If there was one thing that separated us from the FARC, besides barbed wire and wooden fences, it was that we knew how to plan long term. As much as were playing hopscotch across the Colombian countryside and were unable to figure out exactly where we were on the map, we were always able to think strategically and keep sight of our position on the game board.

ELEVEN

Dead

November 2005–May 2006

TOM

From our cage at the Exercise Camp, it was hard for us to see whether Plan Patriota was effective, but by November of 2005, we certainly knew that it was in full force. During the fall of 2005, we had heard the FARC doing a lot of road building, and that activity must have caught the attention of the Colombian military. By November, the OV-10 and Fantasma attacks that always spooked Milton intensified and became nightly occurrences. Milton had a special fear of the Fantasma, which he called "the Pig," but we knew better. Even though it didn't have the deadly weapons system capabilities of the Pig, in many ways the aircraft the FARC referred to as "the Cross" actually posed a greater threat to us.

What the FARC called the Cross was in fact a surveillance airplane manufactured by the Schweitzer Aircraft Corporation. Its long thin fuselage and thin gliderlike wings earned it its name. Schweitzer was known for manufacturing gliders and the Schweitzer SA2 we all spotted above us could easily be mistaken for one. With its long wingspan, it could stay aloft even after the pilot significantly cut power to its engine. A special muffler system further quieted the plane, making it nearly silent. Because it didn't have the distinctive whine of the Pig, didn't send rockets down to crater the earth, or spray bullets like the OV-10, the FARC underestimated its capability. Doing so would prove to be a deadly mistake. The FARC were afraid of missiles. We were afraid of the intelligence that the Cross produced and the rescue attempt or attack that might follow any detection of our location.

Our concern stemmed from the fact that we knew the Cross was outfitted with some of the most advanced surveillance equipment available. Because it could fly so slowly and had a FLIR system that enabled it to effectively penetrate the jungle, the pilot and operator could pinpoint targets with great accuracy. Those targets were then given to the pilots of the Pig and the Kfir interceptors and they executed the precision bombing runs that so frightened Milton. The FARC failed to connect the dots. If it weren't for the work of the Cross, the rocket attacks would not have been nearly as precise. President Uribe was not about to carpet-bomb the countryside. While he said that he would use blood and fire, instead he was using the microscope and the scalpel.

As 2005 drew to a close, we fled the Exercise Camp into the mountains, but we couldn't avoid one bit of news: Lucho and Ingrid had escaped. This led the guerrillas to tighten their security on us a bit, seizing our flashlights and increasing the number of guards on duty. We noticed one equipment change for the FARC. Many of them started carrying compasses. We could tell that we were marching north, but we made frequent stops so that Milton and his brain trust could consult their compasses. It was clear that they had no idea how to follow the heading they were given. The Plumber told us that they'd been instructed to follow a 010 heading—essentially due north. He also confirmed what we'd already figured out: Their trouble with the compasses had caused us to wander far off course during the first three days of what was to have been a five-day march. Every time we marched, no matter how far from that original 010 we'd wandered, we always resumed another 010 heading from that point. Instead of traveling in a straight line as instructed, it was like we were walking up a series of stairs. We might as well have been using an Etch A Sketch to navigate.

To make matters worse, Milton was up to his usual tricks, telling the others that he didn't need a compass, that he could navigate the jungle by using his head. (The only way we figured that would work was if there was still some shrapnel in his old head wound, and that shrapnel was magnetized.) Eventually, we were so lost that Milton sent out an advance scouting party of Mono and Alfonzo to find our destination.

Two days after our five-day march was supposed to end, we arrived at an older camp where we were to stay and resupply. Despite our movement, the pattern of relentless Fantasma attacks continued at this new location much as it had at the Exercise Camp. Milton was clearly stressed and showing it. One night we evacuated the camp at the sound of the Fantasma approaching and emptied into a trench nearby that we had been using as our hideout during the nighttime attacks. The three of us hung back at the end of the line in the trench to give ourselves the best chance of running, if it came to that. The Fantasma hadn't attacked yet. It was orbiting above a position not too far from our own.

Milton began screaming at Rogelio and Cereal Boy, his voice rising until he was nearly shrieking. "What is that airplane doing? What is it doing?"

Neither Rogelio nor the Plumber responded. The plane's purpose was obvious. By circling it was able to receive more information about its possible targets and then wait for the Kfirs to come in. Milton was nearly foaming at the mouth as he barked at his number one and number two.

"If you are ever going to be a commander, you have to make decisions. What is that airplane *doing*!" Still, neither of the pair could say a word. They were either too frightened or they honestly didn't know.

After we'd gotten more provisions and the FARC calmed down, we set out. We were told that we'd been given a week by the Front commander, Efren, to reach a rendezvous point, but it seemed that Milton had simply stopped caring about whether we got to where we were going. He'd halt the march whenever he felt like it and go hunting in the jungle, disappearing for stretches at a time while we waited for his return.

At first, we assumed that with these breaks he was just doing his guerrillas a favor. All our exercise had paid off, making us fit and strong, but now the guerrillas were the ones struggling. Our increased strength and endurance didn't go unnoticed. Milton made several angry remarks to his crew about their failure to keep up with us, using the boot instead of his brain to motivate his people.

When that didn't produce the effects he wanted, Milton took another approach. On one of his hunting stops, we all noticed a group of spider monkeys overhead. Milton took his rifle and brought one down with a single shot. It fell just off the trail. He walked over and grabbed it by its tail and hauled it toward us. We had clustered together, and Milton dragged the monkey into the center of our group.

We could see the monkey's chest heaving. It was lying on its back and was clearly alive. Milton walked over to one of his guerrillas and pulled his machete out of its scabbard. He hefted the tool in his hand, and for a split second it was as though we could see the large knife going through a transformation as it turned from a tool into a weapon.

Milton looked at the monkey and then at us. He raised the machete and rotated it in his hand before bringing the flat of the blade down on the monkey's head. As he did this, he yelled the word *whack!* like he was in a sick comic book and was narrating the sound effects. Blood poured out of the monkey's head and into its eye. Still, it was breathing.

He grabbed the monkey's right leg and began sawing at the socket of the hip. A few of us turned our back at the first blow and more did after he severed the leg. We could hear him hacking his way through flesh and sinew, the cracking of the joint. Our stomachs turned. He continued with the other leg. I turned to look, hoping the animal was out of its misery. The monkey lay on its back, eyes open, still breathing.

The three of us stood and stared at one another. We looked away at the ground, the trees, anywhere but at Milton. I couldn't get the image out of my mind of Milton as the surgeon performing Clara Rojas's C-section. No wonder Emanuel's arm had been broken. I felt bad for the monkey, but in that moment my mind was on that suffering child. Emanuel so frequently lay on his back staring up at the sky, unseeing and, we hoped, unfeeling. As horrific as the scene was before us, I was haunted by the image of Clara standing at the fence in the compound in Camp Caribe as she yelled for her baby to be brought to her.

Milton's butchery was far too much for any of us to bear. We knew he was an uneducated and impoverished man. He grew up in an environment that had formed his mind-set and his definition of cruelty, but we could not excuse what he was doing to that animal, what he had done to Clara's baby, or what he had done to us all.

Milton called for one of the girls to step forward and then one of the guys. He had the guy tie the bloody leg to the girl's backpack. Her eyes were brimming with tears and she was shaking. He did the same with the other leg and the other guerrilla. Then he gave the order to move out. His boot and not his head was still in command. We all filed past the monkey that lay on its back, eyes open, still breathing.

MARC

By the time we reached our next long-term camp, I'd finished the chess set I'd begun almost a year before. We quietly passed the three-year mark in captivity on February 13, 2006, in an area adjacent to an old FARC compound that had become our new camp. Tom and I made a board from a scrap box, and suddenly a game that we'd wanted since our first months of captivity was within our reach. Just as physical activity had taken up much of our time at the Exercise Camp, at what we called Chess Camp, the ancient game of warfare and strategy dominated our time. We had epic matches with one another that lasted all day. Sometimes the guards even gathered to watch, and when they could manage it, they would sneak in a game or two with us.

Tom proved to be a top-notch player, the best among the three of us. Not only was he good, but he was a master of the mind games as well. Whenever he took one of our pieces off the board, he would do so with a flourish—verbal and physical—to let us know that he had just crushed us and any hope we had of beating him. His grin was wicked, and the enjoyment he took in stomping an opponent was off the charts. I was just learning the game, so I wasn't much of a challenge for him at the beginning, but I set myself the goal of beating him someday. Eventually I got so immersed in chess that I would skip lunch if I was in the middle of a game so that I could study the board and plot my next moves. During our marathon, day-long matches, the guards who had gone off duty at the start came up to us later in the day for an update. These titanic struggles between the master and the pupil loomed large in everyone's imagination. I was grateful for the distraction the games provided; they helped me take my mind off of Ingrid and the others. I prayed for her nightly and hoped she was well.

The Plumber also wanted to play Tom, and though he was a bright guy, he was not an experienced player. Tom wasn't about to let up on anyone, and he had the Plumber on the run from the get go. Each time Tom took one of his pieces with that distinctive flourish of his, we could see the Plumber getting more and more flustered and angry. He was playing right into Tom's hands—make the opponent think of anything but what he was supposed to be thinking about. Tom took the Plumber's rook and it was only a matter of a couple of moves before he was going to win.

Taking exception to Tom seizing his last vital defender and tossing it to the ground, the Plumber stood up and shouted defensively, "*¡No hay violencia aquí!*"

As he jumped up, the Plumber knocked over the board, sending pieces flying in all directions. He was clearly upset, but all Tom did was stare at him and raise his palms up as if to say, "Let's not get carried away."

Everybody started laughing and the situation quickly quieted since we knew Milton would freak out if he knew the guards were fraternizing with us in that way. But it seemed odd to all of us that the Plumber would respond so violently while telling us that violence had no place on the chessboard. We'd seen a lot of evidence that nearly every member of the FARC was capable of violence. We were playing a game, but these guys were committing real acts of brutality. Those thoughts didn't stop us from playing chess, but I always kept that image of the Plumber shouting and upsetting the board in my mind. The incident was a good reminder of what his essential nature was—he was a terrorist and would always be one no matter how much contact he had with us. It was dangerous for us to think otherwise.

A short while after the Plumber's eruption, real violence intruded into our lives. One morning we woke up to the sound of bombs detonating near our camp—much closer than usual. The sound of explosion after explosion after explosion rode the waving tops of the trees; we knew a battle was going on, but we didn't know where or who was waging it. Eventually we heard the familiar sound of gunfire from a Fantasma and we knew that something very serious was going on. All we could hope was that the FARC guerrillas were taking their lumps.

The next day the Plumber reported back to us what he'd learned. We were in a region where the FARC had control over many coca fields. Instead of relying on airplane spraying to eradicate the crops, the government had sent in a unit to manually destroy them. The FARC had ambushed the workers and killed twenty-seven policemen. We didn't know the number of wounded or killed among the FARC. We imagined their losses had to be significant based on the intensity and length of the battle.

Later in the day Mono came to Keith and whispered, "Keith, the merchandise is here." At first, Keith wasn't sure what he meant; the guards frequently delivered supplies to us. When he repeated the message, Keith understood. Mono was referring to the cocaine that had not yet been fully refined. Mono claimed that the Front had shipped five tons to our location.

During our years of captivity, we hadn't seen much of the FARC's drug operation up close. On one of our short marches, we'd been inside a lab, but hadn't seen the final product. The news of this massive cocaine shipment explained why our guards had been on longer rotations. Instead of being with us for two hours, they were taking five-hour shifts. The guards we weren't seeing were likely guarding the cocaine. When Keith told us about the amount of coke on the premises, we all thought about the job we'd been doing before our captivity and how it had contributed to the situation the FARC was currently in. They had the drugs at our location, but they couldn't move them anywhere because of the strong military presence and heavy activity. We were glad to know that the combined efforts of the Colombians and the Americans in Plan Patriota were having some effect.

While it was hard for me to visualize what five tons of crystal cocaine looked like, it was easy to picture the devastation that amount of drugs could do to neighborhoods back in the U.S. I was used to seeing photos of kids shot in drug-related drive-by shootings on the streets of just about every major American city. I was used to seeing pictures of crack babies. I was used to seeing pictures of grieving families at funerals for those directly and in most cases indirectly involved in the drug trade. I was used to hearing the outrageous numbers of dollars narco-trafficking produced.

What I had come to see in my time in Colombia was that there was a whole new set of victims of the drug trade. I mourned the loss of those twenty-seven policemen. I mourned the loss of the kidnap victims who were frequently slaughtered because their families either weren't able to make the payments the FARC demanded or refused to cave in to a terrorist practice. I prayed for their families. I prayed for all of us. I didn't pray for the FARC.

Our stay in the Chess Camp was marked by one of the problems that plagued us throughout our captivity—not enough food; only this time it was for different reasons. According to the Plumber, our supply chain had been cut off by the Colombian Army. In fact, the Colombians were so active, between the Front headquarters, supply depots, and our position, that two things happened: Milton went into forced radio silence, and we ran out of food. In our minds, this was a cause for celebration. It meant we were going to go on starvation rations, but it also meant the FARC were as well. They would be even weaker. The fact that they couldn't communicate with their higher-ups only added to our glee.

Meanwhile Milton was too stupid to make a sound decision on his own. We hoped he'd do something that would enhance our chances of them being taken down in a firefight with the army. If the noose was tightening and Milton continued to treat his people like dirt, we might be able to get some of them to fully commit to getting out there and surrendering. With them as our guides and offering some protection, we had a better chance of surviving.

Nearly three months into our stay at the Chess Camp, food remained in short supply. Eventually we noticed that Rogelio and Mono had been gone for several days. Rogelio had been particularly cruel and nutty leading up to his absence. He was in a no-medicine-for-Tom mood and we were all fighting that battle again. With him gone, the attitude in our camp was definitely better and it seemed the same was true for the other members of the Front as well.

Aside from enjoying the relative calm, we didn't think much of Rogelio's absence, but four days after our last little confrontation with

him, we saw his girl, Vanessa, walking toward our part of camp crying. Not long after, we saw Tatiana, Mono's woman, crying as well. We
asked the Plumber what was up. Normally he was an upbeat kind of
guy, but at that moment he looked really downcast.

"Guys, I've got some very bad news," he said, making it sound as if
he was hesitant to tell us because he didn't want us to be upset. "Mono
and Rogelio are dead."

We looked at one another, uncertain of how much emotion to show
in front of the Plumber. He paused for a minute before continuing.

"They were sent to find food and to make contact with the other
members of the Front. They were walking down the road when they
were ambushed by the Colombian Army. They were both shot and
killed." He lowered his head and scanned the ground in front of him
for a few moments; his solemn expression said it all.

I wasn't proud of how I felt back then, but I was glad to hear that
Rogelio was dead. I felt an enormous amount of relief that such a vin-
dictive and evil person wasn't on the planet anymore. As a Christian, I
knew it wasn't the attitude I should have taken, but I couldn't help it.
We all felt that way. It was as if we'd been given a gift.

Though Mono had treated us better than Rogelio, I had no great
affection for him, either. He had killed innocent people, something
he talked about frequently. He had told us about the execution he'd
performed and bragged about several other killings and drive-by shootings. Whether he did the things or not didn't matter, and neither did
the fact that at times he had helped us out and been kind. Either way,
he was still a killer. I didn't mourn his passing, but I did mourn the
waste of a life. I knew that he had joined the FARC as a very young
man and felt he had no other choice. That his opportunities had been
so limited was sad, but I was not about to shed a tear for him.

The Plumber walked away from us, and once he was out of earshot,
we all shared our pleasure in not having Rogelio in our lives. We re-
counted some of the things that he had done to us. In my mind's eye,

I imagined him on that road and wondered what he thought about the moment the first round pierced his body or as he lay in the mud with his life seeping out of him. I doubted he felt any remorse.

The silence lingered among the three of us.

"Can you believe it?" I asked, almost thinking out loud.

Tom and Keith knew what I was talking about because they both said, "No. But that's just how it is."

Though we'd heard of other FARC guerrillas who had died or disappeared during our time in captivity, this was the first time that guards we'd come to know well had been killed. We were all a bit surprised that we'd taken such satisfaction in Rogelio's death. It disturbed me. I found myself questioning whether it was the captivity that had brought out this side of me, or if I was simply changed now and this event demonstrated the new me. Perhaps some very small part of my soul died along with Rogelio. Perhaps his treatment of us had afflicted me in such a way that I'd lost some of my humanity. Perhaps I had to add my conscience to our casualty list.

I didn't dwell on these thoughts for very long. The FARC did nothing to commemorate their fallen comrades. Vanessa and Tatiana very quickly regrouped and moved on. The other guerrillas descended on Rogelio and Mono's belongings and took whatever they wanted, picking through piece by piece until every item was taken.

KEITH

A week after we heard about Rogelio and Mono's deaths, we were on the march again. Instead of it being a real ordeal or getting lost because of Milton's cluelessness, we actually caught a bit of good luck. Whether it was because Milton had lost a couple of guys or somebody higher up in the group figured that the shithead needed a break, we were introduced to a new player. Ernesto joined our bunch, and the scuttlebutt was that he was pretty close to the boss of the whole Front.

Compared to a lot of the guerrillas, Ernesto, at about five feet ten, was pretty tall. He had a barrel chest and a broad face topped by silvery gray hair and matching mustache. Next to Milton, he looked sophisticated, a city slicker rather than some backwoods ruffian—that is, a city slicker who wore a baseball-style T-shirt and sweatpants. He kept his nine-millimeter strapped to his side at all times and conducted himself like a professional—keeping his distance and maintaining a relatively calm and pleasant attitude.

He, too, got sucked into the chess thing, and at one point in his series of matches with Tom (who won nine out of eleven), Ernesto told a long story about the history of chess. It was clear that the guy had some education and could read, but he had obviously drunk the FARC Kool-Aid. His story was that he came from a poor family, and to hear him tell it, everything he learned, he learned from the FARC. To him, everyone benefited from the cocaine trade and he didn't understand our trying to stop it. He sincerely believed that the revolution would equalize things for everyone and that was what all this was about.

From the start, we had Ernesto pegged as an idealist and true believer, but at least he made good on his idea of spreading the wealth. He treated us fairly and intervened on our behalf to make sure that our enclosures were larger. He said of Milton, "One thing that people in charge of prisoners sometimes fail to remember is that the prisoners are human beings."

It was too bad that the FARC had such an uneven policy when it came to respecting people's human rights. On this series of marches, with Rogelio gone and Milton no longer completely responsible for our day-to-day care, the atmosphere loosened considerably. Each day when we bathed, it seemed as if we attracted more and more attention from the female guerrillas. They came down and bathed at the same time as we did, and we were back to being zoo animals in an interactive exhibit. As gringos, everything we did was funny. Because both the men and the women of the FARC had a tendency to giggle when nervous, at times it was like we were men surrounded by a bunch of silly schoolgirls.

One day Vanessa came down to bathe, and when she took off her T-shirt, it was clear that even in death Rogelio had found a way to plague us: Vanessa didn't just display a baby bump, she was full-on pregnant. Having a child was a direct violation of FARC policy, but we knew that Rogelio had to be the baby's father. She'd moved on after his death, but she hadn't taken up with any of the other guerrillas. We weren't certain what was going to happen to the baby, but we knew whatever it was would not be good.

By our estimation, Vanessa was four to five months' pregnant when the word came down that she was going to have to terminate it. Tatiana, Mono's former girl, had befriended Marc, and she filled us in on Vanessa's situation. Tatiana knew what the only outcome could be, but she still expressed her dismay that Vanessa wouldn't be able to carry the baby to full term. She said that Vanessa was resigned to the fact that the fetus was going to be killed.

There was an older woman in camp, Gira, who acted like a wise mother hen much of the time; as it turned out she was also the camp abortionist. The morning that Gira administered the drugs to Vanessa so that she would "spontaneously" abort her child was surreal. As a parent, I was sick at the thought of a four- to five-month-old fetus having its life terminated. Marc and I were angry and frustrated that there was nothing we could do to help her. Sitting in our area and listening to Vanessa's mumbled protests and later her cries of discomfort followed by grief, I felt like I'd reached a new level of disgust with the FARC. As much as we'd all hated Rogelio and hated the idea that some of his DNA was going to be passed on to another human being, we all hoped that somehow the best in humanity could overcome the rough start that kid had been given. We wanted to believe that with the opportunity, even in the incredibly dysfunctional FARC community, this child would have the chance to become a decent human being.

The next time we saw Vanessa, she was a broken woman. No amount of brainwashing could extinguish her maternal instincts. She knew she'd had no choice, that one way or another the FARC would take that baby from her. Just as they had done with Clara's baby, they didn't see a human life in that child; they saw the potential for death. To them, a child was a liability, a crying, mewling presence that might betray their position. One more mouth to feed, one more item to be humped through the jungle. Seething in our area, I hated them like never before.

As we marched away from the Chess Camp and the Colombian military, heading out of the mountains, we knew that we were in for a long one and that some major changes were afoot. In addition to Ernesto, we met another FARC leader, by the name of Pidinolo, a young, lean, athletic-looking guy who didn't seem to belong to the rat's nest of human genetic material that made up the rest of the group. He carried himself like he was somebody, and as it turned out, he was: the right-hand man of the 27th Front's commander, Efren. Pidinolo was said to be the guy in charge of tactical planning for their military operations.

Accompanying Pidinolo were three really young kids, none of them older than fifteen. All were complete greenhorns, wet-behind-the-ears kids kitted up with brand-new gear and clearly in love with being in the jungle with the adults. This was their chance to play war. Shortly after Pidinolo and his young crew joined us, we stopped one day and he ordered that a pig be slaughtered so we could have a nice meal. While the pig was roasting, a few soldiers brought over a bunch of coconuts. As it turned out, we were in an agricultural area and there were farms all around us. The FARC were wolfing down coconuts, and Eliécer took his machete and used it like a set of ginsu knives to carve up a big portion of coconut for the three of us.

The months that had passed since the Exercise Camp had done nothing to alleviate Eliécer's feeling of entrapment. He continued to speak to us about his unhappiness, how enslaved he felt, but still he managed to get up every day and march alongside us. He revealed that he had been tricked into joining the FARC. Through it all, he always impressed us with his humanity and generosity—the coconut was just one small example of this.

That night, we enjoyed the pork and bedded down. Because we were on the move, we set up our hooches in the middle of the FARC guards. Just to our left was where Eliécer and one of Pidinolo's young aides, Duber, were sleeping. Long after we'd turned in, I was awakened by the click of a rifle's safety being switched off. A second later, that weapon discharged and a bullet whizzed over us.

The next sound I heard was the voice of one of the young kids. He was screaming.

"¡Duber se mató! ¡Duber se mató!"

We couldn't believe that one of those young kids had shot himself. The three of them were the picture of innocence, or at least as innocent as a FARC guerrilla could be. Over all the shouting, we heard the Plumber, who was on guard duty, asking, "Who, who?" Then we heard the words that we'd been dreading for almost a year:

"¡Eliécer se mató! ¡Eliécer se mató!"

My heart jumped into my throat. I knew immediately that Eliécer had made good on the suicide he'd threatened so many months before.

The guerrillas assembled and we were told to remain where we were. After a few minutes of conversation, we heard the FARC moving around. I heard the sound of a single spade turning up the dirt and thumping it on the ground just a few yards from where we lay. This quiet rhythm went on until it was interrupted by something heavy being dragged out of the hooch next to ours.

I lay there thinking of Eliécer and how just a few hours before, he'd fed us coconut. Cutting up the coconut for us was a simple gesture, but it demonstrated the kindness we'd come to know in Eliécer. As every one of his fellow FARC members was enjoying their food, reveling in the meal, he was thinking that we were captives, we were trapped. We were unable to enjoy the food without the right tools. The coconut had been exactly the kind of offering that we expected from him.

Just a few months before this, Eliécer had come to us shortly after midnight on Christmas Eve and New Year's Eve, our third in captivity. All of us had our thoughts very much on family and friends and the enormous gulf between us and them. Just as he had done the year before, Eliécer was the only one of the FARC to reach across the darkness to shake our hands and give us his best wishes.

The shoveling stopped for just a moment and we heard a heavy thump as Eliécer's body was tossed into his shallow grave. Then the shoveling continued, an unbroken heartbeat that matched our own.

The next morning, we moved out. I didn't have a whole lot of time to spend standing over the patch of ground that Milton's men had covered over with leaves and branches so that it wouldn't betray our having been there. It didn't matter to me that they did that; I knew that Eliécer had been there. I was wearing a shirt that he'd literally given me off his back. My legs were powered by the food that he'd given me the night before, just as he had shared his meager supplies with us so many other times. That morning, I wished I knew his real name. I told myself that if I had the chance when we got back home, I would contact his family. I wanted them to know that their son, their brother, their friend, had found himself taking part in some fucked-up shit, but his generosity of spirit and human kindness were never casualties. Weeks before, I'd told Marc and Tom that when we were free, if I got the chance, I'd figure out some way to get Eliécer out of Colombia. I'd have been happy to have that big old country boy with the shit-eating grin come and live with me. I'd take real pleasure in breaking bread with him, sharing a cold one, or pouring him a stiff shot of whatever. I knew plenty of other folks who would have welcomed him and enjoyed being around such a good-hearted person.

As we walked away from that camp, I was about as broken down as I'd been in captivity. I had a lump the size of a fist squeezing my throat, and a coal-furnace fire heating my anger. I could live with the sad, but I had to get rid of the angry. It was easier than I thought. I just thought of Eliécer and all he'd done for the three of us. He had died, but what he represented marched on with us. We all renewed the vow we'd made early on. No matter what the FARC threw at us, we'd never stoop to their level. We were tested that very same day when Milton came up to tell us that he'd lost one of his guys, telling us Eliécer's pistol accidentally discharged while he was cleaning it at two in the morning in the pitch black of a jungle night.

Darkness comes in many forms, and what shadowed Eliécer, what finally chased him over the edge, I'll never know. Perhaps it all became too much. Perhaps seeing Pidinolo's kids all lined up and eager just reminded him of how vicious the FARC cycle really was. In the end, though, the reason didn't matter; all that mattered was the light he had shined for Marc, Tom, and me. Like us, Eliécer had chosen, in life and in death, to do the good hard thing.

TWELVE

Running on Empty

May 2006–September 2006

MARC

Our departure from the Chess Camp in May of 2006 began months of
a gypsylike existence, going from temporary camp to temporary camp.
With the supply and communication chains still in flux because of
Plan Patriota, it was often unclear if there was, in fact, any destination
at all.

The longer we wandered aimlessly with Milton, the thinner our supplies got. We nearly ran out of soap completely, and toilet paper became just a memory. To that point, Ernesto's promise that better days
were ahead had proven untrue. We'd become masters of frugality; we
were able to make a tube of toothpaste last six months or longer, and
whenever we could steal something from the FARC, we didn't hesitate.
They'd taken so much from us that a bit of kitchen soap to bathe with
seemed inconsequential. We had hoped that by leaving the mountains
and heading into the flatlands, our supplies would increase, but like so

many times before, these inflated hopes were grounded by harsh reality. This FARC column was barely managing to scrape by.

Every so often we had mirrors for shaving. The FARC frequently confiscated these because they could be used to signal aircraft, and each time I got a new one, I was shocked to see how much I'd deteriorated. Like Tom and Keith, I'd taken on the sunken-eyed and hollow-cheeked appearance of the destitute. We knew that we weren't getting enough fruit and vegetables in our diet and calcium was practically nonexistent. Without much calcium and vitamin D, my teeth were weakened to the point that I constantly chipped them. My nails grew brittle as well, and as they grew they were dotted with tiny holes.

We didn't enjoy the tough times, but we seemed better able to deal with them. One of the things we did to keep ourselves going was talk about what we'd do when we were finally home. I had always had a passionate affair with motorcycles. The night before I left for Colombia to begin my last rotation before the crash, I had taken my bike out for a last ride. The kids were in bed, and I kissed Shane good-bye and took off at about nine-thirty at night. I headed up US 1 and crossed the Seven-Mile Bridge and stopped at Marathon Key. The weather was warm and the breeze felt cool as I whipped along. At that hour, the traffic was relatively light. On my return trip, I decided to open it up a bit. My bike was a Yamaha R-6, what some people refer to as a crotch rocket. While I didn't blast through the atmosphere and into outer space, I did watch as the speedometer's readout climbed past 100, then 110, and by the time I backed off the throttle, I'd hit 137. The incredible bladder-tingling sensation of moving that fast, experiencing that kind of freedom, was something I often returned to while slogging through a march or enduring a long day in an enclosure like the barbed-wire cage.

Tom was also into motorcycles. He had a couple of English bikes; a BSA Golden Flash was among his favorites. I'd never heard of BSA bikes. By the time I was riding, the company had gone out of business, but Tom described what the bike looked like and how the old tried-and-true technology of carburetion and magneto-fired ignition could be temperamental but a joy to someone who enjoyed tinkering and diagnosing and repairing almost as much as he liked riding. We endlessly debated what bike we would each buy when we got out—used Honda Rebels, Shadows, or Nighthawks when we were being realistic, and Harley-Davidsons when we were dreaming.

Gradually our talk shifted to a ride the three of us would take—what we called the Freedom Ride. Like our ambitions about what bikes we might ride, the Freedom Ride started out small. We'd tour Florida. We'd take all back roads, and Keith insisted we hit all the mom-and-pop restaurants and every barbecue joint and greasy-spoon diner we could find. Tom talked about his desire to keep it local and have his wife ride along behind him—just being out and able to throw a leg over a bike anytime he wanted to was freedom enough.

In time, as our liberty and our chances of being released faded, we all expanded our ideas of the Freedom Ride. Forget the cheap bikes, let's go all-out, maybe pick up some used Harleys and tour the Southeast U.S. As our deprivation increased, and we needed even grander dreams to offset it, we thought we could walk into a Harley-Davidson dealership, tell them our story of being held captive, and get a sweet deal on three brand-spanking-new bikes. We'd hit the road and go coast-to-coast.

Even when we stopped for a five-minute rest and could sense that we were dragging or our spirits were down, one of us would say something like, "I heard about this one road in Tennessee. They call it the Tail of the Dragon. Three hundred and eighteen curves in eleven miles. We're going to ride that thing." I would spend the next part of the march there on that road, taking each and every one of those curves. How much we relied on that fantasy and the extent to which we expanded it grew in proportion to the length of time we were held and the degree to which our hope of getting out of there diminished.

When we were in the jungle and supplies were at their lowest, the FARC always seemed to be able to find something to kill and to slaughter. They always served the lousiest cuts of meat right after the kill. They said that meat rots closest to the bone first. In a lot of ways that was true for our mental states during our months of wandering after the Chess Camp. Maybe it was because we were so frequently out of radio contact or maybe it was because the times when we did have access to radios we missed the messages, but we began to despair over the fact that at that point we had been gone for more than three years. In that time, Tom had received fewer than three or four messages from his wife, while in Keith's case and my case, we'd heard only once from Malia and Shane respectively.

Keith and I both worried and fretted over that. In the vacuum created by an absence of information, all kinds of negative thoughts rushed in. If we looked at things realistically, we understood that the likelihood of them having moved on and met someone else was great. We didn't like that idea, but we understood. We also understood that as much as we were starving for information from our spouses, they were likely just as torn up knowing little about what had happened to us. Fair or unfair, we thought that with all the responsibilities that had been dumped in their laps as a result of our absence, life in one sense was easier for them—at least their minds were more easily occupied than ours were. They had fewer hours in the day during which they would think about all the what-if scenarios we churned out with assembly-line-like frequency.

For Keith, it was worse, since he had two families to worry about. As a father of two toddlers living in Colombia, and two other children in the States, his concerns were spread over continents. I continued to wonder about Ingrid and the other politicals, and hoped that Clara and Emanuel were doing all right.

Just as our motorcycle dreams expanded in a positive direction, our optimism for a return to the family life we'd left behind diminished. Getting back home likely meant discovering that our lives were going to be very different from what they'd been when we left. How altered, and how much worse than what they were before, we couldn't really know. On the bad days, when even the Freedom Ride couldn't penetrate our gloom, thoughts of how our lives had been fractured were consuming. I was eventually able to leave those thoughts behind, drown them out in the rush of wind and the high-pitched screaming exhaust note of my mental motorcycle.

In between daydreams and waking nightmares, Ernesto's promised land of supplies proved perpetually elusive for the FARC. Just about the only thing we had going for us in those blurry months after the Chess Camp was that we were being treated better without Milton overseeing us. At one camp, Ernesto gave us radios. At another temporary camp, he loaned us machetes. The three of us were setting up our *coletas,* our little tentlike sites to sleep in, when Ernesto handed the large blades to us.

We all looked at them like he'd handed us the keys to a new motorcycle.

"Well, go cut a tree down." Ernesto put his hands on his hips and shook his head slowly like he couldn't believe how we were behaving.

We each edged a few feet into the jungle and looked over at him as if asking, "Is it okay that we're this far away?" Guards were around us and they had their weapons.

Ernesto let out a heavy sigh. "What's wrong with you guys?" He pointed away from our site, where more promising stake material was growing some thirty or forty yards away. We all walked in that direction, eyeing the guards but still experiencing a thrilling sense, if not of freedom, then of openness.

"Can you believe it?" Keith asked incredulously as we walked farther away from camp with our new blades. "We can't even walk a few yards now without thinking somebody's got to give us the okay. Man, this shit creeps up on you."

Until that point, none of us had realized just how much incarceration had affected us psychologically. We'd come to accept things in this life as "normal" that we'd have never stood for in our other lives. Having someone dictate when we could bathe, when we could eat, where we would go, and when we would start and stop marching had invisibly worked on us. As much as we'd thought about the physical effects of our being held captive, that incident with the machetes served as an important reminder: Like the butchered animals, we would rot from the inside out. We needed to be as vigilant as we could be for any other signs of mental imprisonment.

One psychological effect of captivity that we never experienced was Stockholm syndrome. We all knew what it was—when a prisoner begins to identify and sympathize with either the individuals holding him or her captive or their cause. By being aware of what it was, we were able to fight off its possible effects. In reality, the possibility of us experiencing anything like Stockholm syndrome was remote because the FARC treated us so horribly.

One sign that our hope was not as intense as it had been earlier was our diminished faith that someone would step forward to help us and claim the reward for that information. While in the Macarena Mountains, we'd heard rumors that someone was offering a reward for our release. Later, we saw pamphlets that had been dropped among the campesinos urging them to cooperate with the authorities in getting us rescued. At first, we thought the news was fantastic since it proved that even though we'd been gone for nearly two years, someone was still interested in getting us out of there. To offset that elation was the reality: We'd seen few campesinos and the guards had told us that before we'd moved through any populated areas, the FARC had threatened to execute anyone who laid eyes on us. We'd heard on the radio about a family of five who had been executed by the FARC. We remembered scrambling off the boats one night and running past a small shack along the river where a family of five was sitting minding their own business. The pieces of the story fit, adding to the death toll our presence had run up.

To top that off, the leaflets reminded us of just what simple lives the FARC and the majority of campesinos lived. The total reward was thirteen billion Colombian pesos or about $5 million. The government must have known this was such a mind-boggling figure that most of the campesinos couldn't even begin to fathom its true value. In order to help with that, the creators of the leaflet added simple illustrations of jeeps, mules, and cows so that those contemplating cooperating could better understand the benefits.

The offer had also been broadcast on the radio, and our FARC guards heard it. The Plumber was one of the few who seemed to get it. He told us he thought of that reward every night. We'd tell him that all those things—cars, electronics, watches, and other fine jewelry—could easily be within his reach. He'd be able to live like a king on that kind of money. A few days later, he came to us and asked, "Could I get someone to manage this money for me? I don't think I'd know how to use it wisely."

We admired him for asking such a smart question, and were glad that one thing that rots people from the inside out—greed—was at our disposal. Unfortunately, another corrupting influence got ahold of the Plumber. He was promoted to the position of *oficial*. This meant that instead of being a run-of-the-mill guard, he was in direct command of us. We'd always thought that in the world of the FARC, the Plumber was the one with celebrity potential. A good-looking guy, he became more conscious of his appearance after his promotion. He stopped wearing sweatpants and T-shirts and took to wearing his camo uniform all the time. He suddenly showed up with a silver necklace, an Arafat scarf, and notebook and pen. In the air force, we called keeping your appearance optimal being "squared away" and that was exactly what the Plumber had done.

During this wandering phase, we saw further evidence of the rot that had corrupted the FARC's values. As we made our way out of the mountains and into the flatlands, we came across a far greater number of cultivated fields. That meant more coca-planting areas. We started spending many nights sleeping in temporarily abandoned drug labs. As the crop came in from one area, the FARC moved to that zone to gather and process, leaving behind the fields they had just harvested. While we didn't see anyone doing the actual processing, the equipment and the sites were there.

Witnessing all of this firsthand simply reinforced much of what we'd been able to gather and deduce from the skies. We took as much satisfaction as we could from knowing that we had discovered what in our previous lives we called "ground truth." That the round piles of waste we had witnessed from the air and in our photographs and video were indeed by-products of cocaine production. In addition, we could see that the identification process we used to mark young coca plants by their color—a nearly lime-green color, different from any other vegetation—was spot on. As we walked by these fields we could tell instantly that these plants had recently been put in the ground. They were thriving, but I hoped that someone had them in their target pack. I hoped that it was only a matter of time before they were pinpointed and removed. Hope, it seemed, was still there. I just needed more ground truth to make it real.

TOM

For months, we'd been playing an unbelievably long game of chess with the Colombian Army, moving all around the board but with few pieces being taken. As much as I wanted to believe that a checkmate was imminent, I had only my optimism to support that belief. As far as I was concerned, our erratic and unpredictable marching had switched from being the result of Milton's incompetence to a deliberate strategy of delay. I hadn't been able to see this at the beginning of the game, but as the moves took on a pattern, I could detect, if not the logic to it, then at least how those moves fit into a larger overall strategy. To me, delay was a good thing. That meant we had something to wait for—and I'd been holding out hope that each time we waited, it was for something better to come along.

But after months of marches and temporary camps, things couldn't have been much worse for us. Yet as strange as it sounds, the worse things got, the more reason we had to hope. If things got so desperate for the FARC, maybe they would be willing to work a deal for us that involved some cash. Or maybe the government would give them a DMZ in exchange for the release of some prisoners.

One day, a female guard told us that we were going to be turned over to a new set of guards. She was just a young kid, so we figured we should try to verify her statement. We managed to pressure the newly strict Plumber into giving up a bit of information, and he told us that a few days before, he and a guide had gone out on horseback to meet with Mono JoJoy, Joaquín Gómez, and a few other big bosses. According to what he'd learned, Mono JoJoy wanted us as close to him as possible, so close in fact that Marc, Keith, and I would be handed over to Mono JoJoy and his men at any moment.

Anytime Mono JoJoy's name and ours were used in the same breath, we were intrigued. Besides being in charge of the military operations, Mono JoJoy, we'd been told, had overall responsibility for the FARC's many hostages. If we were being turned over to him, it was a big deal. We had heard a lot of aircraft activity and were near a lot of farms and larger towns, which boosted our hopes that a release might be coming up. We'd spent about twenty weeks playing this crazy chess match, and it was nice to think that it was finally going to end. Whether it meant release or getting away from Milton, we'd still be earning a huge victory.

We really got the sense that some significant change was coming in our last temporary camp with Milton's group. The Plumber came up to Keith and handed him one of the *panelón* radios we'd been lusting after for so long. I called it the Chevrolet of jungle radios. It was an AM-FM model, a Sony, and as reliable as anything out there, especially if you wanted to pick up local Colombian AM stations. He handed Keith the radio, said, "Remember me," and walked away.

The Plumber never did anything without a reason. A couple of years into our captivity, I'd had a conversation with him in which he said that if we were ever able to get out of there, and if he was able to get out of the FARC (he could lose a foot to a land mine or something), he wanted to know how he could connect with us again. I told him that the only way he could contact me was through my e-mail address. I told him he could go into Villavicencio and find an Internet café. I gave him as much information as I could, knowing full well that the odds of any of this happening were pretty remote.

I saw the Plumber for what he was—a schemer. If I had any respect at all for him, it was because he seemed the closest of the FARC to really understanding the situation he was in. He didn't like prisoner duty, but he knew that it was safer than other units. The likelihood of him being killed while with us was lower than it was out in the field taking military action or protecting coke labs. He'd seen his best friend killed in action and that dose of reality got to him. The Plumber understood risks, and just as he would go only so far to help us, he was going to go only so far to put his own life in jeopardy.

When we asked him what he thought about his future, he said something very telling. In a lot of ways, he said, things were worse for him than they were for the others. He understood that by joining the FARC, he had essentially given his life away. Guerrillas got killed and the FARC just recruited more kids to replace them. Sooner or later it would be his turn. That he gave Keith the radio let us know that he still held out some hope that his life might play out differently. We figured it was his way of saying, "If you ever get out of there, keep me in mind and get me to the States somehow."

We didn't have long to wait to see what was next. Some new FARC faces had joined our temporary camp, and when we got the order to pack up, we were the only ones who did so. All of the FARC under

Milton's "command" stood and watched us pack up. Then they formed a kind of rough line and said good-bye. Tatiana had a little chick that she wanted Marc to take with him so that he could finally have an egg layer of his own someday. I found myself feeling a little emotional at the thought of separating from this group. We'd been together for two years and now it was over. It wasn't quite that old line about feeling good when you stop banging your head against the wall, but it was something like that mixed with a little bit of genuine regret.

All of those emotions changed when Milton pulled the three of us aside. He started by explaining that he was turning us over to a new group. He said that Jair, a short blond guerrilla we'd seen in camp the last two days was now going to be in charge of us. We assumed that was all Milton was going to say, but then he went into cover-his-ass mode. Stating that he was only human—which we had seen ample evidence of, what with all his failings—he admitted that he'd made some mistakes. He was aware that he'd denied us the things we wanted most—radios and books—and he claimed that he'd told Jair to provide us with those things. He also said that he'd put in a good word with the new Front. We'd been no trouble to him. He offered his hand. As much as I hated the guy, I figured there was no point in pissing him off. I took his hand and Milton walked away, back to the jungle and the life he seemed to love so much.

Jair led us on a ten-minute march and we met up with a larger group. He struck us as a sharp and energetic guy. With his blond hair and crew cut, he seemed like a gringo who'd been airlifted into the jungle. Still we were concerned about losing the connections to the guards in Milton's group and the information channels that we'd worked so hard to cultivate. The Plumber and the others had been vital in helping us get what we needed and stay on top of our situation. We were all a bit anxious about having to start over.

Immediately we could sense the change in attitude among this new group. Suddenly we were being stared at again—novelty attractions on

display for all to see. We'd been with Milton's guys for so long, we'd forgotten what it was like to be the new kids. But there was good news as
well. Even though losing the connections we had for information was
difficult, Jair's style of leadership was way better than Milton's, and he
was much more responsive to our needs. I got the sense immediately
that this was a big step up for us. They had prepared a bathing platform
for us in the creek and that was more than we could ever have expected
of Milton's lazy bunch. Simple things like soap and toilet paper let us
know that this group was better supplied. The food was more plentiful
and that always helped our morale. Nevertheless, when we brought up
the subject of radios, Jair seemed surprised—so much for Milton letting him know what we needed and wanted.

The very next night, we were given the order to move out. Jair and
his guerrillas were in much better physical condition and clearly better
outfitted than Milton's bunch. They were heavily loaded with supplies,
but when we set out with them, we were moving double time. Before
we had gone very far, we came to a large open field, and standing in it
was an older FARC member, a guy we recognized from our proof of
life. His name was César. He was the leader of the 1st Front and one of
the most vicious warriors in the FARC's history. As we filed past him
he said in English, "Good morning."

We didn't have too much time to wonder what he was doing there.
This group had us on the move, hustling us out of that hot zone as
quickly as possible. Marc had hurt his knee and mine were still painfully swollen, not to mention that I was troubled by an Achilles-tendon
problem. Still, we both wanted to make nice with the new group, so we
did everything we could to keep pace. At times we were actually running, and we estimated that we were moving at a rate of about twenty
kilometers a day for the first three to four days. The odd thing was that
as fast as we were moving and as difficult as that pace was, the guerrillas were being nice to us. They kept saying, "This isn't a forced march.
If you need to stop, we can stop. Just let us know."

From the time Sonia and her crew had captured us to this point nearly three and a half years later, no one had ever said that to me. Just knowing that I could take a break when I needed to and not pay a price for it made it a lot easier to keep pushing on. The FARC were also carrying a lot of the gear Marc and I had in order to lighten our loads. With Milton's bunch, it had been just the opposite; we constantly had to help them out by carrying extra food and other essentials in our *equipos*.

When we reached a resupply point, we were given new boots and clothes. The food was more plentiful than before, but it came at odd hours and with no rhyme or reason. We weren't about to object, but getting beer and bread at 8 A.M. did seem strange. If we'd learned one thing in the jungle, it was don't question too much. We just took whatever food or supplies we were given because you could never predict when you might get those things again.

While we were there, César also showed up. He seemed to like to joke around and keep things light. Before he moved off into the jungle with another cadre of FARC, he told us not to worry and that we'd now be better taken care of. He said that we'd be watching movies, reading, and when we got to our destination, there would be radios waiting for us. We were taking a wait-and-see attitude on that, but so far these guys definitely had lived up to their promises. We spent a few days at the resupply depot with Jair's group, where we learned that one of the reasons we'd been hightailing it was that our new group had come under fire from an air attack just a couple of days before they picked us up. They wouldn't talk about casualties, but it was clear they wanted out of the hot zone as quickly as possible.

With all of us heavily loaded again—Marc and I had to carry all our own stuff again because the FARC were carrying all the food and other materials they needed—we kept up that same intense pace for a few days. We finally slowed down and came to a camp on the edge of a wide, fast-moving river. Across the river from us we saw César and his encampment. Even though we'd been with the FARC for more than three years, I never got used to one particular sight. Like all the other FARC leaders, César shared his quarters with a young woman. He had to be in his midforties and this woman was no more than eighteen or nineteen. I tried to tell myself that given what we knew about the FARC and the sheer drudgery of their life, she was probably wise to pair off with someone of his rank, but it still bothered me that these young women were wasting their lives.

From that point on, we moved on the river. Including all the FARC, there must have been about forty of us plus all our supplies. The FARC only had two of the smaller river-running canoes. As a result, we would travel for a couple of hours downstream and stop. The boats would head back upstream to pick up those left behind and then return. In the meantime, we set up camp and generally took it easy.

In this manner, we gradually made our way downriver, and though we continued to be on the move, it was far less rigorous than it had been with Milton. Our diet was much better thanks to the abundant *caribe* fish. I'd enjoyed eating them from the beginning and Marc and Keith started to nibble at them. For the first time in a while, there were measured stretches of leisure time that gave me the opportunity to take in my surroundings. Even though I'd been held captive in the place, the beauty of Colombia still lured me. At one point, we'd stopped to camp at a bend in the river. We were in what seemed to me to be virgin territory. This enormous elbow of river was spread out in front of us and it opened onto a vast vista of valleys and tree-covered hillsides that stood in row after row until they bumped up against the horizon.

As it turned out, that vista was more than just a pretty sight. It signaled a change in the river. Instead of thick jungle on either side, we entered an area with sheer rock-face walls and enormous boulders strewn haphazardly across the river. The FARC had traveled these waters frequently and had names for some of the rock outcroppings—the Elephant, the Window, etc. We could hear the distinctive sound of white water. Rather than risk running the rapids, we would get out of the boats and walk along trails that the FARC had clearly been using for years. In the less tempestuous waters, a few of us would remain in the boat and run the rapid while the others walked and were then picked up again. At times we abandoned the boats altogether because the water was too low. The FARC seemed to know exactly where these spots were and anticipated them. Sometimes we would travel on foot for a few hours, sometimes for several days, before we got back in different boats that were tied up and waiting for us. Those coordinated efforts were a far cry from Milton's meanderings.

As a pilot, I admire anyone who can handle any kind of craft with skill. When we'd been on boats before, the pilots simply bashed their way through any obstacle. They couldn't do that with the rocks and rapids. Our pilot didn't seem like a FARC member. His long hair, which hung down his back, and his goatee gave him a rock-star look. He was a big guy, and like Rogelio, he was difficult to understand. What little bits we did pick up indicated to us that he was a true revolutionary convert. His nickname, Mantequillo, loosely translated to Butter Boy. Keith couldn't resist needling our chubby boat driver. He kept asking why all the boat drivers were overweight and if he had been stealing instead of delivering the food supplies. Butter Boy didn't laugh at that. He took his job seriously and swallowed the whole FARC reformation-of-the-country ideology in large quantities.

Despite its better organization, this new group still managed to keep things as surreal as ever. One night toward the end of our ride down the river one of the older female guerrillas serenaded us with anti-American propaganda songs. As this came to an end, we were struggling to find an entrance to a camp just off the water. The foliage and vegetation were so thick that even with their spotlights, the FARC couldn't find the entry point to the tributary. At one camp, we'd all seen the cheap horror flick *Leprechaun* and one of the new guerrillas was a spitting image of the evil dwarf of the title. He was a bit of a know-it-all and a chain smoker extraordinaire. He stood in the bow of the boat using a branch to steady himself. Silhouetted by the spotlight, he pointed his short arm and crooked little finger in the direction he thought we should go. His high-pitched screaming lent an air of both familiarity and bizarreness to the night's spectacle. The more things changed, the more they stayed the same when it came to the FARC.

KEITH

I wasn't sure if it was because Butter Boy smelled his mama's home cooking or what, but he finally found the river entrance through the jungle he was looking for. We only went a few yards before we were told to off-load the boat. We set out on a clearly marked trail at about two in the morning and marched for an hour or so before we finally stopped. After a quick dinner of guerrilla rice—their version of Rice-A-Roni—and an egg, we turned in for the night. We only got a couple of hours of sleep before we were awakened and told to pack up again. It didn't take Tom and me long to get our gear together, since we'd both slept in hammocks, but Marc, whose back had been bad since the crash, needed to take his tent down, so he was lagging behind us.

We marched for a couple of hours until we came to a large FARC encampment. Like so many others we'd seen, it likely dated back to the DMZ days when the FARC were far less mobile than now. The place had similarities to Caribe, with a few permanent-walled structures and walkways to keep the guards out of the mud. Primarily, the other structures were typical small, jungle, open-air buildings with roofs. The jungle had tried to reclaim some of the territory, but much of the camp was still intact. As we walked along a boardwalk past where all the FARC were camped, something seemed unusual and out of place. At first, I was too tired to pick up on it, but then it hit me: On the clotheslines strung up around this camp, there were civilian clothes. The arrangement of the hooches was different from that of the FARC in their camp.

Even in our sleep-deprived state, it didn't take long for us to realize that we had been relocated to a camp with other hostages. When I first saw one of their faces I was both excited and sad. I was happy to see some of the military guys who'd been separated from us during the forty-day march after Caribe. Armando Castellanos was one of the first to spot me and he was literally jumping up and down. He was always a really emotional guy, and he started crying and put his arms around me. When I hugged him back, I thought I had my arms around a bag of brooms. Armando had always been a fit guy, but he had gotten very thin. He told me he had hepatitis, and though his skin didn't show any signs of it, he was almost unrecognizable. Despite his physical condition, he was the same upbeat, positive guy.

As was always the case during our captivity, this was a good-news/bad-news deal. On the one hand, I was pleased to see their familiar faces; on the other, it was devastating that these eight military prisoners were still in captivity. All of them had been in custody years longer than we had. In the time since the forty-day march, we had speculated endlessly about what happened to everyone. We'd also wondered a lot of times about when we might get put back into a group of other prisoners. The eight of them seemed thrilled to see us, too, and our little reunion was a mix of handshakes, pats on the back, questions and answers, and a rush of excited chatter. Making things even better was the fact that we were going to be mixed in with a group of military and police guys. Based on our time in the political camp, I knew they conducted themselves the way that I wanted to handle my captivity.

Once I got through greeting the eight of them, I saw two more people standing there—Ingrid and Lucho. Life had not been easy on any of us for the last two years and it showed in all of our faces, our eyes, and in the way we carried ourselves. Ingrid and Lucho seemed as diminished physically as the rest of us, but it was their attitudes that had changed the most. They were genuinely glad to see us and their warm greeting was in stark contrast to their behavior when they'd first seen us two years earlier. Marc used the term *beaten down* to describe them, and I agreed, but I thought that their newfound humility suited them. It didn't seem to me that they'd suffered physically more than the rest of us, but their egos had been knocked down a peg or two, and that was fine with me.

Unfortunately it didn't take long for me to learn that their personalities weren't quite as changed as I'd hoped. Some of the same issues that had plagued us when we were with them at Caribe continued in what we quickly began to refer to as the Reunion Camp. The happy couple reminded me of some people from high school you see at your ten-year reunion. They look different physically, but they're still the same pains in the ass. I trusted them both as little as I ever did, but I was willing to play nice so long as they didn't pull any of the shit they had the first time.

As it turned out, Ingrid and Lucho had already been separated from the rest of the prisoners and each other because of some trouble they'd caused. We didn't get the specifics, but that didn't matter. All we knew was that Ingrid's hooch was at the edge of camp, as far from the other prisoners as possible. Normally she wasn't allowed to interact with any of them, and she could only speak with Lucho briefly each day. Their days of being joined at the hip were done.

During our two-year separation from them, we'd heard a rumor that the pair had attempted an escape. We didn't give it too much credence at the time because the loopy FARC female guerrilla who'd told us about it was a member of the flat-earth society, but early on at the Reunion Camp, we were able to confirm that Ingrid and Lucho had actually made a break and been recaptured. They'd gotten out and traveled at night down the river. Lucho was in poor health overall because of his diabetes, so they could only float for a few hours on their best days. The water was frigid, so to avoid hypothermia, they had to limit their time in it. Each day as they grew weaker, their time in the river shrank. Finally, they were picked up.

Upon hearing this, I gained a bit more respect for them. If they were being separated because they posed an escape threat, then good for them. I didn't like to see how the FARC increased security on them—by using chains on them at night—but at least if they had "earned" that extra security, it was because of something valiant they'd done and not just because they'd been treating people poorly.

Marc, Tom, and I had talked about escape plans endlessly, and hindsight is always 20/20, but I had to admire Ingrid and Lucho for having the balls to attempt what they did. The three of us had always talked balls and brains. If you were going to use one, it had better be in direct proportion to the other. We were not going to do anything that would place additional security on us. If we were going to escape, it had to be as close to a sure thing as possible. Either that or our situation would have to be so dire that the risks of getting caught would outweigh the risks of staying in captivity. I wasn't sure if Ingrid and Lucho had been in a hot zone like we had, but if they made their move without considering the risks of chains in an area like that, then their plans were deeply flawed. There was no way in hell I was going to get myself put in chains and chance being handicapped by them in case of a rescue or an attack. That was one mantra that I clung to: Don't do anything stupid.

Of course, I did stupid things anyway, but at least I was aware of those times and kept them to a minimum. When everyone swapped stories of the previous two years, I realized just how much we'd missed other human contact. As much as we tried to keep ourselves busy, it wasn't possible to fill up the entire day when it was just the three of us. Having ten people to update kept us all very busy. If Miguel Arteaga didn't have a question for us or a story to tell, then Juan Carlos Bermeo wanted to get started on English lessons. Our days went from boring to busy to booked solid.

We'd all heard bits and pieces of what was going on in one another's lives through the message programs. Because we were all in and out of radio contact, everyone filled the others in on what we'd heard. Perhaps

the worst news was about Gloria Polanco. The FARC had executed her
husband. As tough as we all had it as hostages, that poor woman was a
hostage, two of her sons had been hostages, and her husband had been
killed by these same terrorists. That would have been too much for me,
and we all said, and sincerely meant it, that we wished we could be with
her or be able to send her some kind of support. Marc did mention her
in his prayers, and I added a few good thoughts as well.

The news wasn't all bad, especially for me. Ever since I'd heard Patricia's first message, I had continued to wonder about the twins and her.
At the Reunion Camp, I learned that Patricia had taken it upon herself
to send more messages to me. Juancho relayed to me what he'd heard
while I was out of radio contact. Both Keith Jr. and Nick were fine and
still living with her in Colombia. I was, of course, a little worried about
their presence in country, but they were with Patricia and that was a
great thing.

The opposite of this good news was that I had not heard from Malia
in years. As hard as it was, I had started assuming that this silence
could mean only one thing: My relationship was over and done with.
I'd loved Malia and wanted her to be my wife. She was a wonderful
woman, but you can tell a lot about somebody when adversity strikes.
Marc pointed out that she had hung in there with me when she found
out about my affair, and I had to give her credit for that. Unfortunately,
the three of us had crashed before my relationship with Malia had gone
too far down Forgiveness Road.

Thrown into the midst of all this was Patricia. She'd seemingly been
able to put aside all the shit I'd done—cheating on her, getting her
pregnant, getting pissed at her for getting pregnant, and telling her to
forget about any future with me—to let me know how the boys were
doing. That took some courage, and she didn't just say how the boys
were doing, but she also told me that she was hoping that I'd get back
soon. She told me that the boys needed me.

That last statement hit me hard. When you're a captive for a long time, you have to rely on so many other people to keep you safe and alive. I had Marc and Tom, and I knew that they needed me in some ways, but the truth of the matter was that if I was somehow no longer in their picture, they were going to be fine. I took comfort in knowing this, but I also liked the idea that someone needed me. Kyle and Lauren were always on my mind, and I knew I wanted to get back to them, but by September of 2007, I wasn't sure just how much they needed me. They were twelve and seventeen; I'd been fourteen when I lost my mom. I knew it wasn't easy to lose a parent at any age, but I believed they'd be okay.

With Patricia and the twins, I wasn't as certain. Colombia was a pretty volatile place. Their mother was, at least when I was with her, a flight attendant. That meant she was going to be gone a lot. I didn't know how her family was going to react to her giving birth to half-gringo kids out of wedlock. I didn't know what their lives were going to be like once they got to be school age. I knew all too well from my youth that there were asses out there who would give them all flavors of grief for being bastards. As antiquated as that idea might have been in most of the U.S., Colombia was a fairly conservative place when it came to such matters.

Still, the irony that Patricia, a woman I'd parted on angry terms with, was staying loyal wasn't lost on me. It was just hard for me to believe that she genuinely cared for me when my own fiancée wasn't even picking up the phone to send messages. The fact that Patricia seemed to be devoted to me meant something, but what it would mean when I got out was anybody's guess.

"I just hope it's not about the money," I confided to Marc one day after Juan Carlos told me about Patricia's messages. "I told Patricia I'd be there for the kids. She doesn't need to do this for money."

"Who cares about her motives? It's pretty admirable for her to hang in there," Marc pointed out. I thought about his words for a minute, and I thought about the fact that Marc's own wife hadn't been sending messages.

"That does say something, doesn't it?" I responded, asking the question as much to myself as to Marc.

Since we'd been in captivity, I'd had nothing but time to think about my past. I'd thought a lot about why my first marriage had failed, why it had taken me six years to finally commit to marrying Malia, why I sometimes found it easier to go outside my relationships and find comfort in the arms of other women. I'd been running from something, figuring always that if I played it fast and loose, I couldn't be caught in any kind of trap of expectations and demands. I was a pretty selfish son of a bitch, truth be told. I figured that since I was a good dad to my kids and a single parent tackling the responsibilities of being a caregiver and provider, the world owed me my little moments of stepping out and finding pleasure wherever I could.

Funny as it was, it took being captive for me to start realizing that my choices before the crash had imprisoned me much like the FARC had. I also realized that the world didn't owe me a damn thing. What we've got in this life is equal to what we give. I didn't believe that I deserved to be held hostage, but it sure as hell was a huge wake-up call that let me know that standard operating procedure before the crash would have eventually led me to some other kind of crisis. It was time I stepped up and applied the principles the Marine Corps had instilled in me, the principles I'd allowed to become diluted, to my personal life. It seemed to me that Patricia was doing a pretty good job of teaching by example. Just because you do something wrong doesn't mean you walk away; you stick around and make things better.

Whether it was because of Patricia or just because of the order of things, I was on an uptick in terms of hope. I can't say shares were at an all-time high, but they had definitely rebounded with this new group in charge of us. The camp was one of the nicer ones we'd been placed in. Just having guards posted on the perimeter with no fences enclosing us did a lot for me psychologically, and knowing that our border was easily penetrated made it easier for me to put up with some other parts of a captive's life. Being able to go down to the water to bathe whenever we wanted to also helped. Our schedule wasn't as rigid as before. Our new jailer, Enrique, was proving to be a decent *comandante*. His guards were a lot more no-nonsense but at least we were being given some freedoms. I liked how that felt and was developing a greater appetite for more.

The FARC had built a pair of volleyball courts next to our camp. Basically, they had cleared an area of trees and undergrowth and strung an actual volleyball net between two trees they'd left standing. On the other court, they did the same except they strung a vine in place of a net. I'd never been a huge fan of the game, but I decided to participate. Whether we were playing against the FARC or there were hostages and guerrillas on the same side didn't matter to me as much as I'd thought it would.

The first time we played, I was stunned. In the last three and half years, I'd been able to exercise, I'd marched a hell of a lot, and I'd even had to triple-time it a bit. What surprised me was that I was able to move freely, but at first I couldn't. I had no chains on me, but it felt like my feet were encased in stone. I knew I was in good enough physical condition to make a quick move and lunge for a ball, but my mind wasn't agile enough to get me to do it. I'd always loved moving. Whether I was out in the woods somewhere carrying my Baretta shotgun or riding bikes with the kids or standing stock still with my hands inside the guts of a Pratt & Whitney engine torquing down a bolt to spec, I wasn't a sit still kind of guy. Chess was a sit still kind of game, and I eventually got around to playing and enjoying it, but I was a far more active person outside of captivity than I was inside it.

These newfound freedoms at the Reunion Camp reminded me of just how much I was missing out on. Instead of this making me angry, it made me more determined than ever to end this game playing and get the hell out of Dodge. It wasn't going to be enough to just be on the same court as those guys. I wanted to win, win big, and go home.

THIRTEEN

Reunited

September 2006–April 2007

TOM

We entered the Reunion Camp filled with hope—if for no other reason than that the camp seemed to be a more permanent structure. We'd been on the move for so long—ever since we'd left the Chess Camp—that we were all looking forward to a more established routine. After months on the move, we craved living conditions that would make us feel a little more at home, and though we knew the risks involved in being with another group of prisoners, we were confident that the stability would be good for all three of us.

While we knew the military and police prisoners from our time at Caribe and the forty-day march, we became much more familiar with their personalities and their group dynamic at the Reunion Camp. By the time we arrived there in September of 2006, most of the military and police prisoners were heading into their ninth year of captivity. The year 1998 had not been particularly good for the military. Three of the men we were with—José Miguel Arteaga (with us he went by Miguel), William Pérez, and Ricardo (call me "Richard") Marulanda—had been captured during a battle with the FARC that year, during which the FARC killed eighty and took forty-three hostages.

Each of the other hostages had witnessed their fellow officers being killed or taken hostage in large numbers. Jhon Pinchao was the least fortunate of the bunch. During an attack on the city of Mitú, he and sixty of his fellow police officers had been captured. As part of the peace process, the FARC released the vast majority of the policemen it had taken hostage. Jhon was one of only six who remained in captivity.

Raimundo Malagón, another of the military and police hostages, was one of the more unforgettable characters we met. At five foot three, he was pretty stocky and his intense personality contributed to his bull-doglike ways. As soon as we entered their camp, he was insistent that we teach him English. Meanwhile Juan Carlos Bermeo was one of the highest-ranking hostages the FARC held and, by a few weeks, had been held hostage for the shortest period of time. "Juancho," as he preferred to be called, developed a strong relationship with Keith.

From the outset, it was clear that these men had endured a lot. We couldn't imagine what it was like to be in captivity as long as they had. Our three-plus years had been hard enough. None of them was stark raving mad—far from it—but they had developed their own camp quirks. Privately, the three of us compared this group to the characters on the television show *Hogan's Heroes*. It became clear to us after a few weeks that Miguel Arteaga was one of the favored prisoners. He worked for the FARC and was rewarded with things like bags of powdered milk, *fariña* (dried and ground yucca), and a whole host of other little objects and food items. He had a little worktable and tools. The FARC provided him with fabric—jungle camo—which he would cut and stitch into hats. His craftsmanship was excellent and he even made one for Keith. None of us liked the idea that he was helping the FARC and receiving favors in return, but by that point in our captivity, we weren't really going to judge him. We hadn't been held captive for as long as he had. If sewing hats and doing other things for the FARC satisfied his general need to keep busy, so be it; he was just doing what we all were, adapting to his environment and circumstances in order to better endure.

He wasn't alone in assuming the role of a "trusty." William Pérez, another military prisoner, did some work for the FARC as well. The FARC never formally gave that title to either Arteaga or Pérez, but it was clear from how they were being treated that they'd assumed some of the functions of the prison trusty. Like prison inmates being granted special privileges by a warden or guards, Pérez and Arteaga were fed better, granted greater latitude in their behavior, and were generally chummier with the guards than we were. Pérez spent most of his time working on creating the leather weapons vests the FARC wore, but he also worked on fixing radios for them and unofficially serving as their medic—a duty he'd had with the Colombian Army. Pérez was one of the quietest guys we'd met and he never seemed to flaunt his relationship with the FARC. With Arteaga, we felt the need to be a bit more careful. We weren't sure of the exact nature of his role with the FARC. He was a little more obvious about his stash of FARC goodies than Pérez was.

Still, we never knew either of them to do anything to put any of the rest of us in a bad spot, and because we didn't know how their arrangements with the FARC guards had begun, we all kept to ourselves about it. For all we knew, the FARC had approached them and initiated the relationship or the guerrillas were just showing their gratitude for the work that was being done. We took a don't-ask, don't-tell approach initially; as long as we weren't being abused, we didn't mind that they were granted extra privileges.

We always had to walk a very fine line in relationships with our captors. We thought that we'd done a good job with our previous crew of not assisting them in winning their war. Making hats and weapons belts, fixing radios, and treating patients seemed to fall on the relatively harmless side of the line. Though we wouldn't have done any of those things for the FARC, we also weren't going to criticize Pérez and Arteaga too harshly. Arteaga and Pérez didn't seem to get along too well; they seemed to be in competition with one another. I thought of it as the two ass-kissers at any job struggling to be the number one ass-kisser. All we needed was a watercooler and a break room to make the office politics feel more like they had at home.

Stepping into this new situation meant that we had to tread carefully with our fellow prisoners and with the guards. Like we had done with Milton's group, we assessed how we could use our relationships with the guards to our best advantage. As it turned out, we didn't have a whole lot to discuss. This FARC group was far more professional and less likely to interact with us on any level but the most superficial. This was most obvious in our trading for goods. With Milton's nicotine fiends, we were able to work deals with them directly. Though the currency remained the same in the Reunion Camp, the method of exchange was completely different. We had to go through Arteaga to trade cigarettes for what we needed. Arteaga in particular had more supplies—batteries for the radios, bags of powdered milk, sleeves of crackers—than he really needed. That didn't stop him from wanting to accumulate more. He used his role as a go-between to his full advantage. He wasn't greedy; he was bored and needed some form of excitement.

Our fellow prisoners weren't the only ones who seemed to have a surplus of gear and food. The FARC in this First Front were the best-equipped group we'd seen. They had portable DVD players, and one of the first nights in that camp, we watched a Jackie Chan movie. We were mesmerized. After so long without seeing a moving image on a screen, the effect was almost hypnotic. They could have shown a movie with cows grazing for an hour and a half and we would have watched it. The FARC powered most of their electronics—laptop computers, DVD players, and communications radios—with motorcycle batteries wired in a series or a Honda portable gas-powered generator.

In addition they used a solar panel to recharge their batteries. Since we were no longer in the mountains shrouded in foliage, they could set the panels up in a clearing and get direct sunlight for a few hours a day.

As always, that increase in sunlight seemed to power us up a bit, too. We enjoyed the coolness in the deeper jungle, but having bright light seemed to lift our spirits. We became extremely optimistic that our groups being put together meant something. Why would we have been separated for so long if they were only going to put us together for no reason? A day or so into our stay, we turned on the radio. Enrique had loaned us his *multibanda* radio and for the first time in years we had access to AM-FM and shortwave frequencies. The three of us were sitting together with a few of the others listening to the news. I was half paying attention when I heard the word *despeje*. I looked over to Keith and Marc.

"Am I hearing things?"

They both had huge grins on their faces.

"No, sir, you are not. Uribe just announced that he's approved a *despeje*. He wants the FARC back at the bargaining table, so he gave them their DMZ." Keith clapped his hands and stomped his feet.

"Thank you, God." Marc leaned back, looked to the sky, and heaved an enormous sigh.

"We could be home for Thanksgiving. I could be strapping on the Stansell feedbag. How awesome would that be?"

Everyone started talking. The other prisoners were grasping one another's arms, shaking hands, and patting one another on the back. They had all shed years right before my eyes. I sometimes forgot that most of the Colombians there had been captured when they were in their early twenties. They'd spent a majority of what should have been the most enjoyable and productive parts of their lives in captivity. The news that the hard-liner Uribe was willing to grant the FARC a demilitarized zone in exchange for peaceful negotiations made kids of us all.

After that announcement, we stayed glued to the radio. The country was in a complete uproar; Uribe had taken such a firm stance against the FARC for so long that the conservatives couldn't believe that he was caving in to their demands. Moderates were hopeful that a negotiated peace process could bring an end to the fighting, and the leftists were claiming a huge victory for the FARC. At that point, politics was the furthest thing from my mind. I was going home to see my son and my wife and that was all that mattered.

We spent another two days at the Reunion Camp before we got the order to move out. I was so confident we were on our way to being released that I gave away a bit of the junk I'd accumulated over the years. We marched for a couple of days, setting up temporary camps along the way. On the third day, Enrique came up to me and said, "This is something, isn't it? I walk up to this camp and I see three smiling Americans. You guys are getting along good. You get along good with the others. Very nice."

I didn't know Enrique that well, but I could sense that he was looser and more relaxed than I'd seen him before. He was barely able to contain his huge grin.

"Do you know anything more about the *despeje* than we do?" I asked him.

He wagged his head from side to side, looking like a bobble-head toy, raised one eyebrow, and squinted at me.

"All I know is this. I have my orders here. I'm here with you guys waiting for the Catalinas to come. That's all I know."

"Catalinas, flying in here? Where will they take us?"

Enrique held up his hands to ward off any more questions. "If I get the order to put you on a Catalina, that's what I will do."

As hard as it was to believe what he was saying, Enrique's words led me to peel layers off of the cynicism and distrust that had callused my hope for so long. This was the real deal—none of Milton's nonsense. Enrique was in direct contact with the higher-ups in the FARC. We didn't have a long track record with him, but to that point everything he'd told us he would do for us he'd done. I didn't think that anyone could be such a good actor as to make us wholeheartedly believe that our release was only days, and maybe even hours, away.

Now, marching with Enrique and everyone else, we all felt lighter, food tasted more flavorful, the jungle scenery seemed more lush and vivid. We were going home. The words seemed difficult to form in my mind and on my lips. Every day, as we marched along, we'd catch one another's eye and smile and shake our heads. Every task took on new meaning. One day the three of us were in camp, breaking things down after a night in the jungle. I noticed that Marc was done well before I was. That hadn't always been the case. So I said to him, "You've gotten pretty damn good at this."

"Had a lot of practice." Marc hefted his *equipo* on one shoulder and then shrugged the other arm through the remaining strap.

"You don't even need help with that," I said.

"I'm traveling light today, Tom," was Marc's reply.

We both were.

KEITH

For a while before the news of the *despeje,* I'd been shedding some things I either no longer needed or no longer had value to me. Among them was any hope that my relationship with my fiancée was still viable. At the Reunion Camp, I'd heard references to Patricia and me a couple of times on the radio. I was the gringo hostage who was the father of the two kids with the Colombian woman. I couldn't imagine that this was easy for Malia to hear, if she was hearing anything at all. When I did get messages—from my kids, from my mom and dad, my brother, and even my ex-wife—no one ever even mentioned Malia's name. We'd been together for six years when Tom, Marc, and I were taken hostage and it was at about half that amount of time into captivity that I began to shed some of those memories and thoughts of what our future life together might be.

The heaviest thing, the most burdensome thing, the thing that was so difficult to strap on my *equipo* and haul comfortably, was the house Malia and I had planned on building. I'd listened to Tom talk about his new house and all the things he wanted to do with it. I didn't say much about my dream house since it wasn't anything more substantial than a hope and a catalog of images—furniture I liked, a big screen TV to settle down in front of. The funny thing was, when news of the *despeje* came through and I found out how close I was to getting home, all the things I'd dreamed of—the house, the furniture, the TV, the motorcycles, the fishing boat—were as easy to pitch out as the old razors, T-shirts worn to rags, and the rest of the crap we all got rid of when we knew we were waiting on a plane to get us the hell out of there.

I wasn't a pack rat by any means, but instead of just ditching everything, I started thinking about replacing a few of those "back home" items. A few days into our stay at the Reunion Camp, I was again able to hear one of Patricia's radio messages with my own ears. She must have developed a good relationship with the radio stations, because they let her just pour out her heart. She told me how much she missed me and reiterated how much the boys needed me to be around to be their father. She ended by saying that I was *el hombre de su vida,* the man of her life.

That translation doesn't do justice to what these words mean to a Colombian. It comes across a little too clichéd, a little too romance-novel cheesy, but I knew how powerful they were. What was more, actually listening to Patricia's voice carried even greater significance. It was one thing when Juancho had paraphrased her thoughts, but it was quite another to hear her utter them herself. Listening to her, I could sense the genuine care and legitimate concern in her voice. Suddenly I began to shed some layers of my skepticism about her motives and about our future.

As elated as I was at the sound of the word *despeje* and at Patricia's message, I knew I couldn't just leave every part of the goddamn awful shit we'd been through. Those experiences were as much a part of me and who I was as anything that came before that engine failure. Every bit of it was going to be returning home with me to the States. It wasn't going to weigh me down a bit because I thought we'd all done ourselves proud—Enrique's words to Tom had confirmed what we'd thought all along. We'd conducted ourselves as honorably as we could under the circumstances. We'd endured and triumphed. As we marched for those five days after we left the Reunion Camp, I was feeling pretty good about being reunited with parts of myself I'd had to tuck away to protect during the long years of captivity. It was like seeing old friends, good friends, best friends I'd been absent from for a good long while.

On day five post–Reunion Camp, we'd exited a bit of dry jungle and crossed into a fairly large field of slash-and-burn. The FARC had just been through there, obviously getting it ready for drug-growing operations. The smell of burned vegetation and the tang of gasoline was on my tongue. I stopped and spat. Marc and Tom pulled up alongside me.

"Hey, Tom, it's clear here; why don't you flip that thing on?" Marc asked.

Tom took out the *multibanda,* pulled up the antennae, and did a few revolutions trying to get the best signal. He looked around; the FARC guards seemed content to let us have a brief break. When we finally got a signal, we could hear President Uribe's voice, and the word that immediately jumped out at me was *denuncié.* That word did not bode well. It was clear that Uribe was wound up about something.

The day before, October 19, a car bomb had exploded outside a military training academy in Bogotá. Twenty-three people had been injured. Uribe was outraged. I looked over at Tom and Marc, and they looked like I felt, as if somebody had kicked me in the nuts—once so they could hurt me, a second time to remind me of what the pain was like, and then a third time so that I would never want to experience that torturous sensation again.

"Fucking FARC. Fucking Uribe. Fucking olive branch shoved up all our asses."

Marc, Tom, and I sat down with our heads slumped. Minutes passed. The military guys came and joined us.

"You heard?" Marc asked.

They all nodded, every one of them looking as downcast as we were. Juancho sat next to me, and we briefly put our arms around each other's shoulders.

"What do you think?" I asked him.

"Uribe was clear. No prisoner exchange now."

Marc chewed at his lip. "I heard him, man. I heard him very clear. 'The only option left is military rescue.' "

The specter of a botched Colombian military rescue or the FARC's deadly response was our version of the Cross, circling and circling high above, feeding its intel and coordinates to them. Not for the first time, I said to Marc, "We're fucked."

Tom added, "Not just by the FARC. France. Switzerland. Spain. Uribe asked them to end their diplomatic efforts and replace their envoys with a military presence."

Ingrid approached our sullen group and added her take.

"Then there is some hope. A unified effort. Perhaps the French will be able to reason with Uribe."

"It was the U.S. that did it." The voice came out of nowhere and it belonged to William Pérez. "I heard that the FARC are blaming you. They said that the U.S. did it so that they could take stronger military action against the FARC."

I couldn't believe it. I looked at Ingrid and Lucho and then at the military guys. None of them would look me in the eye. It was true that the FARC had not used car bombs before, but we'd heard rumors that they had contacts with other rebel groups and other terrorist organizations. I reminded everyone of what we'd heard regarding an explosion at a munitions camp that had killed a bunch of guerrillas. They weren't messing with that warhead so that they could send a souvenir home.

Tom spoke up. "The FARC have never admitted to anything. Why would they admit to this? For God's sake, we were in a camp where a guy deliberately shot himself in the head and the FARC told us it was a pistol cleaning accident. They don't ever tell the truth."

Eventually the guards got us moving again. The three of us went out ahead of the others.

"We've been here before," Tom said.

I knew what he was saying, and it had nothing to do with our physical location.

"Tom's right," I said. "We're Teflon guys. Nothing sticks to us. This absolutely bites big-time, but we've been here before."

"Absolutely. Déjà vu all over again. The FARC or Uribe will come around again. They have to. This can't keep going on." Marc kicked at a clod of dirt.

"It's like I've told you guys before," Tom added. "Colombian politics are like the weather. If you don't like what you've got, stick around for a day or two. It's bound to change."

"We got nothing better to do than wait," I said.

Marc was all ready there with the bandage. "I was thinking about the Freedom Ride. If we get back before Christmas, it's going to be pretty damn cold. We'll probably have to stay pretty far south to get to the West Coast."

"I can't think that far ahead, Marc," I replied. "Halloween is in eleven days and I've got trick or treat on the brain."

October 20, 2006, may not have been a day that lived in infamy to the rest of the world, but it kicked our asses more than just a little bit. Our exchange of jungle repartee was our first attempt at restoring order. We knew we were running the risk of flying too high. That we'd nose-dived into the ground and then had to dig ourselves out was just a fact of life. We'd become accustomed to taking on that job; it didn't mean we liked having to do it, but we knew what needed to be done. A day or so later, Uribe revealed that the Colombians had intercepted a phone message from Mono JoJoy that proved the FARC were involved in the bombing, and that mostly settled the issue of U.S. involvement.

Adding to our pile of misery was the fact that we also weren't in a permanent camp. Now that the *despeje* had fallen through, we were back to where we were before the Reunion Camp—on the move, roving through the jungle, with no home in sight. To get ourselves back on our collective feet, we resumed as much of our normal routine as possible. The FARC built a temporary camp just a few kilometers from where we'd stopped and heard the bad news. They immediately cleared an area for a volleyball court. If the three of us had one thing in our favor, we were still in the honeymoon period with Enrique. We had been referring to him as Gafas or "Glasses" because of the prominent specs he wore, and we thought he was one of the few FARC we'd been involved with who did have a pretty focused vision of how hostages should be treated.

Enrique's group also provided us with *tablas* to sleep on. Marc was the only holdout among us when it came to hammock sleeping. His back just wouldn't let him do it. He generally slept underneath the spot where I'd strung my hammock. That preserved some space for everyone else in camp. We slept in two rows, with a walkway between us. Ingrid was always kept at one end of the camp and Lucho at the other. Their visiting hours were rigidly enforced and the four guards on duty at any one time made it almost impossible to speak with them.

Despite the fallout from the car bomb, we continued to pass the time much as we had at the Reunion Camp. We still tutored some of the military hostages in English. In some ways, we were as much a language-acquisition exchange program as we were hostages. Each of us had our own set of students and came up with our own methods of teaching. Because we were so immersed in Spanish, we had become proficient enough that we rarely had questions for the Colombians.

Along with tutoring, working out, reading, and playing chess and poker, the radio remained a vital part of our survival. Though we could understand the Spanish-language broadcasts on the radio, we always enjoyed listening to English-language stations. Enrique's shortwave radio allowed us to pick up more English-language programming, and no matter how good we got at Spanish, it was still nice to hear our native language coming over the airwaves. With stations like the BBC and the Voice of America, we got a different perspective on world events. Throughout our captivity, we'd picked up bits and pieces of information about what was happening in the larger world, but it seemed that news about hostages in other parts of the world always grabbed our attention. We were horrified when we found out that an American businessman in Iraq, Nicholas Berg, had been beheaded. We remembered that before him, an American journalist had been kidnapped in Pakistan and suffered the same fate. As much as we were horrified by this loss of life, such events reminded us that our situation could have been much worse.

The radio often gave us small pieces of information that could spur conversation for hours—even days—at a time. We were shocked to learn that a barrel of crude oil had risen in price to $75. We took that tidbit and ran with it, expounding on our theories of geopolitics and oil and the plausibility of alternative fuels like ethanol, electricity, and hydrogen. We had seen ads for new Dell computers that at $850 were many times more powerful than what we'd paid nearly three times as much for. One of the radio programs we listened to had a technology report and from it we learned that there was this music device called an iPod. We heard one advertisement for a car dealership offering a free preprogrammed iPod with five thousand songs on it with the purchase of a new car. Based on that, we began listing the songs we would put on our iPod as an exercise to get through the day.

At about the same time, Marc and I started listening to a program on Colombian national radio that played all jazz and blues. I was a big fan of the blues, not a real aficionado, but I knew what I liked. I thought that Marc might get into it, and he did. We'd lie in the dark at night and

Muddy Waters would come out of that little plastic box. Suddenly a bit of home was transplanted into the jungle. We also listened to Radio Netherlands and a weekly program called *Curious Orange*. After a hard day's march, it was always good to have something to settle down with. Music kept us going during the day—all we had to do was to mention the title of a song and we were off in our heads and out of the mud and the mire.

One night we were listening to Radio Netherlands, waiting for *Curious Orange* to come on. The program was in English, and we heard a mention of Colombia and the FARC. A young Dutch woman had left her family at the age of twenty-two. She told her family and friends that she was going to Colombia to teach poverty-stricken kids. For the past two years, no one had heard from her. She was from a fairly wealthy family, had spent a semester in Colombia, and was fluent in Spanish, English, German, and Dutch.

Marc said to me, "Do you remember—"

I cut him off. "I know where you're going with this. The pretty girl at the proof of life. I knew she was from somewhere else. I thought Cuba, but who knew?"

"That was her. How many other European-looking women are running around with the FARC?"

"How the hell does a young Dutch girl get mixed up with this bunch?" I thought again of Lauren and was grateful that no matter what else, I could count on her not having joined a terrorist organization, unless something had drastically changed at the Delta Delta Gamma sorority.

We listened a while longer and learned that the young woman's name was Tanja Nijmeijer. The description they gave of her fit with what we remembered. How she'd ended up with the FARC was difficult to figure out. She'd said all the right FARC bullshit and she could hardly breathe without uttering something anti-American. That fit with the profile of the young idealist her family and friends described who was so upset with the social and economic injustice she'd seen in Colombia that she'd gone back to help right the wrongs.

By the end of 2006, we hadn't managed to recover our losses from the highs of early October, but the radios and one another had helped us to avoid a complete free fall. If we were a barrel of oil, we were at about forty-eight dollars—not bad but not setting the world on fire, either. None of us was too happy with being on the march again, but as the year came to a close we did manage to enjoy a few moments—even if the enjoyment came vicariously. Christmas Day 2006, the FARC let us rest in our temporary camp. They offered us a bit of their home-brewed fruit-based alcohol. The stuff was pretty good, and a few sips to celebrate the holiday and the relief from the march were welcome. The FARC partied all day, mostly just playing volleyball and drinking. The games got louder as the day went on. We tried to ignore them, and we were glad to hear them yelling, "*¡Pare la bulla!*" at one another instead of telling us to keep it quiet.

At one point, one of the young guards who seemed like a decent guy waddled over to take his post. He was clearly shit-faced, and when he sat down on his platform, he could barely keep his head up. His buddies kept coming by to straighten him up, but he'd list to one side or the other, half asleep and fully buzzed. Finally they gave up and dragged him back over to the volleyball court. I was glad for the distraction and watched the other guerrillas give him hell. Marc was sitting next to me reading, and Tom was off playing chess. I nudged Marc in the arm.

"Merry Christmas, bro." I pointed to where the FARC were playing.

"And Happy New Year, too. That's Ferney. What is he doing here?"

"Look who's with him."

"And 2.5, too? I guess they're having their own reunion."

"Maybe what we've been hearing is true." It was a surprise to see some of the guards we'd left behind at the abandoned hospital after the forty-day march. At one of our camps, some of the military guys had seen a group of four prisoners off in the distance. We suspected that this other group might be the prisoners we'd parted ways with back at the hospital. Now, as we saw their guard crew mingling with Enrique's bunch guarding us, it seemed possible that we'd meet up with more people from Caribe.

Marc stood with his hands on his hips looking across the camp. He shook his head and looked up at the sky. The sun was just beginning to go down and everything was gilded by an amazing late-afternoon gold hue.

"I just hope there's five of them. All I want for Christmas is for there to be five of them."

"Me, too, bro." I got up and stood alongside him. "Regardless, Marc, Julian was a great guy. We owe it to him and everybody else that didn't make it to get the hell out of here."

Just before we'd left Milton's group, Tatiana had told us she'd heard that Julian Guevera, the military hostage who'd been forced to crawl on the forty-day march, had died in captivity. Julian was one of the most heroic of the hostages we'd encountered. He suffered from tuberculosis, and the FARC refused to treat him for it. When Tatiana told us that he'd died, I didn't want to believe it. Whenever I thought I was having a rough day on a march, I thought of him and everything he'd been through—a serious gunshot wound to the head, tuberculosis, being chained through all those days and nights while struggling to march. I didn't have a hell of a lot to complain about in comparison.

Marc had grown real quiet thinking about Julian and what I'd said.

"All we needed was the Catalinas, you know? Enrique said he was just waiting for orders to put us on that airplane. A wing and a prayer, Keith. I got the one covered, we just needed the other. So close. So close."

"I know, I was tasting the turkey. I really was."

"I've got a pack of crackers with our names on it. Let's get Tom and celebrate."

MARC

As 2006 rolled over into 2007, we continued to have at least one blessing to be grateful for. With the exception of the polyester-cord tethers we'd had to wear for a bit, we had never been chained, unlike our Colombian counterparts. None of us knew for sure why the FARC had not chained us, but we assumed that Enrique's statement about us being well behaved had a lot to do with it. After the collapse of the *despeje* in October 2006, President Uribe once again reminded the world that the only viable option for the hostages was a military rescue. Tom, Keith, and I reiterated to one another how important it was that we remain chain-free. The Colombians handled the difference in treatment well, never complaining to the FARC that we should be in chains at night since they were. Complaining about your own bad situation was one thing; doing something to put someone else in a bad situation was another.

Shortly after the New Year, William Pérez and I were playing chess in my *coleta*. William could be unpredictable at times, and we suspected that he was bipolar. On some occasions, he was sullen and silent, and on others, he was energetic and enthusiastic. On this particular day, he was in one of his up periods. He'd come walking through camp shouting, "Marc, are you afraid of me today?" He was a good chess player and he kicked my butt all the time, but I liked the challenge. While we were playing, Moster, our new *oficial* and the FARC guard responsible for us, came in and began talking to Richard Marulanda. We were busy with the game, but we looked over at them and saw that Moster was upset with Richard about something. They kept glancing at us and then quickly looking away. Richard and William shared a *coleta* and were chained together at night. From what I could figure out, they'd had some kind of dispute and now Moster was intervening.

When Moster was through talking with Richard, he went to speak to William. Moster smiled and said, "How are you, comrade?"

I knew that William was a trusty, but the difference between the way Moster spoke to the rest of us and the way he addressed William was startling. It was like the two of them were buddies, not guard and hostage.

"What did Marulanda do?" I asked.

It struck me that Moster had already made up his mind about what happened and was not really investigating the source of the dispute at all. William basically blamed Richard for the problem that had cropped up, but he didn't need to. Moster simply said, "Yes. Yes. Don't worry about it. I'll take care of everything."

The next morning, when the guards came to unlock the Colombians' chains, they left Marulanda chained up. Another guard dug a little trench near his bed, took William's chain, and attached it to Richard's.

We were all sitting and eating, and Keith asked, "What is up with that? What'd the dumb-ass Marulanda do this time?"

I explained what I'd witnessed. Marulanda could get on everyone's last nerve, and he was not Keith's favorite by a long shot, but there was little to justify something like this.

"That's just wrong. The guy's got to shit and piss right there because of what Pérez said." A vein in Keith's temple was throbbing and I knew he wanted to confront William. He looked at Marulanda and then at Pérez, who simply sat eating his food as if nothing unusual were going on. Keith stood up, and I tensed, thinking that he was going to go after William. He didn't; instead he walked over to where our food had been set out for us, ladled out a bowl of soup, and brought it over to Marulanda. For the next week, Marulanda remained in chains. He didn't gripe about it, and just kept to himself. I'd always suspected he was a tough guy and could put up with a lot. Marulanda didn't want to say what the fight had been about, but he eventually told us that William was upset because Marulanda had been moving around a lot at night. His movements rattled the chains and woke William up. They'd exchanged words and that was the extent of it. At least until William took matters into his own hands.

Ever since we'd arrived at the Reunion Camp, we'd known that William was a trusty, but seeing what Enrique and Moster had done to Richard made us realize just what William was capable of. We hated seeing anyone in chains, and the thought that another hostage was responsible for putting someone there sickened us all. After that, I stopped playing chess with William. He seemed to have slipped into a black cycle and I wondered if maybe guilt had brought on his darker mood.

Incidents like this made the ever-shifting dynamics of the hostages difficult to predict. Alliances changed, positions in hierarchies moved, and all the three of us could do was watch as the personalities ebbed and flowed. Of everyone, Jhon Pinchao seemed the least integrated into the group. Like the other military and police guys, he'd been held since 1998, but though we'd spent quite a bit of time with him, none of us really knew much about him. As my language skills developed, I struggled to find common ground with Jhon. I liked him and he was a good-hearted person, but it was still difficult to say that I, of any of the three of us, formed a friendship with him. The one person he seemed to communicate with was Ingrid, and I thought it was great that she had reached out to him.

Jhon always seemed to be on the fringe of any group, and he had a kind of intense expression that sometimes led you to think that he was either thinking very deeply or not thinking at all. At one of our more permanent camps during that spring of 2007, we had access to a deep section of river where we could actually swim. Usually the rivers and streams were too shallow, but the rainy season had flooded the banks of this particular river. Jhon didn't know how to swim when he was first taken, but with the help of other hostages, he started to learn, and that spring he became obsessed with it. Out of all of us, Tom was probably the most comfortable in the water, and watching him trying to teach Jhon, we couldn't help but smile at Jhon's thrashing and kicking, which he did with a ferocity that churned up water like crazy. He didn't move very far considering all the energy he was expending, but as Tom pointed out, the guy just had an inefficient motor—lots of horsepower but no torque. That didn't stop him from practicing, though. Like the chess players and the card players, he'd found something to help pass the time.

While we swam and played chess when we could, on occasion, the FARC would put us to work on projects that were for our "benefit." According to FARC policy, as hostages we were not to be asked to do work for them. Enrique had a way of skirting that rule by telling us that if we wanted something, we had to help build it. Such was the case in early April 2007 when Enrique told us that if we wanted a volleyball court, we had to bring in the sand. All of us got together and carried bags of sand from the river to the camp. We all pitched in. Tom had been really sick for a few weeks, but even he was out there, glad to be able to move at all after weeks in his hammock.

To see every one of us, Lucho and Ingrid included, working collectively boosted morale, but even though Ingrid was hauling dirt with the rest of us, we were still not allowed to talk to her, a point that Moster reiterated numerous times during the volleyball-court construction. As I brought sand up to the camp, I tried to imagine what it was like to be singled out that way. That Ingrid was forbidden to interact fully with the group seemed as harsh a punishment as what Richard had to endure, but instead of a week, she had been punished for months. After years in captivity, I knew that one person's mood or energy level had a profound effect on the rest of us. As we watched her flinch at Moster's reprimands, it was clear that Ingrid was struggling, that the effects of her captivity were taking a toll.

Like Tom, I'd been battling a pretty serious jungle sickness around the time that we were building the volleyball court. Though I was well enough to join in the swimming adventures and the camp building, the illness had forced me to think long and hard about my captivity and the impact it had on me. In between grabbing my stomach and loads of sand, I'd come to a painful realization: I hadn't heard from my wife, Shane, in years. My mother was on the message programs all the time, and I heard from my kids, my father, and my brother regularly as well.

Shane, however, had gone silent. I relied on my faith and told myself that whatever was meant to happen had happened. I didn't want to believe that Shane had moved on, but there was little evidence to the contrary. Keith and I discussed the issue endlessly, and I came to the conclusion that I was essentially a single man again. I was still determined to be a good father to Destiney, Cody, and Joey, but I couldn't hide from the truth anymore: My wife had taken her life in a new direction.

Over the last three years in captivity, I'd been good about following the plan to reform my life that I'd set into motion all the way back at the New Camp. Coming to terms with my relationship with Shane seemed a necessary step in that plan. I couldn't live with illusions of any kind. In keeping with this, I also had to confront the prejudices that I'd developed in camp. The nights that Ingrid and I had spent listening to the radio together had opened my eyes to the way that I'd rushed to judgment on her. My initial impression had been pretty presumptuous, and I wanted to be open to the possibility that there was more to her than I'd thought.

Because Ingrid had basically been in isolation since we arrived at the Reunion Camp, I hadn't been able to give her a second chance. I wanted to believe that the person I'd shared the radio with, the woman who'd comforted me when I'd seen the video of Shane, was the real Ingrid. In some ways, I needed to believe that people were good-hearted but occasionally did bad things. That's what I'd concluded about my wife, and if I could feel that way about someone I'd known for almost twenty years, I could do it for someone I'd only spent a few months with.

A few days after we built the volleyball court, I decided to deal with this issue directly, and I approached Enrique.

"I want to be able to speak to whoever I want to speak to. None of us like having these restrictions placed on us. It's just going to cause problems for us all."

Enrique shook his head and issued the no-surprise response. "I've received orders that the other prisoners not be allowed to speak with her."

I wasn't going to give up that easily. "We'll speak to her in Spanish so everyone knows what's being said. We'll do whatever, but what you're doing is cruel and it's going to cause problems for all of us."

Enrique pulled off his glasses and rubbed the kidney-shaped welt on either side of his nose. "The orders are these: You will be on one side of the camp. Ingrid will be on the other. You will not communicate with her." And with that, he walked away.

On April 15 (a day you can pretty much always remember no matter what jungle you're in), I was sitting in my *coleta* tearing apart an old pair of sweatpants. I had traded for a scalpel, and was using it and the salvaged thread to take in the waist on a new pair of sweats I'd been given. I was engrossed in what I was doing, when I saw a pair of female hands cross my line of vision. Ingrid sat down and began helping me with my project. We whispered hello and looked to see if the guards had noticed us. They didn't seem to, so Ingrid and I kept on chatting—mostly just checking in on each other and how we were doing mentally. At one point, she stopped plucking at the threads and put her hands in her lap.

Tears welled in her eyes. "I'm so worried about my mother. She is not well. She's frustrated. I heard on the news that when Uribe canceled the negotiations for the exchange, she said that he had issued a death sentence for us all."

"I'm sure she's trying to keep the pressure on the government. She didn't mean that literally."

"Regardless, I'm afraid that what she said is true."

I took Ingrid's hand and said, "We're going to get out of here." I told her about the rainbow I'd seen shortly after we'd been taken hostage and the sense of calm I'd experienced.

"That's a nice story. A fairy tale of a kind. Pretty to believe but not based on this reality."

Our conversation was brief and I didn't speak to her again until she asked to borrow my scalpel a few days later. I gladly lent it to her. I wanted a chance to speak with her again, to gauge up close how she was doing. Over the next few weeks, she borrowed and returned the scalpel on several occasions, and each time we got to sneak in a few words of encouragement and connection. The last time she returned the scalpel to me, I noticed that something was different about it, but I didn't have the time to figure out exactly what. I returned it to my stash of things and jumped into a game of chess with Tom. We passed the rest of the day engrossed in one of our epic battles.

The next morning the sound of guards running around rousted us out of our beds. We stood there bleary-eyed as Moster came dashing in, followed by Enrique. They were both completely geared up—weapons, vests, harnesses and chains, their rifles. They were all standing outside Jhon Pinchao's hooch.

"What the hell is going on?" Keith asked.

"Something's up with Pinchao." I shrugged. "You hear anything?" I asked Tom.

"All I can think of is that he took off."

"How the hell could he? He's chained to Juancho every night." Keith took a couple of steps closer to see if he could spot Jhon's body in the *coleta*. By that time, Enrique was done checking things out. He turned to look at all of us and then spoke to his men, his voice quaking with anger. "If you find him, shoot him in the foot. He will not do this again."

Groups of guards charged their weapons and trotted off past us.

"I hope to God he made it out," I said to Keith.

"Desperate or crazy or smarter than the rest of us." I could hear the admiration and hope in Keith's appraisal of the situation.

A few moments later, Ingrid walked up to me and said, "Incredible, no?"

"Yeah. I mean wow. How did he get out of the chains? They must have made a mistake when they locked them. When they put the lock on him, it didn't fully catch or something."

Ingrid had been watching the guards running off. She turned to me and smiled, and all I could think of was the *Mona Lisa*. "Yes. Maybe that's what he did." I realized that she knew a lot more than she was telling. That scalpel wasn't as sharp as it had been, and knowing that it had somehow aided Jhon in his escape made me feel pretty good about lending it to Ingrid. I was also glad to see the gleam back in her eye.

FOURTEEN

The Swamp

April 2007–August 2007

KEITH

For the next few days after Pinchao's disappearance, the camp was in an uproar. The guards were all tense and the little dirtbag Moster was beside himself. The three of us, however, were loving life. None of us knew for sure what Jhon had done or how he'd managed to sneak out of camp without his chains, but we were all rooting for him, no matter what his escape meant for us.

In the immediate, it meant that May Day 2007, three days after Jhon left, was going to be moving day. We weren't sure if our departure was a result of the escape or if it had been scheduled. We packed all our gear and were ordered to stand on the volleyball court. Marc, Tom, and I stood there watching as the FARC completely dismantled the camp. It was the same cover-your-tracks behavior that we'd experienced with Milton.

"I've seen this before," Tom said.

"Yeah, Tom. I guess our cool zone is heating up, guys," I replied. We all watched the guards drag leaves and branches over the walkway.

"They must be afraid that Jhon got somewhere already and has re-layed our position to the military," Marc said. He was probably right on. It would have taken some kind of superhuman effort to get out of the middle of nowhere to someplace he could make contact with the military, but at that point *¿Quién sabe?*

Tom added to our song of praise, "Do you remember how he kept asking and asking for help with his swimming, and none of us saw this coming. Amazing. He slips out of camp and swims off in the middle of the night. That takes some guts."

While I didn't know Jhon's exact plan, I'd been aware that he was up to something for a while. For weeks, the guy had clearly been actively training, both physically and mentally. He had been getting swimming lessons and a cigarette lighter from Tom, while I'd been giving him navigation lessons. Jhon had asked me if we wanted to go with him. I'd considered it for a few minutes, but the odds were so stacked against us that I didn't think it was the right move. He understood, but was determined. For three or four days before he left, he kept coming to me with more questions about navigation. The day before he left, he told me that I was to forget everything he'd been saying. That's when I knew he was going to try to make it out.

A gunshot interrupted our retelling of the Gospel of Jhon. It was followed in rapid succession by five more. We were all stunned, and Moster seemed most surprised. He kept yelling, "*¿Qué pasó? ¿Qué pasó?*" and "Did the man arrive?" He sprinted past us, and a few of the guards started their nervous tittering. A moment later, one of the guards, a guy with one eye clouded over, came up to us and said, "I have some bad news. We were out searching for Pinchao. We heard screams from the river and we saw Pinchao get dragged under by an anaconda."

The instant the word *anaconda* left his mouth, we knew the snake story was a feeble attempt to cover something up. We stood there in silence, stupefied. What we didn't know was if they'd captured and then shot Jhon. That scenario didn't seem plausible; it was unlikely that he'd have stuck around camp for the seventy hours following his escape.

"Keith, I just want to believe that he made it, but I don't know." Marc picked up his *equipo* and let it dangle from his hand.

"I hope he remembered some of the stuff I taught him. Land navigation is tough enough when you're first learning it and you're on solid ground. In this swamp shit, I don't know."

Still high on Jhon's escape, everyone—all the prisoners and the guards—set out on the river, once again in the large *bongos* or canoes. It was clear that Enrique was not happy with what had happened and was concerned about our location being detected. For the first few days after we left, we traveled a lot at night. The FARC wanted as much time as possible to move, so we frequently set up camp in the boats or made quick, hammocks-only camps alongside the river. With the torrential rains of the season continuing on and off for days, the river was constantly rising and nearly everything around us was covered in water. Our boats were skimming along the treetops and we were about as miserable as we could possibly be.

Every time we came to a populated area, Enrique would find "dry" land and have us march along through stinking, boot-sucking mud. We'd skirt the town and then head back to the river, where we'd get on the boat again. I was having a hard time keeping track of where we were going, but it seemed as if we were always heading south downriver. Just how far we could go and still be in Colombia started to play on my mind.

I'd long suspected that Venezuela provided a safe haven for the FARC. The admiration they had for Hugo Chávez wasn't simply because they liked his policies and how he used Venezuela's oil reserves as a tool to get what he wanted. The FARC guerrillas weren't sophisticated enough in their understanding of the politics of the region for that. It seemed to me that there had to be a more direct link between Venezuela and the FARC.

Direct support of a terrorist group is an easy thing to suspect and a difficult thing to prove. We'd known for a long time that our uniforms were from Venezuela and we believed that the FARC's arms and other munitions had to come from there as well. Even before we'd seen the Venezuelan supplies, we viewed Chávez as being, if not sympathetic to the FARC, then at least using them for his own gain. If Colombia's military and other resources were tied up in battling the FARC, they were weaker in other areas.

In the time I'd spent in Colombia, I'd gotten a very clear sense that Chávez wanted to be top dog, not just in Venezuela but in the whole region. Our discussions with the politicians and what we heard on the radios didn't do anything to convince me otherwise. I hated Chávez's depiction of the U.S. as a meddling and corrupting influence. I'd heard a lot of the same shit from the FARC, and as far as I was concerned, there weren't that many differences between Chávez and them. As some of the politcals explained it to me, Chávez would do anything he could do to stir up shit because it took his country's attention away from his failed domestic policies. Flex your muscles, put on a good show, let the region know that you're not going to let anybody kick sand in your face, build national unity and pride at the price of innocent lives like ours. Fucking great guy.

The longer we traveled on the river, the clearer it became that the FARC were taking advantage of Chávez's apparent sympathy for their cause by traversing the porous border between Venezuela and Colombia. Eventually we started picking up Venezuelan radio stations, something we'd never done before. Those stations weren't coming in fuzzy or distorted—they rang through loud and crisp, with the signal getting stronger each day we moved south. In my gut I knew that we had crossed the border, and one glance at Enrique's GPS unit would have confirmed it. I took note of the fact that the guerrillas seemed as accustomed to the terrain in this border region as they were with their strongholds in central Colombia.

Two and half weeks into our boat march, we had bedded down for the night. Suddenly Lucho's voice split the still night air, "¡Marc! ¡Marc! Pinchao está vivo. ¡Está en Bogotá!"

Marc was nearest to him, and he got up to listen. His face split into a huge grin. He tilted his head back and pumped his fists. Everybody was looking at him, and he told Ingrid, setting off a chain reaction of good news: Jhon had made it. According to the radio, he'd wandered around for seventeen days before running into a group of indigenous Colombians who took him to the police jungle commandos who were in the area destroying labs and coca fields. Now Jhon was safely back in Bogotá, dehydrated and malnourished but alive.

I climbed out of my hammock and over some of the others, ignoring the guards' orders to stay where I was. Tom joined Marc and me, and we sat there just relishing the moment. We pounded one another on the back and whooped it up at the thought that Jhon was out of the shit and back home with family. We were sitting along the river, the breeze was fresh, and the air tasted of freedom. It didn't matter that it was secondhand freedom, it was the closest we'd come to savoring the real thing in four years. We figured that with Jhon free, he'd be able to give the Colombian military solid ground truth about our location. The radio broadcast had mentioned something about Jhon being discovered in the Pachoa municipality near the Papurí River. Even though we'd been heading south ever since his escape, just having that little bit of information gave us even more hope.

As joyful as we were at the news of Jhon's success, Enrique was just as angry. The next morning, he issued an order that we all be searched. We all hated requisas. It was a pain in the ass to take all the junk we'd accumulated over the years and dump it out so that we could show the FARC just how piss-poor we all were. To make matters worse, it was raining, so we all had to put up with everything getting soaked and dirty. We protested, but it didn't do us any good. The FARC stripped us of anything that might help us escape, including any extra food, medicine, knives, files. They patted us all down, checked the clothes we were wearing, inside our boots—the whole gestapo deal.

We then broke camp and got into the boats. Instead of allowing us to spread out a bit, they confined us to roughly half the space. Every one of the guards seemed a lot more aggressive and they pulled the plastic sheeting down over us. That kept us out of the rain, but it also exposed us to the fumes from the fifty-five-gallon barrel of gasoline that they were carrying as well as the fumes from the engine. Our heads were swimming and our stomachs turning, but they wouldn't let us out of that toxic plastic bubble. We were crammed in close quarters, and if you were lucky enough to be near the gunwales of the boat, you could lift the edge of the plastic up a bit to sneak some fresh air into the little enclosure.

On top of all that, they started to end their runs at about three o'clock in the morning. They wouldn't let us unpack anything or set up our tents. They stopped clearing any ground for us, and it was sleep in the virgin jungle for an hour or so and then head out again. At one point, we killed a couple of coral snakes. They weren't the giant constrictors, but two- to three-foot devils with the most venomous bite in the jungle. None of us liked the idea of sleeping on the jungle floor, and the threat from snakes, tarantulas, and every other insect in the jungle made it even harder to get any shut-eye in spite of our sleep-deprived state.

As much shit as the FARC were dishing out to us, none of us complained once about the fact that their tightening the screws on us was a result of Jhon's escape. If there had been any yapping about that, I know that the three of us would have shut it down damned quick. How we behaved before, during, and after Jhon made it out was a source of pride to all of us. We didn't come right out and say it to one another, but we all felt that part of us had escaped with him. I just hoped that my part of Jhon was sitting in some nice nightspot in Bogotá enjoying a relaxing bourbon while puffing on a nice Cuban *Belicoso* cigar.

MARC

Jhon's escape and Enrique's subsequent clampdown reminded us that every high also carried a low. I had long ago learned to deal with the ups and downs of jungle life, and rather than dwell on the valleys, I tried to keep my mind focused on what was directly in front of me. Anticipating the bad times only made those times last longer. Rather than get all worked up about what was coming next, I decided it was better to enjoy the view from up top than to tense up for the inevitable drop.

On the boat rides following our retreat from Jhon's escape camp, we were all together in the closest quarters we'd been in. One night we were told to set our sleeping gear in the boat. Sleeping in the hammocks continued to be hard because of my back, so instead I slept on the ground. I was complaining to Tom about my sleeplessness, when Moster interrupted us.

"You, " he said, pointing to me. "In the bow."

Tom frowned and said, "So what? We can't talk to each other anymore?"

Moster ignored him and pointed to my new spot.

"Thanks, Tom. It's not worth it. I'll move."

I followed Moster's outstretched arm and finger to my new spot. I was being placed next to Ingrid. Normally, she was separated from us, but since Moster had been pointing to that exact location, I figured we could talk. I was glad to have the opportunity. I wasn't sure if Ingrid had trouble sleeping in hammocks like I did or if she was just glad for the company, but we chatted for a while, just checking up on how each of us was doing. Eventually, we started talking about Jhon.

"I'm glad he's gone and grateful to God that he made it," Ingrid said.

I detected something wistful in her tone, like there was more that she wanted to say but was afraid to.

"But?" I asked.

Ingrid looked at me and I watched as her pupils narrowed. I felt a twitch in my stomach; it was the same feeling I'd felt in school when a teacher asked me a question and was waiting for my response. I felt like I was being evaluated in some way.

"I wish that I had gone with him. I wish that I was out of here."

I was struck by the simple honesty of her words and the way they mirrored my own feelings. We all liked Jhon and marveled at what he'd done, but there was a bittersweet quality to knowing that he was free and we weren't. Call it envy, call it reality, but I said to Ingrid, "I wish it had been me, too."

"It's hard to keep believing that my time will come."

I decided that she'd opened the door to the subject, so I asked, "Is it hard being outside all the time?"

She looked up into the night sky and said, "No rain." She laughed softly. "I know what you mean, and yes, it isn't easy being the outcast, particularly when you've not done much to deserve that status."

"Do you mean because both of you tried to escape and Lucho's not kept from everyone else?"

"In part, yes. But because I am the only woman here, the FARC use it to their advantage."

I wasn't sure exactly what she meant. I hesitated before asking, "Do you mean they're worried about another Clara? Another baby?"

"Not so much that. It is difficult to explain."

I heard some of the enthusiasm in her voice drain. I'd tried to put myself in Ingrid's position a couple of times, but her comments about being a woman made me realize that I could only go so far in understanding what captivity was like for her.

"Do you miss being with the other women? Having someone to talk to who could understand."

"Not really. Some. I've been around men most of my life. Ambitious men. Powerful men who wanted to control me. The FARC are more crude, but they feel the same way, that I should be kept in my place since they think that I seem not to know where it is myself. I miss my children. I miss my mother. I share more of a bond with them."

Our conversation veered to talk about our families. I was surprised to learn that Ingrid had been in California for a while, that she'd given birth to her son by the immersion method.

"That seems pretty hippy and out there."

"Hippy?" She laughed and the light in her eyes returned. "It is the most natural way to enter the world. From water to water."

She asked about Destiney and Shane, and for some reason, I opened up to her a bit. I suppose it's natural for a man to feel more comfortable talking to a woman about those kinds of things. I told her again that it hurt to know that my wife hadn't been making the effort to keep in contact. I didn't feel like going into it any more deeply, and she put her hand on my forearm and said, "I understand. It's complicated, but I think I know what you mean and how you feel." And I was sure she did.

What struck me was not just that she understood, but how easy I found it to talk to her, to let her know things that I'd kept mostly private for so long. I liked how when the two of us were talking, it seemed as if the rest of the jungle and everyone in it just disappeared. For a hostage, the moments when you don't feel like you are being held captive are so few. Just as I wished that I had Jhon's freedom, I wanted more of those moments with Ingrid when the harshness of our reality dimmed and a brighter perspective rose.

After that night, Ingrid and I talked more frequently. Something about being in that boat on the river made it feel like we were away from everyone and everything else. The noise of the motor, the water running past the boat's bow, and the rush of the breeze cocooned any two people who were next to each other. Only if you shouted or if someone asked you what was being said could you have a conversation with a large group. I knew that Ingrid and Lucho were very close but weren't able to speak to each other. With Jhon gone, I felt like I needed and wanted to fill the void in Ingrid's life. Her role as an outsider touched me in a vulnerable spot. Shane had been dealing with some personal issues when I met her. I felt good about myself because I'd been able to help her through them. We all have a vision of ourselves, and a part of mine was that I was approachable and trustworthy. If Ingrid needed someone to help her get through the horrors and sadness of captivity, I would try to be that person.

In addition to wanting to help, I really enjoyed our conversations. I felt so good about myself when I said something that made her smile; it was as if all her pain and suffering were wiped away. We passed many pleasant hours just talking. She told me a lot about her travels and her boarding-school education. I was fascinated by someone who had been sent off at an early age to another country. I was public school educated, and even though I'd joined the air force, I hadn't seen that much of the world. Getting married at the age of nineteen, I hadn't spent any real part of my adulthood venturing far beyond the duties and the responsibilities of a family man. I had no regrets, but that didn't mean that I couldn't take vicarious pleasure in hearing the stories of a life so different from my own.

After twenty-eight days of boat rides and mud treks, our wandering came to a close. The last month of spontaneous camps had taken a toll on our bodies and everyone was grateful to settle into a more permanent camp. When we were told where to set up our hooches, Ingrid was placed at the end of the line, but not as far away from me as she had been before. She and I took advantage of this to talk more than we ever had before.

Lucho and Ingrid were not allowed any contact at all, and it didn't take any great sensitivity to recognize that he was upset by my time with Ingrid. The three of us had seen his jealous nature at Caribe. I wanted to do what I could to avoid any kind of conflict again, but it didn't seem fair to Ingrid or to me. We were adults who were becoming good friends. We'd shared some intimate moments and we had similar interests. One afternoon, I stopped by her hooch to say hello.

Ingrid was startled, a rosy color came to her cheeks, and her bottom lip quivered. "Oh, hello, Marc." She composed herself and smiled. I could sense that she was nervous, and I was flattered to think that this powerful woman was slightly off balance around me.

We made small talk for a while, and our discussion turned to the Bible. I told her that I believed that Jesus' mother, Mary, was at the tomb on the day of the Resurrection. When the stone was rolled back to reveal the empty tomb, she was there to witness His burial garments lying there and His corporeal body gone. Ingrid disagreed. Each of us reread passages from the Bible, from each of the four books of the New Testament, to bolster our cases. I'd read and reread Sergeant Lasso's Bible, and to have someone I could talk about it with was great. There was no one else at camp whom I felt as connected to and who understood my need to think about and talk about spiritual matters. Ingrid felt the same way. Our captivity was the greatest test of our faith that each of us had ever faced, and having someone to share this element with went beyond the connection I shared with Tom or Keith.

It soon became obvious to us both that other people had been watching as we grew closer and spent more time together. Ingrid was truly the outsider, and for someone like me, who worked hard to get along with everybody, it made perfect sense that I would be the one to reach out to her and for her to reach out to me. Based on how Ingrid had behaved in previous camps, I could see that others might think of us as oil and water, but we were much more complementary than that.

The fact that Lucho and the other Colombian men would be jealous of us seemed ridiculous. I tried not to pay much attention to them, but at times it grew difficult. When Ingrid sat with me to help me patch my tent (she was a very good seamstress and my efforts at sewing were passable at best), Lucho or one of the others would sit and stare at us.

She didn't tell me what had passed between them, but it was clear there had been some breach in their relationship. It was none of my business, so I didn't press her for details. I hated camp gossip and the various allegiances everyone had. I chose to look beyond all that and simply do what I saw as the hard right thing and the thing I wanted to do.

I suppose that what the others were experiencing was another form of the envy that we had all experienced when Jhon had escaped. They saw Ingrid and me taking great pleasure in each other's company. Being able to laugh with someone, share fears and concerns, and connect on a deep emotional level was something we all wanted and needed in order to survive. Unfortunately, the FARC also saw how much time we were spending together and how frequently we were engrossed in one of our "disappearing" conversations. It was a difficult choice, but we decided that we needed to limit the amount of time we spent together. The FARC's divide-and-conquer mentality, as well as their heightened state of alertness following Jhon's escape, made the decision necessary.

"This is not something I want," Ingrid told me, "but I don't want to see either of us get in any trouble because of this."

"You're right, but this seems like just another bit of unfairness piled onto more unfairness."

Ingrid nodded, and I could see that she was fighting tears. I held her hand for a minute before Moster walked past us and shouted at her, "If you keep talking to the gringos, I'm going to chain you to a tree!" He didn't say anything at all to me.

Ingrid rolled her eyes and shook her head. "What is it with these guys? Why do I pose such a threat to them?"

"I don't get it, either. We're just standing here talking. I told them once I'd speak Spanish if that would make them more comfortable."

Ingrid shook her head. "Even before Jhon's escape, or my escape, it was like this. Not just with you. They don't know what to do with me. If I were weak and submissive, they'd like it, but I'm not."

I saw again her vulnerability and her desire to make it seem as if she could handle anything. She was also truly angry, and I could see how she might pose a threat to the guards. She was a strong and fierce woman, and she didn't want anyone or anything to dictate how she should behave. I didn't, either, but I also didn't want to be responsible for Ingrid being punished any more than she already had been.

"Ingrid, Tom, Keith, and I talk about this all the time. As much as I hate Moster and some of these other guerrillas, this isn't about winning or losing these little battles. You can't win them. You can't lose sight of the bigger goal. We win when we get out of here and go back to our families."

Ingrid shut her eyes. I could see her making an effort to compose her face into a smile. Piece by piece she did so. "Thank you, Marc. Thanks for that reminder. If I didn't have someone looking out for me—"

She paused and let the thought remain suspended.

I could probably have put up with the FARC's arbitrary decision to isolate her and forbid her to talk to me if at any time I'd posed a threat to their security. I figured that one of the reasons why Moster hadn't yelled at me was that I hadn't caused him any trouble before. Even though the guards tried to separate us, they couldn't. It was as if they didn't understand that Ingrid and I were on our way toward developing a relationship that transcended our circumstances and the conditions the FARC imposed on us, a similar relationship to the one I had with Keith and Tom.

I wrote her a note after separating, reiterating the things we'd said, and concluded with, "Thank you for the good talks. Be strong. We will get through this."

Ingrid wrote beautifully, and her return message made me feel again as though I was no longer a hostage, no longer struggling alone to understand something that had been forced on me for a reason I couldn't understand. I was learning about the depth of the connection we can make with one another as humans and how circumstances can bring out both the best and the worst in us. I had been a part of the best, and I wasn't willing to let it go that easily.

The next day, I walked out of our hooch and saw Ingrid sitting in her newly assigned area. Our eyes met, and with a single look it was clear that we didn't need to speak to convey our feelings. Just looking into her eyes, I felt how much pain she was in and how desperate she was to be able to keep our connection alive. Even without words, we shared a bond that the FARC could not break.

Maintaining communication meant having to be selective about which guards we could speak together in front of. Even when she and I weren't talking, we'd communicate with a wave or a look; sometimes just seeing each other was enough to keep us going. We'd walk past each other and slip each other letters, using all the methods that Keith, Tom, and I had developed during our months of enforced silence early on. The letters we wrote to each other were important, not just because they were our lifeline, but because they were our chance to speak without the intruding eyes of the guards. The letters gave us a chance to air our feelings about each other and about life in captivity. In the letters we could be honest with each other and with ourselves.

What really troubled me was that it wasn't just the guards who didn't want us talking; it was some of the other prisoners. Every time I spoke to Ingrid or she sat near me, one of the military prisoners, Amahón Flores, was right there. He'd try to eavesdrop and then slink off to report to Lucho. At first it was kind of amusing; we were in such a small area that it was hard for him to be stealthy, but our amusement turned to disgust one evening when Moster came up to me and said, "You were speaking with Ingrid today. That's not allowed. You know this."

It wasn't that I minded Moster getting on my case, but he hadn't been in camp all day. The only time I'd seen him was when he was speaking with Amahón on the outskirts of our camp. That was not the last time Amahón ratted us out—far from it. Eventually Ingrid was moved farther away, to an area about twenty-five or thirty yards from us. It felt like miles. I started to pass time by engaging in little experiments. I'd linger by Ingrid's space and see how long it would take for Amahón to go to the guards. Usually it didn't take very long.

Again, I couldn't understand why Ingrid was the one who was being disciplined and I wasn't. I knew that Tom, Keith, and I had conducted ourselves well, but none of what was being done to her seemed fair. A few days after Ingrid was moved from the main cluster of hooches, I spotted Enrique nearby.

"What's the deal? Why were Ingrid and I able to speak before and now we can't?"

The sun was in Enrique's glasses, so I couldn't see his eyes. I moved to my left, hoping that he would turn with me so that I could meet his eyes. He didn't.

"Those are the rules."

"But why are those the rules now when they weren't before?"

I moved again to stand directly in his line of sight. He folded his arms across his chest and said, "Those are the orders from above."

I was sick to death of hearing that, and to avoid doing something I'd regret, I walked away. I hated that helpless feeling of speaking to a rock. I went to sleep that night with a prayer on my lips for more patience.

The next morning, after I'd exercised, I had my usual little break and snack. I intended to get a cup of coffee. A couple of *coletas* down, I heard shouting. I could hear Lucho and Malagón screaming at each other. I pulled my boots on and ran over. As I was approaching them I could see that Malagón had pinned Lucho to the ground. He was kneeling on top of him and he had Lucho's arms immobilized. Lucho was thrashing his legs and twisting his torso to try to get free. Without thinking, I ran into the hooch, grabbed Malagón, and dragged him off of Lucho. I wasn't really thinking or hearing anything at all. I just saw Lucho staggering to his feet like he wanted to go after Malagón again. I looked to the side and I saw Ingrid shrieking and crying. She was crushing some papers in her hands, and she threw them at Malagón and stormed out of the *coleta*.

The next thing I remember clearly was Keith's voice telling me to get out of there. I walked back toward our hooch. Keith put his arm around my shoulder and sat me down on his hammock. I wasn't hurt, but I was so stunned at what had just happened that I didn't know what to think. Keith waited for everything to settle down before he spoke.

"Marc, I didn't want to see you get into that with those guys. It's a fucking swamp. You can't get out of there clean."

"I didn't want to see Lucho get his ass kicked."

"I know that. Lucho's a grown man. He decided he wanted to throw down with somebody, that's his choice. He's always running his mouth. Maybe he needed to learn a lesson."

"Still, the guy's always talking about how sick he is."

"The whole thing is sick, Marc. Those guys have got themselves so twisted in knots; they're like vipers going after their own tails. Or maybe I should say one tail. You know that." He gave me a chance to let that thought sink in. "I don't know what's going on with Amahón, bro. The guy's like stalking you every minute lately. And Malagón—he's crossed the line."

"What are you talking about?" At first, I was confused by Keith's remark, but right after he said it, I remembered something that had happened during one of our marches. Malagón had grabbed Ingrid a couple of times. He claimed he was just fooling around, but Ingrid was incensed. I always felt it was instances like this that had led Ingrid to send me a note just to thank me for treating her decently. Perhaps this time Malagón had gone too far.

"Armando came to me this morning," Keith responded. "He's worried about Malagón. He showed me these notes that Malagón had written to Ingrid. Just really foul and disrespectful stuff. He's been sniffing around Ingrid for a while, you know that. He just really lost it. I told him so. I said that he was an officer and he had better start acting like one again."

"He didn't listen to you. Ingrid had the notes." I remembered painfully the sight of Ingrid tearing at those sheets of paper and crying. If it wasn't Lucho faking illnesses, it was Amahón interfering with her friendships and Malagón making an ass of himself. It was like she couldn't win no matter what man she was dealing with.

"Marc, bro, you know I don't like Ingrid one bit. In this case, she didn't deserve to be treated that way. But listen to me, man. This is just a stinking fetid swamp here with these guys and her. All you're going to do is get dragged down into it. All this mucking around in the shit is going to come back to hurt you. All you're trying to do is the hard right thing, but that doesn't count for much with all this bullshit."

I got up to clear my head. I'd been working so hard on making changes in my life. I didn't know if I could just walk away and let all this stuff continue. I had no delusions that I was a white knight on a charger rescuing a damsel in distress. As Ingrid had said to me in one of our earliest conversations, everything there, all the hostages' relationships, was complex. I wanted things to be black and white. I wanted to know that it was just the guards, the FARC, whom we had to fight against. That we often had to fight against one another and most often against our own impulses to do the wrong, easy thing was a difficult reality to face.

Part of what made the whole situation harder was that I began to realize that my actions risked getting Keith and Tom in trouble, too. Each night the clicks of the Colombians' chains were audible reminders of what bad behavior would bring. If the threat of chains wasn't enough, it also seemed that the chains had brought about changes in many of the military guys. Whereas before we had seen them as examples to emulate, rifts had begun taking shape causing too much petty crap to come to the surface.

Ingrid and I were thrown into this mix of emotions. Two people in the jungle trying to sort through a precarious chemistry of feelings. As confusing as that was, I could understand why the FARC would want to separate us, but why would my fellow hostages not want us to be happy? It seemed like no one really understood what was going on. I wanted to get everyone together and spell it out for them: Ingrid and I were attracted to each other; we enjoyed each other's company immensely. That should have been obvious, just as it was obvious to them all that at no time did we express those feelings through any kind of physical intimacy other than a brief touch or a held hand. We were trying to balance our desire to do no harm with an impulse to do whatever was best for ourselves; what we didn't know was whether we'd be able to maintain that balance.

The morning after Lucho and Malagón's confrontation, I lay awake fretting over what was going on. I wanted to talk to Ingrid, to speak to somebody who understood. Normally at that hour, the Colombians were released from their chains. Instead of the sound of their chains being folded and their locks opened, I heard the sound of chains being dragged across the ground. I rolled out from underneath Keith's hammock and into the compound.

"Oh my God." The words rasped out of my throat. "Ingrid!" I ran toward where she had been moved. I could see that the thick steel chains were wrapped around her neck.

My guts heaved and I thought I was going to vomit.

Across the way, Ingrid sat slumped and sobbing, the chains from her neck snaking to a nearby tree. Moster had made good on his threat. At that moment I wished that it was my hands around that disgusting animal's neck, choking the worthless life out of him.

It broke my heart to see someone I cared about so much in such obvious pain. I felt helpless, and I knew the image of Ingrid sitting there was one that would haunt me for a long time.

Shortly after the confrontation between Lucho and Malagón, Tom, Keith, and I were lying in the dark. The sweep of flashlights first caught my eye and then I heard the clink of chains. Just from the sound, I knew that these were not the usual FARC chains. Instead of a deep tinkling sound, these had a distinctive metallic thud. I thought of the chains that people used to carry around in their cars in New England to drag one another out of ditches alongside the snow-slick roads. The threat of chains had hung over us for so long; now I thought it was going to be realized.

It turned out the chains weren't for us. A few weeks before, while on the march, Enrique had gotten into a verbal spat with Juancho. Enrique had stormed off, threatening to bring out the big steel for the military and police prisoners. He said that it would be all Juancho's fault. He was finally making good on his threat. I heard a guard named Asprilla, speaking to Keith.

"Tell your friends to keep behaving the way they've been behaving and there will be no chains. We got orders from above to keep you guys out of them unless absolutely necessary. Keep respecting us and each other and it will stay that way."

Keith told him we had no plans to alter what we'd been doing, and he asked if it was really necessary to impose that punishment on the others. He didn't get a reply.

One morning a few days after the new chains came out, Tom heard Amahón and Lucho talking. They were shackled together in their *coleta*. At first, he thought they were having some kind of joint nightmare or were hallucinating together. They kept mumbling about "*los diputados*" and bullet holes and wanting the bodies. Lucho was very agitated and Amahón was doing his best to calm him down, but he wasn't in much better shape himself.

Tom came to Keith and me and told us what he'd overheard. We flipped on the radio and quickly learned what was upsetting Lucho. In 2002, twelve local politicians from Valle del Cauca had been taken hostage. They were referred to as *los diputados*. We'd heard their story a long time ago, but the radio confirmed an ugly new twist: eleven of the twelve deputies had been killed.

The FARC issued a communiqué stating that they had come under an attack by an unknown group and the deputies had been killed in the cross fire. We weren't sure how the one had survived, but we knew this communiqué was just a cover story. The government responded to the FARC's allegations by stating that it had made no rescue attempt. The FARC had been on edge for a while, and we figured they could have stumbled across any other group in the jungle and thought it was the Colombian military. In the confusion, the prisoners had been executed. The families were asking that the bodies be returned to them. It seemed unlikely that the FARC would comply. There would have been too much evidence of their murders.

We didn't have long to dwell on the massacre. The next day we were told to pack up. We brought our *equipos* down to the boat launch and one of the guards began announcing names; he pointed to the left side of the boat or the right and we sat according to his directions. The three of us, Lucho, Juancho, and Miguel Arteaga were all on one side, and the others—including Ingrid—sat on the opposite side. Ingrid and I exchanged a look. This could only mean one thing: We were being separated. I walked over to her.

"The FARC are separating the groups because they don't want the two of us together."

She looked at me and nodded in agreement. We both got increasingly agitated; they were doing this to keep us apart. We decided we would write letters of protest to Mono JoJoy requesting to be placed in the same camp. In them, we would make clear to Mono JoJoy that we wouldn't put up with this abusive treatment, that they couldn't keep us apart and deny us our free will.

When we loaded onto the boats, the FARC tried to separate us by piling all our *equipos* in the center. Ingrid was on one side of the barrier, and I was on the other. We moved through the moonlit night, sensing that we were going to have to part ways. I laid my arm on the *equipos*, and I felt Ingrid's soft hand in mine.

"We won't let them do this to us," she said.

"They can't keep us from talking to one another. Can't keep us from communicating somehow."

We spent a good part of the night on the river before we came to a small temporary camp the FARC had prepared for us. After sleeping for a few hours, we woke up and set up our tents—the six of us—while the others sat and watched. When we were through, it was time to say good-bye.

Over the last four years I gotten used to such hasty departures, but this was particularly tough. I didn't know when or if I would see Ingrid again. We both promised to do what we could to be reunited, but in the end we knew this wasn't much. We hugged and reminded each other to write the letter of protest. A minute later, they loaded Ingrid's group onto the *bongo*. All I could do was stand by and watch as the boat slipped out a sight, feeling very much like a part of me was also leaving.

TOM

I wasn't happy about the other group's departure, but I dealt with it. In the end, my vote was for peace. If we could get rid of some of the tension in the camp, I was all for it. As one FARC guard explained things, "The complicated go and the uncomplicated stay. We don't want any more troubles."

We relocated in a place about four hours from where we'd separated from the others. After setting up camp by midafternoon, Asprilla, the guard who had promised Keith that we wouldn't be put in chains if we continued to conduct ourselves well, came up to us.

"Tonight you are going to be in chains."

"You told us if we kept doing—"

Asprilla plowed right through my objection.

"This will only be for the nights. During the day, you will not have chains. I didn't want to surprise you later."

He didn't look disappointed at being the bearer of bad news. After he left, the three of us huddled up.

"Well, here we are. No surprise," Keith said.

"Let's just hope they take these things off tomorrow morning," Marc said.

"So, look. We've talked about this before," Keith continued, "and nothing is going to break us down. No matter what these fuckers throw at us, they will not break us down. Chains suck. We suck it up. The military guys have been in them for years. We can beat this."

"You're right, Keith," Marc added. "Let's keep our routines. Tomorrow morning when you normally do your English class with Juancho, I'll go with you. We can stretch out the chains so I can get to Miguel's worktable. Then, after breakfast, we'll exercise, just like always. Now is when we really need to work together."

"Agreed. We can't let it divide us. Whatever else is going on among us, we don't let these chains add to it." I looked at Keith and Marc. None of us was happy with this development, but having other people we trusted and respected in the same situation made it a bit easier to deal with.

"We're going to do this. I'm not going to let these things start fucking with me." I liked Keith's attitude and I hoped that each of us was going to be able to walk the walk.

The first time I felt the cold metal around my neck, I found myself thinking of heavy tow chains. The weight of them was bad, but not as bad as I'd imagined. The real problem was not the weight but the grip. They made you feel like you were being choked. Every time I swallowed, my Adam's apple rubbed against the steel. Keith and Marc were chained together, while I was chained to Lucho. From that day on, he and I shared a hooch adjacent to where Marc and Keith slept. At least the proximity would be a good thing.

Shortly after they fastened the chains around us, Lucho and I agreed that we needed to get along no matter what. We had good reason to feel confident that we could do this. In all the time we'd been together—the six months since we had been reunited—we'd never exchanged a harsh word. Now, without Ingrid around to rile up his jealousy, I figured he was the best person outside of Marc and Keith for me to be paired with.

As predicted, the chains didn't come off in the morning or the rest of the day. Even when we went to bathe, they stayed on us. We had a talk with Asprilla and convinced him that the cheap Chinese locks on the chains would oxidize and seize up. Unexpectedly, he saw the wisdom in not ruining the locks and we were free to bathe without the danger of the chains snagging on some underwater obstruction.

If nothing else, the restraints helped us learn to be adaptable. Privacy was always an issue, but the chains were long enough to allow us at least sixteen feet of space. The *orquetas* or forked sticks came in handy for draping them. On that very first morning in chains, I saw Marc and Keith walking on their separate steppers. Their chains hung down from their necks to an *orqueta* strategically placed between them. They did the same with the pull-up bar. Marc put a good spin on the chains by saying, "The extra weight is going to help me get even more buff than before." He'd lost nearly fifty pounds in captivity and looked to our eyes fit and healthy, though I imagine that anyone who didn't see the gradual transformation would have been shocked at his skeletal appearance.

During the first few weeks with the chains, we all learned little tricks to make them more bearable. Sleeping with a chain around your neck takes some getting used to or at least some minor engineering marvel. I had held on to a piece of parachute cord that Jhon Jairo Durán gave me way back on the forty-day march. I looped it around the links and around my waist, putting enough tension on the chain so that it didn't rest on my neck.

Fortunately, along with Keith and Marc, I had another being I could rely on to get me through the savagery of the FARC. Just before we'd arrived at the Reunion Camp, we'd been joined by a small, stout dog

who'd wandered into one of our temporary camps. I immediately identified with the little guy. Like us, he was plagued by *nuches* and insect
bites. He reminded me of a stubby-legged yellow Labrador retriever
with his characteristic "smile" and pleasant disposition. Beneath his
patchwork of fur and exposed skin, I could see his ribs. He smelled
like a hound from hell, but there was something about him that drew
us together.

I gave him the name Tula—which means burlap bag—because of his
color and the coarse, chewed-up nature of his fur. I didn't want to admit
that he hung close to me just because I fed him, but in time I think
he really enjoyed my company as much as I did his. I spread out a bit
of black plastic on the ground, and Tula slept there each night. When
we got to the Reunion Camp, everybody took a liking to the animal I'd
come to think of as my dog. Tula was like any dog, a real chowhound,
but he was respectful, never stealing food and waiting patiently for any
scrap we would toss him. Arteaga was another dog lover, and he helped
me get Tula in better shape. He got rid of the *nuche* worms, and the
FARC gave us used motor oil to clean up his mange. Within a few
weeks, Tula no longer smelled so bad and had started to fatten up; he
provided a pleasant diversion from the stress of camp life.

Tula was a real trooper, and he enjoyed the *bongo* rides, standing up
in the bow of the boat stretched to his full height with his nose held
proudly in the air, looking like the bowsprit on a sailing vessel. Eventually Enrique decided that Tula was better off with him, and since
Enrique had easier access to food than I did, he managed to lure the
dog away from me. Tula still wandered from camp to camp and person
to person, but he no longer slept near me. I didn't mind so much; it
seemed that like us, Tula was doing whatever he could to get by.

Initially, focusing on Tula and keeping to our routine made things a
bit more bearable, but after a few weeks, I realized that maybe the chains
were having a greater effect on me than I thought. About a month into
our chaining, sometime near the Fourth of July, I was sitting and read-

ing *Don Quixote*. Maybe it was irony on top of irony on top of irony that got me, but LJ, a guard, and Arteaga, the trusty, were talking about the FARC and how even though they were down in numbers, they could pick off the military guys one by one and eventually take over the country. Here I was reading a book about a delusional but admirable idealist, and these two guys were running their mouths off about what great things the FARC could accomplish. The fact that one of them was a prisoner who wasn't setting the guard straight bothered me.

"You guys are just a bunch of assassins. You go out and grab innocent people and then, at the first sign of trouble, you kill them. That's your military action."

LJ looked at me and asked, "What are you saying? Do you know what you're saying?"

His macho tone was too much for me. "Hell yes I know what I'm saying. And you should just take your commie bullshit and go to the other side of the camp with it. I don't want to hear it."

"You need to be respectful, Tom. You really don't want me to report what you're saying."

"I don't care. Go ahead and tell Enrique."

LJ went away and returned a few minutes later with Enrique. I was in my hammock when Enrique told me to come out of the *coleta* so we could talk.

"I'm not coming out. If you want me for something, you come in here."

Each of the *comandantes*—whether it was Sombra or Enrique or the lower-ranked Milton—was a mini-dictator in my eyes. Enrique was the worst of the bunch. He was full of his idealistic talk about equality, and I would see him sitting in a chair looking like the lord of the manor with a young girl lounging beside him. He would keep his laptop computer with him and all his troops would gather around to catch a glimpse of *el jefe*'s movie selection.

By not bowing to his command, I wanted to show up the little dictator in front of his troops. He wasn't used to anyone talking down to him, and it gave me a bit of evil pleasure to put him in his place in front of his guerrillas. He stomped off and returned a moment later with his .22 rifle. The FARC often used it for hunting. Enrique sent his *oficial,* Mario, inside my hooch to talk to me. I stayed in the hammock.

"Come outside," Mario ordered.

"No. If Enrique wants something to do with me, he's going to have to come in here himself."

I could see that in addition to the rifle, Enrique had brought another set of chains. Keith and Marc showed up, and Enrique began talking to them. That pissed me off even more and I started shouting at him, giving him hell for every grievance I'd felt since I'd been with him. Over my shouting, I could hear what he was saying to Keith.

"You have to reason with him, Keith. You have to keep your men under control."

Keith stopped Enrique immediately. "We don't tell Tom or anybody else what to do."

"If he doesn't calm down and stop yelling at me and my guards, I'll have to shoot him in the foot. If that doesn't shut him up, then I'll have him dig a hole for himself and he'll live in that."

I didn't think that Enrique would shoot me, but I didn't rule it out. I knew I'd lost control but I didn't care. I was sick of being treated like crap and seeing other people like Arteaga get treated better. I was sick of being lied to, sick of being told that I would be in chains just at night only to have the chains stay on all the time. I had kept so much inside for so long, I exploded.

In the end, it was a pretty hollow victory. I stood up to Enrique and vented at him, but he punished me. For a few weeks, I wasn't joined to Lucho. The guards added another chain to mine, and wherever I went I had to be secured to something—a post, a tree, or a bench. When I went to bathe I wrapped the length of chain around my neck so I looked like I had an enormous, steel turtleneck sweater on. I didn't care. I knew that I'd be able to outlast Enrique. Marc and Keith gave me a few days to cool off before they talked to me. They said that if I didn't cooperate, the FARC were going to dig a hole, put me in it, and cover it with boards.

"Tom, you don't want to be in that hole. Rescue comes, you're just a rat in a box. They'll gun you down so easy. It makes no sense to keep pushing this thing," Keith said.

"Tom, I know what you were feeling. I'm praying for you. I know you don't need it, but you'll get through this."

I looked at Marc and nodded. "I appreciate it. It's over. I'll do my time and we'll get on with it."

FIFTEEN

Politics and Pawns

August 2007–May 2008

TOM

During the third week in August, shortly after my battle with Enrique, we were listening to the Voice of America and learned that Ingrid's mother and several other family members of hostages had gone to Caracas to meet with Venezuela's president Hugo Chávez. Chávez had stated that he was willing to act as an intermediary between the FARC and the Colombian government.

"Why the hell is that leftist red-shirt-wearing bastard getting mixed up in this?" Keith said upon hearing the news. "Hey, I'm all for somebody intervening in this, but why that guy? If Uribe's going to meet with him, it'll be just to shit in Chávez's beret and send him back to Caracas with it as a souvenir."

Keith was right to be skeptical. Putting Chávez and Uribe together was like combining gasoline and a match. A socialist and conservative from two countries who were on the worst terms in decades didn't offer much hope for a productive conversation.

"Maybe it took two years for those two to get over Colombia's arrest of Granda," Marc said. "Much as I hate Granda and the rest of the FARC, how do you think Chávez and Venezuela are going to act when its borders are violated and someone's arrested. You don't just go over someone else's border like Colombia did without permission and snatch a guy and not expect any fallout."

Lucho nodded. "That is the arrogance of Uribe. Granda was a FARC at one time, certainly, but that doesn't mean that the government can ignore the sovereignty of another nation. If Chávez is willing to move beyond that, then this is a good thing, Keith. Though I doubt it will lead to much. "

Lucho's typically insightful but contradictory response was something I'd come to expect. With him, life was a feast or a famine. Sometimes both simultaneously, but you always knew where he stood—even if he sometimes moved around a lot.

"C'mon, Lucho," Keith replied. "Uribe let Chávez believe he won that whole Granda thing. Uribe got what he wanted and then backed off. Chavez is angling for something else."

"Let's keep this in perspective," I said. "There's a chance that they'll get everybody together to talk about humanitarian exchanges. Who cares about the rest of the politics involved."

I looked at Marc, who nodded in agreement. "We can wait and see what Uribe does. Let's just hope this leads to something."

Our fears of the situation exploding were tempered when we found out that Chávez was scheduled to visit Bogotá in the next weeks to speak with Uribe. If Uribe didn't dismiss the idea out of hand, we had even more reason to hope that our captivity wouldn't stretch beyond five years. I'd always had that span of time in the back of my mind as a kind of barricade past which I wouldn't be able to go. Though I hadn't focused on the idea for a while, it may have subconsciously contributed to my eruption at Enrique.

Ten days later on August 31, 2007, our prospects got even better when Uribe announced that he would allow Chávez to act on behalf of the Colombian government in negotiations with the FARC for a prisoner exchange. Chávez stated that he had also received a letter from a high-ranking FARC official asking him to get involved. In a show of good faith, the FARC led a Red Cross delegation to the site where the bodies of the eleven slaughtered deputies were located. The bodies were to be returned to the families after a forensic analysis. Several days after this promise was carried out, Raúl Reyes, the FARC's number two in command, stated that Chávez's participation was a good first step; however, any prisoner exchange would have to take place in Colombia. Chávez vowed that if necessary, he would go into the deepest parts of the jungle to meet with FARC leaders. There'd been rumors that Marulanda was not well and unable to travel, so wherever and whenever Chávez held his meetings was a good thing for us.

Everyone in camp was energized by the news. Even Lucho was cautiously optimistic.

"This is the first time in twenty years that I've seen relations between Venezuela and us even remotely positive," he said. "It has been a long time coming. I don't trust Chávez's motives, but if it can help extract us from this hell, I'd be willing to have the devil himself take my hand."

The radio reported that Chávez stayed twelve hours longer than originally intended and that he and Uribe had wide ranging discussions about a variety of issues of mutual benefit. If the Venezualan president was angling for something else, as Keith predicted, I didn't care. I wanted out of that jungle even if it meant that I was being used as a pawn in a much bigger game.

About the same time that Uribe announced Chavez's involvement, we got word that there would be a new U.S. ambassador to Colombia named William Brownfield. Brownfield was replacing William Wood, a move that could only be good for us. During his tenure as ambassador, Wood only seemed to talk about drugs and counterdrugs, saying nothing about us hostages. Brownfield was different. In an address to the Colombian people, he made it clear that he knew about the three of us and that he was hopeful a solution could be worked out.

The arrival of the new ambassador was encouraging, but lengthy delays in getting the negotiations started set our hopes back a bit. As September drew to a close, the two sides were haggling over things as they usually did. The FARC demanded a demilitarized zone in the south, roughly where we figured we were located, along the border between Colombia, Venezuela, and Brazil. Uribe refused. Colombia wanted proof of life before moving forward with any hostage negotiations, but as far as we knew, the FARC had yet to order any.

As the wrangling continued, Uribe shocked us all once again by naming Piedad Córdoba, a member of one of the more liberal parties in Colombia and a vocal critic of his presidency, as a mediator in the negotiations for hostage release. She made no bones about being sympathetic to the FARC, but no one knew just how deep her ties were. A cloud of suspicion seemed to follow her around in some circles in Bogotá. Lucho was a friend of hers, and he defended her, saying that she was a serious, hardworking, and charismatic woman with good intentions. He said that if anyone could help us out, it was she. She'd once been taken hostage herself by a right-wing paramilitary group and would be very sympathetic to our plight. As questionable a figure as Chávez was, and to a lesser extent Córdoba herself, in the end it didn't matter to us who was doing the talking, so long as there *was* talking. Even Keith, who hated Chávez and everything he stood for, said that he would kiss the man's butt if he could get us free.

The morning of October 20, we were in the river bathing when Enrique hustled down the embankment.

"You have five minutes. You must put on your best clothes. I have received orders to do a proof of life for each of you."

We all looked at one another. Ever since we'd heard those words come up as one of Colombia's demands, we'd known this was coming. The question now was how we would react.

"Look," Keith said, turning away from Enrique. "The FARC have come forward saying they want to do a prisoner exchange. Uribe does an about-face and gets Córdoba and Chávez involved. Our ambassador starts talking about us. Something is up. Let's keep it simple and focus on that."

Marc seemed lost in thought. I asked him what was on his mind.

"Yeah, we have to keep this as simple as possible," he said. "We can't control what the governments of all these countries and all the departments within governments are going to do or say. Do *we* want to do this?"

"I think I need to do it," I said. "I wasn't prepared the last time and I want my family to know that I'm okay. All the other political stuff and what our government is asking for and what doing the proof means to the FARC just doesn't matter in comparison to that. I have to assure my family I'm alive and well."

None of us spoke for a few seconds.

"I know how you feel," Marc said. "I'm torn. I want to let my family know that I'm okay, but after what that journalist Botero did with the first proof of life, I don't know if I can let the FARC use me like that again."

We paused for a moment, all chewing over the memory of how Botero had manipulated us with news of our friends' deaths.

"I'm not the same guy I was then," Marc continued. "I'm not afraid of them anymore. And after what they've put us through, I don't know if I can do anything that might help their cause."

He sat with this chin resting on his closed fists, still shaking his head, looking like a man faced with doing the right hard thing who hates himself for having to do it. Keith threw his hat in the ring.

"I hear you, Marc. I'm not doing it. They want to use our pain, our families' pain, to advance their cause. That's just wrong to me. Tom, I admire you for being able to focus on your family, and you know you don't need me to tell you this, but I'm going to anyway. You do what's best for you and we've got your back, bro."

"I know that, Keith," I replied, certain that we each had to do what was right for us.

"Marc, I'm not trying to sway you one way or the other, but just hear me out. We're human currency here. We all know that. The FARC *secretariado* are likely busting their buttons over this. They got multiple countries wanting to deal with them, legitimizing them in their eyes. We're also more valuable to them now than ever before. I don't think they're going to throw us chips into the pot at this point. Why should they?"

We waited in the water for Enrique, and when he returned, he told Marc he would be first. Marc didn't hesitate a second.

"I'm not going to do it. I don't want to be videotaped and I don't want to speak. I won't answer any questions." When he was through, Marc's jaw was clenched and a vein stood out on his forehead. His eyes never left Enrique's.

Enrique took in his stare for a moment before speaking. "That is fine. But know this: I will have a video of you whether you like it or not. You can be squatting over the *chaunto;* I'll get a video of you there. You can be as you are now in the bath; I'll get a video of you here. It doesn't matter, you will have a video of you done on my terms or you can cooperate."

Enrique walked off a few yards.

"I know he could tape whatever he wants. I'm not going to give him that control. I'll do the video but I won't talk."

Marc waded out of the water and headed up the hill with Keith and me following. He put on a black T-shirt and a pair of sweatpants, hardly the "best clothes" that Enrique had asked us to wear. Marc was determined that the video show how we really were treated and not what the FARC wanted everyone to believe. Enrique hovered around him with his video camera for a few minutes, trying to get the best shots he could. Marc took out the scrap of T-shirt he used as a handkerchief and swatted at a few mosquitoes, never smiling, never looking straight into the camera.

Keith was next, so Marc and I had a chance to talk.

"I really, really wanted to say something to my family," Marc said. "I really did. This just hurts so bad. I feel like I've swallowed a brick and it's lodged in my throat. My kids. What would they think if they knew?"

Keith did the same thing as Marc, as did Lucho. My motivation was wanting to hold my marriage together and not having someone wait for me to be released out of pity. I hadn't heard from Mariana in quite a while, and I wasn't sure what our status was, but I did want her and my sons to know how I felt about them.

Sitting there with Enrique taping me was surreal. Here was this guy whom I hated so much I just wanted to spit in his face, a guy who ordered me placed in chains. And yet there I was speaking words of love to my wife, looking into the camera and trying to ignore who was behind that lens. I handed Enrique a letter that I'd written to my wife. It was essentially a will, so that in case I didn't make it out, my family would be well taken care of. I needed to know that things would be handled neatly and there would as few loose ends as possible. As a practical guy, I needed to have that bit of security in my pocket. I wasn't particularly worried about dying, but covering all the bases would help me rest easier.

The letter also included a list of things my wife needed to do to keep the house in good working order. The gutters needed cleaning once a year so that they wouldn't overflow and ruin the wood siding. There had already been some water damage before the crash and I told her to get a carpenter to fix it. I knew that it was an oddball assortment of romantic and pragmatic stuff, but in a marriage, there's always going to be that mix. I knew she'd understand, and in some ways, she'd know the letter wasn't a fake. I'd been changed by my captivity, but those essential traits that made me a pilot and someone who liked to dot all the *i*s and cross all the *t*s remained.

After the proof of life, camp returned to normal during the fall of 2007. Enrique wasn't happy that we'd ignored his request to tell the world we didn't want a military rescue, but he didn't tighten the screws any further. In fact, a few times he even allowed us to be out of chains to play volleyball. We stayed tuned to the radio and kept up on all the other developments. Chávez had the French government on his side because of Ingrid's dual citizenship. French President Nicolas Sarkozy was doing what he could to encourage negotiations. Meanwhile the FARC had announced a unilateral hostage release as a sign of goodwill.

From what we could tell, there seemed to be a whole lot of talking, flying, and visiting, but no real progress. Chávez had promised the much-anticipated proof of life to the French government before his visit to France, but when he arrived, he wasn't able to produce it. We had no idea why the FARC were holding on to it, and our frustration with the pace of things increased. We also began to see evidence that Chávez's motives were self-serving and two-faced. In radio addresses, he would praise the FARC's founder Marulanda and hail him as a great revolutionary, while we saw him as what he really was—the leader of a terrorist organization.

It seemed as if every day that fall, the news in Colombia was related to the hostages and the FARC. We had other reasons to be hopeful. U.S. presidential campaigns were in full swing. With Senators Hillary Clinton and Barack Obama in the lead on one side, and Senator John McCain rallying on the other, we figured that either way our chances looked good. Liberals were more likely to be sympathetic to our cause and Senator McCain, having been a POW himself, would be willing to focus more attention on our situation. A U.S. congressman, Jim McGovern, had been active in trying to get the FARC to negotiate, and we had hopes that other government representatives would join him. In addition, Simón Trinidad had been convicted in the U.S. the previous July of kidnapping the three of us, but when we heard his sentencing had been delayed, we hoped that somehow it was related to possible Justice Department negotiations about our release.

On November 20, Enrique informed us that we needed to do another proof-of-life video. When we asked him why, he offered a vague excuse about something happening to the other one. It seemed just like the FARC to lose something that various heads of state had been asking for. We had no idea what had happened to the last one, but given the kinds of casualties we'd heard the FARC had taken in the last few years, anything was possible. With the mounting evidence that this proof of life was something that others beside the FARC were calling for, we agreed that it was best to provide our families with the reassurance we all wanted to give them and to satisfy one condition of the possible negotiations. If we didn't know that the French and Colombian governments were asking for the evidence that we were still alive and we hadn't heard for ourselves that our ambassador was eager to work for our release, it would have been a lot easier to reject Enrique's request. We weighed all that out and decided that the scales tipped in favor of doing what Enrique asked.

For my part, I was glad to have another shot at a proof of life. I felt like the previous one had been rushed; in looking back on it, I had some thoughts about what I would do differently, and I incorporated them into the November version. I stole a line from my favorite author, Gabriel García Márquez, which sounded better in Spanish than English. I told Mariana, "*La quiero resueltamente*," which means "I love you resolutely." I also put that line in the written love letter. I was pleased to get that message out in place of my home improvements, especially since I didn't know if I would have a home to return to.

KEITH

I never trusted Chávez. I figured that any military guy who would flee to Cuba wasn't worth much. When he showed up empty-handed in Paris for his meeting with Sarkozy, I knew these negotiations weren't long for this world. Of course, the FARC didn't help matters. If I was certain of one thing, it was that between Chávez and the knuckleheads at the FARC, they would figure out some way to fuck things up. It took a while, but they managed to do it.

It was hard not to let that bit of news overshadow something else we learned. Among the family members who'd earlier gone to Caracas was Patricia. Even if I wasn't at the press conference that Chávez held, my twins were. Apparently, they'd gone with their mother, and "*los tigres*," as they were known, got out of the cage of their mother's arms. They tore around Chávez's presidential palace and interrupted the press conference, so that Chávez left the podium to chase after them. He caught them and played a bit of hide-and-seek around a huge globe on a stand. The press loved it, and the twins served as a reminder that "*los americanos*" were still in captivity even if one of them had twins who couldn't be tamed.

Hearing on the radio that *los tigres* had torn up the presidential palace was a huge boost—especially knowing that the apple hadn't fallen very far from the tree. It was also good to hear that the Colombians had seemed to embrace Patricia and the boys as their own. Whatever worries I had about their being dumped on because of the sins of the father were now gone. All I needed to do was to figure out how to better atone for those sins and stop being a Chávez-esque dumb shit myself.

On November 22, two days after our second proof of life, we heard on the radio that Uribe had officially terminated Chávez and Córdoba as his envoys with the FARC. Happy fucking Thanksgiving to us, pass the cranberries and the mashed hopes. When we heard the news, I held my chain in my hand and said, "That's it. Stick a fork in it. It's over."

All of us sat around the radio listening to the sad little tale of hurt feelings and stupidity. Apparently, Chávez and Córdoba got a little too full of themselves. During a flight together, they got the big idea into their heads that they could take charge of this situation entirely. They called Colombian army commander General Montoya and tried to set up a meeting with him to discuss the hostages and the FARC. What they forgot was that one of the conditions of their appointment as Uribe's representatives was that they not contact anyone or set up any meetings unless they went through him first. He had to approve whatever moves they made. Oops, I guess they didn't read the fine print on the contract, and so because they wanted to hog the spotlight, we stayed in captivity.

Lucho was as pissed off at Uribe as I was at Chávez—not that I didn't think there wasn't enough blame to go around.

"Uribe was merely looking for an opportunity to rescind his agreement. He wanted to embarrass and discredit Chávez from the beginning. A mere technicality and he gets his wish." Lucho had gone red in the face and was looking like he was going to launch into one of his antiright speeches. Fortunately, Marc cut him off before he got too wound up.

"Lucho, the guy is the president of Venezuela. How can you expect Uribe to do nothing when he's talking to the top military man in Colombia without clearing it with him. You don't go over someone's head like that."

Lucho looked near tears, and I wasn't far behind him on that one.

"Then you reprimand him privately and give him an opportunity to do what you requested him to do. You don't issue a public statement terminating him. He's trying to bring down Córdoba and Chávez in the eyes of the people of Colombia and using us to advance his agenda."

Uribe had done plenty wrong in my eyes, so I hated defending him. In his statement dismissing Chávez, he said the Venezuelan was the only one in the world the FARC would respect and hand over hostages to. If Chávez was out of the picture, what did that mean for us? In the days that followed, Chávez and Uribe abandoned their tolerance of each other and fired off potshots. Chávez called Uribe a liar and put relations with Colombia "in the freezer." Uribe accused Chávez of siding with the FARC and with having expansionist intentions. Chávez put things deeper into the freezer by saying that Uribe was a bad president who didn't want peace for his people and was a "sad pawn of the empire." At the same time, the commentators on the radio were speculating that Uribe had only cooperated with Chávez because the Democratic Congress in the U.S. failed to pass a proposed free-trade agreement with Colombia. The commentators figured that Uribe knew that consorting with our main enemy in the region would give him some leverage in America, or at least could slap our wrists a bit.

We were just sick of the rhetoric; what these politicians forgot was that their actions, their finger-pointing, and their manipulating all kept us in chains. Angry as we were, we also knew that things could change again. This was just the latest chapter in the back-and-forth that we'd been living through for almost five years. It was dry season and the waters were literally receding around us, but in our minds, that was just a part of nature's cycle. Just as the political climate had taken a downturn, we knew that it would turn in our favor again. At least people were talking about hostages and exchanges. That was more than what we'd seen in years.

About four or five days before Christmas, a guard told us that we were going to celebrate the holiday early since the plan was for us to be on the march on Christmas Day. By this point, we'd all come to feel like Christmas or any other holiday was just a name on a calendar; we weren't with our families, so the days didn't have the same meaning. The FARC seemed to share that point of view, though they usually had some kind of gathering for themselves on Christmas.

Our pre-Christmas 2007 celebration started off quietly. Eventually, a guard brought in a bottle of a Colombian liquor called *aguardiente*. It was a licorice-flavored drink that was pretty potent. To be polite, I had a shot with the rest of the guys and then stopped. Tom and Marc had a couple more. I was a little worried about them because none of us had eaten yet, and Marc, who had been under the weather, hadn't eaten much for a couple of days. Finally the FARC brought us our food. Instead of just setting a big pot out for us, the cooks served us. For the FARC, chicken was haute cuisine, so that was our special Christmas dinner. This was no succulent Sunday afternoon with the family bird; it was a bit dry and stringy, but better than anything we'd eaten in a long time.

It was then that Enrique came in looking pretty happy. He had one hand behind his back and he told the guard to unlock our chains so we could sit on the ground comfortably to eat. We knew something was up, and as we sat down he brought out a video camera he'd been hiding. We figured what the hell, if Enrique wanted to record us to show the world how well we ate and that we were just chain-free happy campers, then so be it. Of course, it didn't sit too well with any of us, but if he wanted the footage, he'd have to deal with the consequences. With Tom's tongue a bit lubricated, he started in on Enrique.

"You think you can bring us food and drink and expect us to just kiss your ass? What the hell happened to you, Enrique, to make you like you are? You must have been a normal kid, what happened? When did you get this *corazón negro*? When did you choose to follow the dark path?"

Acting like he couldn't hear what Tom was saying, Enrique just kept taping. He was shooting the whole area while Tom narrated the story of Enrique's decline into being an abusive piece of shit. I was sitting back loving all this, when I saw Marc get up. He grabbed a few of the chains that were on the ground, and he wrapped them around his neck. He started walking around with them and rattling them like a ghost out of *A Christmas Carol*. He wanted to ruin Enrique's little sorry-we-can't-be-home-for-the-holidays video. The rest of us were laughing and hooting. Tom continued to read Enrique the riot act while Marc kept inserting himself into the frame of the video. I could tell Enrique was getting pissed. The camera started to shake, and every time he turned it in a different direction, Marc would pop into view with his chain scarf.

Tom was speaking for all of us at that point, and all the disappointment at the unraveling of our expectations came pouring out, along with a lot of pent-up frustration about being put in chains. It was a classic bit of rebellion. We piled up all the junk like it was stacked under our tropical Christmas tree. Enrique slunk out of camp like a cartoon character with steam coming out of his ears.

We knew that he would exact his revenge on us, but we had no idea he would distribute it so unequally. He put Tom in a second set of chains but did nothing to Marc or me. Tom knew that was the nature of the beast. The dark road that Enrique traveled always seemed to lead back to Tom.

Our Christmas "celebration" behind us, we prepared to move out. Enrique came to us on Christmas Day to tell us that we were going to start the march that day.

"We have a ways to go. These marches are difficult sometimes, as you know. I'm sure you will be concerned about your condition. You are responsible for yourselves. We are responsible for ourselves."

Without being direct, Enrique was making it clear that he wanted us to help carry the food supplies. We'd been down this road before. Technically, we, as captives, weren't responsible for ourselves. The FARC were responsible for feeding and supplying us. But his implication here was clear: You don't help us carry food in addition to your own gear, then you won't eat as well. The first rations to be cut, in other words, would be ours. We knew we didn't have much choice. We were in chains and being led on a march. The chains were heavy, about ten pounds, and our packs were far heavier, but if we wanted the one thing that would sustain our energy, we were going to have to take on an extra load.

"We'll carry *your* food," I said, "but we need something in exchange. Powdered milk and *panela*. If I get that, you can pile it on me."

By offering to have it piled on, I was not just getting the milk and sugar I wanted, but something potentially more valuable—the goodwill of the grunt-level guerrillas. Over the years, we'd noticed that the greatest source of dissension among the rank-and-file guerrillas was the perception that some of them had to carry more than others. They were absolutely right. We'd seen guys like Eliécir packed to the gills, while others skated by with light loads. The longer our marches went, the more disgruntled these guys got, leading them to take out their frustrations on us. I figured that if they saw us carrying heavy, they'd be more likely to do us a favor. Usually, if you were transporting food on a march, your load got lighter each day as the supplies were eaten. On this march, I continually asked to be resupplied so that I was always carrying heavy.

As we started out, Tom wasn't able to carry any extras. Enrique had him in double chains on the march and that was tough enough—especially because Tom had a bad knee. Marc did what he could, but his knee was also in bad, bad shape and he'd been sick. I was fortunate to be in about as good a physical condition as I could be, given the circumstances. I wasn't thrilled with the idea of helping out the FARC, but if it meant keeping our asses from starving, then that's what I had to do. With us on the cusp of five years as hostages, we'd become infinitely wiser in the ways of captivity. We were tougher physically as well as mentally, and we knew what the boundaries were.

With the extra weight, the march began rough, but we got a piece of news early on that helped to push us along. On December 28, we got word that the Red Cross and other agencies were pressuring the FARC to release Clara Rojas and her son. What no one on the outside knew was that the FARC had somehow gotten Emanuel to an orphanage, and it wasn't until Jhon Pinchao's escape that the Colombian authorities were able to track down a kid of the right age with a telltale broken arm. Emanuel became a cause célèbre in Colombia and the FARC were taking some serious hits for the kid's condition when he was dropped off and the bad treatment of his arm.

Once Emanuel turned up, the FARC, as usual, still dragged their feet and didn't release Clara, claiming the government had just found any old kid and said it was Emanuel. Clara's mom submitted a DNA sample and that test confirmed that Emanuel was Clara's. Only when Uribe went public with that news about the DNA test did the FARC finally agree to let her go. A pair of Venezuelan helos were given the coordinates of Clara and Consuelo's location. The Red Cross oversaw the operation and the two women were released on January 10.

We needed that bit of good news. By the tenth, we'd been on the march for sixteen full days, and the only other positive development for us was the knowledge that other groups of hostages were nearby. We were in the lead, so we had to set up camp whenever we stopped, but instead of tearing the camps down when we moved out, we left them up for the groups behind us. The guards confirmed our assumptions, saying that there were two groups behind us, one including Ingrid, the five others we'd been separated from, and four other military prisoners.

Every one of us had serious issues with our feet, but Lucho was in the worst shape. A diabetic, he was prone to circulation problems in his legs and feet and that kept even minor things from healing quickly. He'd picked the skin off a popped blister and it got infected. He explained to the FARC about his diabetes. One night, while chained to Tom, Lucho thought he was suffering a heart attack until Tom gave him aspirin. Still, the FARC continued to drive Lucho relentlessly, and the harder they drove him, the worse his foot got. The infection was going deep, and he knew that a lot of diabetics had had to have toes and feet and even legs amputated. He wasn't panicking, but we could all see the legitimate worry in his face.

We'd long known Lucho to be theatrical about his injuries, but it was clear that this was a serious problem. Mercifully, the FARC recognized it, too—the pus and ooze coming out Lucho's foot was as rank as anything I'd ever smelled. I didn't know how he kept going. Soon we came to an old camp, one of the first ones we'd stayed in with Enrique, which looked a lot like it did when we left it.

As we got settled in, we noticed that Enrique and several other FARC were talking to Lucho, who looked very agitated. He came over to us, and for a guy who always wore his heart on his sleeve, it was easy to tell that he'd gotten some bad news.

"They are taking me out of the group, gentlemen. I regret to say that I know no more than that. This may be farewell. I may no longer be residing in the Plenitude."

Marc and I both laughed at his use of the nickname that we'd come up with for the retirement home/hooch that Lucho shared with Tom.

"Well, those of us in the snake pit will miss your presence." I fed Lucho a straight line about the name he and Tom had come up with for the hooch I shared with Marc. He didn't take it.

Instead he said, "I wish you well. Tom, if it is possible to say such a thing under the circumstances, it has been a pleasure. To think that chains can bring us together and keep us apart." Lucho was clearly struggling with his emotions. Marc and I stepped back to let Tom and Lucho have a private moment.

When Lucho was led away, Tom stood next to us and watched him leave. I could sense that Tom was working on something internally. He stood rubbing the back of his neck with his hands, almost as if he wasn't aware that he was doing it.

Marc asked him if he was okay.

Tom pursed his lips and exhaled. "I didn't expect that. I hope he is headed to freedom." None of us expected it, but then again, uncertainty had become our lives. We all shared Tom's hope.

A couple of days later, we were shocked to see Lucho back, this time joined by the two groups that had been following us. The guards kept us segregated in our marching groups. We could wave and say hello, but nothing much beyond that. In one sense, it was good to see Romero, Jhon Jairo, Buitrago, and Javier after such a long time, but mostly it was sad to know they were still being held. When we came to another old campsite, the FARC still kept us in our groups, separating us by about a kilometer or so.

One night, two weeks after Lucho had rejoined us, he and Tom were listening to the message programs in the *coleta* next to Marc and me. I heard him say something that sounded like "Hwmphr." That was followed a moment later by his saying as calmly as if he were telling us the time, "The news announced that I am to be released."

It took a second for his words to register. Everyone—Lucho included—was in complete shock. By the next morning, he was his old self. He went around to each of us encouraging us to write letters, as many letters as we wanted, and he would be certain that they'd get out. We all got to work on writing, and in addition to the letters, Marc asked him to take along a couple of extras for his family. He had carved a wooden plaque with the word *family* on it and had also made some patches with the names of his wife, his daughter, and his two sons on them. Tom and I both had letters to go home, and I also wrote two more letters—one to Patricia and one to her father.

Ever since I'd heard Patricia's first message, it seemed pretty clear to me that she was a woman doing the hard right thing under the toughest of circumstances. From that point on, her messages had given me support that I didn't even know I needed. Before the crash, I'd run from reality. She hadn't. Even after all the time with no word from me, she was mothering *los tigres* and standing by me in a way that I wished I could have stood by her.

This situation seemed to test my resolve about whether I really had been changed by captivity. What kind of person was I going to be when I was out of here? There wasn't anything I could do about the past and the huge hole my absence had put in my loved ones' lives, but I could let Patricia know what I was planning on doing about the future. I could let her know that I saw things differently. I told Patricia and her family that I was going to do right by them. I was going to see if we could be a family, all of us together in some form.

Before he left, Lucho came to me and asked me about my intentions toward Patricia.

"Do you want me to tell her that you want to marry her?" he asked.

"Tell her that I want to do the right thing and support the boys and her. I'd like us to be a family."

"Say no more, Keith. I know how to handle this. I am a Colombian man, I know what to do."

I figured who better than a diplomat and senator to help get my message out. I figured I owed him an honest appraisal.

"Lucho, when we first met, I couldn't stand you. The things you did to the three of us disgusted me. But you know what? I'm glad I got to spend this last six months with you, the real you. I like the person I see now and I'm glad that I saw this side of you."

As happy as we were for Lucho, when we learned that Jorge, Gloria, and Orlando were also being released, we were truly overjoyed. To think that anyone—let alone a group this big—was going home was thrilling. Knowing that the FARC were doing this unilaterally just as they'd done with Clara and Consuelo gave us hope that our time might come soon.

On February 26, 2008, Lucho bid us all farewell. There was very little that was bittersweet about his departure. While a part of me kept expecting the FARC to drop their end of things, for once that didn't happen. With his bags packed and his hope returned, Lucho walked out of our camp that day and did not return.

MARC

On March 1, the Colombian government announced that they had discovered and attacked a FARC camp in the Putamayo region on the Ecuadoran border. The first reports that came in said that sixteen FARC guerrillas had been killed and that among them was Raúl Reyes, the first of the *secretariado* to be killed in battle since the FARC was founded. Keith, Tom, and I rejoiced at this news. Reyes was a vital component of the FARC's engine. Rumor had it that Marulanda was ill and about to step down as the FARC's commander in chief. Reyes was next in line. If nothing else, his death would send shock waves through the FARC.

While this was a positive development, it could also be a bad deal for us—especially because of how it happened. In subsequent days, the radio had more reports about Reyes's death and the controversy that ensued. Reyes and his group had penetrated the Ecuadoran border and had been killed there. Some in Colombia and in Ecuador were upset with the military's crossing the border. After a day or two of angry accusations and denials, Uribe explained that his military had launched a rocket attack from Colombia. Only after they believed that they had hit their intended target did they cross the border into Ecuador—with Ecuadoran president Rafael Correa's permission. Along with the bodies, they also recovered Reyes's laptops, and a series of allegations about the damning evidence the laptops contained began to circulate, including verification of Chávez's longtime collusion with the FARC. If this was true, it could have big implications for us, but all we could do was wonder how it would affect negotiations for our release.

Whether it was because of Reyes's death, Lucho's release, or some other force we were unaware of, in the days after Lucho's departure, we noticed a lot more surveillance aircraft activity. We had been traveling either by boat or by marching along the river. Late one afternoon, deep into a nasty slog a few hundred yards off the river itself, Keith stopped and cocked his ear like a bird dog.

"Hear that?"

I strained my ear and caught something faint; the sound waves vibrated the bones in my chest. "I got something but I don't know what."

"Blackhawks. I'm sure of it." Keith looked like he did the first time he'd received a radio message from his family. "If we spot them and those birds have got the FLIR units on their chins, then we know. My God, honest-to-goodness American forces could be in our vicinity."

As we were talking, we could all hear what we hoped was the distinctive sound of American firepower. We looked at one another and in that moment something wonderful and terrible passed through us all. If we knew the Blackhawks were in the area, so might the FARC. If they knew American pressure was on them, how would they react?

The FARC's Plan A was to run. The tempo of our marches increased and we were punished by the pace. We also moved farther from the river and deeper into the jungle. One night, as we settled down to sleep, Keith was taken to see Enrique. While on the march, they'd discovered some metal tubes on the ground. The tubes had a clear plastic cover on one end and a Cannon plug on the other. Keith could barely contain his laughter when they asked him what they were. He saw immediately that a small camera was inside the lightly pressurized tube. He didn't want the guerrillas messing with it, so he told them that it was a camera—it was so obvious that one of them would have eventually figured it out. He asked to see it, and while examining it, he noticed a North Carolina manufacturer's address printed on the batteries.

To a guy like Keith, it could only mean one thing—Fort Bragg. He figured that the Blackhawks and the cameras meant that some Special Forces units were likely on the ground and definitely in our airspace. As sick as I was feeling, I was thrilled by the news, but we had to keep quiet about it. We convinced one of the guards to pass a note in English to the other hostages alerting them to the fact that something was undoubtedly up. We needed them to be prepared to move in case of a rescue and a FARC response.

As the days progressed, we got the sense that we were being herded by the Blackhawks. They never came close enough that we saw them, but we definitely felt and heard their presence. We also knew that the FARC were being hemmed in by the Colombian military. We had been heading downriver for a time, when the FARC switched tactics and headed back upriver. A sense of urgency surrounded all this. We were running low on supplies. Fortunately, because I was sick, Keith took on extra food and worked a deal with the guards to get some of the last packages of milk and sugar. We were down to meals of four or five spoonfuls of rice. Without those extras, we would have been in really bad shape.

The FARC were in no better condition than we were. They were really on the run, and during the times we were on the river, things weren't any easier than the marches. Trying to get those boats back upriver was a real chore. At some points, the FARC didn't want to or couldn't run the motors, so some of the guerrillas jumped out of the boat and grabbed a rope to tow us. Exhausted and bleary-eyed, they seemed to be drones on the verge of collapse.

If the exhaustion wasn't going to get them, then the fear would. One day we were on the move when we learned that two guards Enrique had sent ahead had been killed. Enrique was getting desperate. We had limited supplies, he was down two men, the Blackhawks were tracking us, and his guerrillas were getting antsy. A couple of days later, a pair of Blackhawks pounded over our heads. We each stood there as they flew past us, reveling in the sheer display of American might. We felt like we were on the flight deck of an aircraft carrier as an F-18 was catapulted into the sky. It had been more than five years since we'd been that close to another American, and almost as much as I missed my family, I missed my country. Even something as faceless as a helo held deep significance for us all.

Those Blackhawks had the opposite effect on the FARC. They were terrified. Milton had browbeaten his troops in the presence of helos and screamed about his underlings' decision-making abilities. Enrique took a different approach. After the flyover, when it was clear that the helos were not coming back, he gathered his guerrillas around him and instructed them to bring out the pots.

"Why are we eating now?" Tom asked.

"I know, I don't get it. We're on less than half rations." Keith shrugged.

A moment later, we heard the sound of something other than rice being poured into the pots. In a few minutes, we heard and smelled the distinctive sound and odor of freshly popped corn. We sat huddled in the forest watching the wide-eyed and nearly trembling FARC drinking their afternoon ration of coffee or chocolate while munching on popcorn.

"Those guys are really shaken up," I said between bites.

"Those Hawks did what they're supposed to. That show of force put a lump in my throat." Keith grinned, then tossed a kernel of corn into the air and caught it in his mouth. "Quite an afternoon matinee."

"This thing is over," Tom said, an air of determination and dread in his voice. "Time is running out on them—" His voice rose at the end as if he was asking a question or leaving a blank that we could have all filled in. "I don't think I've ever been as proud as I was when those helos came over. It was the most breathtaking thing I've seen in five years."

Very early the next morning, the tension was back in the camp. We'd been in total blackout conditions the night before, and Tom had spilled some soup in his hammock. He was trying to get cleaned up when the guards came over and began hassling us to get on our way. Tom said, "Why didn't you just get us up at midnight?"

Enrique's voice cut through the gray predawn. "Who said that?"

Tom responded calmly, "I did."

Enrique strode toward him, his pistol drawn. He leveled it at Tom. "I'll kill you."

"Just do it. I know you don't have the orders to do it. Let's see if you can do something on your own."

Enrique lowered the gun, as if he intended to shoot Tom in the groin.

"That's not going to kill me. If you're going to shoot me, have the decency to make it a clean kill."

Enrique lowered the gun and pointed it at Tom's foot. I didn't know what to do or to say, but Tom stayed completely calm.

"Do that and I can't march."

Enrique said, "Then I'll shoot you in the arm."

"Then you'll give our position away. Thanks."

Enrique was on the verge of completely losing it, but he walked away. A minute later, Tom was double-chained. The look on the guards' faces told us everything we needed to know. We'd seen the disbelief and resignation on the faces of Milton's crew. The guards understood that Enrique was losing it—control of himself, of his guerrillas. They understood that he had crossed the line of needless and excessive cruelty. If he was crumbling under the pressure, they were next in line.

One of the guards took Keith's chain and added it to Tom's. We hadn't been marching in chains to that point, except when Tom was being punished, and now he had double loops around his neck. We were disgusted. Keith pulled a few things out of Tom's backpack, including his tent top, and put it in his. Tom also had to discard a few things that had once been precious commodities.

Keith tried to lighten the mood. "Think of all the cigarettes you had to trade for that shit."

Tom smiled. "With Lucho gone, it's no fun. We had the market cornered. We were setting prices. We had everyone by the balls."

"Just be sure you don't lose yours to fucking Enrique. The guy is not holding up well. If we play our cards right, we might be able to make it out of here. Chains aren't going to help."

I edged closer to Keith and Tom. "There are so many friendlies around here I can feel them. I feel like all we need is five minutes on these guys"—I nodded toward our guards—"and we could be out of here. I can hardly keep my feet from taking off."

As it turned out, we were all speaking too soon. The guards came over to us with a new chain for Keith. No more free marching. The chains went on both of us, and instead of a single guard, we had two of them assigned to us for the next several days.

Just as it seemed the FARC were at their breaking point and the Blackhawks were zeroing in on us, all the helo activity stopped. By the end of April, it was as if someone had flipped a switch and they were gone. We were able to reach a resupply point and for a few hours we simply sat and waited, too exhausted to do anything but eat. We were barely conscious when suddenly Ingrid and William Pérez emerged from the jungle. "Now what is *that*?" Keith asked. He was clearly irritated by the sight of them.

I was relieved to see Ingrid looking about as well as could be expected after our month on the run. It was the first time that she and I had seen each other since that night on the boat. I was pleased to see her again, but when she greeted me, I knew immediately that something had changed. She was not the same woman that I'd held hands with that night on the *bongo*. The light that I'd seen in her eyes was no longer there.

Based on the way William was looking at me, I sensed it had something to do with him. Ingrid didn't treat me coldly, but there was a distance that hadn't been there before. She seemed to be looking at and acting around William the way that she had with me, but she was openly affectionate toward him in a way she had never been with me.

One of the things that Ingrid had shared with me was how difficult it was for her to be a woman in captivity. We'd seen how easily and casually the FARC had coupled literally and metaphorically, and from the outset, it seemed as if Ingrid allied herself with one man in each of the camps. Maybe it was a way to be protected, maybe it was a function of loneliness, but she'd complained to me that she didn't like being forced into a position of helplessness. She shared some of her thoughts about this in letters she'd written to me. I had tried to be honest with her and told her that as much as I understood what other people were doing to her, she was responsible for herself. She was a strong woman and she could stand up to anyone. She told me that she was done with feeling afraid and intimidated. She was capable of being alone and not relying on anyone else.

Now that she appeared to be with William Pérez, I was sad to see that she had reverted to form, that whatever forces were at work on her in the jungle had again reduced her to seeking refuge in someone else instead of in herself and in her faith. I had always had the impulse to fix things for people and to fix people themselves. I didn't consider Ingrid a project, but I wondered if some of her fragility was due to her being on her own for the first time in her life. As much as she had traveled and as much as going off to boarding school at a relatively young age had helped her gain independence, like a lot of adults, she'd never truly been on her own. What I sensed in her was also true of me. I'd been married at nineteen. Being taken captive was the most protracted period of self-reliance that I'd ever experienced. I was pleased to find that I had discovered a strength inside me that I might have never seen if I hadn't been tested in this way.

I couldn't presume to know what Ingrid had been through, but I saw someone who had led a life that, until being taken hostage, was by most people's standards one of relative ease. We'd all been tested, and it seemed like she had taken the less difficult route, fallen back on habits she'd claimed she wanted to break.

During his time as a prisoner, William Pérez had done what he could to make his life in captivity easier. Taking all the favors he did from the FARC, acting as a trusty, Pérez relied on someone other than himself to survive. I struggled to understand why Ingrid was drawn to someone like him. We always said that life in the jungle as a captive would strip us bare and reveal us for who we are. The accomplished, charismatic and ambitious Ingrid I knew and liked and respected very much seemed to exist side by side with the proud, haughty, and very insecure Ingrid I felt sorry for. It may not have been fair to judge her, and I tried to be charitable, but I just couldn't get past the feeling that all the things we'd talked about, all the visions she'd shared of a better life and a better Colombia, rang false. I wasn't sure if it was the politician or the woman I was disappointed in, but it seemed impossible to separate the two.

In the days following our reunion, Ingrid approached me to explain what had happened and why she'd changed. She said that the other camp had been very, very difficult. William was the only one of the group she could speak with. She needed someone out there.

Listening to her, I bit my tongue. I wondered how she could fix a country that she thought needed fixing when she wasn't willing to put in the effort to help herself; it seemed as long as there was someone around to do things for her, she'd never merge the image of who she wanted to be with who she really was.

SIXTEEN

Fat Camp

May 2008–June 2008

KEITH

Not eating is a strange thing. The less you eat, the more attuned you become to what you're feeling on the inside. You focus on the sheer pain of emptiness, so much so that it's easy to forget the toll that it takes on your appearance.

When William and Ingrid joined us in early May 2008, we could see that they'd endured exactly what we had, since their group had been on our heels every step of the way. When you witness yourself starving day by day, the changes are gradual; when you see someone who has been absent for a couple of months of starvation marching, the effects are startling. Seeing them made me reevaluate my appearance. I was definitely at my lowest weight. Sometimes people talk about someone having chiseled features, but the three of us looked more like we had whittled features. We were sticks that someone had taken a knife to and hollowed out our cheeks and necks.

As bad as the three of us looked, starvation appeared to have taken a greater toll on Ingrid. We all had the same skeletal bodies, but it seemed like something had been extinguished inside of her—maybe it was the fight in her eyes. Before, if someone said something she disagreed with or didn't like, you could see flashes of anger and indignation; now those lightning bolts had been reduced to the dim sparking of an empty cigarette lighter's flint.

Given our malnourished state, it was lucky for all of us that our camp was settled at a little *estancia* along a river. In more than five years of captivity, we'd eaten fruits and vegetables about a dozen times, but at this camp we had a bumper crop. It became clear almost immediately that the FARC wanted to fatten us up. That worried me and had me thinking that I was in worse shape than I thought. All day long it seemed as if the guerrillas were bringing us more food. We had boxes of vanilla-filled shortbread cookies, more rice and beans than we'd ever seen. At every meal, we ate until we couldn't force down another bite and the guards teased us for not being able to eat any more. It was like our mothers were there urging us to eat.

This was one time when we weren't intentionally going against the FARC's wishes. Even when our stomachs got used to the idea that we could fit more into them than a few tablespoons of rice and a few sips of unknown-origin broth, we still could not down all that the FARC brought to us. We began to stockpile extras, something we hadn't been able to do in a long time. We were being as frugal as possible, hoarding whatever we could for the next inevitable famine.

Food wasn't the only bounty we received. One morning Enrique came into our section of the camp. The six of us were together with the other hostages somewhere nearby but not visible to us. Tom and I were talking, and Four Eyes said to me, "Keith, this is for you." He handed me a Sony multiband radio. We'd been asking for radios for more than five years, and finally here was Enrique handing me the king of jungle radios. I held the thing in my hand, and it felt like I had been given a half pound of gold. I wasn't about to kiss Enrique's ass, but I did say, "That's great."

Enrique looked at Tom and smiled. "And one for you." From behind his back he pulled out a tiny little green radio that looked like something you'd give your toddler so he could pretend he was listening to something. It was cube-shaped and had a little foldout solar panel to recharge the batteries. Tom didn't rise to Enrique's bait. Instead of getting on him for what was clearly a slap in the face, he simply flipped the switch on the radio. Some Christian ministry or another must have had them made, because only two stations came in. In place of a dial, it had a little button you pushed to change between the two frequencies. Both stations played religious programming twenty-four hours a day. At the first word out of that radio, Tom smiled a big toothy grin at Enrique. Unbeknownst to Enrique, on our recent march, Marc had traded cigarettes to get a radio. Now, with Tom's and my new radios, that brought our count up to three. We no longer had to rely on other people for news.

Through much of April, we'd only had spotty radio reception, but one of the things we learned immediately was that the FARC were taking their lumps and so was Chávez. The Colombian intelligence agency or the military had seized and then analyzed the contents of the laptops that Raúl Reyes had with him when he was killed. According to Colombia's top police official, the computers showed evidence that the Venezuelans had offered $300 million to the FARC. The official also accused Chávez of accepting financial support from the FARC for the previous fifteen years, going all the way back to when Chávez was in prison following an attempted coup d'état. To answer accusations that Uribe had planted evidence on the laptop, the Colombians had Interpol examine the computers, and they determined that the Colombian government hadn't tampered with them.

Everyone knew that $300 million wasn't lunch money for the guerrillas; Chávez must have been expecting something in return for it. Ingrid said she believed that Chávez had grand designs on dominating the region and uniting nations into a Bolivarian Gran Colombia. I figured the guy had a big enough ego that he'd want it named Chávezlandia.

In addition, we found out that the FARC's *secretariado* had taken another hit when Iván Ríos, the head of the central bloc, was killed by his own security chief. He brought Colombian officials Ríos's severed right hand, his ID, and his laptop to prove that Ríos was dead. Eventually, fingerprints confirmed that the hand belonged to Ríos. The U.S. had a $5 million bounty on Ríos, and the security chief who reportedly turned in his boss—or at least that one part of him—asked for the reward. We were never sure if he got it, but we were sure of one thing. One less was good enough for us, especially a big important one like Ríos.

Good enough couldn't adequately describe our reaction to the news that the FARC's number one man, Manuel Marulanda, had died back in March. The FARC said that he'd kicked because of a heart attack and this was plausible. After all, he was seventy-eight years old, and we'd heard that he hadn't been in good health for a while. Rumor had it that the guy who would replace Marulanda, Alfonso Cano, was highly educated, a psychiatrist, and according to the FARC guerrillas we talked to, a bit "softer." They told us that he was the guy in charge of the FARC's "ideas." Cano had founded the Clandestine Colombian Communist Party, and the whole CCCP initials and the reference to the former Soviet Union's CCCP was kind of clever. Our hope was that injecting some new blood, and shedding more FARC blood, would bring about some positive changes that might lead to our release.

MARC

Finding out that Marulanda, Reyes, and Ríos had all died within a short time of one another helped us to understand a number of things. Suddenly it was clear why the FARC had us on the run. Furthermore, we now saw why Enrique had become so much more vile in his treatment of all of us—especially of Tom.

It was easier to really feel good about someone dying, someone we considered evil, when we didn't know him personally. In the case of the hideous guard Rogelio, we were glad he would no longer be around to plague us or any other hostages. We took a great deal more pleasure in the deaths of those three FARC leaders, because it seemed to us that the FARC, as a viable organization, was dying. We could imagine some impoverished family in the boondocks of Colombia viewing Marulanda as a hero. To us, and to the rest of the world, the guy was a murderer. Under his leadership, the FARC had kidnapped thousands, killed thousands, and ruined the lives of thousands more of their own people. As Keith often pointed out, "The guy gave up his right to be thought of as a human being a long time ago. He's nothing but an oxygen thief at this point."

Aside from debating the implications that these developments had for us, our time at the Fat Camp was one of the few periods when we didn't fully engage in a lot of other activities besides eating, reading, and listening to the radio. We needed to recoup our energy. We exercised, but not with the intensity we had at the Exercise Camp. We played chess, but not with the passion we had at the Chess Camp. It seemed like we were taking our cue from the FARC, and they were in a low-activity mode. We were balancing out the flurry of activity that had taken place politically in Colombia.

We were encouraged to learn that Governor Bill Richardson of New Mexico had traveled to Colombia to discuss our situation. We didn't know if it was because he was Hispanic himself and felt comfortable with the language or if one of our family members had been able to get his attention somehow, but we were grateful nonetheless. Being able to add his name to the growing list of Americans involved in some way helped to offset the disappointment we felt when the Blackhawks stopped coming around.

The FARC also seemed to pay closer attention to Ingrid. Even Enrique, who had little regard for her previously, was acting much friendlier. Having William in her corner also helped. Ingrid benefited from the special treatment he'd long been receiving. Just by getting to watch a DVD, William and Ingrid were ahead of us. In addition to William's presence, it was easy to figure out why the FARC were going out of their way to please her. In her November proof-of-life video, she had looked frail and weak. Compared to how she looked in May, that video showed her in great spirits and in top form. If they were going to use her in another video, they had to get her healthier.

I was concerned about Ingrid as well, but I looked at the situation from the energy perspective. The FARC had set up this rest camp to get us back in physical shape. I needed to be better mentally and spiritually as well. I decided that Ingrid's choices and decisions, as much as I might have disagreed with them, were hers to make. I had enough to do to get my own situation squared away.

All six of our group were housed under our tent tops in a confined area. When we slept, there was barely a foot to eighteen inches between us. As a result, contact with Ingrid was unavoidable and not unwelcome, but not something I sought out. After a few weeks of the fattening-up routine, I noticed that she was paying more attention to me. I was polite to her, but suspicious, too. When she realized that I wasn't responding to her the way I had before, she stopped being subtle and came out and told me what she wanted from me.

"Marc, I would like the letters and notes I sent to you."

I looked at her and could see that some of the old, original Ingrid had returned. Though she said she "would like" those things back, it was clear that she meant "give me." When we'd gotten close, she'd dropped the I'm-somebody-and-you're-not tone. Now it wasn't fully back in place, but enough of it was creeping in around the edges to make me uncomfortable.

"I don't understand, Ingrid. What you sent to me is mine. You can't have them back. You gave them to me."

Ingrid persisted, and I asked her to please respect what we'd shared and leave it at that. For days, she wouldn't, and I could tell that she was getting angrier and angrier. She and William segregated themselves from everyone as best they could and the mood of the camp plummeted. We were back to where we'd been before and none of us was too happy about it. Some of the old issues among the Colombian hostages started to surface, but Juancho did the right thing. He came to Keith and said, "I can feel it coming on again. Why it is that when we have a woman in the camp things get this way I don't know. I'm staying away from her. We all should."

I didn't like having to do this, but I knew that for my sake and the sake of everyone else in the camp, I just had to avoid any more confrontations with Ingrid.

We were all spread out in our small area working away when Mario, the guard in direct charge of us, came up to Keith, Tom, and me and said, "Guys, you need to get all your stuff together." He led us back to our hooch.

"Where are we going?" I asked after I'd packed everything up.

"Come with me and bring your pack." Mario led me out into an open area.

He pointed to a spot where the FARC had spread out black plastic sheets. "Not this again," I muttered.

"Come on. This is ridiculous. You guys just searched us." Tom's agitation was clear and uniformly shared. We knew the civilians were coming to speak with us and maybe the FARC needed to search us again for security reasons, but since we had been segregated from the other captives, we had not been in contact with anyone else. We couldn't have possibly gotten our hands on anything new.

"Mario, what is going on? Why are we being searched again?" I asked.

Mario looked around and started in on some lame excuse about Enrique and following orders.

"Empty it."

I did what he asked.

I had knelt down and started to pull everything out of my bag when I saw Ingrid approaching. She was walking with her head down and her arms folded across her chest. She looked up and caught my eye, holding my glare for a second and looking as defiant and arrogant as I'd ever seen her. That was when I knew what was up. Mario had been feeding me a line of bullshit about Enrique and orders from above. The orders for this search had come from Ingrid.

Mario took every piece of paper, every note, every notebook, and scanned the pages before handing them to Ingrid. He then asked, "Are these the documents you are looking for?"

Ingrid looked each item over, and said, "No."

"Look, you're not going to find what you're looking for. I burned everything," I told them.

Mario continued tearing through my stuff, handing every scrap of paper to Ingrid. I could tell he was getting frustrated. He started indiscriminately tossing my things on the ground.

I was furious and couldn't believe what was going on.

Mario finally stopped and said, "There is nothing."

"I know that he has them. He didn't burn them. He told me he would give them back to me."

"Mario," I said, "I don't have them. I did burn them."

I heard Ingrid heave a huge sigh of anger and disbelief.

"I would have given them back to her if she would have given me mine."

Ingrid stormed off, her long hair swinging like a pendulum. In a way, I could understand why she was so angry. After I refused to return some of the letters she had written to me, she'd given back a few of my letters to her. I'd decided that if we each agreed to return every one of them, I'd be okay with it. Her response was to have the guards go through my things and subject my friends to the same harsh treatment.

After Tom and Keith were searched, they returned to the hooch. I was still stunned, and I could tell that Keith was really angry.

"In my five and a half years of captivity, I've never seen anything like this," Keith began. I could tell he was just taxiing down the runway. His anger was going to take off. "I've been in chains for months, I've been starved, pushed past my physical limits, had every one of my human rights violated by the FARC, but none of that can compare to the feeling of having someone who is allegedly on my side collaborating with the enemy. And for what? Because she wanted some notes and letters back from you? You told her she couldn't have them, and she couldn't find a way to get them out of you. So, like a schoolgirl, she went to the teacher to rat us out."

"I know. I know," I said, "I think it was William. You know how he is."

It was a violation that went beyond any we'd seen before. With a handful of exceptions, most notably when William had Richard put in chains, trusties never used their connections to the FARC against other prisoners. With this stroke, the line between us and them had been obliterated. These were terrorists we were dealing with. We'd had our lives threatened by these people, and now it seemed as if she was using them to get some notes and letters back from me. I couldn't believe that Ingrid was treating us like she was on the FARC's side. It wasn't like her, but I could believe that William would instigate it.

Worse, we had expressed our feelings for each other in those letters. Asking for them back was like trying to take back those thoughts and emotions. If I'd learned anything in captivity, it was that we all escaped from reality for moments at a time. Whether it was the Freedom Ride, thinking of our houses back home, or whatever, we all had places to escape to. Ingrid and I had gone to one of those places together, but to dismiss what we innocently shared or to cast it as something we should regret or could do us harm down the line was a distortion of the truth. We'd done nothing wrong, and I hated what she seemed to be implying by asking for them back. I wasn't one of the many kinds of "them" that Ingrid might imagine were after her or out to hurt her. I'd been helping her, at great risk to myself and the relationships I had with the other hostages. Denying this was not something I could do.

"Marc, bro, I am so sorry. That was the sickest thing I've seen out here. You've just been betrayed by someone who you reached out to in the goodness of your heart when no one else gave a fuck about her. You did the Christian thing, the charitable thing, the hardest, rightest, most stand up thing in the world, and this search is how you've been repaid."

"That's just how some people are. It's almost like she can't help herself. She put her image and her fear of it being damaged above our friendship. I don't really get it." My voice started as a whisper but picked up in intensity as I spoke. "I'm so pissed I can't even think straight. If there's one thing you don't ever do it's going to the enemy like that. Unbelievable."

"Did she get what she was after?"

I hesitated for a moment before a smile crept across my face. I shook my head. "No. No. They couldn't put their hands on anything. Nothing and no one is going to touch me now."

Later that day, our chief guard came to us and said, "Pack up. We're moving all of you." None of us was ready for another march. We stowed all our gear and waited for the order to move out. The head guard and three others approached us. I didn't think much of that since each of us typically had his own person watching him. Instead of marching us out of the camp, we were told, "*Requisa.*"

"Not this again." Tom sighed. "We just stowed everything."

"I wonder what it means?" I asked.

"Wonder if there was another escape?" Keith picked up his backpack and shook the contents onto a sheet of black plastic the guards provided. At least our things wouldn't get all dirty. The thing we'd noticed about the searches was that they weren't especially professional and thorough. Going through a line at the airport in the States was a lot more invasive and productive than what the FARC did. This one, though, was a little more thorough. With the search complete, the six of us marched fifty yards into the woods to make camp.

TOM

Ingrid's initiation of a search on Keith, Marc, and me did one thing. It made the three of us realize that no matter what, we could at least count on one another. Maybe the shared experience of the most recent starvation march and all of us doing what we could to help one another out to get through it also contributed. We were united in a way that we hadn't been before. I didn't want to think about it too long or analyze it. I just wanted to enjoy the goodwill and keep whatever positive energy we had flowing.

As far as we were concerned, whatever tension was in our group of six wasn't a result of anything we had done. We decided to just get past being singled out for another search after the one Ingrid had initiated. Also, we'd been searched many times previously and it was likely that we would be again.

"Given all that happened with the FARC, the escapes, the killings, it made sense that they were shaping up a bit," I said.

"Too little too late for these shitheads. They're never going to shape up. How the hell they can—"

" 'Think of themselves as soldiers. When I was in the corps . . .' " We all laughed at Marc being able to recite chapter and verse of one of Keith's favorite sermons.

Marc said, "Remember the time you were using that flight-instructor stuff with Jhon and Juancho? Those guys were in the land of nod and you kept going on and on."

It felt good to be able to laugh about some of those things. We'd been together a long time. It's difficult to reminisce about an experience as painful as captivity, but with the two of them there, it was possible.

The weeks following our brief separation from the other three passed in much the same way as they had at Fat Camp. We listened to the radios but the news about our release had begun to stagnate. We were still eating well, and one evening Marc had been served too much rice. He wandered over to the trash hole. He came back and I could tell something was up. Keith must have also because he asked, "What is going on, bro?"

Marc sat down near us and checked to see how close the guards were. I moved my eyes but kept my head facing Marc. "There was a cardboard box. It had letters cut out of it. It spelled '*Acuerdo Humani-tario Ya.*' They weren't just cut out, but they were like traced, stenciled. They had red spray paint on the edges."

"Are they making signs or T-shirts or something?" Keith asked.

"Humanitarian Agreement Now." I tossed the words around in my head. That was something we'd all been hoping for, but it seemed odd that the FARC would stencil those words on anything unless it was intended for public display. "Keith's right. It has to be signs or T-shirts."

"You think they would make us wear those in another proof of life?" Marc asked.

"If they're as desperate as they seem, why not?" I figured that as a piece of propaganda, a bit of video with all the hostages wearing T-shirts or carrying signs demanding an exchange of prisoners was pretty good.

"Well, we said before, with all the food and better treatment, they wanted us to be camera-ready," Keith said.

"We did get asked our clothes sizes again. They must be making us each a shirt." Marc's voice carried a note of finality.

We all agreed we should take advantage of this next proof of life. At this point, it was best not to do anything to diminish our chances. The videos weren't of interest to us; instead we focused on writing letters to our families. We hoped that there would be some way to get them sent out. For the next two days, we did little besides eat and write. The guards seemed to be noticing our sudden interest in literary activity, but we kept on in spite of it.

When our proof-of-life clothes arrived, there were no "Humanitarian Accord Now" T-shirts. Mario brought them to us, and we just about lost it. At first, we thought it was funny, but then we got upset thinking that Enrique was trying to make us look like we'd crossed the line to the other side. Our new clothes consisted of cheap blue jeans, the kind we'd seen poorer Colombians wearing when they came into the city in their good clothes. With the pants, we were handed campesino-style western dress shirts. All we needed was a straw hat and we would have looked like we'd stepped off the set of one of the Mexican B movies we'd watched on the DVD players.

"I'm not wearing this." Marc shook his head and tossed the clothes to the ground.

Mario looked completely surprised. "Why not? What is wrong with them? They are in your size." He was acting like he'd gone out and shopped for us himself.

"Because this isn't how I'm dressed when I'm out here. I want to look just like I look now." Marc pulled at one leg of his sweatpants and then tugged at the collar of his T-shirt. "I can't go marching around wearing jeans and a shirt. We're all heavy-loaded as it is. I'm not going to wear them and I'm not going to carry them."

If I were Marc, I would have had the same reaction. Mario had brought him a hideous pink shirt.

Keith tossed his down as well. "Not going to do it, either."

Mario shook his head and left.

We were certain that Enrique would come back later that day and read us the riot act, but he didn't. Two days later, he did come to our camp, but he was calm.

"Here is the news. An international commission will be arriving. They are going to look you guys over to make sure you are well. Medical checks. They will want to speak with you."

We all quickly glanced at one another. This was our chance to get the letters we'd written to our families out of the country. We were just going to have to figure out how to get them in the hands of the commission without the FARC knowing.

Enrique continued, "You will be allowed to write letters. Be very careful what you write. If you do anything that gives away our location, I promise you this. If you fuck us, we will fuck you."

Enrique's pupils narrowed to BBs behind his thick glasses. "You understand me? We're trying to be nice to you. We bring you clothes. Some of you aren't accepting them. You don't want those clothes, then we'll have problems."

Marc spoke up. "I'm the one who didn't accept the clothes. Don't get on these guys for that. I'm not going to wear them. I'm an American. Let me dress like an American. I'm not a Colombian. I'm not a *campesino*."

Enrique set his jaw and pursed his lips. "You should be so lucky as to be a *campesino* and not an imperialist."

He went on for a bit, but we tuned him out. All we could think of was the great news. We'd be able to get word out to our families. Over the years, we'd written so many letters in our heads and on paper; until now they'd never had a chance of getting out. This time would be different. It had been nearly five and a half years since I wrote something thinking that others would read it. Now all I had to do was press my pen to paper and I could make myself heard.

SEVENTEEN

Freedom

July 2, 2008

KEITH

As we came up on July, we were staring five and half years in captivity right in the eyeballs. Knowing that some international observers, medics, aid workers, or whatever were coming to see us for the first time could have signified one of two things: Either the FARC had caved in to pressure for a more strenuous proof of life so that our value could be upped, or a deal was in the works and our new "owners" wanted to be sure they weren't getting ripped off before they put down their cold hard cash. Either of these was good enough for me. Ever since the flurry of activity with Chávez and Córdoba, I figured that in about a year's time we'd be out. Knowing how the FARC stalled, how they'd messed up with the first proof-of-life videos (we learned eventually that the Colombian military had seized them), and how their organization was riddled by deaths to their leaders, my estimate was conservative but one I was comfortable with.

Like everybody in the camp, I was excited about the visit. To actually be able to talk to someone face-to-face who wasn't involved in this mess was enough to have me riding a small high. We were all busy working on letters, conferring with one another on what was appropriate to say or to not say—we weren't concerned about Enrique's warning; we just wanted to be sure that we didn't do anything to alarm anyone.

July 1 brought us one day closer to our favorite holiday—the Fourth of July. We'd heard a rumor from one of the guards that members of the international committee had already been on the ground in our area trying to make contact with the FARC. If they were that close, we figured we didn't have long to wait. Each time the guards came to us with new instructions, they seemed more relaxed and let a little more information slip. We were each brought a small knapsack and told to bring two changes of clothing and any other essentials. That was it. We'd get the rest of our gear when we returned. One of the guards let me know that we'd be taken to a permanent structure where there would be mattresses, a pool table, and good food. All of that sounded fine with me, and I had to laugh when the guard told us that we'd be spending a night in an old whorehouse.

We returned to the structure where we'd first been held with the other Colombians. Everyone was eager to get going, and anticipation was at an all-time high. We'd been joined by four other hostages—Jhon Jairo Durán, Julio César Buitrago, Javier Rodríguez, and Erasmo Romero, bringing the total number of hostages in the camp up to fifteen. We were especially glad to see more of the military and police guys with us. If anybody deserved the chance to be in contact with their families, it was them. They'd been held for so long and yet they continued to carry themselves with dignity and character. Durán was the most selfless person I'd ever met. From the very beginning, he'd been great, and he and Tom had developed a special bond that just amazed me. Two guys of very different ages and backgrounds, one a devout Christian and the other a professed atheist, but none of that mattered. Durán walked the walk in ways that humbled me—the only one among us who wouldn't snag extra food from the FARC's supplies.

We gave one another some shit about the civilian clothes the FARC was making us wear. It was like we were all going to a school dance, or something. Ingrid was off with William and not mixing in, but the rest of the guys all stood around busting one another's chops, talking about what was to come, and burning off a whole bunch of pent-up energy.

Arteaga let everyone know about my wedding plans.

"Patricia has invited dozens and dozens of people, every day more, as the news says. It is going to be a grand celebration."

Talk turned to my new life situation, and I let the boys have their fun with it.

Apparently Lucho had taken it upon himself to propose to Patricia on my behalf. He greeted her at the airport in Bogotá with a bouquet of flowers and my "declaration of intentions." The first I learned of said intentions was during a radio broadcast. When I heard about the captive American who had proposed to his Colombian girlfriend, I was stunned, but knowing Lucho, and remembering his words—*I know how to handle this. I am a Colombian man*—I should have guessed what he was up to. After the proposal, Patricia's messages took on an even more tender tone, and her declarations of love hit me hard and in all the right places. I wasn't sure that a wedding was in our immediate future, but I was eager to see her again, and she wasn't going to be simply a monthly notation in my checkbook—she was going to be someone I would spend significant time with.

The FARC fed us lunch and it was as loud as a school cafeteria in that little enclosure. Arteaga and Armando were among the most vocal in their delight that we were being given the opportunity to do another proof of life. We all speculated about what the international aid workers would be like. I didn't think a lot about it, but every time any of the

FARC mentioned the visitors, they always used the word *international*. Typical of them, they were jacked up simply because they were getting some attention and "good press."

After lunch, we were loaded into a *bongo* and taken up a good-size river. Though we were moving during daylight, the FARC didn't cover us up, and I was able to take in the scenery. No matter how many times I was out on the river, I never got tired of getting out from underneath the jungle canopy. In some ways, those river trips reminded me of being out in the Everglades—the air smelled the same, a mix of mud and fish and rotting vegetation. It wasn't an unpleasant odor—it just seemed as if everything was either fully alive and blooming or dead and decaying. We were clipping along at a decent pace, and the fresh breeze made it seem like the whole world was exhaling along with us.

The building where we were brought might have been a whorehouse at some point, but now it looked a lot more like a warehouse. We were taken into some kind of stockroom where long, wide shelves lined the walls. On top of the shelves were some thin mattresses on which the guards told us to sleep. There weren't enough mattresses, so some of us had to double up, but considering I hadn't been on one in years, I figured it would be like sleeping on a cloud. Our field trip was just beginning, and until well past dark, we chattered excitedly like kids at a sleepover.

The next morning, we got another surprise. Instead of being served breakfast in a large metal pot from which we had to fill our own small cups, the guerrillas brought out our meal in actual porcelain bowls. Marc, Juancho, and I were seated together, and you would have thought they'd brought out their heirloom silver serving bowls the way we reacted. They also set out some decent silverware. It felt odd to be touching something that wasn't pitted, gouged, or dented. Marc tucked his new spoon away.

"That's just rude, bro. Our hosts bring out the good china and silver and you're going to swipe it."

Marc laughed and then turned serious. "I'm going to need this thing. The first one I had lasted me five years. Who knows how long I'm going to have to eat with this one."

After breakfast, Tom and I sat and watched as Marc played chess with Jhon Durán for a bit. None of us knew where things were going from here, but Arteaga seemed to be the center of attention among the group. Eventually he walked over to us and said, "We are going to go on a helicopter today. One of the guards told me. Expect helicopters."

"Really? Helos? They're going to take us out of here to do the exams and stuff?" I suddenly felt the urge to pee, and I walked away from everybody to do my business. Suddenly, as I was standing there, I heard the familiar noise of helos dropping down.

"Keith! Helos! Keith, helos!" I heard Marc yelling for me. I zipped up, confused as hell about what this meant. For years one of the worst sounds coming out of the jungle was the *bhwhup bhwhup bhwhup* of a helicopter's blades slicing up the air. The adrenaline started pumping, and the hairs stood up on my arms. As I looked out over the tops of the trees ringing our clearing, I saw two Russian built M–17 helos descending and going into hover.

If Arteaga hadn't told me just minutes before that helos were coming I would have run. As it was, I was torn. I kept looking at the guards, waiting for them to fan out so they could cover all of us with fire. Instead of doing that, each guard called out a single name: "Raimundo with me," "Erasmo with me," "Flores with me," "Tom with me"—all the way down the line. I wondered if this was how they did it. All of us paired up with a guard who would then shoot us. I could see they'd prepared for this and were ready for us. For once, the FARC seemed disciplined and organized. Maybe that was all they were good for, killing hostages when the rescue helos showed up. Tom was taken near the front of the line, while Marc and I were at the back end.

Marc looked at me. "Do we go?"

I shrugged. "At this point, yes. But we've got to be smart."

We were all loaded onto a boat and ferried directly across the river, where we waited near a small shack on the border of a coca field. Standing there was César, whom we hadn't seen in more than a year. He lingered by us, watching the helos prepare to land.

I didn't understand why the first Front's leader was there, but I had a more immediate concern on my mind. Now that the helos were close, I could see that they were painted white and the wheel wells were red, but something was missing.

"Where are the crosses?" I yelled to Marc above the noise of the motors.

Marc frowned and shrugged, signaling that he couldn't hear what I was saying. As one of the helos landed, its engine settled into an idle. I led Marc to the very back of the irregular line of hostages and guards that had formed. Tom continued to stay toward the front near Durán and Juancho.

"If that's the Red Cross, then where the fuck are the crosses?"

Marc kept pivoting his head between me and the helo.

"What's going on?"

"I don't know, bro, but we may be fucked."

MARC

Keith and I stood frozen, weighing our options. Nearly everything in me said to run, but something held me back. Maybe it was just the idea that as far as we knew, the FARC had no helicopters. Whoever was coming in would likely be better than the guerrillas.

"Getting on a helo can't be a bad thing. Let's see how this plays out when we get off the helo," Keith said, echoing my thoughts.

"I'm with you."

When I first heard the helos approaching, I thought it was the sound of freedom. Now that we were waiting for the clamshell doors to open, I wasn't so sure. When the international team filed out, all of them were wearing brown vests, but one man caught my eye. He had bleached blond hair and a heavy five-o'clock shadow. His mirrored Ray-Ban sunglasses obscured his eyes and reflected the jungle behind us. The sun glinted off the earring he wore, and when he raised his arm to shield his eyes, I saw that he had a bandanna wrapped around his wrist. He was followed by a journalist carrying a microphone and another with a large professional video camera. They went straight toward the guerrillas and began to interview them.

A guy wearing square-framed glasses broke from the group. He approached us and said in Spanish, "I'm the doctor. Is everybody okay here? Does anyone need immediate assistance? Any emergencies?"

We all shook our heads no. Whether it was the reality of seeing someone other than a hostage or a guerrilla or the smell of aviation fuel was getting to me, I don't know, but I was suddenly feeling excited at the prospect of being able to fly somewhere.

"Marc, this has got to be good," Keith repeated. "They wouldn't be here with these helos and flying us somewhere unless this was good."

One of the humanitarian workers stepped up to us. "Cross the barbed-wire fence and we will load you in the helicopter."

We all stepped over the low strands of wire and into the coca fields. We collected in a small group. I looked back and saw César being interviewed. I could see that the camera had a Telesur logo on it—a Venezuelan media outlet. We took a few steps toward the helo. Another aide worker raised his arms and a couple of other guys and one woman spread out alongside him.

"As one of the conditions of your proof of life and evaluation, you must be placed in restraints." At that point, he held up plastic wire tie wraps—the kind that policemen in the U.S. sometimes use in place of metal handcuffs.

"No way, Keith," I said. "I'm not letting them do that to me. These are supposed to be humanitarian aid workers. We've been chained and they want to do this to us? What is going on!"

We were at the back of the line and several others had already been tied. I could hear Tom's voice above the engine noise: "Everyone just be calm and cooperate. This is just a precaution. Get in the helo quickly so that it doesn't burn too much fuel."

Jhon Jairo Durán was sobbing and yelling, "I've been a hostage for ten years. Why are you doing this to me? How can you tie us up?"

He flung himself to the ground and Tom knelt over him, talking to and trying to soothe him. When Jhon stood up, I could see that he was so agitated that foam and spit had coagulated on his lips. Tom put his arm around him and tried to hold him still. Jhon had been such a stalwart throughout his captivity that seeing him like this really shocked me; out of everyone, I would not have bet on him to break down at that point.

Keith walked away from me and stepped in front of the camera. Enrique and the guards started shouting that somebody should stop him, but before anyone could, he shouted, "Tom Howes. Marc Gonsalves. Keith Stansell. We are three Americans being held. We are well." Keith hustled back toward me and the two of us stood there, still uncertain what to do.

In the meantime, the aid worker with the mirrored sunglasses walked up to Keith and me. He said to us in English, "My name is Daniel. You see this?" He took a laminated card that was hanging from a cord draped around his neck and showed it to us. "This is my ID. I'm Australian."

Before I could respond, Keith grabbed the ID and looked it over.

"Bullshit. Who the fuck are you and what is going on? You're not Australian; you've got a fucking Colombian accent. What is going on? You are *not* who you say you are."

Daniel stayed very calm and said to us, in English again, "I am going to get you out of here. Do you want to go home?"

"Hell, yeah," we said in unison.

Keith turned to me and said, "Screw the tie wraps. Put them on. Let's get the fuck out of here."

I wasn't completely convinced. I asked Daniel as he was busy tying Keith's wrists, "Is this for our freedom?" Daniel didn't look up; he was too intent on getting Keith's ties done.

Then he yanked one end of the strap, pulled up his sunglasses for a second, and said, "Trust me. Trust me."

He stood up, and as the helo's motor began to wind up, he looked at Keith and me and said loud enough to be heard over the noise, "Do you understand what I am trying to tell you? *Trust me.*"

I stood there, adrenaline pounding through my veins, as he cinched the plastic bands around my wrists. Keith was just ahead of me and the rest of the hostages were already seated in the aircraft along each sidewall. I could see that Keith had already worked his way out of the ties. I couldn't believe he'd told me to let myself get tied up and he had already broken out of his. He was holding his wrists together to make it look like he was restrained, but the bands were gone. I sped up a bit and got past Keith, turning to see from his expression if there was something else we should be doing besides boarding. He mouthed words, but in all the noise and confusion, I couldn't make them out.

Walking up the ramp to the helo, I had no idea what to think. I saw an open seat, and the next thing I knew, someone had lifted me up and tossed me into it. A darker-skinned guy wearing a Che T-shirt yanked my boots off and flung them to the other side of the helo. This is what humanitarian aid workers do?

I was stunned and yelled at him, "Calm down. Stop it."

I looked toward the middle of the craft and saw Keith about to sit down next to Tom. The next thing I knew, one of the other aid workers picked Keith up and threw him down in the back of the helo. He ripped off Keith's boots and then tie-wrapped his feet. I could hear the pull of the plastic strap as it ratcheted along the teeth. Keith had a confused look on his face, and when the aid worker turned around, I could see why. The guy had on a Che Guevara shirt just like we'd seen so many of the FARC wearing. What was this deal? Were we being taken by another guerrilla group, the Venezuelans, some right-wing Colombians?

When Keith's guy moved on to bind the next person's legs, Keith raised his arms and separated his hands to show me that he was free of the ties. He did the same thing with his legs. He'd already snapped his leg ties and was spreading his legs again and again to show me how to get out of mine. I was wondering if the three of us were supposed to break out at that point. There were fifteen hostages and not counting the pilots, only five of them. Before I could figure out everything that Keith was trying to tell me, I saw César step into the helo. He was about to take a seat next to me when the Ray-Ban guy stepped in front of him.

"No, comrade. Sit here, comrade." He pointed to a jump seat at the front of the cabin that faced the rear. César took the seat and was directly across from me. With the door not yet completely closed, we started to pull pitch and leave the ground. I looked over my shoulder to see out the window and we were airborne for the first time in more than five years. Almost immediately the feeling that we were in a car and speeding over a hill welled up in the pit of my stomach.

When I turned back around, all hell had broken loose. Bodies were jammed up in front of me. I could see Keith, Jhon Jairo, and one of the aid workers struggling with César. César was in his fifties, but he was a tough old guy and I could see him trying to get his pistol. No one else had a weapon that I knew of. Keith threw a punch and Jhon Jairo tackled César.

For the last five-plus years, I had barely raised my voice above my normal speaking volume. With everyone else in the craft yelling, and the noise from the rotors and the motor churning, I shouted so loud my throat was burning and the muscles and tendons in my neck felt like they were on fire. I had no idea if anyone could hear me.

Above the sound of my own voice, I heard several other people shouting in Spanish and English, "Colombian Army! Colombian Army!" Suddenly I felt that same sensation I had whenever I got a message, that a voice and a presence were touching me from a great distance. In an instant, all the dreams, fantasies, and visions I'd had of what it would be like to be rescued flew through me at Mach 2. I went from completely empty to completely filled.

The fight continued. Whoever these friendlies on board were, they were giving César a serious beating. One of them was punching him behind the ear, and then I heard the spark-snapping sound of a stun gun. The guy who had introduced himself as the doctor looked at me and told me, "Get the shot! Get the shot!" I stood up, forgetting that my legs were still tied. I nearly fell over.

The "doctor" pointed to the seat next to me where César had tried to sit down. Under it, I found a bag and a hypodermic needle. I handed it to the doctor, and he jabbed it into César. In a few moments the Front commander was out.

Keith rolled out of the pile on César and then so did Jhon Jairo. Tom knelt down next to them, put his arms around them, and said, "Damn, Keith. We're free now."

There was a soft thump behind us. Enrique had lain down on the floor and one of our rescuers tied him up. He had just sat back and watched while César fought like a tiger. Enrique surrendered without even a whimper.

Tom saw him and stood up. The rescuers put Enrique in a seat. As Tom walked toward him, Keith and I looked at each other. For all the hell that Enrique had put Tom through, we were expecting a punch, a kick, a slap—something. Instead Tom just squatted down in front of him. He patted Enrique on the chest and said, "Good luck."

Keith and I stood up and nodded. Nothing else needed to be said. We had won.

I sat back down and looked across the cabin at Tom. He'd retaken his seat, a huge smile spread across his face. I felt the same way. I had no idea who these people were, but they had just set us free. Everyone on the aircraft was yelling, and I tried to get the attention of the one woman who was with the guys who'd done this for us all. She finally came and cut my leg restraints. I walked back toward Tom, and a moment later Keith joined us. We all took turns embracing. Keith had blood on his hand, and when I pointed it out to him, he laughed: "Just one blow for freedom, bro."

"My God," I said. "I can't believe it. This is it. We're free."

"I can't believe it, either," Tom said, still smiling.

One of our rescuers came up to us and pointed at the backpack Keith was holding. "Hang on to that. Important stuff in there."

Keith nodded and clutched the backpack to him. He smiled and said, "It's César's. I grabbed it during the scuffle. Must be something valuable in there."

"You know," I said, "the first thing I thought when this thing took off was I hope this Russian bucket of bolts holds together."

The thought of crashing had occurred to all of us during the rescue. It had taken just a few minutes and it was executed as flawlessly as any of us could have imagined. The Colombian military had devised a scheme that must have been months in the planning. In the time it took us to lift off and get airborne a few hundred feet, fifteen souls had been lifted out of the jungle, and two FARC terrorists were on their way to whatever hell awaited them.

Keith looked at the two of us in turn. "Have you ever felt this light? This relaxed? Man, it's like I've been carrying the weight of the world on my shoulders for five years. It's gone. It's gone." He turned to look out the window.

"I wonder when we'll be able to get to a cell phone. I want to talk to Destiney. I have to hear my girl's voice and let her know I'm coming home." My voice caught in my throat for a moment. I looked around the helo. All fifteen of us were smiling and laughing, and a few were brushing away tears of joy. I was with them, in spirit and emotion, but a part of me was still back in the jungle we were flying over, worrying about the hundreds and maybe thousands of other hostages the FARC still held. We were one step closer to getting home, but none of us would really ever be fully there until all of us were reunited with our loved ones.

TOM

The chess match was over. We'd won. It was as if the FARC had never even played the game before. The setup and execution was so perfect and the kill so clean, I didn't need to swipe the pieces off the board in a flamboyant display of triumph. It was enough to just sit back and admire the swiftness of it all. How could five years and four months of agony come to an end so quickly?

I didn't want to linger on the question. I just wanted to savor the moment. Everyone was dancing and jumping up and down, and Jhon Jairo and I grabbed each other by the biceps. All we could do was laugh and smile. It felt so good to see him like that. He was a young kid who had spent the prime of his youth in captivity. I can't say that the years slipped from his face, but there was a spark of life back in his eyes, a spark that had dimmed briefly before we got on board the helo.

"You gave César hell, Jhon," I said.

He frowned and pursed his lips. "I only did what was necessary to make sure he didn't harm anyone else. God will decide the rest."

We tried to say more to each other, but the Colombians had burst into song, a patriotic tune I'd heard before but never really paid much attention to. We expressed our thanks to the heroes who'd rescued us. Each time I tried to convey my gratitude and admiration, they simply said that we were the heroes. I didn't really look at it that way. We were the victors. We were the survivors. Doing the hard right thing doesn't make you heroic, it just means that you'll eventually come out on top.

Taking in the whole scene, I thought of something that Enrique said many times along with a number of the other guerrillas. He always said that if he saw the end coming, he would not submit meekly. He had the old they'll-never-take-me-alive mentality. To see him sitting on the helo stripped to his underwear and with his limbs all wrapped up, I couldn't help but think of him as a pig. A pig's an intelligent animal, and as yellow as Enrique proved himself to be, he'd made the intelligent choice. He couldn't have fought us all off. In the end, I think he realized what we all did about the FARC: Their cause was not something worth losing your life over.

After a brief twenty-minute flight, we were on the ground in San José. Without any fanfare or delay, we were loaded onto a Fokker jet that had once been the Colombian president's equivalent to *Air Force One*. We were seated in the front part of the plane, the first-class cabin. The rest of the former hostages were in the rear of the plane. We sank into the cushioned leather seats. In my life, I'd been on too many commercial flights to count, but never had an airline seat felt so comfortable. A small contingent of Americans were on the plane with us. They were partly responsible for our rescue and worked at the embassy in a highly classified capacity. They were great to us and filled us in on some details of the operation. Essentially the FARC were undone by their own people and their own flawed and antiquated communications systems. It was good to know that some members of the FARC had been corrupt enough to cooperate. The FARC had been duped into believing that a humanitarian contingent had come to visit with all of us, but in fact, our rescuers were highly trained members of an elite Colombian army squad. The doctor was real, but the TV guys were soldiers who'd volunteered for this dangerous mission.

We drank clean bottled water for the first time in years and sat back, letting everything sink in. We heard quite a celebration going on in the back of the plane, and walked in that direction to enjoy the spectacle. General Montoya, the chief of the Colombian military, was speaking through a megaphone: "Stop it! Stop it! Silence!" Things would quiet down for a bit and then he would scream, "Glory to the Colombian Army!," causing the cabin to explode again in revelry. When he finally got them all to calm down, he said that we were going to begin the flight with a prayer. A Colombian priest was on board and he led us all in a prayer of thanks. At the end, I did manage to say amen.

After the prayer, General Montoya got them all singing again. I couldn't imagine an American general letting loose with that kind of emotion, but I was so glad to see him respond that way. He should have been happy; they'd just delivered one of the biggest blows ever to the FARC. Their most valuable hostages were no longer in their grasp.

After takeoff, Ingrid came into the forward cabin. She walked up to Marc and hugged him.

"I'm so happy we are all free." She paused for a bit. Then, a look of regret passed across her face like a cloud shadow. She continued, "I hope that we will be in touch again in the future." They hugged again and she walked back to the rear cabin.

Someone mentioned that we would be landing at a military base in Tolemaida. The Colombians would be going their own way from that point.

"It's going to be weird saying good-bye to them," Marc said.

"It's also going to be good," Keith responded, and Marc and I waited for him to explain.

When he didn't, Marc said, "Whatever happened happened. I can move on from there. When I heard the guy shout, 'Colombian Army! Colombian Army!,' the last five years just seemed like they had lasted a few minutes. I don't hold any resentments. I'm just happy to be free. No animosity. Just get home."

Keith said, "That's what I meant. I can get over just about anything, but I don't know about Ingrid. Forgive? Yes. Move on? Yes. Respect? No."

We asked if we could go back to say good-bye to the Colombians. When we landed, Keith immediately went to his buddy Juancho. They bumped fists and Juancho said, "Hey, don't forget to call. I'm going to need that truck." The two of them had talked about Keith shipping his old Toyota pickup to him. All of the military ex-hostages were trying to move forward and there was a contingent of other Colombian military personnel on board in addition to the rescue team. I wanted to say good-bye to them all, but we only had a few moments, so it all felt rushed and out of control. I managed to find Jhon Jairo and we said a quick farewell and good luck.

When we deplaned from the Fokker, we were immediately loaded onto an American C–130 for a quick flight over the mountains to Bogotá. As we boarded we were greeting by Ambassador Brownfield. He was from Texas and it was strange to hear English spoken with that accent. We could tell he was thrilled by the success of the rescue mission and he was proud of the role he'd played in helping bring it about. We thanked him for all his efforts and for the bottles of Lone Star beer he'd brought on board with him. Our heads were spinning. I looked at the cheap Casio watch I'd picked up on one of our marches. Only a couple of hours had passed since the helos had first set down, and we were descending into Bogotá. I'd had dreams that lasted longer than this new reality.

We didn't know what to expect when we landed, 1,967 days since we'd taken off. When the loading ramp lowered and we walked down it, we saw Fast Eddie's in front of us. Cordoned off from the parking area where our planes usually sat, there was an enormous crowd. It was as surreal a moment as when we'd first crashed and found ourselves in the *Planet of the Apes.*

As soon as we saw some of our old crew from the company and from the embassy, we broke into a jog. We were all a bit taken aback by how emotional everyone else seemed to be. We were happy, but people were sobbing and laughing. Brian Wilkins, a guy who had started with the company at almost the same time as Marc, was shouting, "We never left. We never stopped working on trying to find you guys."

Ed Trinidad, the man who had been on the other side of our mayday calls that day in February 2003 was there, as was Mike Villegas, another coworker of ours from before the crash. They were both in tears and their voices choked with emotion as they repeated a variation on what Brian had said.

"We never stopped. We never stopped."

We were overwhelmed by the emotion and the thought that these people had suffered, too. Not only had they lived through our crash, but they had lost another crew. And still they kept flying, doing orbits to track our location. It made me realize yet again something that I'd tried hard to block out over the years: So many other people besides the three of us had suffered because of the FARC. I couldn't even begin accounting for the damage they had done to us all.

Everything happened in a rush and a blur, and we only had a few minutes with everyone there before we were escorted to a C-17. When we were on our missions and we'd successfully flown over all our targets, Keith was always the one to let our people know we were RTB—Returning to Base.

Our colleagues were crying like crazy, and through the muffled tears of joy, I could hear Keith say, "It's okay, it's okay. We're RTB. We're a little late, but we're RTB."

EIGHTEEN

Homecoming

July 2008–October 2008

TOM

From the moment we set foot in the air-force C-17 transport, we were solely in the hands of Americans and on familiar turf. Only a little of the euphoria had begun to wear off, and just being back in an aircraft felt so good that I asked if I could join the crew on the flight deck.

"I'll check on that for you, sir," one of the flight engineers said as he headed back to the cockpit.

"You remember what happened the last time you were in the cockpit with the two of us in the back, don't you, Tom?" Keith laughed and I gave him my best, "who me?" look. It was wonderful to laugh, and we knew we were in good hands on this flight. The flight engineer reemerged from the front of the plane.

"Mr. Howes, you can make your way up to the flight deck, sir. The PIC has given her approval for you to join the crew there."

"Mr. Howes? Sir? I'd almost forgotten I had a last name."

Keith and Marc could only shake their heads.

I'd been in a lot of aircraft that day, but sitting in the cockpit of our C-17 transport, I enjoyed looking at the airplane's sophisticated avionics. It felt good to be out of the Stone Age and in my world again. I leaned back, relaxed, and let it all sink in. Just hearing the quiet exchanges of the flight crew on a routine, uneventful flight did a lot to scrub away the memory of that day back in February of 2003. My mind didn't rest on those thoughts for very long; they passed beneath me like the landscape below. Everything was below me at that point. The intoxicating sense of being free was so great that nothing could drag me down or have me descend. Over the years, I'd taken a lot of grief from various FARC members, but in the end, they were still in the jungle fighting for what they thought of as freedom, and I *had* mine. We'd won. I'd won.

As we passed over the dark, inky water of the Gulf of Mexico, my anticipation grew. Until February 13, 2003, I'd never been a rah-rah kind of patriot, but words weren't enough to describe just how much I was looking forward to seeing the shores of the U.S. again. About fifty nautical miles from land, I could see the first few pinpricks of light from the Texas Gulf Coast spreading out before me. As we drew closer and the glow grew brighter, I had to still my leg as it bounced from a combination of eagerness and fatigue.

We touched down at Lackland Air Force Base in San Antonio and were ferried by a Blackhawk to Brooke Army Medical Center (BAMC) at Fort Sam Houston, adding to the tally of flights and aircraft we'd been on in a twelve-hour period. Because the doctor who examined us on the C-17 flight couldn't be certain that we didn't have any infectious diseases and we had visible signs of lesions (both Keith and my leishmaniasis was clearly visible), the staff at BAMC had cordoned off an entire wing of the hospital in anticipation of our arrival.

As another part of our reintegration, the army's specialists had arranged it so that the three of us would stay together that first night.

They believed that it would be better that way until we'd been reoriented a bit more. When we were settled into our room, I found that my energy had returned more forcefully than I expected. After I flew, I could never just go right to sleep. It was as if my mind had raced ahead to my new location, but my body was still lagging behind. That first night felt a lot like that.

I was eager to call Mariana, but I wasn't able to reach her. The first familiar voices from home I heard were those of my brother, Steve, and my sister, Sally. We talked for a few minutes, but it was getting late and I had other phone calls I wanted to make. Before I knew it, the exhaustion of everything caught up with me and I was out.

The next day began with a battery of physical exams and several forms of psychological evaluation. We were all amazed by how kind and compassionate the staff was. Without stating it directly, they made it clear that Marc, Keith, and I would not be separated from one another for long periods of time. Some of our question-and-answer sessions were done individually and others as a group. The thinking seemed to be that only the three of us could really understand what we'd been through, and not having one or the other of us to rely on might be too disconcerting for us.

After being treated indifferently at best and inhumanely at worst by the FARC's "doctors," it felt wonderful to be in the hands of amazingly talented and compassionate physicians, nurses, orderlies, and technicians. I was never so glad to be subjected to so many tests, answer so many questions, and have so many people concerned about the various fluids and by-products my body produced. I almost laughed whenever someone tending to me said, "You're going to feel a little pinch here." Or "You may feel some discomfort." I felt nothing but wonderful and alive and well.

My son, Tommy, had been with some of my in-laws at a remote farm in Peru, so it took a few days for him to arrive. Mariana's mother accompanied him into the room, and as much regard as I had for her, it was almost like she didn't exist in those first few moments. The years apart could not break the special bond that Tommy and I had shared since he was born. We held on to each other and time disappeared. Neither of us could speak. Before the crash, if I'd wanted to hug him, I had to kneel. That day in July, he was big enough to bury his head in my chest. I bent my face down and breathed in the smell of his freshly shampooed hair. After a few moments we parted a bit to let his grandmother join in the embrace.

The next day, Mariana and I saw each other. I was nervous during the hours leading up to the meeting. I didn't have high hopes for an intensely romantic or dramatic greeting. I knew that she had been in Brussels when I'd been released. Always a cool, somewhat reserved, and refined woman, she wasn't capable of a public display of emotion and affection. Holding in your arms a woman you've loved but been estranged from for so long was odd. I wanted so much for it to feel familiar and right, but I'd also been prepared by the psychologists not to expect too much too soon. Mariana and I were cordial with each other but our exchanges felt scripted—a kind of forced politeness between two people who were hoping to keep up appearances. Gradually, as we spent more time together, it seemed as if some of the tension began to ease, but until we got back on our home turf, everything was going to feel a bit strange.

As part of our reintegration, we were gradually introduced to social settings through brief trips to off-base locations. The highlight for me was a trip to the local Harley-Davidson motorcycle shop. We had never stopped talking about and dreaming of the Freedom Ride. Walking into that dealership, Marc was like a motorcycle addict in a chrome shop. Row after row of gleaming new bikes and parts sat spotlit and glinting.

"Guys," Marc said to Keith and me, "I think I'm in motorcycle heaven." I inhaled the aroma of rubber, leather, and the faint scent of motor oil coming from the dealership's shop.

"Unreal. Look at all this." Keith turned a tight three-sixty with his head thrown back and his arms wide, "Two floors of nothing but the finest the motor company can produce."

I immediately walked over to an Electra Glide and sat down on it. "Someday," I said with a resolve that surprised even me.

The staff at the dealership was as kind as could be. We were never sure how much advance warning they had of our arrival and how much they knew about us, but they provided us with hats, T-shirts, and pins to commemorate our visit. We may have worn out our welcome by sitting on just about every bike in the place, but we saw no sign of it.

On July 7, we agreed that we were ready to do our first formal press conference at what the army called its Yellow Ribbon Ceremony. We each got a blue sport coat. I'd never felt that comfortable getting dressed up, but when the three of us stepped on the raised dais in front a few hundred folks gathered to welcome us home, it was very easy to stand tall. Mariana, her mother, Tommy, and my stepson, Santiago, joined me in front of the assembled staff and members of the public.

We all posed for photos in front of a large American flag. Having a lump in my throat at the sight of that potent symbol was something I'd not experienced since the days just after 9/11. I was never prouder to be an American and never more appreciative for what the governments of Colombia and the U.S. had done. Later, as the motorcade drove us to the jet that Northrop Grumman had provided to take us back to various points in Florida, I found myself wishing that I had been able to spend more time in Texas, getting to know the people who had helped me come home. I was equally indebted to the heroes of the Colombian military who, at great risk to themselves, pulled off a chess move that not even I was capable of. Operation Jaque—Operation Checkmate in English—gets its name from the move in chess when the king is in jeopardy and must be moved out of the line of direct attack. I could not have played the game any better than they did, and I remained confident that a checkmate against the FARC was soon to follow.

During our time in captivity, Keith, Marc, and I really had become brothers, and just as in some families where feelings remain unspoken or not demonstratively paraded in front of everyone, it was fitting then that our farewells were low-key. At each airport where we were dropped off, we hugged one another, slapped one another on the back, and said a quick "see you later." With upcoming visits to the White House, various meetings and reunions with coworkers, debriefing sessions, and sit-downs with military personnel who had connections to our situation, we were going to see one another quite often. Our farewells were a bit anticlimactic, but some bonds don't need to be massaged to remain strong.

Walking through the door of my house, I couldn't help but think that I'd spent five and a half years thinking about this place, but I'd only spent two weeks actually living in it. My first few days at home were occupied by my attempts to get reacquainted with the space that I'd traversed in my mind so many times throughout captivity. I would close my eyes and move from room to room. Upon opening them, I'd find myself shocked to be staring at an actual room and not the green of the jungle. By the time the novelty of the rooms wore off, I had resumed a somewhat normal routine. Once school started, it was a real pleasure to take Tommy there, to be up in the morning ahead of him to have his breakfast prepared and his lunch made.

For Mariana and me, that routine was harder to establish. I don't think you can take any two adults, let alone two with independent streaks as prominent as ours, and expect them to bridge a five-year gap. We'd both grown in different directions, and after a nearly three-month period of failing to adjust, it became clear in late September that it would be better for all three of us if she and I ended the marriage. In the jungle, I'd told myself that no matter what, I was going to do everything I could to keep our family together. My son deserved to have an intact family, and if I just worked hard enough at it, I could make the marriage last. The reality didn't work out that cleanly, but with everything I'd been through, in some ways, I was ready for it. I didn't want my son to live in anything less than a good and positive environment. He and I are still as close as it is possible to be, and in the end, that's all that matters.

Meeting President Bush and President Uribe was an honor, and it felt good to express my gratitude toward them both—in particular to Mr. Uribe—for their support and the amazing job the Colombian military did in deceiving the FARC and rescuing fifteen hostages without a single shot being fired. None of us wanted to see any more lives lost, and we were enormously impressed and grateful that Operation Jaque had accomplished that.

Perhaps my greatest joy these days comes from my motorcycle—not my old bike, but a new one. During an interview we did with CNN, we mentioned the Freedom Ride, and someone at Harley-Davidson heard about our story and our desire to ride the country. They contacted each of us and invited us to Milwaukee for the company's 105th anniversary celebration. Hanging out with all kinds of fellow enthusiasts was great, and the generosity of the people at Harley was unbelievable, especially when they told us we could each select a model of our choice from our local dealer as a gift.

It was an amazing gesture. Every few days, I take my new bike out and go for a morning cup of coffee at a shop called Osorio. There's nothing all that swanky about the place, but being able to go out and get cup of coffee in a paper cup just because I can is pleasure enough. In some ways, Osorio reminds me of where I'd grown up in Cape Cod. Chatham is a nice little touristy village, and Cocoa Village, Florida, has much the same feel. I enjoy the leisurely pace of life down there. I can sit in the sun and watch the other coffee drinkers come and go. For now, I've got no better place to be, and I like that.

When my cup is empty, I don't linger for long. The ride home in the steadily warming air is always refreshing, but nothing beats pulling into the driveway of my house. One thing the hostage experience taught me is the pleasure of the hammock. I have one alongside the pool where I can see the citrus trees in my backyard. Fruit was a rare treat while in captivity, and so being surrounded by orange, grapefruit, lime, lemon, and mango trees, and lying in a hammock perfumed by those scents, is just about every bit of the peace I craved when in the hands of the FARC. For a guy who spent most of his adult life in the pursuit of adventure and a way to get a leg up financially, I'm enjoying having both legs up in my hammock, appreciating the time I have before I immerse myself in household projects.

I haven't flown since I've been back, and though that was one of my life's passions, I know that rushing around in a headlong dash to achieve what someone else might define as success is not for me. In my mind, I've already won whatever game I was playing, and there is no greater demonstration of that than exercising my ability to choose whether to swing or lie still, answer the phone or let it go to voice mail. Nothing is too important to let it interfere with the comfortable bubble I've found in my private tropical paradise.

KEITH

"Keith, welcome home and welcome to Fort Sam Houston."

From the first words that Major General Keith Huber spoke, I knew that we were being reintroduced to gallantry and service. His firm handshake and intense blue eyes underscored the fact that the brutality that had marked our lives for so long had finally come to an end. General Huber set the tone for everyone else at Fort Sam Houston. The folks there at the BAMC exceeded our expectations in every way, and so much of this had to do with the compassionate command of Major General Keith Huber. From the moment we set foot on that base to the day we left it, General Huber was there—whether it was offering us his advice and wise counsel or driving us from one location to another.

This was my first real extended contact with a man of his rank, and the man had no airs about him, even if I was a lowly ex-Marine.

As we settled into our room on that first night, I ate a cheeseburger that a full-bird colonel had been nice enough to rush from home to prepare for me. In between bites, I anticipated the next day. I'd managed to get ahold of a cell phone from a colleague while we were still in Bogotá, and I spoke with my mother and father in Florida. Our conversation had been brief, but their excitement and relief at hearing my voice stayed with me through the rest of the day. They promised that I'd be seeing them the following day.

The next morning, they arrived, along with Lauren and Kyle. All of them were led into a conference room where they found me sitting at a table. We all grabbed one another in one big huddle and had a good cry. Kyle was now sixteen years old and stood six feet six inches tall. I could not believe that my boy had gone and eaten one of Jack's beans and become a beanstalk himself. Lauren was now nineteen and about as beautiful a young woman as any man could be proud to claim as a daughter. Seeing them and their transformations was almost too much, and after I'd quieted everyone down, I felt the need to say something.

"You guys. Listen up, all of you. I can't thank you enough for the messages. You have no idea how much your words meant to me—hell, meant to all of us. You were with me when I needed you and I will never, never be able to thank you enough, but I sure as hell am going to try."

My dad's an intellectual, the kind of guy who lives through his books. I'd never seen him so choked up, and just looking at him with tears running down his cheeks was enough to bust me up inside.

"Dad, I'm on the other side of it now. I'm bulletproof from here on out. Nothing, nothing can touch me anymore." I reached across the table and grabbed his arm.

He put his hand on mine and said, "So many things I want to say. Should have said before—"

I cut him off. "You said it all in those messages. You took care of my son and daughter. You looked after things for me."

"I know but . . ."

Only during the next few days did I learn what he meant when he said "but." I'd suspected from early on that Malia had jumped from the sinking ship to save herself. I didn't really blame her. My dad was worried I'd expected her to be waiting for me with a dozen roses and a bottle of champagne, and he didn't want to bring me down. But he didn't have to say a word. I'd long known the truth and confronted it in the jungle. I hadn't heard from her for almost four years. Marc, Tom, and I had all said that we didn't expect anyone to put a life on hold because of us. I knew that even before the crash, I'd put my relationship with Malia in jeopardy, and I didn't have any illusions about what would happen now that I was free. We always said that captivity would reveal the truth about ourselves. Well, the same was true for the people we left behind. When I told my dad I was bulletproof, I meant it. I'd already moved on.

The second day back, Patricia and the twins were scheduled to visit me, and before they arrived, General Huber came to our room to talk to me.

"Keith, listen. I'm a family man myself, blessed with a loving wife, two great kids, and my first grandson. I want you to be sure you're ready for this. Meeting those two boys could be real tough on you. I just want to make sure you're ready."

"Yes, sir. I am. I'm their father and I need to see them. They need to know who I am." I'd thought a lot about the twins while in captivity. The radio mix-up regarding whether or not they'd both survived the birth had made me worry, but later I just generally wondered what their lives were like with Patricia. Through Lucho, the world understood that she and I were engaged, but this was reality and I knew it.

My heart was in my throat as I walked from our room to face Patricia and the twins. General Huber stepped in front of me just as I was about to open the door. "You're sure?" he asked. I could see the genuine concern he had etched in his eyes.

I nodded and he smiled and swung the door open. The first thing I saw was two young boys sitting on the floor playing with cars with their backs to me. When they turned around at the sound of the door opening, they jumped up and ran to me, yelling, "Papa! Papa!" They each grabbed a leg, and I swear to you, it felt like both of them could have taken me down. I was so weak-kneed and rubbery-thighed I just wanted to sink down right there and cry. Instead I went down on one knee and let them put their arms around my neck. I looked at Patricia and that cemented in my mind what I'd been thinking about for the last few months: Here was a woman who knew how to do the hard right thing. For all the shit I'd put her through, for all the walls that I'd put up between us, and for all the tangled mess that had been my life in captivity, she found a way to break through and embrace me in a way that no one ever had before.

To see that gorgeous woman sitting there with her hands in front of her mouth and tears welling in her eyes, I knew that one person had failed me but another had delivered in ways beyond belief. I was not about to consider questions of deserved or not, I just wanted to hold in my arms a woman who really understood what it was to love and to forgive.

"How did they know?" was about all I could manage to squeeze past my constricted throat.

"I had a photo of you on the wall in their room. Right between their beds. I told them all about you. I told them about the bad men who had you, and that was why you weren't with us."

We sat down and I took her hand.

"But how did you know?" I alluded to the fact that she had no way of knowing what my feelings for her were.

"Before Luis Eladio came home, I didn't know. I just trusted—and hoped."

The first night that we were in the hospital, I'd taken my first hot shower in five-plus years. I couldn't believe that I could actually turn a knob and hot, clean water would come out a showerhead. Actual soap and shampoo were there for me, and not laundry soap. Staying in that soothing stream of water for hours felt like the best way that I could begin to scrub off the layers of accumulated filth that had marked my experience with the FARC.

Sitting there with Patricia and my two boys made me feel like I'd been given another chance. I wasn't going to squander that opportunity to be washed clean, to remove some of the layers of selfishness and ego that had been building up on me long before I'd crashed in Colombia. If I hadn't gotten the message that giving of myself to others was a necessary and beneficial thing that enabled us all to survive our captivity, then Patricia's selfless devotion drove the point home so that even this big dumb country boy wouldn't forget it.

When I finally got back to Florida and started to set up a household with Patricia and my reconfigured family, it was a real joy. Being with Patricia and the kids confirmed what I'd long suspected in the jungle: Feeling safe and secure in a relationship beat the hell out of running amok and trying to prove things to myself or other people that had no real meaning to them or to me. I wasn't about to sit down and recite a long litany of my sins and atone for every one of them—there are only twenty-four hours in a day, after all—but our captivity had given me time to do some assessing. I didn't talk about it much, but just as Tom had sat and thought about his house and each of the rooms and all the things he needed and wanted to do to them, I'd done the same with my own house, the self I'd lived with, and my whole life. I didn't think that I needed to be torn down and rebuilt from the ground up, but there was some fundamental structural damage that needed to be addressed.

In the jungle, I'd gone through an honest evaluation and admission of who I was and what I'd done with my life to that point. By the time we'd gotten to our final year in captivity, I'd filled notebook after notebook with all kinds of thoughts and reflections. One day I decided that having spilled my guts for that many years, it was time to stop thinking so much about the past and focus on the present. I burned those notebooks, and while I didn't think that I'd rise phoenixlike from those ashes, I was aware that I was one lucky guy who had received a major tap on the shoulder from the universe. Maybe that's why I was always able to sleep so well in captivity—I was a little bit like a newborn with a clear conscience.

With Patricia, it's been easier than I ever thought to be a devoted dad and mate. Before, I'd been able to manage just the dad part. I think I found some strength in that jungle, came to understand that carrying heavy for another person could pay dividends for us both.

During my first weeks back home, I spent a decent amount of time learning what I could about Operation Jaque. I still keep in touch with Juancho and have even exchanged e-mails with Lucho, so it's not as if I wanted to put Colombia out of my mind completely. I admire anyone who does anything skillfully, and the Colombian military really pulled off an amazing feat. I knew that it was U.S. supported and technically assisted, but the guys on the ground who executed the mission, and whoever higher up in the hierarchy who was responsible for command and control of the operation, have my admiration.

Operation Jaque relied a great deal on the groundwork that the Colombian military had been laying for years, as well as unpredictable things such as various FARC mistakes, the pressure from the U.S. ambassador, and the deaths of the three FARC leaders. I still don't know how all those pieces fit together, but someone up there was looking out for us. The key to the whole thing was that the Colombians had been able to turn two FARC guerrillas to the good side. Without that level of human intelligence, we'd likely still be in Colombia. The military had been intercepting FARC radio transmissions for a while. We knew that to be the case going all the way back to when we were with Milton, and one of the reasons we'd spent so much agonizing time wandering aimlessly was that the FARC realized their communications security had been breached. As a result, they had to resort to using couriers to hand-carry messages from the Front commanders to the guys in the field. Whether it was Mono JoJoy or César who were issuing them, those orders were slow in arriving and that gave the military another edge.

As much as it seemed we were hustling from place to place and being tracked, we didn't know how close we'd come to friendlies on the ground. Finding the camera and the battery pack was a good indication of that and so were the helos overhead, but at a reception held for us, I learned that some U.S. Special Forces guys had spotted us once while we were bathing in one of the rivers. Another told me that he'd been on the ground and the strangest thing had happened—he could smell popcorn. I couldn't believe that Enrique's attempt to calm his outfit was sending smoke signals to our guys in-country. Even knowing all that after the fact made me feel better.

But while the U.S. Special Forces were behind the scenes and in the shadows, the Colombians were the masterminds. They were smart enough to know that they had to test whether or not their spy/couriers would be effective. They forged orders to see if the FARC would actually follow them, and a few of our movements from site to site were the products of those fake orders to Milton and Enrique. In fact, it was the Colombian government and not anyone in the FARC high command who issued the order for William Pérez and Ingrid Betancourt to rejoin us shortly before the rescue.

The Colombian military also took advantage of something else. Independent of their efforts, an actual humanitarian organization was on the ground in our area searching for us on foot. Those remarkably committed folks inadvertently played a big role in the ruse that the military created to rescue us. We had been hearing on news reports that this group was trying to find us. So when the military issued fake orders that we be taken to that location and loaded onto helos, it corroborated what the FARC had already heard about the humanitarian organization on the news. With fake orders issued from the high command, Enrique had no choice but to do what he was told. As tired as we'd grown of hearing that lame-ass excuse, in this case it actually saved us.

Enrique and César are still in custody, and their disorganization seems to be in more disarray than ever. I'd like to think that our being taken and then rescued will contribute in a small way to their downfall. We can only hope that somehow our rescue leads to the release of additional hostages. Most of my thoughts about the FARC now concern making sure that those hostages who remain in captivity are not forgotten in this country. The three of us remain as committed to them today as we were the day of our release. I'm not sure why, but for some reason, here in America, we tend not to think much about our neighbors to the south. It's only when Chávez is tweaking us or threatening to cut our supply of oil that we pay much attention to what goes on down there. I hope that what happened to the three of us serves as a lesson that politics is personal and that human-rights issues strike very close to home.

On the whole, I try not to obsess about the FARC too much these days. A few weeks ago, I had a chance to do something that I absolutely love (besides riding my new motorcycle, of course) with a good buddy of mine. I love the fall in Florida and South Georgia. We don't get the same kind of weather and vegetation changes folks up north do, but the temperatures are moderate and some mornings it is downright brisk. On this particular day, I was out hunting deer, sitting in a tower stand that overlooked a bean field. A bit of ground fog cotton-balled the field, and the early-morning sunlight had torched some of the dew, making it look like the land was on fire. A couple of does and a buck were nibbling at the grass along the edge. My gun was at my side, but I left it there and just continued to soak in the scene.

My buddy nudged me and said, "You got a good shot at that buck. You going to take it or not?"

I shook my head. "No. It feels good just to sit here in all this." I raised my arms to indicate the terrain where I'd spent the better part—no, make that the best part—of my life.

"I hear you," he said.

"You know, for the first time I think I can really say this."

"What's that?"

"I'm not carrying heavy anymore. I'm back."

MARC

"I feel like E.T."

As I said those words, I meant them in more ways than one. To start with, we'd walked through a plastic-sheeted doorway of the quarantine room and all around us stood masked and gowned figures who were applauding and waving. It was overwhelming to be in the presence of people who were genuinely interested in our well-being, and more than anything that had me feeling a bit alien. When you've had a group of people abusing you for as long as we did, even the smallest kindness seems out of proportion.

After things calmed down and we settled into our room at BAMC, I tried to reach my family members again. Earlier in the day, I'd called everyone, but I hadn't been able to reach them. No one was home at my mother's number, and I was dying to speak to my kids, but I hadn't been able to. No one was home at Shane's number, and I couldn't leave a message. Finally, that night I was able to connect with my dad. To hear his voice after all that time, it was as if somehow some kind of liquid had been transmitted over the phone and had been poured into my ear, working its way down through every part of my body. Relief doesn't begin to explain what I felt, but there was a sense of calm and security that I hadn't experienced in so long.

My dad was understandably very emotional, and he told me how happy he was and how much he loved me. It wasn't a time for eloquence, it was simply time to immerse ourselves in the emotions of the moment. The people responsible for our reintegration program only wanted me to speak to him for a few minutes; they'd been through this before and had a specific program designed to keep us from being too overwhelmed. I said good-bye to my father regretfully, and without realizing how strange the words sounded, I said I would see him tomorrow.

I learned from my father that my mother was in France. She'd gone there to participate in several peaceful protests and to take part in various ceremonies designed to bring attention to the plight of the Colombian hostages. Part of the plan was to climb to the top of Mount Blanc to place photos of hostages at the highest point in Western Europe. She had been informed of our rescue, and with the aid of Northrop, was on her way to Texas.

Sleeping in a real bed for the first time was wonderful, but even that comfort couldn't prevent me from having a nightmare. All through captivity I'd dream at night that I'd been rescued. That first night in the BAMC I awoke from a nightmare in which I was in the jungle and everything that had just happened—the rescue, the flights, the return to the States, the conversation with my father—everything was only a dream and my reality was that I was still in the jungle. As clichéd as it may seem, that vivid and disturbing nightmare startled me awake, and in the darkness, I wondered if everything in that hospital room was a product of my imagination.

On day two of our return, I got to see my mother and stepfather, Mike, as well as my father, stepmother, and stepsister and brother. Again, all the visits were carefully regulated and somewhat brief. When my mother clamped her arms around me, I thought either I had become that frail or she'd become that strong. I felt like she could crush my rib cage, but I didn't mind.

"I am so glad to see you. My prayers have been answered. I love you so much." She kept repeating those words, and with each repetition, she held me tighter. When I was finally able to create a little bit of separation between us, I could see that the years I'd been gone had not been easy on her. I tried to tell myself that after not seeing someone for more than five years, there were bound to be changes, but her worry and anxiety had physically punished her.

"You know, Marc, we are in San Antonio—Saint Anthony. We pray to him when we lose things so that he can help us find them. You're found."

The following day brought my long awaited reunion with my kids. As soon as the door opened, Destiney ran into my arms and I felt my heart jump up to greet her. The little girl I'd left behind had grown so much I could barely believe it. Beneath the new hairstyle and makeup was still a kid who'd missed her dad as much as I'd missed her. Throughout our twenty-minute meeting, she clung to me.

Destiney told me the story of how she'd found out I had been taken hostage. Our bond had been so tight that when I was first abducted, Shane didn't know how to break it to her. She told Destiney that I was working all day long and was only able to call very late at night. (I used to call home every single day.) At first, Destiney didn't understand, but as the days passed by without her talking to me, she began to miss me more and more. She was only nine years old at the time. She was told that I was calling late at night, so she started to stay awake, waiting for my call. Each night she would stay awake later and later, waiting for me to call, until she was up all night long. But I never called.

Hearing this account of her suffering filled me with an intense and straining pain that nothing could alleviate. To be angry and hate the FARC didn't help, to regret my decision to fly in Colombia didn't help, to look to the future didn't help, because none of those things would take Destiney's suffering away. There were so many nights of my captivity when I prayed and gave thanks that it was me there in that jungle and not anyone in my family. But hearing Destiney speak, I realized that it wasn't just me in that jungle; they we were all there—my mother, my father, my little Destiney—suffering with me.

Hugging Cody, I was surprised that he was nearly as tall as I was.

"Hey. Welcome home," he said with a huge smile.

When he spoke those words, it was the first time I'd heard his post-pubescent voice, and I felt the rumble of it rattle my collarbone. Joey hugged me and I was amazed that he still looked just as he did before I left.

"You guys, I just can't tell you . . ." I paused and in that instant a universe of emotions washed over me. "It is so good to see you guys."

Through my tears, I saw Shane standing off to one side—nervously folding her arms and looking around the room, her eyes avoiding mine. When I approached her, she smiled wanly and said, "It's good to see you. I'm glad you're okay."

From her tone and her rigid posture, the way she seemed to flinch when I put my arms around her, I knew that what I'd long suspected in the jungle was true. Shane had moved on in her life. I didn't blame her, but it made me sad to think we'd been so deeply in love. There would be time to deal with the fallout of the end of our marriage, but it wasn't now.

"I'm happy to see you, too. I missed you so much." Both of us spoke like I'd just been away for a few days on a business trip; not for sixty-five months. I'd prepared myself for this moment, but I was still surprised at how much it hurt—mainly because when I looked at Shane, I sensed that the years I'd been gone hadn't been good to her either. With Destiney clinging to me so tightly, I wondered what Shane had experienced, how painful my absence from her life must have been.

Several days later, when we were all moved into an apartment in the married service personnel's quarters, that gulf that existed between Shane and me became even more evident. Even in that relatively small space, it felt as if I was still in Colombia and she was in Florida. The awkward silences that passed between us reminded me of the times when Tom, Keith, and I were without radios or radio reception. At least then the white noise of the static held out some hope that a transmission signal was somewhere in the area. Between Shane and me, there was only the dead silence and the recognition that I was coming back to a fractured life.

Unfortunately, what had fractured my marriage couldn't be repaired, and Shane and I are no longer together. While this turn of events saddened me, like Keith and Tom, I had long been prepared for it. The years that had passed since Shane's last radio message had signaled to me that things would never be the same. In captivity, I had readied myself to face it. Despite the reality, my bonds with Destiney, Cody, and Joey have never been stronger. Having them in my life every day has reminded me of what I spent five years surviving for. There's not a day that goes by that I don't thank God for allowing me to be an active part of their lives again.

Of all the amazing things that have happened since our return, our trip to Harley-Davidson and their kindness ranks among my favorites. When it came time for me to pick out my free bike, I didn't want one of each in each color and level of accessories. All I wanted to do was ride, to throw a leg over and again feel that rush of wind in my face, and the distinctive *potato-potato* sound of that twin-cylinder engine propelling me down a twisty road. For so long the thought of bikes had been our coping mechanism. Now they were our reality.

The euphoria of rescue continued for days and weeks, and was gradually replaced by a feeling of security and contentment that I'd never known. I moved back to Connecticut to be near my mother and father and the rest of my family. I was thrilled for my mom when she was awarded honorary Colombian citizenship for all her work—not just to get the three of us freed, but all the other hostages remaining in Colombia. They remain very much on my mind to this day. Meanwhile Northrop Grumman has done everything it possibly can to ease my transition, even though I'd only been their employee for a brief time before the accident. In Tom and in Keith, I have brothers with whom I have forged a bond that goes deeper than blood and bone to spirit and soul. We continue to talk frequently, and every day I remember anew how our friendship made survival possible.

I'm a different person now. Inevitably, we all change, but those five-plus years worked on me in some very good ways. I have a new-found appreciation of and patience for just about everything I do. The other day, I had to go to the hospital for an MRI. (I still have trouble with my knee and my back.) I was told to arrive at 9:30 A.M. for a ten-o'clock appointment. I sat in the waiting room and watched as time passed. An hour went by without my name being called. Several other patients groused about their time being wasted. I smiled at the thought that any time was a waste. At twelve-thirty, my name was finally called.

The technician was an attractive Hispanic woman who seemed no older than eighteen. As she led me down the hallway to the exam room, she kept apologizing for the wait.

"No me importa. Ninguna necesidad de disculparse." I told her that I didn't care and that there was no need to apologize.

"Your Spanish is very good, as is your accent. Are you South American?"

"No," I said, laughing, "but I've spent some time there."

She began explaining the procedure. When she was done, she asked, "Will it bother you to have to lie very still? Some people find being in the machine very confining."

I shook my head and said, "No. I'll be okay."

When I got back home after the test, I climbed on my bike. I had no particular place to go, and no particular destination in mind. Before, when I had my sport bike, my rides were tests of courage and speed, hurtling down interstates as fast as I could on those arrow straight strips of Florida asphalt. All that's long gone now; my adrenaline rushes have been satisfied. That day, I rode along State Route 66 enjoying a crisp and clear New England fall day. The colors of the maple trees were vibrant in the waning afternoon sunlight. Heading north, I passed along Columbia Lake, and as I cruised from shadow to sunlight, it was as if the trees in Nathan Hale State Forest were like fireworks bursting into flame and then extinguishing.

Though I'd had no idea that this was the route I'd take, as I rode along a curved ribbon of road and enjoyed the rises and falls, it somehow seemed appropriate to pass an area named for one of our country's great heroes—someone considered our first intelligence operative, a soldier and a martyr of the revolution who gave the one life he had for this country. Thanks to him and so many others, I could just ride and enjoy the day with nothing better to do than be enormously appreciative of my freedom. I rolled on the throttle and banked into a series of tight turns, and then with my thrill-seeking satisfied, I headed for home out of captivity at last.

Acknowledgments

The three of us learned a lot about relying on each other while in the jungle. In the last few months as we've worked on this book project, we've put those lessons to good use. We've been fortunate to receive the guidance, support, and efforts of a team who helped us get this book done in what seemed to us to be record time during one of the busiest periods in our lives. We're deeply indebted to so many people. If we were to thank you all individually, we'd end up with a book twice as long as the one you hold in your hands. Please know that we are enormously grateful to everyone who offered up a prayer or good thought for our safe return, to those who offered a kind word or gesture to our families while we were in captivity, and to those who since our return have embraced us as we've made the adjustment to life out of the jungle. Even though we can't possibly name each and every one of you, we are grateful to you for your contribution to our lives.

We would be remiss if we didn't thank some people and organizations by name. We are deeply grateful to the government, the military, and the people of Colombia. In particular, General Mario Montoya, Colombian Minister of Defense Juan Manuel Santos, President Alvaro Uribe Velez, and the brave men and woman involved in the planning and execution of Operation Jaque deserve mention. To those in the U.S. military and government who also contributed to our release, you have our deep and abiding thanks. When we returned to the United States, we were warmly welcomed and cared for by General Keith Hubert and his staff at the Brooke Army Medical Center at Fort Sam Houston. Also, Mr. Doug Sanders was particularly helpful during this time. We are indebted to everyone who participated in our reintegration process. Your amazing compassion and concern overwhelmed us and enabled us to make the transition to life outside of captivity much more easily.

The folks at Northrop Grumman helped take care of our families during our absence and have been incredibly supportive and accommodating of our needs since our return. We especially want to thank James Pitts, Ronald Sugar, and Michele Magaletta, Jr., for their contributions. To our colleagues back in-country in Colombia who never lost faith and continued to search for us—Brian Wilks, Mike Villegas, Jim Pabon and Ed Trinidad—we salute you for your effort and for never forgetting.

We also thank everyone at Harley-Davidson and at our local dealers for their enormous generosity and support of our Freedom Ride. We hope to see all of you on the road.

Wade Chapple and Doug Sanders were instrumental in helping us get some of the terrific images together for the photo insert. Our thanks go out to both of them for sending us their pictures and allowing us to use them.

Our lawyers Newt Porter and Tony Korvick were crucial to guiding us through the initial stages of the publication process. Through them, we met a number of publishers. We're very glad that we found a home at William Morrow/HarperCollins. From the moment we spoke with the William Morrow team, we felt we'd found the right fit and our gut reaction proved true. We've benefited enormously from our editor, Matt Harper, and his steady and insightful shaping and shepherding of our book. His timely and wise suggestions made this a book we are all proud of. We'd also like to thank Lisa Sharkey and the countless others at HarperCollins who had a hand in the book's production, promotion, and sales.

Finally, we'd also like to thank our cowriter Gary Brozek for all his hard work in bringing our story to life on the page. This ambitious undertaking wouldn't have been successful without his dedication and his magical ability to transport himself into the jungle with us as he told our story.

TOM

It's just about impossible to express my gratitude to the countless people who offered support and encouragement during our captivity and the reintegration process. I'm sorry that I can't single you all out, but please know that your contributions are not forgotten. I do want to make note of my siblings—my sister, Sally, and my brother, Steve—it is great to be back with you again. My son, Tommy, continues to share a special bond with me, and I'm so proud to see the kind of young man you've grown into and I'm eager to share more of my life with you. My stepson, Santiago Giraldo, did a wonderful job of watching over our family in my absence, proving once again what a remarkable man he is.

KEITH

If you've finished reading this book, then you know that there is one person among the thousands (and can't possibly be named—I'm grateful to her for unending support and devotion. Patricia, I thank you for having so much faith in me and for being *la mujer de mi vida*. To my daughter, Lauren, and my son, Kyle, I can never tell you enough how much I love you and how proud I am of who you have become. I always knew that you guys could take care of yourselves, but I'm so glad I can be here with you now to watch you both do your thing. Mom and Dad, the two of you did so much for my family during my absence that I can never repay you (and I know you did all those things without expecting anything in return) for helping to hold together my life and family here in the States. You amaze me and continue to show me day after day how taking the hard right path can be its own reward. To Keith, Jr., and Nick: circumstances were never easy for the two of you, but as "los tigres," you've shown the kind of tenacity that makes this former Marine's chest swell with pride. It's going to be a lot of fun from here on out.

Tommy Janis, Ralph Ponticelli, Tommy Schmidt, and Butch Oliver have joined the list of America's fallen but unsung heroes. It is men like you who, having made the ultimate sacrifice, have added your names to the list of those who have made this country great. By quietly doing a dangerous job that most Americans don't even know about, you give us all reason to be proud. God bless you and your families. I will always carry you all in my heart and in my mind. Tom and Marc: We made it!

MARC

It is no longer a fantasy; now I am free. I want to thank all of those who prayed, who wrote, and who remembered us. Miracles do happen. One thing that I learned in the jungle is the true value of family. I especially want to thank my mother, Jo Rosano, who is my champion on the battlefield. I heard your voice, Mom; I heard it in the jungle. To my father and stepmother George and Monique, and my brother and sisters Michael, Denise, Corina, and Misty, I love you all. No more suffering. To my precious children Joey, Cody, and Destiney, I am so thankful to our Lord for allowing me to see you again. We have a lot of time to make up for, but we have all of our lives in front of us to do it.

I would never wish what happened to me on even my worst enemy. But having said that, I can tell you all one thing: I would not have survived alone. Tom, Keith: I didn't pick you to be my fellow hostages, but I am so thankful that I had you with me. You can't pick your family members, you're born with them. The same goes for your fellow hostages. We are family now. And together we did it; we survived. I love you, my brothers. Let's ride.